Wilder: Hold Fast to Dreams

DONALD P. BAKER

WILDER: HOLD FAST TO DREAMS

A biography of L. Douglas Wilder

Seven Locks Press
Cabin John, MD/ Washington, D.C.

ISBN0-932020-81-X (Cloth)
ISBN 0-932020-80-1 (Paper)

Cover design by Wendy Ross.
Text design by The Publishers Service Bureau.
Printed by McNaughton and Gunn.
Set in Times Roman and printed on acid-free paper.

SEVEN LOCKS PRESS
P.O.Box 27
Cabin John, MD 20818
(301) 320-2130

Acknowledgment: "Dreams,"by Langston Hughes, copyright 1932 by Alfred A. Knopf, Inc., and renewed 1960 by Langston Hughes. Reprinted from "The Dream Keeper and other Poems" by Langston Hughes, by permission of Alfred A .Knopf, Inc.

CONTENTS

WILDER: HOLD FAST TO DREAMS

To Nancy, Lisa and Mandy
and to all the Miss Beulahs.

Hold fast to dreams
For if dreams die
Life is a broken-winged bird
That cannot fly.

Hold fast to dreams
For when dreams go
Life is a barren field
Frozen with snow.

-Langston Hughes

Introduction

The first time I met Doug, it was quickly apparent to me that he had his sights set on a goal higher than average. It was in 1962, at a convention of our college fraternity, Omega Psi Phi, an important and exciting time—just before passage of public accommodation laws and after the Supreme Court decision ordering the integration of schools. I already was active in the civil rights movement, having organized lunch counter sit-ins in Greensboro, and was anxious to talk to Doug, who was starting to build his successful law practice in Richmond.

We were just in fraternity politics then, but you could determine leadership traits and qualities. You could identify some of the guys in what I call the breakthrough generation, those who were determined to be the first to break through, such as the first black to go to the university. It was already too late for us in that regard—both Doug and I had been barred by law from attending our home state universities.

Doug did not settle for being average, even then. He stood out at that convention. Among his peers, and among those who were much older, he already had carved out a niche of respect for himself. He had standout qualities—an aptitude for leadership, and an understanding of the need to build coalitions. And he still has those qualities.

The people who are the first always have got to be overqualified, to be able to survive the double and triple standards, and obviously Doug was prepared to match those standards, to make a breakthrough.

When he became lieutenant governor, I was delighted, but not at all surprised. Because I had seen Doug as early as 1962, at that convention in Denver, Colorado, taking the necessary steps—exhibiting powerful ambition, showing determination to understand and set policy—to go straight to the top.

By the time Doug became a legislator, developing within the context of the black base, he also showed a sense of outreach, of coalition building beyond the black base.

Bicultural relations are familiar to most black officials from an early age. You live on one side of town and work on the other side; you live on one side of town, you caddy at the country club on the other side of town; you live on one side of town, you wait tables in the other part of town.

The difference is, that for a black person—Birch Bayh's son can run for governor of Indiana without the political burden of a racial standard; Dan Quayle can become vice president without the political burden of race—for Doug Wilder and Jesse Jackson to be the first out of the box, we have an extra burden.

You do the best you can as a black person to allay people's fears. You do that by being fair, being non-racist. Some white Democrats have tried to protect themselves by trying to discredit blacks. They did that to me. They did that to Dr. King as well. I'm in good company.

For the most part, blacks vote for whites in great numbers, but whites do not vote for blacks in great numbers. We face the challenge of reciprocal voting, and legislative slate-making. Doug was on the cutting edge of demanding fairness, demanding reciprocal voting, demanding that he be included in the legislative slate-making. Black politicians have gone out in the social clubs and in the churches, in the parks, and on the media, and convinced other blacks to support a white, based upon their knowledge of that person and trust. They haven't just endorsed the whites, they have worked to popularize them.

Blacks running for statewide office is the new breakthrough, sometimes running in their party, sometimes running as independents. If a black candidate challenges leaders in his party, it is because, for the most part, blacks have been attacked more by white Democrats than by white Republicans. When Doug thought about running for Senate in 1982, he met resistance. Every time he came up with the idea of running, he met resistance. The challenge to white Democrats is to be reciprocal in voting, to be expansive, to be inclusive, to be fair. They have been the beneficiary of black investment and now blacks are demanding a fair return on their investment. It's a reasonable demand.

If white politicians who receive black votes would be as fair to blacks as blacks have been toward them, if white Democrats work as hard to convince whites that Doug is fair and good for the state, as he as done for whites for years, he'll win. That is the key. Reciprocity. If that happens, blacks will take their place as governors, senators and president. In my last campaign, I got 25 percent of the votes. I won in New York and Alaska; in Michigan and Mississippi, so that process is taking place.

People expect me to stand for the civil rights of blacks, but not at their expense. They sense that I want to be fair.

You seek common ground.

If you're running in Virginia, you run on a platform of fair prices for farmers, adequate resarech for the tobacco industry during its transition, pay equity for women, a higher minimum wage for all workers. And a better education of our children, all children. Day care and prenatal care and head start on the front side of life is cheaper than jail care and welfare on the back side of life. You take a strong position against the flow of drugs and access of guns in the hands of unauthorized people and criminals. You are for affordable housing. Those issues are not characterized as ethnic. They affect everybody positively. That's how you do it. You run in search of solutions, common ground.

But you should never abandon your natural base when you reach out. That's not right, and it's not good. But you don't have to. You can still stress better education of black children, because that is good for everyone, because education produces the kinds of citizens who pay taxes, and lack of education does not. It's better to spend money to keep young people in high school at seventeen, and in college after that, than in jail at twenty-seven. So it makes sense to invest in Virginia State and Norfolk State.

It's good for Virginia's productivity to drive away drugs and crime. It's good for everybody. You've got to articulate those issues. You've also got to challenge discrimination, whether it's race, sex or rural discrimination. You've got to stand for that. You can't just be warm spit. You've got to stand for something.

African-Americans aren't monolithic. Yet we're always projected in five really devastating stereotypes: As being less intelligent than we are; less hard working than we are; less universal than we are; less patriotic than we are, and more violent than we are. Such stereotypes are unfair, untrue and unAmerican.

There are some issues that may still be distinctively black, but there are

Introduction

civil rights organizations, and other ethnic leaders, to keep the pressure on on those issues. To ask a man who could be governor to be the state's top civil rights leader all at the same time may be asking a bit too much.

The New South must shift away from being a battleground, to economic common ground, to moral higher ground. And it is in that vernacular that everybody wins. You maximize everybody's security level, you minimize the discomfort level.

It's more likely to happen in the South first because the ground has been plowed more thoroughly. And when the ground is plowed more thoroughly, you get a better crop. Plus, in the South, the political equation demands a different relationship between blacks and whites.

Blacks and whites are in the same political boat. Either one can capsize the boat. So they reach an accommodation. Given the black-white ratio in Virginia, it lends itself to a new equation.

Doug knows he has the ability to be governor of Virginia. But he also knows he has to bear the double cross of being politician-public servant, spelling out his vision and ideology, and facing the headwind of being told he can't win. But you can't win political victories posthumously. So you can't wait.

When Doug was elected lieutenant governor, he surprised a lot of people who told him he couldn't win. They didn't know him, didn't see his breakthrough qualities that I saw back in 1962.

Now Doug dares to see himself as an equal. He dares run for governor. Whatever I can do to help Doug, I'll do it, whether it is by proximity or distance. When you volunteer to help someone, you get as close as they need you to be, as far away as they need you. Again, it's a delicate situation. I'm sensitive to his burden. The registration we did in 1984, and our victory in Virginia in 1984, laid the groundwork for Doug's victory in Virginia in 1985. Our Super Tuesday victory in 1988 in Virginia laid the groundwork for future victories.

There have been amazing changes already in my lifetime. I remember the first time I went through Richmond. It was in the early sixties, and we were driving from Greensboro to Washington and stopped there for the night. We couldn't use a hotel or motel. Doug couldn't go to the University of Virginia in Charlottesville, but now two of his children are graduates of UVa, and one of my sons is a student there, and Doug is the lieutenant governor.

Now Doug dares to make a difference again. Simply by running, he sets a pace, he sets anchor. In so many ways, he can't lose. He dares to make a difference.

And if he wins, the inauguration itself will lift the sights of millions of people around the world. Just the inauguration. Not to mention what he can accomplish as governor. The aspiration level of people everywhere will be heightened.

Great changes have been made in my lifetime, and more are coming. We truly are the breakthrough generation. I'm so proud of Doug. I glory in his gain.

The Rev. Jesse L. Jackson.

PREFACE

Six weeks before the 1989 Virginia Republican gubernatorial primary election, one of the three white conservative men vying for the nomination, former state attorney general J. Marshall Coleman, ran into Doug Wilder at a sheriff's association meeting at Kings Dominion, a theme park north of Richmond.

Who would ever have thought," Coleman said with genuine admiration, "that the way to get the Republican nomination in 1989 would be to say that 'I'm the only guy who can beat Doug Wilder?' You've come a long way, Doug," Coleman said to Wilder.

By mid-year, Wilder was an even favorite to defeat Coleman, who won the June 13 Republican primary, and to become the first black elected governor in American history. (In 1872, Pickney B. S. Pinchback served one month as acting governor of Louisiana during the impeachment of his white carpetbagger predecessor.)

This in Virginia, the Old Dominion, the former Capitol of the Confederacy, where every sleepy courthouse town covets a memorial "to our Confederate dead," where less than a generation ago some of the public schools closed rather than allow black children to attend with whites, and where, despite Wilder's acknowledged prowess as a barrier-breaker, the racist lyrics of the state song, "Carry Me Back to Old Virginia," remain intact.

Like its native son Wilder, Virginia too had come a long way in the decades of the 1970s and 1980s. What had been a quiescent southern state, known by tourists as a commonwealth that virtually deified its sometimes glorious, sometimes inglorious past, had transformed itself into the New Dominion, a relatively progressive, almost Eastern, state, leading the New South toward a new century.

And nothing typified the change in such stark—even black and white—terms as the presence of Doug Wilder, a grandson of slaves, a savvy, smart city slicker of a lawyer who was forced to get his law degree beyond the border of his native land because of the color of his skin, at the head of the ticket of the Democratic party of not just Madison, Monroe and Jefferson, but also of Robert E. Lee, Stonewall Jackson, Jefferson Davis, Harry Byrd Sr. and Mills E. Godwin.

1. From the Kitchen to the Stage

The slight, immaculately dressed black man, in the grasp of a state trooper, strode off the freight elevator, glided around an obstacle course of hanging pots, walk-in freezers and grease-coated gas stoves, and pushed through the swinging door.

As he entered the hot, crowded room, he was greeted by scores of sweaty, outstretched palms, seeking to touch him, and bombarded by pleas for recognition from hundreds of voices hoarse with joy.

The ornate ballroom of the John Marshall Hotel in downtown Richmond, and its adjoining kitchen, were familiar territory for Doug Wilder. As a dollar-a-day waiter in the late 1940s and early 1950s, he had worked many an evening there, serving banquet meals, busing tables and dutifully responding to an occasional command of "more coffee, boy" from diners in the all-white crowds.

Waiting tables was just one of many part-time jobs that Wilder, next to the youngest of eight children of a poor-but-proud family from Richmond's Church Hill neighborhood, held to help pay his tuition at nearby Virginia Union University, where he was studying chemistry. A church-operated, all-black school, founded during Reconstruction, Union was less prestigious and more expensive than Virginia's highly touted major public colleges, but Wilder was barred from attending them because of his race.

So it should hardly be surprising that, in frustration, the otherwise efficient, light-skinned young waiter occasionally spilled coffee or dumped a tray on an obnoxious patron, or, a decade later, as an angry, battle-scarred veteran of Korea, contemplated more serious actions—sprinkling poison on the salads of his white oppressors was one idea he toyed with.

But this night, November 5, 1985, was different: Squeezing through the cheering crowd, his plainclothed bodyguard clearing a path, Lawrence Douglas Wilder bounded onto the stage, stretched his hands skyward in a double V that was at once the traditional victory signal and a silent acknowledgement of a dream come true: This grandson of slaves had just been elected lieutenant governor of Virginia by nearly 50,000 votes.

"Looking at that audience was more beautiful than anything," he reflected several years later. "Young, old, white, black, of every description. And the rancor and bitterness of the campaign, even of all the years, dissolved into the crystallization of the moment, of the realization that it's all possible."

That night, Wilder spoke extemporaneously, which he does best, and convolutely, which he does often.

"Many, many years ago, in this room—there may be some of you here who were with me," he said, scanning the shoulder-to-shoulder crowd for glimpses of relatives and former fellow waiters, "when I used to listen to political speeches, as I would wait tables on this floor, as well as in the gallery (cheers from the balcony), little did I believe that one day (pause), I just might be, your (pause) lieutenant governor (cheers). I give thanks to God for having brought me this far along the way.

"I can only hope that my mother and father were here to witness this moment. But I can see my mother's face (smiling, momentarily lost in reverie) as clearly as if she were here (a thought that unleashed that broad, infectious grin that had soothed a thousand suspicions during the just-ended campaign) and she

1

would tell me, 'Don't let your head get too big (applause) because you know you didn't get there by yourself.' And God knows I didn't."

2. First Families of Virginia

Doug Wilder is a third- or maybe fourth- or fifth-generation Virginian. When the Wilders first came to Virginia—a state that treats the genealogy of its white citizens with reverence and meticulous record-keeping—cannot be determined because his paternal grandparents and two of his aunts—his father's oldest sisters—were slaves. Slaves first were brought to Virginia in the late 1600s by a Dutch trader, so it is conceivable that the Wilders came to Virginia early enough to qualify, except for the color of their skin, for membership in the First Families of Virginia (FFV). But, as a curator at the state archives put it matter-of-factly, there is no official document detailing the arrival of the Wilders in Virginia because "they didn't keep track of their property in those days, any more than we keep track of people's automobiles today."

This much is known: Doug Wilder's grandfather, James W. Wilder, was born November 18, 1838, in Goochland County, just west of Richmond, and his paternal grandmother, Agnes W. Johnson, was born December 8, 1839, in Richmond.

A marriage certificate, pressed into the family Bible along with a color reproduction of the Emancipation Proclamation, records that they were married April 25, 1856, at Braggs Farm in Henrico County, north of the capital city.

James and Agnes Wilder's oldest two children were Emma, born August 15, 1857, in Richmond, and Sallie, born the same date four years later, in Hanover County.

Some time after their marriage, James Wilder and his young wife were sold separately, with Agnes taking her two young daughters with her to a house in Hanover County, the next county north of Henrico. "So trustworthy was James that he was given a white pass, which permitted him to cross the county line and visit his wife each Sunday, (when) he walked from Henrico to Hanover County," wrote Sarah Laverna Jones Sharp, a neighbor of the Wilders on Church Hill, in a paper titled, "Genealogy Challenge to the Black American." It went on:

"Agnes was a house servant. Her master had a handicapped child (who) was her complete responsibility. Whenever she was not caring for the child, she had sewing to do for the entire family....A tutor came at regular intervals to teach the child. During these times, Agnes would sit in the sewing corner (where) she absorbed all of the lessons taught to the child by tutor. In this way, she became quite literate. Each night she went back to her little hut, to her own babies."

Some time after January 1, 1863, when President Abraham Lincoln ordered the manumission of slaves, the Wilders were reunited. The census of 1870 recorded that James Wilder, age thirty-two, a teamster, and his wife, Agnes, thirty-one, lived in Richmond.

None of the Wilders now living remembers Sallie, who died in 1892, but several older members of Doug's generation remember Aunt Emma Reed, who lived in South Fulton, not far from Church Hill, until her death in 1932, when Doug was one year old.

Wilder's father, Robert Judson Wilder, the youngest of James and Agnes Wilder's thirteen children, was born in Richmond on July 10, 1886. At the time, his mother was forty-six and his father was forty-seven.

In Richmond, James and Agnes Wilder accomplished the incredible feat of saving enough money not only to raise thirteen children, but to build and own a house, in the Church Hill section of the city. He died on March 8, 1912, and his wife died June 9, 1919.

Except that they were free Negroes, less is known about the lineage of Wilder's mother and her family. Beulah Olive Richards was born April 26, 1892, in the hamlet of Ruthville, in Charles City County, near Williamsburg. None of her children knows anything about their maternal grandfather, except, presumably, he was named Richards.

Beulah's mother, Mary Richards, brought her to Richmond when she was a baby, where they lived briefly with Beulah's grandmother, who was called Pinky. Douglas and his sisters don't know if Pinky was a nickname, her first name, or her last name. Shortly thereafter, Mary and her daughter, Beulah, moved to Newark, N. J., where Mary worked as a live-in domestic for a family that owned a brick company. While living there, Mary Richards met and married the family's chauffeur, Robert Tolan.

Beulah attended the integrated public schools in Newark, and was a student at Sumpter High School. When Beulah was fourteen or fifteen, her mother died. Beulah returned to Richmond and lived on Church Hill with her grandmother Pinky and her Aunt Kate, who worked as a domestic for a white family.

When she was about twenty, while buying groceries at Harvey Peace's store, near her house, she met Robert Wilder, who delivered groceries for Mr. Peace via horse and wagon. They were married July 8, 1913.

3. Gentle Poverty

After their marriage, Robert and Beulah Wilder, Douglas Wilder's parents, moved into Robert's parents' house, which was known in the family as the Old Homestead. There they joined an extended family that already included Douglas's grandmother, Agnes, his Aunt Mary and her husband, Foster, who already had set up housekeeping there. Douglas's grandfather, James Wilder, had died in 1912.

Douglas's parents bought the house in 1919, but it wasn't long before they decided it was time for a new house. Robert Wilder signed a contract for the new house on October 2, 1923. The builder, E. Roscoe Bailey, promised to construct a frame house "according to plans and specifications furnished by Mr. Robert Wilder, on the southeast corner of 28th and P streets, for the sum of $2,875. To be paid as follows: $175 when contract is signed; $900 when roof is on; $900 when building are (sic) ready for plaster, and remainder when house is completed. Will utilize all old materials, stripped down and suitable to complete job in a first-class, workman-like manner."

Roscoe Bailey was a man of his word. The new Wilder residence was one of the handsomest houses on the block. Its pillared front porch, which faced 28th Street, ran the thirty-foot width of the house. Its wide concrete stoops quickly became a favorite gathering spot for the children. On the P Street side were upstairs and downstairs porches, partly enclosed with siding, and connected by exterior stairs. Beulah Wilder could watch the comings and goings on busy P Street from her kitchen window. When neighbors stopped by, they entered through the gate in the tall backyard fence and onto the porch, which had doors to both the kitchen and the hallway.

Inside the front door, a foyer, often adorned by fresh flowers from the yard, led to the stairs, and to a hall past the dining room to the kitchen at the rear. The living room, with its three big windows, looked out on the front porch. Upstairs, the lone bathroom was between the girls' bedrooms in the rear and the parents' bedroom was above the living room. A door from the boys' bedroom to the upstairs porch provided a convenient entrance on those nights when Douglas or his older brother, Robert, would sneak in after curfew.

The house was finished none too soon. The Wilders had four children by the time they moved in—two others had died in infancy—and four more were born in the next nine years.

The first two children born to Robert and Beulah Wilder didn't live beyond infancy: Elizabeth, the oldest, died of a childhood disease when she was about three years old; the second, a boy, lived only a few days, not even long enough to get a name.

Then came eight healthy children, the next to the youngest of whom they named Lawrence Douglas Wilder, in honor of two great American Negroes, poet Paul Lawrence Dunbar and abolitionist-orator Frederick Douglass. In later life, people would remark that Lawrence Douglas, would exhibit traits of both of his namesakes.

The Wilder's second son, born January 17, 1931, was called Lawrence— his mother would abide no nicknames—until Beulah Wilder discovered that a neighbor was slurring her baby's name to "Larnce." That was unacceptable. After that, the boy was Douglas—never Doug. To this day, while he is referred to as Doug by millions of people, most of whom have never met him, he remains Douglas to his family.

Beulah Wilder not only insisted that her children be addressed by their first names, not Bob or Doug, and also that she and her husband be referred to properly. She was called Mrs. Wilder, or Miss Beulah by her friends, and her husband was Mr. Wilder to those outside his immediate circle of friends.

Miss Beulah worked on-and-off outside the home, as a domestic, and as a "salad girl" in the dining room of a downtown apartment building. Douglas's sister Olga, who was named after a Russian classmate of her mother's at Sumpter High in Newark, remembers visiting her mother at the dining room and hearing someone refer to her as Beulah. "So me and my fresh mouth, I said, 'That's Mrs. Wilder.''

Because his brother, Robert, was ten years older, it seemed to young Douglas that he lived in a world of girls—teasing, bothersome, irritating sisters and their friends. For most of his childhood, four sisters were at home: Olga, eight years older; Agnes, six years older; Beulah Berthel, who preferred to be called BB, or, as a compromise to her mother's formality, Berthel, two years older; and Jean, two years younger. Jean alone was born in a hospital. The three older children, Naomi, Doris and Robert, all deceased, were, respectively, sixteen, fourteen and ten years older than Douglas.

Wilder gave his sisters a fit, as he described it, and they gave him a fit in return. Two or three of them would gang up on him, and he'd try to grab them by the arm and sling them. When he complained to his mother, she replied, "whatever these girls do, you can't fight them." When he said that they took advantage of him, she said, "I'll have to punish them. You tell me what they've done."

The Wilders grew up in what they now describe as the "gentle poverty" of a segregated neighborhood in the former capital of the Confederacy.

Although their father's salary never exceeded fifty dollars a week, Robert Wilder Sr. had what his contemporaries viewed as a good job, especially during the Great Depression. He sold insurance, door-to-door, and collected the weekly premiums, usually a nickel, dime or quarter, for the Richmond-based Southern Aid Insurance Co., the oldest black-owned insurance company in America.

Later, when he was promoted to a clerical position, he sometimes allowed Douglas to tag along with him to the Southern Aid's headquarters on Second Street, in the heart of Richmond's "colored downtown." Visiting the four-story brick building, with its high ceilings and ornate trim, was like going into a bank. The young boy was impressed that blacks owned the building. He also was impressed with the company's stylish president, a Mr. Jordan, who wore spats, patent-leather shoes and striped trousers.

Robert Wilder hadn't intended to stay in the insurance business. He had struck a deal with his brother, Charles: He would help Charles become a doctor and then Charles would help Robert become a lawyer. Robert and Beulah Wilder carried out their part of the bargain, helping Charles pay for medical school by taking out a mortgage on their house. But Charles Wilder was unable to live up to his part. After graduation, and an internship at Freedman's Hospital in Washington, he returned to Richmond and began his medical practice, setting up

Gentle Poverty

his examining room in a corner room of Robert and Beulah Wilder's house. But before he could make enough money to allow Douglas' father to quit his job and read for the bar (one didn't have to go to college in those days to become an attorney) he contracted pneumonia and died, at age thirty-two. His death dealt a bitter, as well as emotional, blow to Robert. He had no recourse other than to stay in the insurance business.

Because of his steady job, Douglas' father often was called on to help some of his older brothers and sisters during the Depression. He could be counted on to provide food from the barn-like shed—he called it a stable—at the back of their house. A relic from Douglas' grandfather's days as a teamster, the stable was taller than the house and filled more than half of the backyard. The Wilders raised an assortment of fowls in it at various times: Chickens, guinea hens, ducks, geese, about two hundred homing pigeons. Inexplicably, his father tore the stable down when Douglas was about nine years old.

Douglas' father was a fanatic about keeping things freshly painted. It fell to Robert and Douglas to whitewash the fence with lime, which their father explained preserved it and made it look good. Like Huck Finns, though, the boys would slip off to play ball. When they'd come home, "I'd get a whipping, and Bob would get two whippings, for letting me go along," Douglas said.

The Wilder house knew no strangers.

Miss Beulah was fond of saying, "this is not my house, it's the family's house, and all are welcome." And over the years, various relatives, and some who just acted like relatives, took her up on the offer.

Because there was no central heat in the house, on cold nights, the kitchen, with its big wood-burning stove, was the warmest room in the house. It was there that the family gathered to listen to the radio, or do homework. One of the after-school chores in the winter was collecting the bark from the yard of a neighbor who cut lumber, and being careful not to shake off the sawdust, bringing it home for the stove. Their father also occasionally brought home a bag of coal.

There was enough difference in the girls' ages—Naomi taught Jean in first grade at George Mason elementary school—that two bedrooms reserved for the girls, one with twin wrought iron beds and the other with a double, were usually sufficient for the number living at home at any given time. Douglas and Robert shared the smaller bedroom in the front of the house.

"We never went hungry, and we had indoor plumbing and there were many homes that had outdoor facilities," said Jean. "You never felt you were poor. We all had clothes, and food and heat, and we all went to school every day, and no one said they were poor."

The stability of the family was a source of pride to the Wilder children, many of whose playmates were constantly on the move, living with a changing array of parents and step-parents. At the start of the school year, when the teachers at George Mason elementary school traditionally asked the children to stand and introduce themselves, the Wilders were happy to be able to say that they lived in the same house as the year before, with both their mother and father, as well as brothers and sisters.

The chores were divided, and well defined. And too many to suit young

7

Douglas. He remembers ducking work and lying on the floor by the screen door, watching the rain, and allowing his fertile imagination to conjure up all sorts of dreams, including escape from the incessant chores.

"I'd think, somebody's going to come and pick me up someday. I don't belong with these people. Once, I told my mother, 'Some rich people left me here, didn't they? They're coming back for me, aren't they?'" She laughed, so he told his sisters the same thing. "I'm not going to be here with you long." And they'd laugh too. "They would crack up," he said.

The chores included polishing the nickel on the kitchen stove, washing and drying dishes, washing and pressing clothes, and hauling the ashes from the two stoves. The Wilders didn't get central heat until 1956, the year Olga got married. "And we got it then only because Dad said he didn't have any more kids to carry out the ashes," she said.

The demands for cleanliness extended beyond the front door. Robert Wilder not only required his children to sweep the sidewalk in front of the house, but also the street. "See that stuff (trash) there," Wilder said on a recent tour of his old neighborhood. "That wouldn't be there. 'Sweep it and pick it up,' he'd say. 'Not toward the culvert,' because that would stop it up. I used to stop it up purposely, because I'd like to see the water coursing."

Even though she had a house full of daughters, Beulah Wilder seldom asked them to help with the cooking. The only exception was on Sunday mornings, when the girls prepared breakfast, while their mother got ready for church. And then, wearing clothes reserved for the day, they'd all set off for services at the First African Baptist Church, a historic edifice that was the site, in 1867, of a freedman-dominated Republican state convention that fired the flames of Reconstruction in Virginia. It was a healthy walk down Church Hill to Fourteenth and Broad streets, downtown. The family never had a car, and neither parent learned to drive.

Stalling around on Sunday morning didn't result in a reprieve from attending church. Anyone who was late was required to attend services across the street from their house, at the Fourth Baptist Church. Dr. Robert L. Taylor, who was pastor at Fourth Baptist for thirty-four years, remembers seeing various Wilders slip into the back pews. "They were frequent visitors," he smiled. And although the Wilders were not members, the children often participated in social events there.

The Wilders are a musical family. There has been a Wilder family member in the choir at First African as long as anyone can remember. Douglas' cousin, Mary Lucas Winston, passed the half-century mark as a choir member in 1988. Douglas' father sang in the choir until he became a deacon. And for many years, he also sang in the Sabbath Glee Club, a twenty-five voice *a cappella* group that earned an international reputation in the first half of the century. Although Douglas made a name for himself as a singer at church socials as a boy, and in bars as a young man, he never joined the choir, which, along with not becoming a preacher, disappointed his father.

One of the money-making ventures that was passed down through the family was selling the Richmond Planet, the weekly black newspaper (later renamed The Richmond Afro-American).

8

Gentle Poverty

The Planet's carriers didn't have regular routes, like the youngsters who sold the daily News Leader or Times-Dispatch. Instead, its sales boys and girls went to the newspaper plant downtown every Thursday and bought a supply of papers, for a nickel a piece, and then sold them door-to-door for a dime.

During the time that Wilder was selling the Planet, the newspaper company, which also published editions in Washington, Baltimore and New Jersey, held a sales contest, with first prize being a week-long trip to New York City. The winners from Richmond were Doug Wilder, a girl named Janet Jones, who lived in Jackson Ward, the most prestigious of Richmond's black neighborhoods, and an adult man, who doubled as chaperone.

Robert Wilder accompanied his son to the Richmond, Fredericksburg and Potomac railroad station on Broad Street, where Douglas joined the two other local winners for the trip. The young Wilder was not bothered by the segregated facilities at the train station—they had to purchase their tickets at the colored window, wait in the colored section of the waiting room and then ride in a car reserved for colored passengers—but by his father's frugality and lack of excitement about the trip. Robert gave his son $5 and said, "don't spend it all."

In New York, the lack of spending money didn't dampen Wilder's enthusiasm for the big city. The wonders he was seeing were mind-boggling: the Statue of Liberty, the Empire State Building, Radio City Music Hall, Rockefeller Plaza. And the Automat. They ate all their meals at Horn and Hardat. The young Wilder was amazed. "Put five cents in it and out came a piece of pie."

After a week in New York, Douglas was anxious to tell his family about his adventure. His father dutifully met him at the railroad station, where, before his star-struck son could begin spouting off the glories of New York, he inquired, "how much money you got left?" Douglas had spent all but a few cents. "Boy," his father said, "you threw all your money away."

Beulah Wilder, a tee-totaling Christian woman, didn't allow whiskey to be consumed in the house—although she made an exception for her homemade wine, although she did not drink it. The abstinence rule, observed Douglas, lead to "a lot of nipping in the back yard" by his father.

Robert Wilder was a deacon in his church, but he also was a weekend drinker who stashed his booze in the chicken house, which was the remaining section of the stable at the back of the lot. On Saturday afternoons, he and his cronies, from the church, Masonic lodge or the neighborhood, slipped back there for a few jolts and then, sufficiently lubricated, returned to the side porch and offered solutions to all the problems of the world. Douglas called those sessions his father's "town council meetings." His father's favorite perch was on the side porch, facing P Street, from where he could look down at those who passed on the busy sidewalk. "He liked to be higher—literally—than the others, over them," Douglas laughed. "Even when people came on the porch, he'd stand or sit so they'd have to look up at him," like the king of Siam demanding that his subjects keep their heads lower than his.

Their salutations befitted a royal court, Douglas said, imitating their exchanges. "'How are you, my Lord?' 'Fine, your grace.'" Inside the house, his mother, with mock criticism, lamented, "Listen to them out there." One night, a friend became a little inebriated and suggested that he and Robert continue their

9

party somewhere else. Jean remembers the incident. "Mother never bossed Daddy around, or anything like that," but when the visitor urged, "Oh, come on Bob," Miss Beulah came out scowling and said, "If you got a home, you better go to it."

Robert Wilder's pals sought his advice as though he were a sage, and he dispensed it in like manner. Between puffs on his pipe, or a cigar or cigarette— he smoked whatever was at hand—he would respond in a voice so deep and low that they were required to strain to hear the wisdom, a technique his politician son later would employ effectively.

The porch also was the site of informal practice sessions of the Sabbath Glee Club, which performed in churches and lodges throughout Virginia, and sometimes as far away as Ohio and New York. The Sabbath Glee, as it was known, was founded and directed by Joseph Matthews, a toothless, white-haired self-taught musical genius, who worked days as a porter at the Federal Reserve Bank in Richmond and arranged music at night. The great Marian Anderson was among those who dropped by to ask him for a special arrangement. On a trip to Washington in 1939, the Richmond chorus was hailed by the director of the National Folk Life Festival, after its performance there, as "one of the best vocal groups in the U. S." And when the British Radio Corporation recorded the choir's most popular spirituals, including "Swing Low, Sweet Chariot," "Ezek-iel Saw the Wheel," and "Roll, Jordan, Roll," for an album, British prime minister David Lloyd George called it "one of the best male choruses I have heard, I'm almost certain it was the best." (One of the songs on the album was "Carry Me Back to Old Virginny," which, because of its lyrics, was the target of stinging criticism by State Senator Wilder in his first term in the Virginia General Assembly.)

After many of those informal practices, Robert Wilder, a bass baritone, and his fellow choraleers would reward themselves with a trip to the chicken house.

The chicken house always had plenty of laying hens, for fresh eggs, and as many as 200 homing pigeons, as squab was considered a delicacy in the Wilder house. Douglas relished the messy chore of killing the chickens. "I loved to get the hatchet," he remembers. And when he had chopped off a chicken's head, said, "I liked to watch them flop." His mother, ever economizing, cautioned him not to chop too much of the neck away.

Until Douglas was about four years old, his father kept horses in the stable, which he occasionally rented for riding. He had learned about horses from Douglas' grandfather, who made a living selling meal around Church Hill from a horse and wagon. Sometimes Douglas was sent across the street to the blacksmith, a Mr. Burke, to have two pieces of metal forged. He watched wide-eyed as Mr. Burke drove nails into a horse's hooves in the shoeing process, while their owners waited with their wagons.

When his brother came home from World War II, during which he had become an accomplished rider as a member of the cavalry, he and Douglas and their father liked to go to the country, to visit Fred Faulk, a deacon at their church, who rented horses. Wilder's dad, who was an expert rider and jumper, would say, "Fred, get us some spirited horses," said Douglas, who didn't want a spirited one. "I wanted one I could get on," said Douglas, who by then was in his early teens.

Gentle Poverty

Douglas later romanticized his riding feats, so much so that his sister Jean said "he now tells people he had a pony when he was a boy. He never did. He just imagined it, he wanted one so badly."

Douglas' father was the disciplinarian in the house—and beyond. Spankings were common, administered by both parents. If there was a squabble, Miss Beulah gave the spanking. And if anyone giggled over the misfortune of a sibling, and their father heard it, he'd say, "Come on, you need some too." And the giggler got it too.

Robert Wilder summoned his children by whistling. No matter where they were, if they heard his whistle, they went home. Rules were clearly spelled out. They knew when and where they could go. They were not allowed to read the paper before their father read it, but on Sundays, when he slept late, they sneaked a look at the comics and folded it back up before church.

Robert Wilder was as conservative with praise as he was liberal with punishment. "You were expected to do well," said Olga. "He never directly told us. But he had high expectations." Jean once overheard her father, leaning across the fence, tell a neighbor, "Jean's home from college, made all A's. I'm so proud of her." Jean said she ran to her mother said "Mom, he's proud of me!" Her mother said, "Yeah, I guess so." It was the first Jean knew of it.

Olga and her older sisters complained that their parents went easy on Douglas and Jean, because they were the youngest. Jean, agreeing partially, told how Douglas took her to the movies on Saturday. "He'd drop me off," Jean said, and then go off on his own, leaving her to sit in the theater all day while he played with his friends. When he picked her up, Jean said he threatened, "If you go back and tell Momma I made you stay here all day I'll never take you again." When her Mother asked, "Why did you stay so long?" Jean replied, "well, it was a good movie." Then her Mother said, "Douglas said he wanted to bring you home." "That's right," Jean said, biting her lip, "but I refused to come."

While Douglas was getting away with such stunts, the girls suffered from what they considered excess restrictions. They were not allowed to wear lipstick. Or bangs. Or have a boyfriend. "You were being a flirt," said Olga. "And no stockings and makeup, and dating, you had to be sixteen," complained Jean. They also weren't allowed to drink coffee or tea. "By the time I could drink the coffee," admitted Olga, "I was into gin."

Like laziness and rudeness, sickness was not tolerated. If you were ill, you got up and went to school, according to Jean, who said she has followed that practice with her own children. If one of the children complained of not feeling well, their father said, "You'll feel better once you get to school" Or church. Headaches didn't count. There was not a lot of aspirin dispensed, or other home remedies. When Berthel got a severe nose bleed, the only permissible treatment was to put ice on her nose. If the complaint were severe enough, their mother had a cure: An aspirin, a half teaspoon of soda, and the same amount of spirits of ammonia, in half a glass of water.

On those rare occasions when outside help was deemed necessary, their mother called Dr. Fred Brown, who had been a childhood friend in Charles City County. When he came, it was not just to treat the person. Long after he had dispensed his treatment, he sat in the kitchen and talked about the old days.

(Douglas's sister Doris later married the doctor's brother, Tom Brown.) Dr. Brown typically prescribed a diarrheic. A favorite was: Scrape an apple and banana, put them in rice water, boil and feed. "Rice water was the salvation," Jean said.

Once, when Jean was terribly sick with intestinal flu, her crying kept everyone awake. Her unsympathetic father yelled "Shut up that noise; people got to sleep." Olga and her mother bathed Jean to keep her quiet. "Daddy didn't think you were supposed to cry," Olga said. "I just think it was his upbringing. He didn't get sick. So no one else should."

4. An Ordinary Family

The most extraordinary thing about the Wilders, according to the Reverend Robert L. Taylor, who watched their comings and goings from his vantage point at the Fourth Baptist Church across the street, was that "it was an ordinary family, a typical, representative black family. They demonstrated the things you expect of family: They believed in sending their children to Sunday school and church, and to public schools; they aspired to average family goals....What is most admirable and significant," he continued, drawing on thirty-four years of observation, is that "one of our average, representative families—not one of the most wealthy, not one of the poorest—has produced the individual who is the highest black elected official in the United States."

Because of the size and stability of the family—Wilders lived at the corner of Twenty-Eighth and P, on one side of the street or the other, for about a century—they were well known on Church Hill. Everyone spoke as they walked by. And passersby knew their home; "That's the Wilders," they would say, nodding.

David L. Temple is the unofficial historian of Church Hill. He began writing the weekly social notes column from Church Hill for the Richmond Planet, as a high school student in the early 1930s and, with a few breaks over the years, was still writing it in retirement more than a half century later. Temple gave the future politician his first publicity. On May 4, 1934, under the heading "Kiddies Unite," he reported that Douglas Wilder, then aged three, and his sister Berthel were among guests at a birthday party for "little Willie Wilson Jr." The children enjoyed "a pleasant evening at the home of Mr. and Mrs. Wilson on East O Street. " It was to be the first of many mentions of Wilder in the Planet and its successor, the Afro-American.

Wilder's older sisters were regular social butterflies, as reported by Temple in the mid-1930s: Miss Doris Wilder spent weekend in Chester at First Union School, where Miss Naomi Wilder is a teacher. She was the dinner guest of Mrs. Hanna McComas; Miss Naomi A. Wilder spent some time in Petersburg last week, attending commencement at Virginia State; Little Miss Berthel Wilder was ringbearer in wedding of Hazel B. Williams and James Sims of King William County.

Helen Temple, David's wife, remembers a politician in the making. She was visiting his parents when Douglas came home after a ball game, his baseball cap turned backwards. She said he stopped and said, "'Oh, Mrs. Temple, I'm so happy to see you. You're looking so charming.' I said, "get out of here before I hit you. You're either going to be the biggest liar in the world, or the best lawyer.'"

There were Wilders scattered throughout Church Hill. Two of Robert Wilder's sisters were neighbors: Auntie Catherine lived across the street and Aunt Mary was four blocks away, and Miss Beulah's aunt, Kate Watkins, was just down the street. Every evening, at least one of the Wilder children was expected to walk to Twenty-Eighth and T to see what Aunt Mary wanted. "And don't take any money from her," their Mother cautioned.

They hated to see their Aunt Catherine coming. "She would tell on us, and anything bad anybody told Daddy about us he believed," Olga said. Jean recalled getting a whipping because someone told her father she had passed them without speaking. After that, Jean said, she waved to every house she passed, thinking somebody might be at the window. "You weren't going to disgrace; you were *Wilders*," emphasized Jean.

They were expected to achieve. "My daddy thought he could have been president, if you'd given him half a chance," Olga said. "And he could build a house if you gave him a hammer, a nail and a piece of wood. We were taught to be black and be proud long before, long before it became popular. It wasn't something you went around with a banner and advertised. It was just something that was expected."

While their father set the expectations, it was their mother who saw that they were carried out. Beulah Wilder had not completed high school, but she had high hopes for her children. It was she who spent the time with them, helping with their homework, encouraging them, seeing that they satisfied their father's orders, and her dreams. Helen Temple, who often visited the house, said Miss Beulah was the strong influence in the family.

On Friday nights, assorted relatives and friends gathered around the big kitchen table, to play cards and games—pinochle, rummy, spades, five hundred, dominoes, Chinese checkers, whist, mah-jongg and a Ouija board were among the possibilities—or listen to a favorite radio program.

"We did a lot of sharing around that table," said Douglas, whose mother especially seemed to relish those times, with everyone dipping into the ice box for cold drinks and snacks, and trying to keep in the conversation. "We don't lie, because we talk too much. We'd get caught. I may be mistaken, but I don't lie," said Berthel. Added Olga, "In this family, if you want in the conversation, you have to jump in."

Douglas loved teasing his sisters. When they played cards, he'd rile them by repeatedly asking one of them to pass him a needed card. "He was talking all the time," said Berthel. She'd say, "Douglas, shut up." The third or fourth time he'd ask, she'd throw the cards at him. His sisters in turn teased their younger brother about his vanity. Always conscious about his dress and looks, he stayed in front of the mirror more than his sisters did. Olga said he would ask, "How does this look?" and she would reply, "Smells good."

Miss Beulah was an avid game player. Monopoly and Scrabble were her favorites. If one of the children was losing at Monopoly, she might give them part of her pile of money. She took special pride in Douglas. "The two of them used to play word games all the time," Olga said. "He would come home and call out, 'I got one (a new word) for you.' Then he'd give her a word to define. And she would have another one for him. Like 'Can You Top This?'"

Their father seldom joined in the games. He went to bed very early—eight or eight-thirty—leaving the games, and the supervision of homework, to his wife. Beulah Wilder enjoyed those quiet times, after the younger children had gone to bed. She often stayed up very late, listening to the radio and working a crossword puzzle, or talking to the older children.

Meal times found as many as ten Wilders squeezed around the oblong dining room table. When one of them went off to college, or got married, the rest moved up closer to the head of the table. They always ate together, even if it meant waiting for their father, who often worked late. Meals began with grace, intoned in a mumble by their father. "Mother would say, 'Robert, it's time to start,'" Berthel said. "Daddy would bow his head, and move his hand across the top of his head as he prayed." It was difficult to hear him; he seldom spoke above a whisper, a habit that his children—even his politician son—lapse into still. But when his hand reached the bald spot near the back of his head, the children, peering above folded hands, knew he was finished.

As the meal progressed, their mother would ask, "Robert, have you had enough?' He'd say, 'I've stopped.' He'd never say he had enough. He'd say, 'I've stopped,'" Douglas remembered.

Douglas developed a dislike for fish because it seemed he was constantly getting bones caught in his throat. When that happened, it sometimes meant a trip to the doctor. By then, the family physician was Dr. V. J. Harris, whose office was about two blocks away. Douglas recalls creating a scene, being carried or dragged through the streets, to get bones cleared from his throat. After a while, when the others were having fish, his mother would fix something different for him. It was the same with soup. He hated potatoes cut up in the vegetable soup. When their mother fixed something special for Douglas, it angered his sisters, who complained, "Why's he got to have something different?" His father also mumbled his dissent.

Like many a child in those Depression days, Douglas survived—thrived—on a diet of Campbell soups, baloney sandwiches and peanut butter. Milk was served only on Sundays. A special treat in the days before homogenization was to get to the bottle of milk before the others and lick the cream off the top. "Oh man, that was good," recalled Douglas, smacking his lips.

Douglas's Aunt Kate prepared and delivered food to construction workers, and he considered it a treat to accompany her. Her staples were hot soup, pigs feet and baked potato pies, which she took to the construction sites in her Model-T Ford.

Douglas said the rhythmic swinging of picks and axes, as the workers grunted and dug ditches, usually for a new sewer or street, "was like Paul Muni in 'I Was a Fugitive From the Chain Gang,'" although unlike the movie, the workers his aunt fed were not prisoners. Not only did Douglas enjoy the rare chance to go for a car ride, but he knew going along increased the likelihood that his aunt would send him home with one of her extra pies.

Aunt Kate was constantly sending food to their house. And if a few days went by without a visit from her, Douglas or his sisters would pay a courtesy call, and in no time she'd hand over a tray of food to take home.

"We never were hungry. And we were never cold," Douglas said. "We had patches, but our clothes were clean. We all put newspapers in the bottoms of our shoes when we got a hole in them. And it was understood you didn't wear your Sunday clothes other than on Sunday, unless you had to go somewhere."

All of the children took music lessons, whether they wanted to or not. Olga, who played the piano, said, "Douglas has a very good voice. He was a big imitator. He used to copy singers."

Their Aunt Kate regularly hosted "silver teas"—so named because a silver offering was taken—at her house, or at the church, and her nieces and nephews provided the entertainment. Douglas sang and his sisters played and sang and accompanied him. Irene Wilson, a former neighbor who now teaches at George Mason Elementary School and directs the choir at Fourth Baptist, remembers Douglas singing "The Battle Hymn of the Republic" as a young adult.

Douglas also recited poems. He was so proficient at memorizing—a trait he inherited from his father—that in school the teachers always called on him to play the role of the prince, or the king, or the person who had the most to say. He hated it, he says now. "You're always up front." He also was embarrassed because he was always paired with a girl, the queen or the princess. "You know how little boys are. They don't want to be with girls. They want to be with the boys." But performing came easy, and it was good training.

There was never any worry about graffiti on the whitewashed fence, or about crime in the neighborhood. No one ever marked up the fence; it was that simple. Similarly, the children heard nothing of crime. The Wilders locked their doors, but the doors were flimsy, with a single pane of glass, and no bolt on either front or back. "No one was coming in your house unless you knew they were coming," Douglas said in later years. The only crime that any of the Wilders can recall occurred after all of the children were grown, when a boy snatched Miss Beulah's purse as she walked home from the grocery store. He was arrested a short time later, and her purse and keys were recovered. When Miss Beulah went to court to identify the purse-snatcher, it was the first time she had been in a courtroom, although by then her son had been practicing law for a couple of years.

The house, whose address was 933 North Twenty-Eighth Street, was torn down in the early 1970s. All of the narrow, two-story frame houses in the neighborhood were replaced with one-story, twenty-by-forty-foot brick-and-frame suburban ranchers, with chain-link fences enclosing what used to be two lots.

Because it had been the home of then-State Senator Wilder, there were suggestions that the house be preserved. Wilder didn't encourage it. He thought tearing down the old houses was in the better interest of the neighborhood, but when he made his first visit back, after the houses had been razed, "it really hit me." There was nothing familiar but the old tree in the back yard.

5. Life on Church Hill

In Richmond during the 1930s, nearly everything came in pairs, separate and unequal facilities and laws for blacks and whites. The city had two school divisions, two sets of libraries, two sides to a courtroom, two sections at the jail, two drinking fountains (painted black and white, for easy identification) two sets of rest rooms, two waiting rooms in the bus station, two ticket windows in the train depot, two places to sit on the trolleys and buses. The duplication even extended to the sections of the city. There were two downtowns, two North Sides, two West Ends and two Church Hills.

The Church Hill of Patrick Henry, where he delivered his fiery "give me liberty or give me death" speech that became a rallying cry of the American Revolution, was part of the smaller, white Church Hill that offers panoramic views of the James River to the south and the white downtown to the west.

Black Church Hill was, much like the folks who lived there, largely invisible to tourists or to the city's white residents. And there was little reason to visit black Church Hill: It had no vistas, no monuments, no acknowledged history.

Its boundaries were clear: Twenty-Fifth Street on the west, Thirty-Fourth Street on the east, Nine Mile Road on the north, and Marshall Street on the south (where white Church Hill began), a total of about a hundred blocks, with about five thousand residents. The black Church Hill of Doug Wilder's childhood was a self-contained community, and to a young boy who seldom ventured beyond it, it had everything. "You name it," Wilder remembers with enthusiasm, "and I could quick run out and get it. Just within a little area, no more than two square blocks."

The bustling neighborhood spewed a cacophony of sounds and a medley of smells: The whir of steel blades from the saw mill, next to the print shop that adjoined the Fourth Baptist Church; across the street, the clanging hammer of the blacksmith, and the neighing of the awaiting horses. In the next block west was Barnett and Richardson's hardware store, whose two white owners walked to work from their homes on Oakwood Avenue. Then came Simmons Laundry, Evans Bakery and two or three butchers. A block farther away was the ice house, to which the Wilder children were frequently dispatched in those days before the family had refrigeration. Douglas' mother occasionally got after him because he would "sit and run my mouth" with the workers at the ice house, while his purchase melted. There was big trouble if he hung around the fish house, because the operator was jailed periodically for selling corn whiskey.

There were no drugs on Church Hill in those days, although marijuana, heroin and, to a lesser degree, cocaine were available downtown on Second Street. For his childhood vice, Douglas tried smoking corn silk, but it made him sick. He didn't begin smoking cigarettes until he went to college, and continued for about fifteen years.

Billy's barber shop was what Wilder called "my stadium." It was there he first participated in political discussions. It was a place where men, and sometimes boys, gathered to talk seriously, to philosophize, to learn, to speak publicly on every kind of issue. Old-timers credit the late Edward (Jim) Carter, a bricklayer, with teaching the future politician how to debate.

WILDER: HOLD FAST TO DREAMS

Douglas was the youngest of the regular orators in the shop. He started speaking up when he was a shoeshine boy, no more than nine or ten. Because he listened carefully, he soon was able to engage older customers in serious conversations, whether the subject was baseball or politics.

To join the inner circle of barber shop philosophers, newcomers not only had to demonstrate proficiency in speech and a knowledge of a topic, but those old enough had to be registered to vote. The barber shop had a long tradition of emphasizing learning. Kids who stopped by with good report cards were rewarded by the owner Billy Alexander, and his regular customers, who understood the importance of education. Wilder returned to the shop after he was older, often stopping in after he had begun law practice in a nearby building.

Next door to the barber shop, at 2816 P Street, was Uncle Ned's shoe shine parlor, where Douglas shined shoes for tips. Around the corner on Twenty-Ninth Street was the pool hall where he developed a pretty good game (which he still plays, on a table in his home). His mother detested him going there, and, to his embarrassment, would come in and make him go home. "What can you learn there?" she asked. "You'd be surprised," he'd answer, laughing.

A new movie house was built on the corner of Twenty-Ninth and Q streets in 1937, when Douglas was six. It was named the Robinson Theater, in honor of Richmonder Bill "Bojangles" Robinson, who placed his footprints in the cement near a plaque that identified him as "the world's greatest tap dancer." (His dancing silhouette on the front of the stucco building is now fading on the cracking paint, and his footprints have long since been cemented over. The theater has been closed since the 1950s, but a new tribute to Bojangles, a statue in Jackson Ward, was dedicated a few years ago, by then-State Senator Wilder.)

The relationship between whites and blacks was "almost gentle," to use Wilder's description. Although the larger stores were owned by whites, blacks owned a number of mom-and-pop businesses: the saw mill, blacksmith shop, the barber shop, a cleaning and pressing shop, one of the printing plants and one of the two drug stores, which were on opposite corners of the same intersection. Both pharmacies had their loyal customers, and they did not often select the store by the skin color of the owner.

But the white-owned stores employed few blacks on a regular basis, not even what everyone referred to as the "Jew stores," whose owners had a reputation of being more sympathetic than other whites. About the only jobs available to blacks were as baggers at the A&P, or as shoe shine boys or errand runners. There were few role models: Even the firemen at the hose house were white.

An empty lot across the street from the blacksmith shop provided a ball field, where Wilder and his neighborhood pals played touch football. But sometimes Wilder's mother insisted that he play with the neighbor girl, Jean Harris, in her yard. "Douglas," she would say, "you've got to go around and play with Jean." The other boys, dirty from playing football, sneered as a cleanly scrubbed Douglas played unhappily with Jean.

St. John's Episcopal Church has been the main tourist attraction on Church Hill for two centuries, but to a boy growing up amidst reminders of American history that largely ignored, if not distorted, the contributions of blacks, the attraction was not the church, or its walled cemetery, or its view of the city. Rather, it was a black man, Spencer Rawls, who served as a guide there for years. Douglas had little interest in Rawls's lectures on Patrick Henry's speech, or the church's role in the American Revolution, which Rawls recited to visitors. What intrigued young Douglas was the jingle in Rawls's pocket, a jingle caused by the coins that tourists daily rewarded Rawls for his history lesson.

At four-thirty in the afternoon, the time that Rawls left the walled church yard—you could set your watch by him—Douglas would position himself across the street, and as the old man in the high-topped shoes set out on his regular route back home to the black section of Church Hill, the boy would greet him, and fall in lockstep with him.

"Hello, Wilder Boy," Rawls would say. "How are you?" He always called him "Wilder Boy."

"Fine, Mister Rawls."

And then Rawls would reach into his pocket and give Douglas a nickel. "He gave me a nickel every time he saw me," said Wilder, who, coin in hand, would skip off to P Street to buy candy or other treats.

His mother caught on to Douglas's trick—the ever-present parental spy network in action—and scolded him. "I understand you're begging." "No, mamma, I'm not," answered her son. It was true. "I never had to ask."

Years later, Rawls came to Wilder's law office as a client. And it was evident that he hadn't given away all his coins. He asked "Wilder Boy" to search a title for a house he wanted to buy, with cash.

The rule of two of everything in Richmond, one black and one white, didn't extend to playgrounds. There were none—not a swing or a slide—in black Church Hill. So Douglas and his friends ventured into white Church Hill, walking about three blocks beyond the boundary of their neighborhood, crossing Marshall and Broad streets. They played in Libby Hill Park, at Twenty-Ninth and Franklin streets, in the shadow of an eighty-foot -tall Confederate Soldiers and Sailors Monument, atop of which a fifteen-foot-tall bronze Rebel soldier, musket in hand, stared down on them.

"It was our park," he recalled. "It was in a white neighborhood, but we claimed it."

There were no actual fights with whites. "White kids didn't come into our park, and we didn't go into theirs." There were times of tension, however. If Douglas and his friends descended on a park and others were using it, some rocks occasionally were thrown or names were called.

But it wasn't whites who posed the major threat to the Church Hill blacks. It was blacks from other neighborhoods. Douglas and his friends from Church Hill felt somewhat isolated. They would not go down the steep steps that led to Fulton, or farther east to Fulton Hill, black neighborhoods on the other side of Stoney Run, a tributary of the James River. They knew that if they crossed those boundaries, they would have to fight.

The city's black neighborhoods had a pecking order, and there was a degree of snobbishness. South Richmond didn't measure up. Fulton absolutely didn't measure up, while Church Hill, maybe, had a few families, a very few families, who were considered upper crust. The Wilders were not one of them.

WILDER: HOLD FAST TO DREAMS

Richmond's black aristocracy, typified by Maggie Walker, the first black woman in America to own a bank and an insurance company, lived in Jackson Ward, near the black section of downtown, which was centered on Second Street and Leigh (not Lee, suh) streets. Next in prestige came a loosely defined area known as the West End, which was not to be confused, either in location or cachet, with the white West End, the bastion of the FFVs, First Families of Virginia, and their official watering hole, the CCV, Country Club of Virginia. (Richmonders are not totally humorless about their past: a flourishing cookie company is called FFV, for First Flours of Virginia.)

Not only did Wilder have to fight boys from rival neighborhoods, but because he is light-skinned, he also had to prove his worth to darker-skinned classmates. "They assumed you were a pantywaist, weak, not strong enough," if you were light-skinned, he said. "There was a demarcation at school. Not by the teachers—we were taught that we were all colored, that was the word—but the kids, they'd say, 'you old black so-and-so.' And they called people of my color 'you old yellow so-and-so.' That schism would go on. The kids taunted each other. Then someone would say to me, 'you're half white.' Because I associated with my brother and other older people, I learned early on to fight, to resist those things right away."

6. Richmond in Black and White

For most blacks, the way out of Church Hill, literally and figuratively, was via streetcar. The other most popular way was to walk. Few had automobiles.

Two trolley lines connected Church Hill with the rest of the city, the Jefferson line and the Venable line. Douglas's first exposure to the harsh realities of segregation came on the Jefferson Street trolley.

Because their house was near the end of the line, the streetcar was always empty, or nearly empty, when the Wilders boarded. Wilder remembers getting on with his mother, and sitting down the first place he came to, which was somewhere near the front. "She'd motion for me to get up and go with her to a seat in the back. I'd say, 'Why,' and she'd say, 'Just come on back. I'll tell you later.'" But his mother never explained. As he got a little older, his sisters took him to town, and when he asked them the same question, they said things such as "because we're supposed to."

"I just couldn't understand it. I was five or six years old. 'Why is it that we can't sit here?' I'd ask. It's that child-like simplicity that solves most of the problems of the world, because no one can ever give a plausible response." Thinking back, Wilder said, "Even looking through all the laws, and the constitutional interpretations, it comes down to simplicity: Tell this kid why he can't."

Unlike some other cities in the South, such as Montgomery, Alabama, where Rosa Parks was arrested for sitting in a section of the bus reserved for whites, there were no designated sections on the trolleys and buses of Richmond. Everyone was supposed to know the rules: Blacks filled up the seats from the rear, whites from the front. Blacks could come as far forward as space allowed, which meant that on the routes that ran through the black neighborhoods, they often could sit near the front.

Problems arose only when people didn't follow the rules.

Dr. Taylor, pastor emeritus of Fourth Baptist, recalled an incident involving Wilder's father. The streetcar was crowded, and Robert Wilder Sr. and he were standing next to each other. A black woman boarded and took the last remaining seat. It happened to be next to a white man, who was sitting in the row that divided the blacks from the whites. As far as Dr. Taylor knew, there was no law that said a black and a white couldn't share the same row—the rule simply said that blacks could not sit in front of whites. So the woman may have figured, if he doesn't like it, he can stand, Dr. Taylor surmised.

But the white man didn't like it, and said so. "He made some remark to her, like, 'You'll have to get up,'" Dr. Taylor said. "Mr. Wilder heard that, and leaned over to her and said something like, 'You sit right there.' Then he looked at the white man, and said something threatening. I couldn't hear the exact words. But I saw the racial fire. When it came to encroaching upon the rights of this black woman, Mr. Wilder stood his ground." The white man never opened his mouth, and the black lady stayed put.

Over the years, Dr. Taylor said, "I saw this deep concern on Mr. Wilder's part whenever he thought some black person was being taken advantage of."

Blacks often stood in the middle of the car, as the back section filled. But Douglas' playmate, Jean Harris, recalled that her mother "would never stand, and she would keep us from standing," even if it meant risking a confrontation

21

by sitting in front of whites. "She had a fiery pride," Harris recalls, but as a child, she remembers "the underlying fear that someone might strike you." The streetcar conductors were "a very rough bunch," according to David L. Temple, who waited tables at Cease's, a lunch shop near Byrd Park that was next to the car barn where the trolleys were kept overnight. A lot of the conductors were regular customers. "They were very hostile toward blacks," Temple discovered. They might come in and yell, "'You nigger, give me an egg sandwich, and hurry it up.'" Didn't he want to dump coffee on them? "Yes, sometimes. But you didn't. It was the Depression, and I needed the job."

Temple's wife, Helen, said blacks often had to stand on the streetcars, despite empty seats, because some whites wouldn't move forward into empty seats. When that happened to her, she didn't make a fuss because "after standing all day at work, I was too tired to argue, and besides that, I didn't want to get arrested." When she got a job at the Linen Mart in 1942, she became the first black sales clerk at a white, downtown store.

Florence Neal, another schoolmate of Douglas's, could not understand "why we couldn't be served in restaurants and could not sit anywhere we wanted on the bus." When she questioned her parents, "they said it was the law." Then they talked about her great, step-grandfather, who was a child during slavery, and said whites discriminated against blacks "because they do not feel blacks are able to excel. So it's important to go school and get an education."

The segregated seating pattern was the basis of much of the contention. As arguments about segregated seating began to occur more frequently on the trolleys and buses, the Greater Richmond Transit Co. organized an advisory committee to deal with the problems, and Dr. Taylor was named to it. "I think I was the only black appointed," he said. At one time he suggested that many of the problems could be resolved if the company would employ some black drivers. "The response was, 'We can't do that, because if we did, all the white folks will stop riding.' It was just that sharp."

The city's two bus stations had segregated waiting rooms, just as the train stations did when Douglas won the trip to New York. His sister Jean remembers the Trailways station, because she met the bus there when she was attending Virginia State College, about thirty miles south of Richmond. "It had a little, bitty waiting room (for blacks). That was it. And it was always crowded." In the 1960s, as a young lawyer, Wilder got a telephone call from a college friend who had been arrested for sitting in the white section of that same bus station. Wilder, who seldom handled civil rights cases, took that one, however, eventually to the United States Supreme Court, where his victory ended segregation in waiting rooms throughout the South.

Just as they did in the small shops of Church Hill, blacks noticed a difference between the big stores downtown that were owned by Jews and other white owners. While neither of the city's major department stores, Thalhimers or Miller and Rhoads, welcomed blacks with open arms, blacks have not forgotten that Thalhimers, owned by a Jewish family, treated them with more respect than the waspish Miller & Rhoads.

Douglas remembers that the water fountains, which usually were located near the escalators in the department stores, "always said white or colored, never

Richmond in Black and White

Negro or black. Always colored."

Janet Jones recalled shopping with her Aunt Sue in the basement of Miller and Rhoads, the part of the store where blacks were welcome, and trying on a yellow, pillbox hat, an action that violated protocol. Like the signs in an antique store that say, "You break it, you've bought it," the unwritten rule for blacks in downtown stores was, "You try it on, you've bought it." So when the clerk came rushing towards Janet, "I jammed it all the way down over my eyes. And then we bought it," she laughed. "It's not what they said, it's what happened," said Jean Harris. "They didn't want us to try on clothes and shoes. And you could not get a drink except at the colored water fountain. But my mother deliberately, absolutely challenged the system. She would not let us drink from the black-topped fountain. We always drank from the white one, and mother stared at anyone who tried to stop us." She brazenly dragged her children up to lunch counters and ordered food. Whenever a black deigned to do that, the white clerks responded by bringing the food on paper plates, but "mother went to places that didn't have paper plates. They would have to serve it on a real plate," she laughed. Jean Harris said "it took me years to overcome the feeling of being second-class. But I'm not bitter. You make peace as you grow older. But you never forget. The experience is just beneath the surface."

Douglas's sister Jean recalled that when their sister Doris died in 1970, she and Olga went shopping to find something appropriate for her to be buried in. "We were distraught, attending to those kinds of things, and we couldn't find what we wanted until we went into Montaldo's," one of Richmond's better clothing stores for women, which had been totally off limits to blacks when they were growing up. "I looked at Olga, and she looked at me, and we walked out. We said 'thank you,' but we just couldn't bury her in a dress from a store that she couldn't go into when she was alive."

Blacks could ride in only one of the elevators at Miller and Rhoads, but they could work in any of them, if they had the proper qualifications. "They would hire you only if you had some college, and were light-skinned," said Olga, who qualified on both counts, and worked there summers during college, as did several of her sisters. "It was not on the application, but it was an unspoken criteria. They had some brown-skinned girls, but they had to be very attractive."

"They expected you to be intelligent, and they measured your intelligence by how well you talked," added Jean, who also ran an elevator at Miller and Rhoads.

The city's hospitals, which also were segregated, provided employment to blacks as elevator operators. Jean's first elevator job was at St. Phillips Hospital, to which black patients of the Medical College of Virginia were assigned.

Every child in the family was expected to have a job, so when Jean saw a newspaper advertisement (the ads also were segregated) for a "colored elevator operator," she applied. A job at MCV carried prestige, she thought. "It was a big thing (for MCV), hiring a colored operator," Jean said.

When she went in for the interview, a sympathetic white elevator operator told her the secret to getting the job was being able to wear one of the available uniforms. The hospital certainly wasn't going to spend money buying a new uniform for a colored operator. The only uniform on hand was far too big. But with the help of the white operator, she folded up the hem, tucked in the waist, and got the job.

For a while, three of the Wilder children—Agnes, Olga and Bob—were operating elevators at the same time.

Integration came slowly to Richmond, and in stages.

The year Douglas graduated from high school, 1947, the main public library was integrated. His sister Olga remembers returning to Richmond and hearing the news. "That was phenomenal. Growing up, we had only one library, on Clay Street. It was called the double-O library," so named because of its address, in the middle of the block that divided addresses by east and west. For readers such as the Wilders, "it would have been great to have used the big library," Olga said, after years of trying to look up things, to do research for school from books that were torn or outdated or simply not available.

In 1948, a black lawyer, Oliver W. Hill, was elected to the nine-member City Council; in 1950 the city got its first black fireman; a black was appointed to the city school board in 1953, the same year the first black police officer was hired. The Greater Richmond Transit Co. hired its first four black drivers in 1952, and four years later, segregated seating ended on the buses and trolleys.

The pace picked up in the early 1960s. Blacks first sat at the basement and first-floor lunch counters at Thalhimers and Miller and Rhoads in 1960; the next year the department store restrooms were desegregated, Thalhimers hired its first black sales clerk and a couple hotels began accepting black guests. The Reverend Martin Luther King Jr. spoke at the John Marshall Hotel in September, 1961, to nine hundred people at a banquet meeting of the Southern Christian Leadership Conference. Picketing of Richmond's downtown theaters that year resulted in their integration.

The first, halting step to integrate schools occurred in the 1960-61 school year, when two blacks were admitted to previously all-white schools. The tennis courts were integrated in 1960, and interracial competition began on the courts in 1963, but both of the public swimming pools were closed in the early sixties, averting integration. Parker Field, home of Richmond's minor league baseball team, which had gotten its first black players a few years before, allowed blacks to sit anywhere for the 1963 season. That same year, two black musicians joined the Richmond Symphony and two black soldiers were admitted to the Virginia National Guard.

Virginius Dabney, the longtime editor of The Richmond Times-Dispatch, writing in the Saturday Review in 1964, praised these actions, many of which followed peaceful picketing and a series of law suits, saying they put the city "in the interracial vanguard among Southern centers of population." They resulted from the "sane and reasonable character of Richmond's Negro leadership...and the tradition of genteel behavior of courtesy and fair dealing for which Richmond is known." The accomplishments were even more noteworthy, Dabney suggested, because they occurred in a city that had more Negro residents (forty-two percent) than any other Southern city and even though "the preponderance of white sentiment in Richmond, as elsewhere in the South, was opposed to desegregation. It is precisely the point, that this occurred despite such sentiments," wrote Dabney.

Richmond in Black and White

Dabney concluded that Richmond was "an example of how sane, level-headed, peaceable and dedicated white and Negro leadership can achieve impressive results on the interracial front in a short time, without stirring up ferocious animosities that could rob any apparent gains of all meaning."

As Wilder and his friends got older, the Jefferson trolley line became an integral part of their lives, as they rode the street car to high school and college. From downtown, the streetcar came to the East End, of which Church Hill is a part, east across the Marshall Street viaduct, a high bridge that spanned an industrial valley that was criss-crossed with railroad tracks that now is the route of Interstate 95 through downtown Richmond. In the middle of the bridge was a depot, or waiting room, and an elevator that took pedestrians to the balley, or Bottom, below. Automobiles also used the viaduct, and the depot was a good place to hitch a ride to Church Hill, after walking there from school.

Over the years, as the viaduct deteriorated, it was closed to trolleys and other vehicles, and finally, even to pedestrians. Now, no vestige remains. It has been replaced by a wide, concrete bridge, built in the early 1970s, and named for Dr. King. Naming the bridge for the slain civil rights leader created a furor among establishment whites. But with the support of blacks on the City Council—including Henry Marsh and Walter Kenney, who grew up on Church Hill –a trail-blazing Republican governor, Linwood Holton, and State Senator Wilder, the tribute to Dr. King prevailed.

7. Growing Out Of Knickers

Douglas' father, in another example of his frugality, had a policy of providing his children with one-way streetcar fare—seven and one-half cents—to high school, leaving it to their ingenuity to manage the other half of the trip. So Douglas usually rode to school, because he often was late and in a rush, and walked or hitchhiked home, because he was not in a hurry to do chores or homework. The walk home was more than thirty blocks, but once he got as far as the Marshall Street viaduct, it was usually possible to get a ride. If not, he and his friends, there were usually three or four in his group, alternately ran and walked the full distance, which took about half an hour, without fooling around.

But there were plenty of distractions enroute. At the corner of Leigh and Saint James, the Armstrong Confectionery dispensed delicious milk shakes and club sandwiches, and Harry's, at First and Leigh, offered sweet potato pie, sweet potato meringue and Royal Crown Cola, which Douglas preferred because it came in a twelve-ounce bottle, twice as much as Pepsi or Coke. The RC "would wash your belly for days," he grinned.

Getting spending money usually wasn't a problem for the industrious Douglas. By high school, he was buying the things he wanted, and that included, except for the things he got at Christmas, clothing. In addition to shining shoes, he had built up a pretty good newspaper route. A talented artist, Douglas also had a sign-painting business, lettering windows around Church Hill with the names of offices and businesses. If a business already had a lettered window, the streetwise Douglas resorted to a scam service. "I'd wash the windows with ammonia, and it would remove the lettering. Then I'd get a job painting the new lettering."

Like many bright youngsters, Douglas was skipped a grade in elementary school and, combined with the fact that there was no eighth grade for blacks (the eleven-year curriculum saved money for the city and helped perpetuate a black underclass), he was only twelve years old when he arrived at Armstrong High in the fall of 1943. "I was the only boy in the freshman class who wore knickers," Douglas admitted with embarrassment. "My father said I was too young to wear long pants. I hated them. I *hated* them. In the whole school, no one else had on knickers. None of the girls wanted to have a date with me. My father said, 'You're sixteen before you wear long pants.' Well, I was going to be out of high school at sixteen."

He couldn't wait that long. As he approached his sophomore year, he concocted a plan to buy a pair of long pants and change into them at the home of his sister Doris, who lived near Armstrong. But before he had to implement the scheme, his mother prevailed on his father to relent on the dress code.

Charles A. Johnson, one of Douglas' friends at the time, said "it might have seemed that way to Doug, but we all wore knickers our freshman year. Corduroys. After that we got long pants."

Once he began wearing long pants, which included a new fad called blue jeans, he became Doug, or Dugo, to his friends, even though he remained Douglas at home.

To get to Armstrong High, a three-story brick building located at Leigh and Prentiss streets in Jackson Ward, Wilder and the other East Side black students had to pass the tall, impressive columns of John Marshall High School, the city's top-rated white school, from which Armstrong got its textbooks, "when they were finished with them," Wilder said. That rankled Doug and his sisters. Jean said she was sure they were always a year behind because of the outdated books and inferior equipment. "That's what got me," said Berthel. "Every morning and every evening, passing John Marshall on the streetcar. We also had to pass George Wythe Junior High, which would have been an easy walk from our house."

Despite those daily reminders of separate-and-unequal education, Doug was proud of Armstrong, which was organized in 1865 by the Freedmen's Bureau to serve free Negroes. The school was named for General Samuel Chapman Armstrong, the founder of Hampton Institute. When Doug arrived at Armstrong, it was one of two high schools for Negroes in Richmond, and had an enrollment of fourteen hundred.

"It was a tremendous school," he said. All eight Wilder children graduated from Armstrong. Berthel was a year ahead of him, Jean a year behind. To show their appreciation, they established a small scholarship in their mother's name after her death.

By the time Doug got to Armstrong, all of its teachers were black, and although they had to endure a discriminatory wage scale, many of them were talented and dedicated instructors. But Armstrong still had a white principal, W. W. Townsend, the last remaining white administrator in a black Richmond school. Townsend retired the summer after Doug graduated, but blacks had been calling for his dismissal for nearly two decades.

In 1932, Josephus Simpson, a columnist for the Planet, writing under the heading, "Getting Them Used to It," said Townsend "probably considers himself a benefactor of the children at Armstrong by virtue of the acts which deny them practically every opportunity to assert themselves. Mr. Townsend has now taken upon himself the duty of naming the class officers. Denying the children a chance to vote in high school will probably accustom them to being denied this chance on reaching maturity. Mr. Townsend is really preparing these children to take their 'place' in society." Simpson concluded that "two things are needed badly at Armstrong: Relief of the overcrowded conditions...and the removal of W. W. Townsend."

Townsend was succeeded in the summer of 1947 by his black assistant, George Peterson Jr., who spent forty-four years at Armstrong before retiring in 1974. He remembers the Wilder children as fine students. As a resident of Church Hill, Peterson also knew their parents, "ideal people" who instilled fine qualities in their children, he said. Doug, he recalled, was a very good student who got along well with students and staff.

One of Peterson's first actions as principal was to stop the practice of sending second-hand books to Armstrong from John Marshall. "The first day they delivered some," he said, "I sent them back."

Relief from overcrowding came in 1939, when Maggie Walker High School was opened on the edge of the campus of Virginia Union University. But in opening another school, Doug said, the whites who controlled the educational destiny of blacks in Richmond managed to provoke a schism within the black community. Maggie Walker was designated a trade school, where students were taught auto mechanics, home economics, barbering, tailoring and bricklaying.

Armstrong was designated the academic high school for Negroes. In the sixties and seventies, Walker produced some of the greatest athletes ever to come out of Richmond, including pro-football Hall of Famer Willie Lanier, Washington Bullets' basketball star Bobby Dandridge, and most famous of all, Arthur Ashe Jr., the first black to win the tennis championship at Wimbleton.

But in Doug's days, as he and his friends perceived it, the "haves" were supposed to go to Armstrong, the "have-nots" to Maggie Walker.

Wednesday and Friday nights were date nights, a chance to show off new clothes and new friends. Doug was among the sharpest dressers. He might wear a reindeer sweater, dress shirt without tie and gabardine trousers, plaid socks and pointy-toed shoes. His date—frequently Ruth Manning, a mortician's daughter—might wear a cardigan or pullover sweater, fake pearls, a plaid skirt and penny loafers or saddle oxfords with white ankle socks. They would catch a movie at the Booker T or Walker theater or go to the Y, at Third and Leigh streets, which held "canteens" on date night. In addition to playing games, they could dance to the latest 78-rpm records. "Doug fancied the women," said Henry (Buddy) Taylor. "He was real good at that, didn't miss a beat."

But there was little formal dating. "We ran around in groups," said Florence Neal, another high school friend. "We may have invited someone to the prom, but most of the time we were all sort of together." Janet Jones added, "All our parents had similar rules, such as keeping the lights on and no alcohol at parties." She remembered one exception, when some boys got into a liquor cabinet at another home.

World War Two was in full tilt when Doug and his classmates arrived at Armstrong, and with patriotism rampant, a man or boy in uniform was accorded special treatment. So Doug joined the Cadet Corps, a para-military organization formed the previous spring. Doug was assigned to Company D, and participated in the drill competition against Maggie Walker High.

His other extra-curricular activities were the cheering squad, which helped spur the boys' basketball team to the Negro state championship his senior year; artist and cartoonist for both the Spirit newspaper and the Rabza yearbook, the latter named for Armstrong's first superintendent, Rabza Morse Manney, a Union Army chaplain from Vermont; and the senior class play.

LaVerne Wingo was in the play, "Rebecca," with Doug, and even now, when she sees Doug, he greets her with a line from the play: "Mrs. DeWinter, I didn't mean to startle you." Doug was "very popular, likable," said Wingo, who was voted both "most brilliant" and "most innocent" in the "perfect senior girl" contest by her classmates at Armstrong.

Doug wasn't voted most perfect anything, but his grades were good enough to get him elected to the National Honor Society, which was reserved for the top fifteen percent. "Work came easy to us," Doug said of himself and his friends, "and we made pretty good grades." Pretty good is about right, according to Charlie Johnson. "We got good marks intermittently. All of us had good minds, but we weren't particularly good students. We were not the studying type, and we didn't have good study habits." Ludwin Branch, another friend, admitted, "Nobody bragged about us."

Doug's talents were obvious to his friends, however. Delores Allen remembers Doug "being in his books," studying with another boy. "He had fantastic recall," said Ludwin Branch. "He could recite poetry and passages from the Bible." Added Florence Neal, "Doug was a great orator." John (Booty) Taylor said he was "a politician even then, a street-corner lawyer, for sure. He loved to talk, to express his views. He was a little one-sided. His views were the only way."

But being a lawyer, much less a politician, was not on Doug's mind. His ambition, according to the 1947 yearbook, was to be a dental surgeon, which explains why he majored in chemistry in college.

When Doug and his buddies encountered a dynamic teacher, as they did in J. Rodman "Little Joe" Ransome, their professorial-looking history teacher, they rose to the occasion, according to Johnson. Ransome "kept everybody hyped up about black politics, he was so vivid with his illustrations." Johnson went on to teach retarded children in the Philadelphia schools for thirty-five years before retiring.

But not even an inspiring teacher could get Doug, or his buddies, excited about politics. They were more interested in sports and girls. Booty Taylor, who lived on Twenty-Sixth Street, said Doug "always wanted to be a football star, but he wasn't big enough." So they played sandlot games on a field on Twenty-Ninth between R and O streets—it's still there—pretending like they were on the high school team. They also played intramural sports and pickup basketball games, and they were ping pong and pool fanatics, which they played at the YMCA.

"We got into a little devilishness, had a few beers, but no one knew about drugs, and we didn't get thrown out of school or anything like that," said Henry "Buddy" Taylor, a varsity football player, not related to Booty, who took his nickname from Buddy Young, the black All-American at the University of Illinois.

All of Doug's pals were confident, but Doug was first among equals. He had "a big ego. I guess we had that in common," said Johnson. "He was always more sure of himself than the average person, including myself. He had an arrogance, a cockiness that made him a popular personality. People seemed to enjoy that."

William W. (Bill) Jones Jr., brother of Janet Jones, recalled a couple of incidents that he said typified Doug's confidence. When they were freshmen or sophomores, they went to the Monroe Center, an armory across the street from the school, to learn how to dance. Waiting for the lesson to begin, Doug got impatient. "I'm going on out on the floor," he said, strutting toward a clump of shy girls who lined the opposite wall. "I'll find someone," he called, and of course he did. It was the same way when they went to take swimming lessons at Brook Park, the city park for Negroes. Awaiting the arrival of the instructor, dangling their legs over the side of the pool, Doug announced, "Let's show 'em how it's done" and dived in. "Of course he didn't know how to swim," Jones said, "but he went in anyway."

It also was at Brook Park that Doug brags that he used to "run Arthur Ashe off the tennis court." Ashe, who grew up to become the top-ranked tennis player in the world, confirmed that story, but pointed out, "I was about five years old and Doug was fifteen, and he and his friends would come on the court and yell, 'Hey, kid, beat it,'" laughed Ashe.

As a child, Doug was "totally uninhibited, nothing bothered him," said Ludwin Branch. He recalled a birthday party in the Wilder back yard—Ludwin and Berthel were born a couple days apart and celebrated their birthdays together—when Douglas picked bees out of the flowers with his fingers. "They'll sting you," warned Branch. "They won't bother me," replied Douglas. He kept picking them up and they never stung him.

When they played baseball, Branch said, Douglas "always managed to wind up on the winning side, even if it meant switching teams near the end of the game." That knack stayed with him, Branch said. Years later, on the way home from Bill Jones' wedding in Brooklyn, Doug, who had been driving Branch's car at speeds of eighty to eighty-five miles an hour on the New Jersey Turnpike, suddenly pulled onto to the shoulder and asked Branch to drive. Just as Branch pulled back on to the turnpike, a state trooper stopped him for speeding. "Doug must have seen him coming," laughed Branch.

8. Right Stuff, Wrong Place

A few months before Doug Wilder was born in an upstairs bedroom in the Wilder house on Church Hill, Thomas Kennerly Wolfe Jr. was born in Johnston-Willis Hospital in Richmond, after which he and his mother returned to their home on Confederate Avenue, an address that even today some people will still pay extra to get. The Wolfe home was in the middle-class neighborhood of Sherwood Park, near where Wilder now lives.

In addition to the accident of birth, in time and place, those two Depression babies shared other characteristics. They attained similar, if not comparable, educations— both graduated from high school in 1947, from college in 1951 and went on to earn graduate degrees—after which both men established a name for themselves in their respective fields, Doug Wilder in politics, Tom Wolfe in letters.

But to therefore believe that Doug Wilder and Tom Wolfe had common boyhood experiences is to not understand the American South in the mid-Twentieth Century. Wolfe was born white and privileged; Wilder was born black and poor. "It was apartheid," Wolfe said of the Richmond of his youth, the 1930s and '40s.

Both Tom Wolfe and Doug Wilder had paternal grandfathers who were scarred by the Civil War: Joseph Lewis Wolfe was an infantryman in the Confederate army who served a couple years in a Yankee prison camp in Elmira, New York.

Tom's father, Tom Wolfe Sr., a Ph.D. agronomist, taught at Virginia Tech, where he became a pioneer of modern techniques for increasing yields through the rotation of crops and co-authored a standard college textbook that is still in wide use in Third World countries. In 1927, he became editor of The Southern Planter, a farm journal, and he and his wife, Helen, moved to Richmond, where the magazine was published.

At the depth of the Depression, when Tom Jr. was about four, his father quit the journal and helped found the Southern States Cooperative. While it became one of the largest businesses of its kind in the South, because it was a true cooperative, Wolfe did not get rich off it.

Yet the Wolfes lived comfortably. Tom Jr. attended Ginter Park Elementary, his all-white, neighborhood public school for six years, and then enrolled at Richmond's premiere college preparatory school, St. Christopher's.

Race was not a topic in young Tom Wolfe's upbringing. "You certainly were aware of it, but it wasn't a live topic. I don't remember all of this being discussed. Maybe by the adults it was, but not at my house. I never heard a derogatory reference to blacks in my house," he said. Other than the half-dozen blacks who worked at St. Christopher's, and Landolia Nizer, the cleaning woman who came to his house, he had no contact with members of a race that constituted nearly half of the population of segregated Richmond. "I guess I didn't know anything about Landolia other than that she lived someplace on Clay Street," in Jackson Ward, Wolfe said.

Whereas Wilder could hardly ignore Tom Wolfe's white world—it slapped him in the face daily, as he walked past the white high school or was shunted to the rear of the trolley, or warned to drink only from the black-topped water fountains—Wilder's world was barely visible to Wolfe. He and his friends

31

never thought about segregation, or its victims. It wasn't a matter of being racist. Blacks in Richmond were, like Ralph Ellison's "Invisible Man," out of sight and out of mind.

As teenagers, Wolfe and Wilder both rode the city's streetcars, but to say that they had that in common would be to say that a judge and a defendant had the law in common. They were on different sides, or in the case of the trolleys, at different ends.

Where Wilder's memories of the trolley relate to being told where he could or could not sit, Wolfe's recollection conjures up a world of innocence.

Tom Wolfe took the streetcar on his first date, with a very pretty girl named Grace Wallace, who later became a top model, and as Miss Rheingold. "It was a frightful experience. I was a nervous wreck," said Wolfe, perhaps because already, at the tender age of sixteen, he had acquired an idiosyncratic style of dress. In an age where less self-assured boys never wore hats, gloves or boots, no matter how inclement the weather, Wolfe wore a hat that night.

"I don't know where I picked up that eccentricity," said the Richmonder who became famous, not only for being "the most skillful writer in America," according to William F. Buckley Jr., but for the affectation of wearing a white suit, amended in recent years to off-white in deference to the grime of his adopted home town of New York.

But on that summer night just after World War Two, Tom Wolfe was just another scared, awkward kid on his first date when he boarded a trolley with Grace Wallace, after seeing a movie at one of the whites-only Broad Street movie palaces, for the trip home to Ginter Park.

"There were some rude boys lounging in the back of the trolley," he recalled. "As we walked by them, they said something, not terrible, but more like unseemly sniggers, probably about my hat. It was all very uncomfortable. As I was getting off the trolley, one of them flipped my hat from behind, and knocked it off my head." The wind caught Wolfe's chapeau, resulting in a dilemma that may have foreshadowed his coming dandiness. "I had to make a choice of staying with Grace by the side of the road," to protect his date should the garrulous gang alight from the trolley, "or retrieve my hat. The ignominious thing was," Wolfe admitted with a modicum of embarrassment, "I retrieved my hat, went running in the trolley tracks after this hat. Worse than the boys, though, was in my mind, the sight of me chasing that hat. Those boys hadn't said anything terribly bad. It was an innocent era. Take your first date home on the trolley."

Almost as an afterthought, Wolfe explained, "Oh, the boys were white." He so seldom encountered blacks that he saw little need to mention the boys' race. Blacks only rode the trolleys that went to their neighborhoods, and Ginter Park, in 1947, was not one of them. Nonetheless, Wolfe unconsciously divided the world into two categories: Those who were white and those who were not.

When he took his first newspaper job, in 1956, at the Springfield (Massachusetts) Union, after earning a bachelor's degree at Washington and Lee University in Lexington, Virginia, and a Ph.D. in American studies at Yale, Wolfe was asked by the other young reporters, "What are you?"

"The question took me by surprise," admitted the waspish Wolfe. Having grown up in the segregated society of Richmond, he was tempted to answer, "'I'm white, of course.' They meant, what ethnic background are you? Are you

Right Stuff, Wrong Place

Italian, or Russian, or Lebanese, or Jewish? What are you? I had never thought of it. In the South, in Richmond, people were black or white."

9. College Days

After graduating from high school in 1947, Wilder and a couple of his friends considered joining the navy. While patriotism was still high, a residue of World War Two, their motivation was hardly idealistic. They noticed that the eight returning servicemen, who were called GIs (for government issue), who graduated from Armstrong with them had money to buy cars and nice clothes, plus the new "GI bill of rights" to pay for college.

But because Wilder and his friends were not yet eighteen, they needed their parents' permission to enlist, and even then Doug would have to wait until January, when he would turn seventeen. "We had taken a pledge," said Charlie Johnson, "that we'd all meet at the recruiting station or at Union." And because their parents refused permission for them to join the navy, they met in September by the stone gates of Virginia Union University, which, like Armstrong High, had been founded just after the Civil War with the help of the federal Freedmen's Bureau, to assure Negroes a chance for a liberal arts education.

Wilder and his pals were hardly enthusiastic about college. "None of us got the scholarship we thought we deserved," he said, "so we ended up at Union. We treated college like we did high school. Things came easy. When we got there, all we wanted to do was party. It looked like all of us gave up. We were just playing around." The kids from Richmond "just kind of went along," according to LaVerne Wingo. "It was like a carry-over from high school."

Because none of their parents had a lot of money, the largest chunk of college-bound seniors at Armstrong, about twenty, ended up at Union so they could live at home. A few went to Virginia State, the public Negro college about thirty miles south, which was considered preferable to Union if for no other reason than it was away from home. Several went to Hampton Institute, a more prestigious private black school, about seventy miles away. Only a lucky few went north to Washington, to Howard University, which was called "the capstone," the highest level of Negro education in America.

A couple of Wilder's sisters went to State, but they to rode the bus back-and-forth each day between Richmond and Ettrick, the black enclave at the edge of the lily-white little city of Colonial Heights where State is located. But for Doug, the reason for going to State was to live on campus, and he couldn't afford that. Academically, Union was considered better than State in the same way that Armstrong was thought to be superior to Walker. Union was strictly liberal arts, plus a divinity school, which gave it its claim to being a university. State was a land-grant college and offered trade courses, in tailoring, hair beautification and agriculture, in addition to the standard academic fields.

While Union wasn't Howard, it was mentioned along with Morehouse, Lincoln and Hampton when talk turned to "the great schools" for blacks, Wilder said. Union students took pride in the number of college presidents their school had produced – eighteen— and more than one-tenth of all the trained ministers serving black Baptist churches in America. "People knew you by your school," Wilder said. "They'd say, 'He's a Union man.'"

"Union was a blessing, a godsend," said Florence Neal. "We got a very good education there. It was like a family. We were all children with the same goals. We knew the route we were going. We had a lot of fun, but we all had goals."

34

College Days

The only cost was tuition, which was one hundred dollars a semester—fifty dollars for students who maintained a C average—plus books and carfare, which Wilder's father again paid one-way. Wilder remembers going to the bursar's office during registration with twenty-five dollars in cash and a note from his mother that said she planned to pay his tuition in installments. The firmly written note was an explanation rather than a request, and the bursar, who appeared not to have encountered such resolve before, shrugged and went along with Miss Beulah's plan.

"As I look back, I was really lucky," Wilder said. "If it hadn't been for my mother, I wouldn't have gone to college. I'd have gone to the navy or something."

And if it hadn't been for him wanting to pledge a fraternity, he wouldn't have stayed. There were very few social outlets for blacks other than the activities sororities and fraternities presented. To join a fraternity, a pledge had to post a C average, and Wilder wanted badly to join Omega Psi Phi—"We don't seek men, men seek Omega" is its motto—one of the "big four" national black fraternities. After a slow start, he rose to the challenge and got his grades up long enough to be eligible to pledge a fraternity and get the reduced tuition.

Frat life at Union around 1950 could not be confused with the Animal House movies of the 1980s. None of the four Greek letter organizations had a house. Instead, they met once a month in the basement of Kingsley Hall, the boys' dormitory, in rooms next to the laundry. Nonetheless, the choice of a fraternity had lifelong implications in the black community, because many members remained active as alumni long after they left the campus. For instance, Wilder and Jesse Jackson, who went to North Carolina Agricultural and Technical College, met at an Omega convention ten years after Wilder had graduated from Union.

After being successfully installed in the fraternity, Doug slipped back into the habit of cutting classes, partying, playing ping-pong and intramural sports. On the sandlot football field he fancied himself a passer, the star quarterback, and even today considers himself a brilliant strategist and Monday morning quarterback. "He really wanted to play on the (varsity) team," said Bill Jones, but he was too small. So Wilder settled for throwing the ball around on campus, often taking a mid-day break to play in an intramural game.

He and Jones were in the same German class their freshman year, and occasionally their professor, John M. Moore, who considered sports a waste of time, saw them playing on the campus. Once, as Jones struggled through a recitation in German—Wilder had already waltzed through his—Moore yelled, "Herr Jones, I'm giving you an F today because you and Wilder played football instead of studying."

Biology Professor Walter O. Bradley Sr. remembers Wilder as "a poor boy—I used to tease him about his one blue suit—yet he dressed better than most of the students." As a young faculty member, Bradley and his wife, Verdelle, a librarian at the college, saw a lot of the students outside the classroom, and he remembers that Wilder was a good dancer and liked to play tennis. In later years, Bradley became a friend of Wilder's, often challenging him in bridge and pool, two activities at which Wilder excels. Of Wilder's pool sharking, Bradley said he was one of the best at the Club 533, a downtown bottle club of which Wilder subsequently served a term as president.

WILDER: HOLD FAST TO DREAMS

Thanks to early training at his aunt's silver teas, Wilder seldom stumbled when it came to recitations. One of the few times he ever lost his confidence was in a speech class at Union, as he was reciting John Masefield's "Sea Fever." Florence Neal and LaVerne Wingo remember watching Wilder stride confidently to the podium and dramatically launch into his presentation. "He was really showing off, and at first he was excellent," Neal said. But after reciting about four lines, Wilder forgot the poem. He stopped cold. "La Verne and I just died. We could not keep from giggling," Neal said. "I don't believe you all are laughing," Wilder wailed at Florence and Laverne after class. "But you were funny, Douglas," teased Neal.

Once Wilder and Bill Jones cut classes to see a movie, "Kiss of Death," which was playing at one of the Negro theaters on Broad Street. They were in a silly mood that afternoon; Jones remembers that when Richard Widmark pushed an old lady down a flight of stairs, he and Wilder snickered, prompting an older woman behind them to scold them. On the way back to the campus, Jones, a biology major who, like Wilder, was giving some thought to medical school, said a serious Wilder turned to him and said, "You know, we don't want to be any doggone doctors. As good as we talk, we ought to be lawyers. I know I'm going to be a lawyer."

Neither Jones nor Wilder abandoned his science studies immediately, however, although they both later chose different careers: Jones went into business, becoming a trailblazing executive with Thalhimer's department store, and later Xerox, and Wilder went into law and politics.

In conversations, Wilder exhibited "a knack for affecting a very positive stance," Jones said. No goal was out of his reach, "irrespective of any inner insecurity he might have felt." Jones noticed that Wilder "could sucker hero worship out of some of our comrades, but he did not show affection," a trait noted by his critics when he became an adult. Wilder was "not much of a follower, definitely a leader," Jones noted.

The lives of many of Wilder's friends from those days remain linked. LaVerne Wingo became a laboratory researcher, studying hypertension and hemotology at the Medical College of Virginia. She married William Cooper, one of Doug's "big brothers" in the fraternity, who became the first black to graduate as a pharmacist from the Medical College of Virginia. Florence Neal, who married Cooper's brother, Lawrence, got a master's degree in pathology at the Medical College of Virginia, and became director of Virginia's Sickle Cell Anemia Awareness Program, which was funded as the result of legislation intorduced in 1979 by then-Senator Wilder.

Union was a placid place in the late forties and early fifties. The closest thing to a protest during Wilder's time there occurred in the fall of 1950, when Union's football team beat arch-rival Virginia State for the first time in seventeen years. Union's students asked for a half-day holiday to celebrate—students at one of the state's major white colleges had been given time off after beating its arch-rival—but Union's president, John M. Ellison, refused. On Monday morning, in an unprecedented act of civil disobedience, a number of Union's students marched to Pickford Hall and clanged the huge bell housed in a free-standing tower next to the administration building until Dr. Ellison acceded. But even in victory, the students were required to spend the time cleaning up Hovey Field, where the game had been played.

"That was the extent of our rebellion," Florence Neal said. "We came from families that were against fighting, against defying. We didn't have that fighting thing that the young people had in the sixties."

In his last year or two at Union, Wilder began to notice the stirrings of tension and discontent with the old ways. He was upset when the city of Richmond finally hired its first black police officers and assigned them to patrol exclusively "the colored section" around Second Street. They were given specific instructions, Wilder heard, that they could not arrest whites. And Wilder was bothered about reports of injustice involving the Martinsville Seven, a group of young blacks who were executed, despite appeals for executive clemency to Governor William Battle, for a gang rape in that Southside Virginia city. They went to their deaths protesting their innocence.

The emotional lightning rod for what little foment that was taking place in the early 1950s was the National Association for the Advancement of Colored People, and while it had a campus chapter at Union, Wilder did not join.

The intellectual experience that challenged Wilder on a regular basis at college was the Friday chapel program. Union had a network of alumni who returned to the campus to speak — renowned lawyers, physicians and educators. Among the greats that Wilder heard was the multi-talented Negro singer Paul Robeson. Because of his international reputation, Robeson, who had been an All-American football player and Rhodes scholar at Rutgers University, was booked off-campus at the Mosque, a large auditorium formerly owned by the Masonic lodges that had been taken over by the city. Both blacks and whites attended, but they sat in separate sections—blacks in the balcony. Wilder said that when Robeson came on stage, he looked over the audience, and "in his big bass-baritone said, 'I had made it known that I would not appear before a segregated audience,' and walked off." Wilder, who was with his sister in the balcony, watched anxiously as members of the black sorority that had sponsored Robeson's appearance ran back stage and begged him to reconsider. After a few minutes Robeson appeared, to great cheering, and announced that he would perform, reluctantly. "But first he raised hell" about segregation, Wilder said.

Throughout his years at Union, Wilder earned spending money by working as a waiter. At the private Westwood Club in the white West End, he was able to study and still make thirty-five to forty dollars a month "for doing nothing." One of the better deals was working a banquet in the crystal-chandeliered ballroom of the John Marshall, then the city's leading hotel, where nearly forty years later he would celebrate his election as lieutenant governor. With tips, he could make as much as three dollars a night.

Another hotel that hosted big meetings was the William Byrd. In 1952, a Republican luncheon there featured Ohio Senator Robert Taft, who was competing with General Dwight D. Eisenhower for the GOP nomination for president. Guy Friddell, a reporter for the Richmond News Leader, dictated his story to the afternoon newspaper from a phone in the lobby, and then headed for Taft's next speaking engagement, at Virginia Union. He gave a ride back to the school to three students who had served as waiters at the luncheon. Enroute, one of them grilled Friddell about his reaction to Taft's speech. Had he heard the speech, Friddell asked the youth. "I always listen," was the reply.

After Taft's speech at the college, Friddell again saw the student, who complained about the moderator's refusal to take questions, including his own, from the audience. The youth also was troubled by what he saw as inconsistencies in Taft's speeches. At Union, the student pointed out that Taft emphasized his support of various legislation he thought benefited blacks, while at the luncheon he said that although he opposed segregation, he didn't think the federal government should force any state to abolish it.

Friddell suggested to the earnest student that the best way to influence change was to get involved in politics. Oh no, the youth said, "I'm a chemistry major." Anyway, he said, he was about to be drafted and sent to Korea. So Friddell wished him luck, and asked his name. As he headed off across the campus, he turned and said, "Doug Wilder."

10. Basic Training

College was so much fun that neither Wilder nor his buddies Bill Jones and Charlie Johnson graduated in June of 1951, with the rest of their class. "We had such a ball; we took it as a big party," admitted Johnson. He and Jones got their diplomas in January, 1952, and Wilder, who had to repeat a calculus course to achieve the requisite grade-point average, finished in August, 1951.

Not that there was any reason to be in a hurry to leave the comfortable confines of the campus. The "police action" in Korea had escalated, and suddenly military service, which had seemed so adventuresome and unattainable to a sixteen-year-old, was, at age twenty, as unglamorous as it was inevitable.

Wilder waited tables, shot pool and waited for his greetings. They came shortly after the New Year. He was in good health; the only question when he reported for the physical examination at the recruiting station on Lombardy Street, just off the Union campus, was which branch of service would he draw. Army was the answer. Wilder was ordered to report to Fort Meade, Maryland, in March, 1952, for processing.

The military services had been integrated by order of President Harry S. Truman in 1948, but the law of the land was not yet the spirit of Fort Meade when Wilder arrived. Hundreds of draftees assembled in a room and a sergeant barked out the names of the military companies—Able, Baker, Charlie, Dog—and assigned recruits to report to their respective units. After a while the only men left in the room were black. "What's going on?" asked one of the recruits, William C. Watson, who was to become Wilder's best army buddy.

"There is no discrimination in this man's army," responded the sergeant.

Watson remonstrated. Fort Meade was Fifth Army headquarters, he pointed out, and "we ought to have some integration right here," before they were shipped out on troop trains for basic training. The other blacks were not sympathetic; several called Watson a Communist. The sergeant assured him that when they got to basic training their outfits would be integrated. And they were. Fort Meade apparently had not gotten around to changing the procedures.

Wilder didn't meet Watson until they arrived at Fort Breckinridge, Kentucky, but after Watson's performance at Meade, Wilder wanted to meet "this radical." At Breckinridge, they had plenty of time for that. While other soldiers were hurried overseas with only eight weeks' basic training, Wilder and Watson underwent the full sixteen-week training course. They discovered they had similar backgrounds. Like Wilder, Watson had grown up in the South (Tuscaloosa, Alabama), in a working-class family (his father was a shoemaker) in which his parents encouraged him to get an education. And he was a graduate of a small, black college (Alabama Agricultural and Mechanical College).

Wilder and Watson hung out together in their off hours, shooting craps and throwing bull in the barracks. "Doug was pretty good (at craps), but I was running the game," bragged the more worldly Watson, who had learned gambling, and lots more, during the two years he had worked on the waterfront in Philadelphia. Watson had lived above a house of prostitution, where his experiences were more than a match for Wilder's skills, honed at the barber shop and pool hall on Richmond's Church Hill.

Although blacks and whites were integrated during the training sessions, Breckinridge was still largely segregated after hours. It even had separate noncommissioned officers' clubs for blacks and whites, and while Wilder, Watson and a few other blacks were not refused admission to the white NCO club, they got the unmistakable impression that they were not wanted there. So on weekend passes, they usually set out for Evansville, Indiana, about thirty miles away, not only because it was the biggest town around (population about 140,000) but because it was, technically, not in the South. Black soldiers were tolerated at many of the downtown clubs, but Wilder and most other black soldiers preferred the joints around Lincoln and Governor streets in what was euphemistically called Baptist Town. They weren't concerned about integration, they were concerned about enjoying the weekend.

Neither Wilder nor Watson had any desire to be a hero, so they began looking into assignments that would keep them out of combat. Wilder decided to offer himself as a singer and Watson tried out for the boxing team. As a crooner, Wilder was good enough to perform with a band in the black NCO club, and he also sang and cadged drinks at bars in Evansville. A good mimic, he did a particularly popular imitation of Billy Eckstein. Watson's career in the ring was short-lived. In his first, and last, match, his opponent hit him with three quick lefts; Watson retaliated with a haymaker; his opponent ducked, and gave him three more lefts. That was it; Watson hung up the gloves. Having been passed over for special services, after four months of basic training they got orders for Korea.

After visits home, they met in Seattle for the trip overseas. While waiting to sail, the two of them went over the fence for an unauthorized furlough. Wilder is uncharacteristically reluctant to talk about the episode, but he chuckled when he heard Watson's version. "I don't know where we were," Watson said. "I think we were up in Vancouver, British Columbia. Anyway, we missed the boat. What were they going to do to us, send us to Korea?" Their sergeant threatened, "You miss the next boat and you'll see what happens." Watson was trying to get court-martialed. He figured the maximum he would get would be six months in the stockade, and then he'd be sent home. His cockiness was jolted, however, when he learned that one GI who was court -martialed was sentenced to six months, but the time was suspended and "they flew his ass to Seoul."

It was a fifteen-day trip to Japan, enroute to Korea. Two thousand soldiers were jammed on the ship, cramped into sleeping quarters with bunks stacked six-high to the ceiling. Many were younger than Wilder and Watson, teenagers fresh out of high school. The food was awful; they dubbed the ship "the USS Stew," and a premium was placed on having a friend in the kitchen who could slip out fresh fruit at night. As bad as the food was, it was worse to have to stand in line to get it. Wilder and Watson "played this dirty game of pretending to be sea-sick," They went forward and pretended to throw up, which prompted a bunch of others to run to the rail, and when they did, "we grabbed their place in line," Watson said.

The troops also lined up for the nightly movie, and one night, Wilder and Watson managed to be at the front of the line when "two white guys tried to get in front of us," Watson said. "Doug grabbed one of the guys. The other guy grabbed Doug around the neck. And I grabbed him. Doug said later that all he remembered was that the guy who had him suddenly relaxed his grip. That was because I had a hammer lock on him. I don't remember the movie. I just knew we were determined to be in the front row."

In quieter moments, they whiled away their hours reciting poetry. While Watson was no match for Wilder, he could summon up several verses of Kipling. And they played cards and shot dice.

When they arrived in Yokohama bay, "I thought it was the most beautiful place I had ever seen," said Wilder, who like most of the soldiers, was getting his first glimpse of a foreign country. The thrill was dampened, however, when the troops were told there was not enough time for leave; they would go to Tokyo for processing and then sail for Korea in a day or two. Once again, Wilder and his buddy adopted a what-can-they-do-to-us attitude. Realizing that they might never see civilization again, they slipped out, along with what appeared to them to be half the division. On their way back to the compound, as Wilder held the wire fence up for Watson to crawl under, a guard put a shotgun in his face.

"Don't shoot, don't shoot," Watson pleaded. He and Wilder did not know at the time that the Japanese guards had locks on their guns. The guard told Wilder, who was still outside the fence, to follow along until they reached a gate, where both of them were turned over to another guard. That guard ordered them to march to the guard house. He was armed only with a stick, however, so Wilder and Watson made a run for it. On a count of three, they fled in opposite directions, as the guard yelled "halt, halt." Watson ran into the first lighted barracks he came to. "It was the damned guard house," he bemoaned. Wilder exhibited good instincts by running in the other direction.

The only solace for Watson was that when his fellow captives, many of whom he recognized from the boat, asked if he had been caught on the way to town or coming back, he could answer, "mission accomplished."

There were so many in the makeshift brig that they were hauled away in a truck. For punishment, Watson—but not Wilder—spent the remaining hours on detail, emptying butt cans and the like. The next day, they were flown to Inchon.

11. Korea

Private (E-2) Wilder was assigned to A Company, First Battalion, Seventeenth Infantry Regiment, Seventh Division, which landed at Inchon, Korea, in late August of 1952.

President Harry S. Truman's order to desegregate the military had caught up with the forces in Korea in the winter of 1951, when Major General William Kean, commander of the Twenty-Fifth Division, disbanded the all-black Twenty-Fourth Infantry Division, whose combat performance was rated the worst of all units on the American side, according to one account.

"There was no patriotism in my being there, as there was with the guys in World War II," admitted Watson. Like many soldiers, Watson realized that the "United Nations police action," as the Korean conflict euphemistically was called back home, was a war that America was not committed to win. "We hadn't been attacked. What am I doing here? Why? These are the questions you ask out on patrol.'"

Wilder had similar questions, and considered several alternatives to avoid combat. He could go into chemical warfare because of his college studies, or into special services as a singer. He had sung on the ship coming over and could have continued that soft life, with hot meals, behind the lines. But the appeal of those assignments was diminished because the length of time a soldier spent in Korea was determined on a point system: You got to go home when you accumulated thirty-six points. Four points were awarded for each month served at the front; two for each month in non-combat zones. An assignment to chemical warfare or the band meant eighteen months in Korea.

Shortly after arriving in Korea, Wilder spotted a friend, who had just come back from the front. Wilder asked him how long he had been at the front and what it was like. He said it was quiet, and that they were getting to come back to the base camp three, four or five times a month. Wilder told him about his opportunity in chemical warfare—he had been given one last chance to reconsider—but the friend advised him to "get it over with." Wilder agreed.

When Wilder got to the front, indeed everything was quiet. It was hilly country, made barren partly because of prolonged artillery barrages. But it was peaceful. Wilder wrote to his mother, "It won't be long." He began accumulating four points a month. He also was drawing combat pay, an extra forty-five dollars a month, which he was sending home. The troops lived in "hootchies," shelters dug halfway into the ground. The top was covered with sandbags, and rocks were placed on top of them, so if a bomb hit, the rocks would detonate it before it went through the sandbags.

The military tactics employed in Korea were more like those of World War One than World War Two. The combatants moved through tunnels and trenches, dug like fingers in the barren hillsides, and then they holed up in the hootchies. By the time Wilder arrived at the front, little premium was put on gaining territory.

"Once the Chinese had our hill, they'd leave it," Wilder observed. "They never wanted the hill. They just didn't want us to have it. Theirs were higher. They were always above us. But they had come down to destroy our bunkers and our communication lines. They would hold it long enough for us to come back and try to take it. Then they would go on back to their hill. It had reached stalemate proportions. We weren't capturing any of them, and they weren't taking any of us. So it was just a matter of holding your own."

The worst duty was the listening post, an outpost about half a mile in front of the main body of troops that always was the first to get hit. Squads of nine to eleven men took turns going there at dark, staying until dawn. Wilder and his buddies quickly learned that the Chinese and North Koreans never fought during the day, "so you had to get accustomed to seeing at night. I got to be very good at it. You'd be surprised what you can see. Even without a moon."

One night, Wilder was in a hootchie, and a soldier he had just met, Skinner, was outside pinging away, shooting into the darkness. "Just freelancing," Wilder said. "He shouldn't have been doing it." But no one returned his solitary fire. Immediately.

A couple hours later, Wilder heard a shot hit Skinner. "ZZZwham. I was about twenty feet away. I came out of the hootch....Without trying to be brutal, have you ever seen a chicken with its head cut off? He's still running. Well, that's what happened to him."

Suddenly, everything got quiet again. Then, as quickly, "all hell broke loose over the entire front. In the process of that fight, my platoon (thirty-six men) was literally wiped out. When I say wiped out, I mean lots had been wounded. More wounded than killed. So they pulled us off the front."

The next day, Wilder went to the company commander and said, "I've been thinking about that proposal for chemical warfare. I think I'd like to go do that...." Laughing, the officer said, "Wilder, you're stuck here."

The practice was for the troops to go on the line for two months, then come back for a month. The first time Wilder was pulled off, he went to Koje, an island off the southern coast of Korea, to guard prisoners whose rioting a few months before had led to one of the many suspensions of peace talks. The POWs were kept in compounds, one thousand to an area, fenced in by concertina wire and surrounded by machine-gun towers. Wilder volunteered to go in with so-called "goon squads," platoons of about thirty-five soldiers who conducted spot searches on groups of prisoners, one thousand at a time. They lined up a hundred men, ten to a row, put them in the anjou position—hands in the air—and searched for weapons. Compared to the front, it was easy work: Clean, indoors and "you got to change uniforms."

Wilder recognized that combat had affected his attitude toward the prisoners. "When you first come off the line, you have an atavistic view of prisoners, and everything else. You're mean; you push the prisoners around, and slap them around, and are generally mean and ugly to them. Matter of fact, when they're in that anjou position, you do mean things to them; poke them in the ribs."

The prisoners were stoical, hardly evincing pain at such treatment. Wilder found their reaction "rather disarming. Punch a guy in the ribs and there's nothing—no reaction." When he punched one prisoner, the fellow said, in perfect English, "'Why are you angry with me? What have I done to you? I was a clerk at Pyongyang (the capital of North Korea). I haven't done anything to you.' Perfect English. I hit him again and said, 'shut up.' And he said, 'is this what your Mr. Jefferson and Mr. Lincoln taught you?' And you *know* what he was referring to.

"'What will you do when you go back home?'" he went on. Wilder flailed him. "'Shut up, shut up.' I slapped him. You met others who were great students of American government. They'd whisper, 'Tell me about Mr. Jefferson, tell me about Mr. Lincoln.'"

Wilder determined that the South Koreans attached to the U. S. troops—called KATUSAs (Koreans Attached to the U. S. Army)—whispered in Korean when an American punched a prisoner in the ribs, "It's not nice what you're doing. He's Korean, I'm Korean." Wilder asked, "Whattaya mean not nice? These guys have been trying to kill us."

But after a few days of slapping prisoners around as part of a "goon squad," Wilder said the Americans became somewhat sympathetic to the prisoners. "You start becoming more humane." The rotation to the POW compounds eventually ended, "because we were being depleted" on the line, Wilder said.

Back at the front, he encountered problems with his new platoon sergeant, a Mexican-American named Quiros, who kept him on patrol inordinately. When on the point, Wilder was in touch with the sergeant by wire communication. Wilder would complain, "You know, I've been out here a lot," and Quiros would respond, "Well, you know the terrain." Which was exactly right. Wilder had found "some nice little caves" where he could take cover. Suspecting that Wilder was not on the point, Quiros, back at the main line of defense, would test him. "He'd say (whispering), 'tell me what you see.'" Responding from the safety of his cave, Wilder answered, "'Three Sisters.' We had hills named for Marilyn Monroe, Jane Russell and I forget the other one. I got so I had memorized everything, so I could tell him what I saw, and he wouldn't know the difference. And the men (on patrol) got so they liked it."

But Wilder didn't want to stay in the outfit with Quiros. "He was after me. You become a different person. You start thinking about yourself. I began thinking, I've never done anything to him." Wilder didn't believe that Quiros was racially motivated—the other black soldiers considered the Mexican-Americans black also. In fact, Quiros purposely went out of his way to be nice to another black in the outfit. Wilder felt that Quiros was after him because Wilder was always talking to people about things that Quiros didn't quite understand. Quiros was well-read, but he was a career soldier, and Wilder decided he resented college people.

Eventually, Quiros asked Wilder to select the men to go on patrol with him. Wilder didn't like that a bit. "People start hating you," he said. He had become friends with a Californian, Jim Cunningham, a big white man in communications who would come by to talk about home, and philosophize. One day when they were on Pork Chop Hill, Cunningham asked Wilder to go with him to restore some wires. It was daytime. Wilder said, "No, I'm working nights, and I want to get some rest." Cunningham said, "Oh come on, things are quiet." Wilder went.

There were wires down all over the place. The two men talked as they worked. On their way back, the Chinese began lobbing in artillery and mortar fire. The sounds were unmistakable. "Wooooooe-urremph. Wooooooe-urremph," Wilder imitated. The whine of artillery can be heard from a long way off. With mortars, which go straight up and then come down, if you hear it, you're already in trouble.

The mortars started falling all around them. "Come on, let's move," yelled Cunningham. Szz-bumb, szz-bumb. "Jim, we better watch it," responded Wilder.

Korea

He wanted to follow Cunningham, but Cunningham pushed him through the door of a hootchie, came in behind him and fell on top of him. The hootchie was dark. They lay there perhaps a minute or so, until the rounds were over. Then Wilder said, "I think maybe we can go out now."

Cunningham said, "I'm done for." Those were his only words.

Wilder looked at his face. It was white. He called for a medic. Everyone was running through the trenches as Wilder yelled, "Medic, medic." They came in to the hootchie and looked at Cunningham, who was still lying on top of Wilder. There was nothing they could do. They freed Wilder and asked how he was. He was all right, he said.

It had been a percussion mortar that killed Cunningham, Wilder said. Without breaking the skin, it had "literally torn him inside out."

Wilder was in shock. Rather than get up, he crawled into the trench. The shelling was still going on, and the medics were putting the wounded in the trench too. "Everybody was wounded but me, and I'm still in there," Wilder said. "I guess I stayed in there maybe an hour, hiding.

"I couldn't get over it. Because if Jim hadn't pushed me, it would have been me."

When he finally came out, his sergeant, named Bette, told Wilder he had to help carry the wounded down the hill. Wilder argued, "We can't carry them down there, we'll have to go through that small-arms fire." Bette said, "You just have to do it." Wilder admits that he thought he might have to do something to Sergeant Bette. "You harbor things. And people were doing that. You'd be surprised the number of guys, if they didn't particularly like someone, would slip into their hootch, put a grenade in there, and blame it on the Chinese. It became self-survival."

As Wilder was helping load the wounded onto stretchers, Sergeant Bette came running by, screaming and yelling. He had been hit between his legs and he wasn't wearing a protector. Wilder admitted it was a relief, because he was freed from the order to carry the wounded. "We found another way to get the guys off the hill.

"You have so many of these things happen that you couldn't explain," Wilder said later. "And other people, better soldiers, were killed or wounded. So you're lucky."

Back at the camp, Wilder went to Watson's hootchie to see if he had gotten a box from home. Watson's revolutionary zeal had spurred the two of them to follow the exploits of Jomo Kenyatta in Kenya. They exchanged letters at the front, signing them, "The Burning Spear," which is what Kenyatta called himself.

Watson remembered one such meeting, when Wilder, like the little boy who knew the bees wouldn't sting him when he plucked them out of the flower, told him, "I'm not going to get shot." "What do you mean you're not going to get shot?" Watson responded. "I'm not going to get shot," Wilder repeated. "I'm going to shoot the son-of-a-bitch first who's going to try to shoot me."

When Wilder got back from that visit, his hootchie was gone. "It literally looked as if it had never been there," Wilder said. "You couldn't find anything of it. Blown up. I looked around to see what had happened. It had taken a direct hit. Three of us had shared it. I wondered where they (the other two) were. But they had gone somewhere too."

By the time the fighting on Pork Chop Hill ended, in May, 1953, it had been picked as clean as Old Baldy. Military historian S. L. A. Marshall said the fighting there had been the most intense since World War II. "Its cratered slopes will not soon bloom again, for they are too well planted with rusty shards and empty tin and bones. Never at Verdun were guns worked at any such rate as this...the operation deserves a place in history. It set the all-time mark for artillery effort," Marshall wrote.

In bull sessions during lulls in the fighting, Wilder discovered that a common complaint among black soldiers was their failure to win promotions. Many felt they had been passed over in favor of white soldiers, including some who were fresh to the front whose inexperience jeopardized the soldiers under them.

Wilder, although still a private, had been serving as a squad leader, a position often, though not always, held by a sergeant. He took the complaints to a black sergeant, who though sympathetic, wasn't willing to make waves and pass the gripes up the line. But Wilder got the sergeant's permission to carry the message himself. To accomplish that, he needed to get an appointment with the battalion commander, Major Earl C. Acuff.

The only way to speak to the major was to go over the head of a lieutenant who Wilder thought would block the request. Wilder managed to bypass the lieutenant by telling him he needed to see the major on "a personal matter," a request that usually was not questioned under army protocol.

Wilder arranged to meet with the major on a Saturday. To bolster his plea, he lined up about a hundred black soldiers who said they would go to the meeting and air their gripes. But when the day came, "about half of them ducked out, saying they wanted to take a shower, or some other lame excuse," Wilder said. He convinced those who showed up to dress in full battle gear and march to the major's tent.

Watson was in the group. Looking back at it, he said, "I could see the politician in Doug, initiating a meeting about the discrimination and racism that was going on." Watson noted that Wilder also displayed other characteristics at the time that so many successful politicians seem to master: "He remembered everybody's name, and Doug had a good command of the English language."

Major Acuff greeted the black soldiers warmly. Wilder summarized the complaints, but when Acuff asked the men to take turns spelling out specific examples, they fell silent. So Wilder told of his own experience. Within a few minutes, Watson and some of the other men joined in. Acuff appeared to be genuinely concerned and promised to redress their grievances. Within a matter of days, promotions started coming through, including one for Wilder, who first moved up to corporal and subsequently to sergeant.

After the two-hour conference, Acuff assembled his officers, including his adjutant, who was black, and told them what he had heard, and said "it couldn't go on. Not just because it was my policy. The army is founded on citizenship, and you can't have second-class citizens in it." The battalion had just come off a big battle, having recaptured Pork Chop Hill, and had lost quite a few men, "fine soldiers, many of them black," Acuff recalled. "They were fighting just as hard as anyone else. I owed them a lot. I felt really bad that someone who was fighting alongside another could discriminate against someone because of color. I was sad, almost ashamed, for the army."

Acuff, a native of Iowa who wound up his thirty-three year army career as a colonel assigned to teach military science at Virginia Tech, remembered the incident clearly, but was unaware that the black soldier who led the delegation was Wilder. Upon retirement in 1974, Acuff became commandant of Tech's corps of cadets. When Wilder ran for lieutenant governor in 1985, Acuff read that he had fought on Pork Chop Hill and realized "he must have been in my battalion," although he didn't make the connection with the meeting of black soldiers.

For Wilder, who had grown up in a totally segregated society, Acuff's response "was an experience that helped me realize that not all white guys were against us; that you could rely on their word." It was a lesson that Wilder would carry with him after he got home from the service. And along with the vivid memory that his life had been saved by "this big white guy from California," it helped foster an attitude that later allowed Wilder, the practical politician, to work successfully with whites of all persuasions, including several with notable racist histories.

About three months before Wilder was shipped home from Korea, he was involved in an action for which he won the Bronze Star.

The official commendation reads:

"Cpl. Lawrence D. Wilder, US52137240, Infantry, United States Army, a member of Company A, 17th Infantry, distinguished himself by heroic achievement near Sokkogae, Korea. On 18 April 1953, Corporal Wilder and his comrades were moving into friendly-held positions with the mission to relieve and hold the positions. Corporal Wilder continually exposed himself to deadly enemy artillery and mortar fire while he aided the wounded from the other units. During the course of the ensuing action, Corporal Wilder moved about the area, placing men in fighting positions and assisted in capturing, searching and guarding prisoners. Then, later in the action, Corporal Wilder aided his comrades in clearing out enemy bunkers by throwing hand grenades into the apertures. The heroic actions of Corporal Wilder reflect great credit on himself and the military service."

Wilder tells it a little differently:

"There were three of us, actually there were four us starting off. A fellow named Wyatt, from New Jersey—he was a private, I was a corporal—and there were two KATUSAs.

"We were going back up on Pork Chop Hill to get our wounded off. We thought that the hill was ours, that the Americans had it all. As it turned out, the Chinese had half of it and we had half of it. But how could you know?

"In the process, one of the little Koreans, who were ahead of us, got taken down (killed). Swwwitt. The second little fellow who was with us, the other Korean, he got wounded. Wyatt called to my attention that the fire was coming from this hootchie. A pretty big one. I asked Wyatt to go around to the back.

"We had WP (white phosphorous) grenades and thermite grenades, which are heat. I told Wyatt, 'Take your bayonet and dig through the sandbags and put the thermite grenade in there, and I'll cover the aperture,' waiting for someone to come out.

"He did. Wyatt went around there, exposed himself, did all that. He got around the back, pulled the pin and shoved it in (the hootchie). A thermite grenade produces a great deal of heat, and fragments. We used the thermite rather than the white phosphorus because the WP produced a smoke screen, and we didn't want that.

"They (the North Koreans) started hollering. We had learned the Korean equivalent of 'don't move or I'll shoot.'—'Hi-e-yan-do'—I've forgotten, but I had rehearsed it," Wilder laughed. "When they came out, there's still no more than two of us, Wyatt and me. Guess the other guy's wounded and the other one's dead. I thought there would be one or two in there. And they thought we were a whole bunch of people.

"They paraded out, and I yelled, 'Drop your weapons, hands up.'

"I was about fifteen feet away. I kept looking around, but there was nobody up there but Wyatt. So each time one would crawl out, I'd recite that little litany, (yelling)' hi-e-yan-do,' and by that time, you really mean it.

"We ended up with twenty. That's when it is important to have an automatic weapon. But Wyatt was the BAR (Browning automatic rifle) specialist. I was carrying an M-1, which is a semi-automatic weapon. You can fire once. So if one of those guys fired at me, I would have gotten off one shot and then it would have been over for me."

Wilder and Wyatt then had twenty prisoners of war—their weapons stacked in a pile in front of the now-empty hootchie—but they faced a thirty- to forty-minute hike down the hill to their squad. "And we've still got mortar fire," Wilder went on. "So I called down (by radio) and told the company commander, Lieutenant Alves—I'll never forget his name—that we had these prisoners, and a lot of wounded people up here. He kept saying, 'how many'? and I told him, 'twenty,' and he said 'are you sure,' and I said 'yes.' I even counted them again to be sure."

Wilder told Wyatt, "I'll lead down the hill, and you cover these people.' I wanted to be in front, to be certain we weren't ambushed from the front." Wilder told the taller Wyatt, who would have a better view of the prisoners as they wound down the hill, "make certain we're not hit from behind."

With Wilder in the lead, and the twenty North Korean prisoners spread out in a line, walking in the anjou position, their hands folded behind their heads, they set off for the base camp. "Don't move your hands," barked Wilder.

At one point on the way down, Wilder heard a shot.

"I turned around, but I couldn't see anything. We were in single file, about five yards between each prisoner, so we were spread out a long way."

When they got to the bottom and approached the base camp, Wilder counted the prisoners again.

"There were only nineteen," he said grimly.

"I looked at Wyatt, and said, 'Wyatt, there were twenty people.' And I could tell by the look on his face: One of them had probably said something smart to him, and he got a little excited. All he had to do was push him off the side of the hill, and that's probably what he did. Wyatt had developed a real hatred for the Chinese and the North Koreans. It happens to people in war."

Lieutenant Alves also could count. "There's only nineteen here," he said. Wilder grimaced. "I almost said 'there must be a mistake.' Instead, I said 'I guess I counted wrong, lieutenant.'"

Despite the "loss" of one prisoner, Wilder believed that Wyatt deserved a medal. "I told Alves about the KATUSAs and that Wyatt had exposed himself considerably. First of all, he detected where the fire was coming from, because you really had to see it to know where to go. He went behind the hootchie, pried the sandbag open and put the thermite in. I said, 'He deserves a commendation.'"

Although Alves wrote up a report, Wilder heard nothing more about his recommendation until he was back in the states. With the war ended, Wilder was whiling away his final days before discharge at Fort Meade, preparing to take a leave for home one weekend, when a sergeant came by the barracks and told him he would have to remain on base to attend a division review Saturday on the drill field.

"You're getting a medal," Wilder was told. He was awarded the Bronze Star "for heroism in ground combat," the citation said.

And to Wilder's great surprise and chagrin, Lieutenant Alves got a medal too, the higher Silver Star, apparently because Alves wrote himself into the action when he submitted the report. "The guy wasn't even there, wasn't anywhere around," squealed Wilder, his voice jumping an octave. As for Wyatt, "Wyatt got nothing. Not a damned thing."

12. Welcome Home

By the time Wilder had enough points to go home from Korea, everybody got to go; the war ended the day he was at the port of debarkation. In fact, he and Watson and the others got stuck at Inchon a few extra days because the ships scheduled to take them home were being used to transport prisoners of war. They waited in fear that new fighting would break out and they would be called back, despite the fact that they had the points to go home.

When they finally left, three thousand war-weary GIs were packed onto a rusty troop transport for the trip back to the states. They hadn't been at sea long when Wilder and Watson noticed that men who had put aside differences of nationality, education and background to fight side-by-side, to save each other's lives, began to resegregate themselves. "The white guys wandered off in little clumps, and so did we," observed Wilder.

"The closer we got to the good old U.S., the more the racism came out," Watson said. "Guys you had lived with, and fought with—by the time we got to Hawaii, it was getting worse and worse and worse. Like a couple of white boys from Georgia who swear I saved their lives. One of them said he was not letting me out of his sight, as long as he lived. These were guys who were going to be buddies forever. This wasn't going to happen. But it did."

At one time or another, everyone was sea sick during the fifteen-day trip, but they were able to ignore the mal de mer, and their racial differences, long enough to participate in one of the perpetual games of poker or craps. Wilder and Watson had sharpened their skills in Korea, where there was very little else to do when they came off the line, but so had lots of others. Wilder had a run of luck, but for every dollar he won, Watson lost one. At least one. "Watson was snake-bitten," Wilder laughed.

When they weren't gambling, or being on the brink of a fight about the gambling, Wilder and Watson lay on their bunks and talked about the future, which was approaching as quickly as the California coastline. The war had radicalized both of them, and what had more or less begun as a game—the notes sent back and forth signed "the Burning Spear," mimicking Jomo Kenyatta's *nom de guerre* in Kenya—began to take on a reality. Most of the soldiers didn't understand the reference. It required "an awareness that was a little above the normal of the guys that we were around," Wilder said.

Wilder and Watson began plotting elaborate though implausible schemes in which they and other like-minded revolutionaries would assemble groups of boys, "get them around age ten or eleven, when their minds were still malleable," Wilder suggested, "and teach them military tactics and survival skills." Training camps would be set up in the woods, and on appointed days they would be unleashed in the cities– roving bands of killers trained to slay the white oppressors.

A less complicated plot called for Wilder and his pals to make use of their experience as waiters to get jobs at major banquets, where they could wipe out large segments of the establishment by "sprinkling poison in the salads."

Wilder later dismissed those ideas as the rantings of soldiers too long in the field, but he acknowledged that the non-violent protest movement of the sixties held little appeal to him. "I never thought it could be accomplished peacefully," he admits, explaining why he eschewed Martin Luther King Jr.'s philosophy, and was not motivated to make the one hundred mile trip to Washington for the 1963 civil rights march.

By the time they arrived at Fort Ord, California, it was clear that they were going home to an unchanged world. The whites were on one end of the ship and the blacks were on the other, Wilder said. The malaise was lifted temporarily when they saw the dock jammed with wives and girlfriends, like a scene from a movie. It made them feel good, even those like Wilder and Watson, who had no one to greet them.

Wilder flew to Richmond, but there was no celebration awaiting him there either. That was the way he wanted it. Twice he had sent letters saying he was coming home, only to have his arrival postponed. Rather than disappoint his family a third time, he didn't write again. He arrived in Richmond about ten-thirty at night, and took a cab from the airport. At the house, he knocked on the front door. He knew he could go in the back door, which was seldom locked, but this was special, so he knocked. His mother, the night owl, was still up. She embraced him and cried. His father had to be awakened. Biting down hard on his pipe stem, he mumbled "welcome home son," and gave him a quick hug. It might have been a scene right out of a black version of Norman Rockwell.

There was no hero's welcome for Wilder because no one knew he was a hero. He first mentioned his Bronze Star publicly when he ran for the state legislature eighteen years later.

Wilder had sent money home to his mother for her use, but she never touched it. She had put it in the bank for him. So he decided to use it to buy a car. His mother suggested there might be better ways to spend the money. "That might be true," he told her, "but I'm going to buy a car." He found a two-door, 1950 Buick Riviera hardtop, pale blue with black top, automatic. A three-holer. He paid eight hundred dollars for it. Cash.

After a brief reunion in Richmond, Wilder, who still had six months to serve in the army, reported to a familiar site, Fort Meade. But he was so protective of his car that he didn't take it with him. At Fort Meade, his field promotion in Korea to first sergeant, courtesy of Major Acuff, was made permanent. Meade was a repro-depot, a reprocessing station, and in those days there wasn't much to do. With the fighting over, the military awarded extra credit for those who had served in Korea, thereby cutting Wilder's time by a couple of months. As a result, he was discharged in December, 1953, instead of the following March, and he got home in time to spend Christmas with his family. He was a month shy of his twenty-third birthday.

(Watson subsequently earned a master's degree from the University of Pennsylvania, and became a professor of criminal justice at the University of the District of Columbia. He and Wilder have kept in touch. Watson took his students to Richmond to meet Lieutenant Governor Wilder, and the lieutenant governor visited Watson in Washington, where Wilder observed that the embers of the "Burning Spear" remained: Watson lives in a house that he has painted black.)

Wilder quickly realized he hadn't had enough time at Meade to decompress. He was still acting as if he were in the army. "My attitude was bad; my patience was thin; I snapped at people. I had become accustomed to dealing with nothing but rough, hard men. So I talked like that to people." Wilder lay around the house a couple months, doing virtually nothing. He didn't want a job. All he wanted to do was to be left alone. His mother was very tolerant of that, but his father was not. "How long you going to sit around?" he grumbled.

The cost of maintaining the car and going out on the town every night soon wiped out his savings, which had been augmented by about six months' mustering out pay from the army and an occasional stint of waiting tables. When he came home late at night, he tiptoed in the back door so as not to wake his father. His mother often waited up for him, and the two would spend much of the night talking.

Finally, in April, down to his last one hundred dollars, and encouraged by two of his brothers-in-law (the husbands of Doris and Naomi) who were mail carriers, Wilder applied for a job at the post office. He was hired as a substitute carrier without having to take a test. He worked various parts of town, but mostly on Church Hill. There he got a quick lesson in the economics of poverty. "On the days when the welfare checks were supposed to be in, if you didn't have them, they'd kill you. They'd be waiting." Some routes were so rough that the regular carriers had permission to carry weapons, Wilder said.

It was good pay, and no one was pushing him to do better. "My mother was just glad I was back home." Getting up early didn't bother him, but staying out late began to take its toll. Wilder began to consider alternatives. He didn't have a specific career or goal in mind, despite those proclamations at Union that he was going to be a lawyer, but he knew he should take advantage of the GI Bill.

So he enrolled at Virginia State College, which had just initiated a master's program in chemistry. On the first day of classes, he discovered that he was one of only two students in the program. It didn't take long for him to decide he didn't want to be a chemist. The other student, Charles Bond, was also a Korean vet, and had been a year ahead of Wilder at Union. After about a month of school, Bonds' father-in-law, who worked at the state employment office in Richmond, tipped off Bonds about a good job that was open, for a technician in the state medical examiner's office. But Bonds was determined to get his master's (he went on and got a doctorate and moved to Washington) so Wilder checked it out. He liked what he saw, dropped out of school and took the job.

The starting pay was about $2,700 a year, with an increase to $3,000 in a short while. The job was in toxicology, "the science of poisons," Wilder explained to friends. His tasks included analyzing the alcohol content of blood samples taken from suspected drunk drivers; checking for seminal stains or spermatozoa in rape cases, and determining the causes of unknown deaths. The work fascinated him, and he felt he was getting some benefit from his chemistry studies. He particularly liked the forensic aspects of the job, and admired his immediate supervisor, the late Elmer Gordon, who later became the chief toxicologist for the city of Rochester, New York.

For the first year or so, Wilder enjoyed the work a lot. His supervisors said he was good at it, and he liked "wearing my little white coat." And his mother was pleased because he was living at home.

Although Wilder liked the work, he didn't love it. He thought it was a dead-end job; if he were to advance, he needed a graduate degree. The office had an arrangement where he could continue working at the lab and work toward a master's next door at the Medical College of Virginia, which by then was admitting blacks. But Wilder realized that both the chief medical examiner, a Canadian physician named Geoffrey Mann, and his assistant, Tom Jordan, were lawyers, so Wilder told them he might go to law school. Dr. Mann didn't encourage him, but when Wilder pointed out that "it's easy for you to say that," because he already had both his law and medical degrees, Mann agreed. In May of 1956, Wilder made the decision to go to law school. Once that was settled, the question of where was easy.

Virginia's two public law schools technically had been open to blacks since 1950, when a federal court ordered the University of Virginia to admit a black, which it did. One. But the experience of that lone black student, John Merchant, was so bad that others were discouraged from applying. Black Virginians who wanted to go to law school were offered a scholarship to attend out-of-state schools that would accept them. The plan required blacks who sought a graduate education to first apply for it at Virginia State. If the program were not offered there, as was the case with law and medicine, the applicant then was awarded a scholarship that amounted to either the difference between the costs of the out-of-state school and the costs at the Virginia school, or the equivalent of the tuition of the state school. In Wilder's case, he got $210 a year, which was determined to be the additional cost of attending Howard University in Washington over the University of Virginia.

Howard was by far the most popular choice of the few black Virginians who went to law school in those days. About a dozen Virginia students went there during Wilder's three years there. Occasionally, a black was admitted to such prestigious and expensive schools as Yale and New York University, but most blacks opted for Howard because of their lack of preparation. "I doubt seriously that I could have passed the LSAT (Law School Admissions Test)," Wilder said, "not with my background." Howard did not require the test. "They expected that most of their students would not pass, because of inadequate training as undergraduates," Wilder learned. "Not only that, they sort of expected you would not necessarily have the usual grades, or the usual dossier for background in law."

Furthermore, Wilder wanted to go to Howard. Oliver W. Hill, who had argued one of the cases that led the U. S. Supreme Court to rule that segregated schools were unconstitutional, had gone there; so had another outstanding black Richmonder, Spottswood W. Robinson III. "All the legal giants were being produced at Howard," Wilder said.

When he was accepted, Wilder told his mother, thinking she would be pleased. But she said, "you've got a nice job here." He had just been promoted to specialist. But Wilder said, "I want to be a lawyer. I'll only be in Washington. It's only a hundred miles away."

Wilder arrived in Washington in August, 1956, about a month before classes began at Howard, and moved in temporarily with a friend of his brother's, Otis N. (Petey) Paige.

Paige had met Robert Wilder Jr. in the army during World War Two, and while stationed at Camp Lee, near Richmond, visited the Wilder home on weekends. Paige was struck by the warmth of the family. The large gatherings weekends. Paige was struck by the warmth of the family. The large gatherings around the kitchen table reminded him of his own family. Paige grew up in Fairfax, Virginia, across the Potomac River from Washington, in a section called Hortontown, a poor, black version of a family compound, with houses occupied by his mother and father and their thirteen children; by five of his mother's sisters and their families, and by his maternal grandmother. His father worked as a caretaker at a private estate and for the federal government.

Paige and Bob Wilder got different assignments after Camp Lee, but when Paige came from home the fighting in the Pacific, he was sent to Fort Bragg, North Carolina, and he visited the Wilders enroute to his home in Fairfax. In 1946, Paige and Bob Wilder were discharged from the army. They reunited in Washington, where they got jobs as messengers for the federal government, and shared a room with Paige's aunt. Even after Bob Wilder married, and moved to Connecticut, using the GI Bill to enroll in the New Haven School of Photography, Paige kept in touch with the Wilders in Richmond.

By the time Doug Wilder came to Washington in 1956, it was natural for Paige, who had married by then, and his wife, Alyce, to invite Wilder to stay with them. Wilder told Paige he also would need a job. "You got one," at Bolling Field, said Paige, who worked nights at the air base's officers' club as a waiter. Wilder's experience as a waiter was evident, and he made good such good money that he stayed on after school began.

Because classes had not begun, Wilder fell into a habit of doing the town with Paige after work. They made the rounds, from the Hollywood Club to the Departmental Club, on the Ninth Street strip in downtown D. C.

The Paiges had a nice apartment in the Mayfair Mansions complex, which was in what was then a tranquil neighborhood off Benning Road in Northeast Washington. But it was a one-bedroom unit, so Wilder had to sleep on a couch, but he didn't mind because the arrangement was temporary. He would move out, he said, when his checks under the GI Bill began arriving. But the Paiges urged him to stay on—why pay a lot of rent someplace else—and he succumbed to their hospitality.

The social life was exhilarating, but perilous. "That was the worst thing I ever did," Wilder said. "The partying almost ruined me. I was getting familiar with the Washington social circuit. You could go to a party in Washington every night if you've got the time, and I found the time. I just started off on the wrong foot." He succumbed to the evil of, for the first time in his life, having too much money. He traded in his 1950 Buick for a 1953 Buick, noting that he was always three years behind the current model. He was getting the GI Bill; he was drawing a small retirement nugget from his employment at the medical examiner's lab; the state of Virginia was paying him hush-money to go out of state to school, and thanks to Paige, he had a job and a place to live. And no bills. He stayed with the Paiges from August to December.

When he finally moved out, it was not for a more sedate environment. Paige had arranged for him to share a house, at 2063 Tenth Street NE, with a friend, Preston Thomas, who had split up with his wife. Thomas had taken in a second tenant, a fellow named Roach, a cousin of the jazz drummer Max Roach, whose wife also had left him.

It was a very nice house, with a bar in the basement. Wilder learned to cook from Thomas and Roach, who were older and fairly accomplished cooks. Each did his own cooking, recalled Wilder, whose reputation as a gourmet cook springs from those days at Thomas's house.

Roach and Thomas, who had clerical jobs at the State Department, sat at night for hours complaining about their wives. Once, when Wilder chuckled at their misery, Thomas, nodding knowingly to their unmarried tenant, said knowingly to Roach, "He doesn't know anything about it, but he'll find out."

Wilder had been living there several months when Thomas came home and announced, "I've got bad news for you. My wife and I are getting back together." Wilder, nonplused by the reunion after all the tirading about women, inquired, "how's that bad news?" Thomas said, "It's bad for you because you're going to have to leave." Both Wilder and Roach left. Roach moved in with a girlfriend, and Wilder moved to Slowe Hall, a new three-story, brick dormitory on Howard's handsome hilltop campus.

13. Law School

On the first day of orientation at Howard, the student next to Wilder reached out his hand in friendship and said, "I'm Henry Marsh from Richmond, Virginia."

"That's my home," answered Wilder. "What part?"

"Twenty-ninth Street, Church Hill," said Marsh.

"Do you know me?" asked Wilder, who grew up on Twenty-eighth Street. When Marsh said no, Wilder laughed. "Well, you can't be from Church Hill then." His ego was such that he did not believe it was possible for any black from Church Hill not to know him.

Marsh, grinning, shot back, "Well, you don't know me either."

Thus began a friendship, born in rivalry and a clash of egos, of two men who over the next several decades would become Virginia's best-known black politicians.

Even though he and Wilder obviously had played on the same playgrounds and walked the same streets growing up on Church Hill, Marsh had been a quiet and introverted youngster. And, unlike Wilder, it was possible he might not have been known outside his immediate circle of friends.

Marsh, whose father was a waiter (and later a preacher) is three years younger than Wilder and went to a different high school, passing up Armstrong in favor of Maggie Walker High because "I didn't want any assumption that I wasn't tough enough to make it at Walker." Marsh said selecting Walker was the best thing that could have happened to him. It gave him more opportunity to exercise more leadership. "At Armstrong," he said later, "if you were smart, you were just lost in the pack. At Walker, if you were smart, you were a leader. So I was a leader at Walker." By the time Marsh got to high school, a twelfth year had been added to the Negro curriculum, so he graduated in 1952.

Like Wilder, Marsh lacked the money to go away to school, so he enrolled at Union in the fall of 1952, and immediately immersed himself in politics and civil rights causes. As president of the student body, he testified before a joint session of the Virginia General Assembly—the only student to do so—against proposed legislation that would permit public funds to be used to finance private, segregated schools, as part of Virginia's program of massive resistance to integration. The legislation passed.

Although he had argued in behalf of a losing cause, Marsh's effort resulted in a personal victory, the first of many he would record as a civil rights leader. He became a hero around the campus after his picture and highlights of his remarks were published in the daily newspaper.

Oliver Hill, the chairman of the NAACP legal staff and one of the top black lawyers in the country, introduced himself to Marsh after his speech. Hill asked, "What you going to be when you grow up, boy?" "A lawyer, sir," answered Marsh, who had made the decision after watching Hill and Spottswood Robinson argue a civil rights case in federal court. "Why don't you come back with me when you finish," said Hill. "I got a job for you."

Marsh graduated from Union in the summer of 1956 and enrolled at Howard law school that fall. He kept in touch with Hill, and eventually joined Hill's firm in Richmond.

While Marsh and Wilder had much in common, they had different goals, and approached their studies in different ways. For one thing, Marsh was going to be dedicated to civil rights; Wilder was going to dedicate himself to making money as a criminal lawyer.

Marsh was a serious student. He often went to trials in Washington to watch lawyers in action. Wilder had other interests, including working nights at Bolling Field. Thanks to an older sister who helped pay his tuition, Marsh didn't have to work much in law school, other than during the holidays, although he too had worked hard during undergraduate school, busing tables, washing dishes, driving taxis, parking cars and carrying mail.

Marsh could tell by the classroom discussions that Wilder was very bright and articulate. Although he didn't have a reputation of being studious, Wilder was smart enough to make decent grades without having to work too hard. Wilder was active in several student activities. He was a cartoonist for the Barrister, the law school newspaper; editor of the law school section of the Bison, the Howard yearbook; a member of the Student Bar Association, and active in his fraternity. Both Wilder and Marsh performed well, although neither was among the eight (of twenty-seven) seniors chosen for the law journal.

Wilder seemed to have a knack of nurturing rocky starts into lifelong friendships. He first met Lewin Manley, a graduate student from Savannah, Georgia, before classes began his first year. Manley was reading when Wilder stuck his head in his dorm room, and in an attempt to make small talk, asked if he could see the book Manley was reading. "No" was the curt reply. "All I want to do is look at it," Wilder said. "No," repeated Manley, barely looking up, "and just please get out of the doorway, you're blocking my air. That's why the door is open."

Manley's caustic attitude struck a responsive note with Wilder, who obligingly unblocked the doorway and managed to engage Manley in conversation. The young men discovered they had the same birthday, although Wilder is a couple years older, shared the same tastes in reading, and thought a lot alike. Sometime later, a grinning Manley asked Wilder what he thought of him the first time they met. "I didn't," replied Wilder.

They became fast friends. When they went to a bar at night and talked, invariably they attracted others who wanted to join in. Whether it was philosophy, history, law, science, they went from bar to bar and engaged in conversation half the night.

Manley, a tall, handsome fellow, was a voracious reader, and provided a cerebration that Wilder today recalls wistfully. "He was always ahead of people. He had a way of getting to the kernel of something. No nonsense. He didn't like anyone to know something he didn't know." Manley became a dentist in Atlanta, and remains an intellectual sounding board for Wilder.

For a while, Wilder had a room in the dormitory next to Manley's. Although he quickly became accustomed to, and enjoyed, the communal life of Slowe Hall, Marsh soon suggested they get an apartment. Wilder resisted, but Marsh persisted, explaining that his girl friend, and future wife, was coming to Howard in the fall, as a dental student, and they wanted a place to spend some time together, Howard in the late 1950s being a place of single-sex dormitories and rigid rules of fraternization between women and men.

"I don't need an apartment," teased Wilder, telling Marsh that Paige and other friends had apartments where he could entertain dates. Finally, one day Marsh announced that he had found "a nice spot" for them in a good neighborhood, within walking distance of the campus. "Henry had it all lined up," Wilder laughed. When they went to inspect the apartment, the landlady, who lived upstairs with her granddaughter, greeted Marsh by name and said to Wilder, "This must be the nice young man you told me about." Whereupon she showed them the apartment, and Wilder agreed it was quite nice.

"I think we ought to take it," Marsh said, not to the surprise of Wilder. As Wilder pondered the decision, Marsh added, "I think she wants a down payment on the rent." Wilder agreed and reached in his pocket for his share. "Where's yours?" he asked Marsh, who stammered and gave Wilder a sorrowful look, asking Wilder if could advance him his share. Wilder shrugged and dug back in his pocket. "Oh," added Marsh, feigning an afterthought, "we're also going to need bed linen and things like that."

"I think we will," grinned Wilder, who realized Marsh didn't have a dime. Later, Marsh came through with his share.

The apartment was at 80 U Street NE, where Florida and Rhode Island avenues converge, and right around the corner from a drug store where they could buy an excellent breakfast for practically nothing.

An unexpected bonus of their partnership was, Wilder discovered, that Marsh was an excellent cook. He could make bread and biscuits and loved to do it. Wilder occasionally brought home food from the officers' club—"things that people didn't particularly need" he said of such heists—and they would call Manley and some other friends and enjoy a late night repast prepared by Chez Marsh. Because both Wilder and Marsh stayed in Washington year-round— Marsh worked summers at the post office and Wilder at the club—their dinner parties became the center of their social life.

Wilder's lackadaisical approach to law school was spotted early by one of his professors, Herbert O. Reid. On a day when the students in his class should have prepared briefs on six cases, Wilder, hung over from a night on the town, showed up without any.

After Wilder had repeatedly failed to be able to explain any of the cases, Reid observed, "It must be pretty hard to find it at the Hollywood," one of the clubs on Ninth Street that was a favorite party spot. Following several such shoddy performances, Reid called Wilder aside after class and told him, "You got a good mind, but I'm going to fail your little ass." When an innocent-looking Wilder asked why, Reid said, "because you're lazy, and you're not productive, and you're not going to cut it."

Wilder knew that Reid meant it, and that it was true. He hadn't studied. "I partied all year," he admitted. He was a member of a study group, but his partners were leaving him behind. In courses such as civil procedure and contracts, where the entire grade depended on the final test, it was difficult to cram. When he finally attempted to participate in the study sessions, he wondered what they were talking about. He was frightened.

One day after study group, Wilder was walking home, up a hill, pondering the deep hole he had dug for himself, when he encountered, in another kind of deep hole, enlightenment. Workmen were in a ditch, repairing a broken water main. As he watched the men dig, it struck him: He was going to end up digging ditches if he didn't straighten up. The revelation prompted him to consider his good fortune: He felt lucky to come back from Korea in one piece, and lucky to get into law school. He determined, on the spot, not to muff his opportunity. In as close as Wilder gets to praying, he vowed, "If I ever get passed this semester, I'll never have any more problems. Never." He sweated out the rest of the term, bluffed his way through the exams, and passed all his courses, including Reid's. It was the last time he had trouble with his studies.

Howard Law was an exciting place to be in the late 1950s. First of all, the physical facilities were excellent. After years of being consigned to the basement of the library, while the university concentrated on building up its medical and dental schools, a new law school building was opened during Wilder's years there.

The facility's crowning glory was the moot courtroom, with tall ceilings, fifties-modern blonde paneling, a microphone in the witness box, inlaid lighting and a huge screen behind the judges' bench for showing films and slides.

Many of the legendary civil rights litigators, black and white, used the moot courtroom to hone their arguments before appearing before the U. S. Supreme Court. Wilder and other students dropped in and watched them: Thurgood Marshall, who later became the first black Supreme Court justice; Jack Greenberg and Robert L. Carter from the NAACP Legal Defense Fund in New York; James M. Nabrit Jr., who had come from Texas to be the dean of Howard's law school; Louis L. Redding from Delaware; Arthur Shores from Alabama; Floyd McKissick from North Carolina; and Oliver Hill and Spottswood Robinson from Richmond.

"They took turns playing devil's advocate," a wide-eyed Wilder noted. "It just did so much for us to see those guys."

Wilder couldn't wait for his chance to get in there, stand before the bench and the jury box, and try out his skills. But the courtroom was kept locked except for special occasions. The dean treated it like a real courtroom, and insisted he wasn't going to have it torn up. That drove Wilder crazy. He wanted to go in there and work out, "aim my voice at various places and hear it come back."

In the moot court competition, Wilder initially was most impressed by the flowery arguments, but as time went on he discovered that those speakers often weren't dealing with the real issues. The judges who graded the presentations gave the best marks to the better-prepared student lawyers, no matter how stolid their oratory, who accompanied their rhetoric with written briefs, often prepared by student assistants. Wilder revised his view of the importance of rhetoric, and discounted students who popped off in class—himself included—realizing that their loquaciousness often was an effort to mask a lack of preparation.

"I thought you had to have the gift of gab, and that if you couldn't talk, you couldn't make it. But the best lawyers are those with the best thoughts. In moot court, you cannot get the balance and substance of a person. You hear them and it doesn't present itself. The best qualification for a good lawyer is an analytical mind," Wilder decided, and his training in chemistry and experience in the lab proved valuable. "Law schools don't teach you how to be a good lawyer, they teach you what the law is. You have to learn how to be a good lawyer on your own."

In the quarter of a century after his graduation, lawyers who witnessed Wilder's performances—and that's what they were—in the courtrooms around Richmond might have wondered why Wilder didn't follow his own advice: His detractors contend that not even his most dazzling summations and arguments could cover what often appeared to be a lack of preparation.

Just as he did at Virginia Union, Wilder enjoyed attending chapel at Howard, not for religious purposes, but to hear the visiting speakers who flocked to "the Capstone" to share their experiences with the next generation of black leaders who were enrolled there. Although the giants of the burgeoning civil rights movement routinely spoke at Howard's chapel sessions, the speakers who fascinated Wilder were the practicing lawyers, whom he would corner afterwards and ask about his favorite topic—how to make money. Wilder was torn between making money and serving "the cause." He thought it should be possible to do both, "that you didn't have to starve to contribute. Sort of like you can't make rabbit stew until you catch a rabbit," he explained. Too many dedicated black lawyers and their families made major sacrifices in time and money. Wilder never wanted to get involved in the actual marching and demonstrations, and even passed up Martin Luther King's famous 1963 march on Washington (though he attended the twenty-fifth anniversary of the event.) Wilder wanted to be "the guy who got them out of trouble, if they got in trouble. I wanted to be on the cutting edge, whenever it was necessary to have that view articulated. And to choose to fight or lead the fight if I wanted, but not just automatically to be involved."

Petey Paige said Wilder never talked about civil rights issues, or the handicap of race. "He never talked that he couldn't do it because he was black. He never seemed to worry about that. Oh, no. He was going to make some money. He wanted to be the best lawyer."

A weakness in Howard's curriculum concerned the practical aspects of practicing law. There was very little training in office management, apparently because nearly all black lawyers worked alone, or with a single partner, and one or two secretaries. Wilder found that over the years a lack of management skills plagued the black business community. He said some lawyers, and their clients, mistakenly measured the accumulation of state-of-the-art equipment, whether it be dental supplies or law books, as success. But "your ability as a lawyer is not determined by the books in your library, or the car you drive, or the house you live in," he said. Although he prized all of those trappings, Wilder was fiscally conservative enough not to accumulate them until he could afford them. The inability to delay such gratification, he found, put a number of young black professionals in financial straits.

When a client comes in the office, Wilder said, he wants help. Period. "I wanted to be known as a lawyer," and all that connoted, he said. He tells the story of the young man who, after taking the bar exam, went home and told his aunt, "I've got some good news for you. Took the examination today, and I'm a lawyer.' And she said, 'Yes, but to a lawyer, are you a lawyer?'" The test, Wilder said, is "when you walk into a courtroom, does the courtroom know that a lawyer has come in. Does the judge respect that person when he makes a presentation?"

14. Eunice

In his first year at law school, Wilder met the woman who was to become his wife. Their relationship grew out of a discussion in the Howard cafeteria. Wilder and his graduate school buddies were holding forth about the affairs of state, much as his father had done on the side porch on Church Hill, when a young woman at the next table had the temerity to interject herself into their lofty conversation, suggesting, in fact, that they were wrong about something. It was the kind of challenge that Wilder couldn't resist, and the fact that such audacity came from a beautiful young woman made it all the more inviting. Her name was Eunice Montgomery. She was a sophomore economics major from Philadelphia and about seven years younger than Doug.

"Eunice was what we called a fox," Henry Marsh said of the statuesque twenty-year-old, who had a stunning figure. She also was smart, although Wilder wasn't attracted to her initially by her brains. Marsh said he knew it was going to be a serious relationship from the start. At least from Wilder's perspective.

But to Eunice, "it wasn't love at first sight," she recalled years later, pointing out that it was six months between their first and second dates. Wilder doesn't recall that it was that long.

Petey Paige's wife, Alyce, in a self-appointed role as surrogate mother, "had to pass approval over whomever I was dating," Wilder said. And at first, Eunice didn't pass muster, primarily because she didn't fawn over Alyce, or Doug, the way some of his other dates had. Alyce meant well, but she succumbed easily to flattery. Alyce had been won over by Ruth Manning, whom Wilder had been dating before he enrolled in law school. Ruth ingratiated herself with Alyce by bringing a gift when she stayed with the Paiges while visiting Wilder, who was living in the dorm at the time, and sending a note to Alyce afterwards. Ruth also was a great favorite with Wilder's family. Wilder had known Ruth since childhood—her father ran the most successful black funeral parlor on Church Hill—but they didn't date regularly until he worked at the medical examiner's office. When he moved to Washington, his mother and sisters urged him to get engaged. Wilder tried to talk to his family about his career plans "and all they wanted to do was talk about Ruth." Wilder had no plans to rush into marriage. And Ruth didn't wait around; she got married shortly after Wilder finished law school.

The strong-willed Eunice didn't dislike Alyce and Petey, but she saw no reason to curry their favor. She didn't much curry Doug's favor either, which may have been the root of Alyce's doubts about her. Ruth and the other women Wilder had dated doted on him. Eunice demanded more of an equal partnership, and she stood up to Wilder, who was used to having his own way in his relationships with women. "I don't think anyone was ever domineering over Doug," Marsh said, "but Eunice had her own personality." Marsh said he was sure that her independence was part of her attraction to Wilder.

Eunice not only stood up to Doug intellectually, she also more than matched him in height. Although only slightly taller, she carried herself so regally that she appeared to tower over her five-foot, eight-inch tall husband. To compensate, Wilder tried to stretch himself when he was with her, even telling people he was five-nine, although others guessed that he was closer to five-seven than five-eight.

WILDER: HOLD FAST TO DREAMS

As their relationship became more serious, one of the decisions they had to sort out was where they would live after they finished their schooling. Before he met Eunice, Wilder and Lewin Manley began thinking about going to California after graduation. Wilder had seen the West Coast only going to and returning from Korea, but he thought fast-growing Southern California offered opportunities for a young lawyer, especially if he spoke Spanish. Although Wilder didn't, he was confident he could learn the language quickly. They were encouraged by a fellow student, Marcus Tucker from San Diego, who said his mother was a real estate agent who could find them a place to live that they could afford. But Eunice balked. She wanted to stay closer to home. Wilder's original idea of living in Richmond was fine with her. Although she was born in Philadelphia, her parents were Virginians; her mother was from Tappahannock County and her father, who worked in a factory in Philadelphia, was from Petersburg.

After classes ended for the 1957-58 academic year, Eunice went home to Philadelphia and Doug remained in Washington, working nights as a waiter at Bolling Field. During the summer, they took turns visiting each other on weekends, and Wilder admitted that Marsh's insistence on taking an apartment "made it convenient for me to see her." Before the summer ended, they decided to get engaged, although they didn't make any formal announcement.

They were married in the fall, on October 11, 1958, in an Episcopal church in Northeast Washington. The ceremony was performed by the Reverend James West, who once had dated Wilder's sister Naomi. Petey Paige was Wilder's best man.

Doug and Eunice's first apartment was on First Street NE, half a dozen blocks from the one he had shared with Marsh, and within walking distance of school. As a newly serious student, Wilder discovered that "the more I studied, the more I found out how much I needed to know." While his work at the club helped them live comfortably, it was interfering with his studies. So he quit.

Wilder quickly felt the loss of the money, which had permitted him, among other things, to take up golf and tennis when time permitted. But he couldn't afford to borrow money and he didn't want to ask his parents for help. He knew Petey would have lent him money, even it if required him to borrow it—"from a loan shark if he had to," Wilder said—so he decided to sell his car, the 1953 Buick.

Without asking or telling Eunice, he slipped out and sold it. On the way home, he picked up a bottle of liquor. When he unwrapped the bottle, Eunice asked what they were celebrating. "I just thought we'd have a little better evening," he said, not mentioning the car. The next morning, as they set off for school, to which they usually took the car, he nonchalantly told Eunice, "Oh, we're going to have to walk." He began muttering about how hard it had become to find a place to park, and how the police seemed to be giving more parking citations and... Eunice interrupted. "You sold the car, didn't you?" Sheepishly, he admitted he had.

On May 19, 1959, Eunice gave birth to a daughter, whom they named Lynn Diana. That same month, Wilder got his law degree, and Eunice received a bachelor's degree in economics. The young family, still without a car, piled in Petey Paige's and moved to Richmond.

Eunice

Wilder now had a wife, a baby and no job.

He was satisfied with the formal legal training he had received at Howard, but he had no prospects of a clerkship, and even if he should be fortunate enough to pass the Virginia bar exam, he felt ill-prepared to work as a lawyer. He had no role models other than the professors he had met, and he certainly wasn't in a position to emulate them, at least for some time to come. He had been "the most improbable person to go to law school—I had never even been in a courtroom," not even, as had some of his friends from Church Hill, as a juvenile defendant. Growing up, the only lawyer he had even heard of, other than a friend of his father's who had read some law and claimed to be a lawyer, was Roland D. "Duke" Ealey, a Howard graduate who later was elected to the Virginia House of Delegates.

There were no opportunities for joining a white firm, and virtually no black firms existed. In looking back at the hurdles, Petersburg attorney Robert H. Cooley Jr., a 1937 graduate of Howard, said, "It was sink or swim in a sole practice." William T. Mason Jr. of Norfolk, who served as president of the black Old Dominion Bar Association from 1969 to 1971, said no black attorneys were employed in public agencies or by private employers such as banks or corporations. Richmond lawyer James E. Sheffield added, "The commonwealth's attorney was not even an option."

In his classic study of Negro lawyers in the 1940s, Swedish sociologist Gunnar Myrdal found that in the South they often were "not allowed to appear in courts, and even when they are allowed, they tend to stay away. Most of them seem to be engaged in settling matters outside of court or working in real estate or insurance offices or giving legal advice. Their white business is mainly restricted to debt collection among Negroes....Negro clients know that a Negro lawyer is not much use in a Southern courtroom."

Opportunities had improved somewhat by the time Wilder graduated, but as late as 1965, there were only fifty-one black lawyers, five of them women, actively practicing in Virginia, eleven of them in Richmond. Of the total, thirty-seven were sole practitioners, and one-fifth didn't even have a secretary.

The first challenge after law school was to pass the bar exam. Although no one would admit it officially, it was common knowledge at Howard that no matter how many blacks took the bar exam in Virginia in any given year, only one would pass. Inexplicably, the quota appeared to have increased to two a year for a while in the 1950s, but by the time Wilder graduated, it had slipped back to one. Part of the problem could be assigned pure and simple to racism, but another factor, while rooted in discrimination, was because none of the black applicants had taken any courses in Virginia law, having been forced to study out-of-state. One way to prepare for the exam was to enroll in one of the two "cram" schools in Virginia that admitted blacks.

Wilder followed another path, which had proved successful for his friend William A. "Al" Smith, who was the only black to pass the Virginia bar in 1959. At Smith's suggestion, he took a job as a clerk to a Newport News lawyer, the late W. Hale Thompson. Smith told him it was a chance to see a real lawyer in action. The job paid thirty-five dollars a week, before taxes. Wilder rented a room on Marshall Avenue, where his landlord, a Mr. Myers, "talked me to death about baseball every morning" before Wilder set off on the fifteen-block walk to

Thompson's office. On weekends, Doug and Eunice took turns making the seventy-mile trip by bus to visit each other. Eunice and Lynn were living with Doug's parents on Church Hill.

Thompson had a thriving practice, with a lot of personal injury work. Wilder planned to stay with him long enough to figure out how a lawyer conducted himself, and then return to Richmond to study for the bar exam. But in the two months that Wilder worked there, Thompson mostly ignored him. Thompson resented Wilder because of Wilder's friendship with Smith, who after learning at Thompson's knee, had left and set up a practice in competition with Thompson. But Thompson got over his initial qualms and proposed that Wilder join him in a partnership after he passed the bar. Although Wilder had grown to like Newport News, and felt that the Tidewater area was going to thrive, he had no intention other than to practice law in Richmond. He was going to be the first lawyer on Church Hill.

On October 4, 1960, after working about four months for Thompson, Wilder returned to Richmond to give himself two months of concentrated study for the test, which was December 8. He holed up in his parents' house, in the corner room that had been used briefly by his Uncle Charlie as a physician's office, and studied. Eunice had gotten a job as a bank teller, and Miss Beulah took care of Lynn during the day.

One night Eunice came home and excitedly announced that another teller's boyfriend was in a group that met nightly to study for the bar and test each other. At Eunice's urging, Wilder attended the next session. But he came home angry. The participants spent most of the evening complaining about how the deck was stacked against them, how it didn't make sense to study so hard for an exam that only one of them would pass. Wilder listened for a while, and then stood and announced he was leaving. If only one black was going to pass, he said, they were looking at him. And he didn't need their help.

And he did pass on that first try.

The next time the exam was given, Henry Marsh was the only black to pass, making it three in a row for the friends from Howard.

"I don't believe that there was a conscious effort to fail blacks," Wilder said. "I couldn't believe that, because that would mean no one would ever pass. If I had believed that (in 1959), I wouldn't have passed. You'd just go in thinking you wouldn't pass."

Much of the problem, Wilder said, was because "no question—many (blacks) weren't as well prepared." When the Old Dominion Bar Association looked into the problem a few years ago, Wilder discussed it with his former professor, Herb Reid.

"Yes, they (blacks) do have a rather bad record in passing the bar," said the uncompromising Reid, "and it's for two reasons: One, the examination is printed in English, and two, it unfortunately asks questions pertaining to the law." Wilder recently asked Reid if he had revised his opinion. "I stand on the record," Reid chuckled.

15. The Lawyer

Wilder found his first client close to home. He rented space above a restaurant, Ike's Shrimp House, two blocks from home, at the corner of Thirtieth and P streets, and began fixing it up for an office. One of his first purchases was gold-leaf lettering, so he could paint his name on the side door that led upstairs to his space. "Got to have it," he said of his first status symbol. He acquired paper and yellow pads—a la his days at the officers' club—from a friend who had connections at an office supply store.

One day, as he was cleaning the place, a city inspector came by and asked to see his zoning permit. He didn't have one, so the inspector told him he would have to vacate the premises. Wilder discovered—no attorney ever before having sought to practice on Church Hill—that a law office was a non-conforming use. So he had to appear before City Council to get the zoning changed.

"It was my first case, and I won," he said proudly.

Wilder bought a set of used law books and a desk from the office of J. P. Carter, who had been president of the Consolidated Bank, the black financial institution founded by Maggie Walker.

While awaiting the approval of his zoning petition, and the transformation of the open space above the restaurant into a business office—Wilder provided most of the labor himself—he took advantage of an offer of temporary space from Frederick Charles Carter (no relation to the other Carter), whose law office was located along the traditional black business row on Second Street. Carter, who was much older, invited Wilder to stay on, with the suggestion that he could take over the practice once Carter was gone. But Wilder was determined to practice law on Church Hill.

The one offer that tempted Wilder came from Spottswood W. Robinson III, who had returned to his hometown in 1949 to practice law and pursue civil rights causes after ten years on the faculty at Howard. "He called and said he wanted my assistance," said Wilder, who knew that Robinson, along with the older Oliver Hill, was considered the Virginia counterpart to Thurgood Marshall of Maryland, whom Thompson had assisted in preparing the landmark *Brown v. Board of Education* case before the U. S. Supreme Court. It was a tremendous honor, Wilder told Robinson, who had earned the highest marks ever recorded at Howard Law.

But there was a hitch. "I don't have any room in my office," said Robinson, who had just moved into the Southern Aid office building, where Wilder's father worked. Robinson was overrun with work. He had inherited a lot of clients from his father, who had been a successful lawyer and real estate broker, and much of his practice was commercially oriented. Trash, he called it.

"I can load you up with trash," he told Wilder, "but you don't want that." Wilder, anxious to pay his mounting bills, said, "Just send it to me. Send me as much work as you can, send the trash." Robinson had told the truth. It was trash. But Wilder learned a lot from it.

At first, Wilder did the work for Robinson in Carter's office, which prompted Carter to ask, "Is Spotts trying to steal you from me?" Wilder responded, "Fred, I don't belong to you." With Robinson shuttling work to him,

WILDER: HOLD FAST TO DREAMS

Wilder was off to a tremendous start. He was living rent-free with his parents, his mother was babysitting Lynn and his wife was working at the bank.

In those early days, Wilder spent lot of time going to meetings, speaking to civic associations, fraternal and Greek letter societies, and lodges. "Going around," as he called it, was essential to a young lawyer, because the more people he met, the more likely one of them might need a lawyer, or know someone who did.

Much to the joy of his mother and sisters, "Lawyer Wilder" and his growing family became regulars in the pews at the First African Baptist Church. Never mind that his motive was business related. He became a Mason, and always made sure to mention he was a member of the order, including, along with his associations with his fraternity and church, in printed biographies.

Wilder's lifelong association with Omega Phi Psi fraternity became a mainstay of his family's social life, with its parties, poker games and dances—"everything else was still segregated"—and provided an introduction to community leaders, businessmen, bankers and physicians. Because all of them had joined the fraternity as college students, the alumni chapter served to "transcend age and relationships," Wilder learned.

With the zoning problems settled and the renovations completed, Wilder left Carter's office and returned to his office above the shrimp house, fulfilling his dream of being the first black lawyer on Church Hill.

One of his early clients was a man involved with show business personalities who was more familiar with part of the law than Wilder was, because he had sued, and been sued, so often. But the man couldn't read. He was suing singer Marvin Gaye for money he owed for lights, amplifiers and other props, which Wilder's client had repossessed after a concert in Richmond the night before.

Gaye, who was en route to a concert date in Norfolk that night, came to Wilder's office to work out a settlement. Gaye brought his entire band along.

"Let's talk about this, Doug," Gaye said in a confidential tone to Wilder, who said "you'd gave thought we had known each other for years." The sociable Wilder, hoping to conduct business in a relaxed atmosphere, offered Gaye a drink. "Do you have sherry?" asked Gaye in a high-faluting manner. When Wilder said yes, Gaye took a drink and passed the bottle around to the band. "They drank up all my sherry," lamented Wilder.

With a celebrity in the office, Wilder's secretary called her friends, and soon the outer office was filled with giggling admirers, whispering, "Marvin Gaye's in there."

Gaye drank Wilder's booze and used his phone to call around the country to get commitments to pay Wilder's client. After a while, Wilder's client said he would accept the promises, which Gaye put in writing, but he also needed some cash. Gaye and the band members emptied their wallets and came up with about two thousand dollars, along with a couple rings and watches. "It was like a creditors' hearing," laughed Wilder. "'Got a ring?' Put in on the table."

The Lawyer

At the beginning, much of Wilder's business came over the telephone, often in the middle of the night. The callers often were those unfortunates who were picked up for drinking, vagrancy or other minor offenses. "The phone would ring at three or four in the morning and it would be someone wanting me to bail them out of jail," Wilder said. The ringing of the phone and the sounds of their father getting dressed often woke the children—by the mid- 1960s, the Wilders had three children—and Eunice would have to sit up with them while her husband went downtown to arrange for bond to be posted. He might bring back twenty-five or thirty dollars, and then spend the next month trying to get another twenty-five out of it for working on the case. Criminal cases were worth little or nothing. If he got fifty dollars for going to court, he was satisfied.

People called at all hours and seldom apologized. "Get the bail bondsman," a voice on the other end of the line would plead. The requirements of bond at that time were outrageous for such minor offenses as vagrancy, maintaining a common nuisance, frequenting a common nuisance, gambling and visiting a nip joint , or after-hours drinking spot.

Those early encounters with the legal system stirred Wilder's sense of fair play. Many poor people ended up in jail for taking part in activities that were condoned by the legal system if they occurred at the expensive and all-white Country Club of Virginia or the downtown Commonwealth Club. But when they took place on Second Street, when a poor black wanted to play a little poker or take a little nip in a state that didn't permit liquor-by-the-drink, he could end up in jail.

Years later, Wilder noted with amazement, the state eliminated a number of petty crimes that formed the basis of his early practice, and legalized and institutionalized gambling through a lottery and pari-mutuel betting.

Wilder literally bumped into his first murder case while checking a bulletin board at the courthouse. A man walked up and asked if he were a lawyer. Told he was, the man said he was looking for someone to handle his case. "What's the charge?" asked Wilder. "Murder," said the man. "Sure, I can handle it," said the cocky Wilder.

His client, Charlie Chambers, owned a pool hall on West Leigh Street in Jackson Ward that had been burglarized several times.   Chambers was charged with killing a man who was breaking into his business. Wilder didn't think the case could be too complicated. "A man has a right to protect his property," he said. But as he prepared for trial, he discovered that his client had not been on his own property, but lying in wait in the dark across the street. "That's an ambush," Wilder admitted. "The question," he smiled in the retelling, "was whether my client had used more force than necessary." He tried the case before a jury and got him off. Wilder admits that his client was "absolutely just lucky." He said he charged the man less than a thousand dollars, which Wilder said was "just crazy, not to get a thousand for a murder case."

The first of a series of sensational trials that helped Wilder gain a reputation as a flamboyant and brilliant defense attorney was dubbed the Milkman Murder Case by The Richmond Afro, which loved to banner crime stories. It occurred in the days when milk still was delivered to homes by truck.

WILDER: HOLD FAST TO DREAMS

Four teenaged boys attempted to rob a milkman while he was making his deliveries in a residential neighborhood. In the scuffle that ensued, one of the boys shot the milkman through the back. Wilder's client hadn't pulled the trigger, but he was there. At the trial, Wilder tried to convince the jury there were mitigating circumstances—his client didn't know the heist was going to result in a murder—but he was found guilty and sentenced to twenty years in prison. "He got out in five," Wilder said matter-of-factly.

Wilder's most famous, or infamous, early client was one of two brothers, the Penns, who were charged as serial killers. Between them they were accused of eleven killings. "They were senseless kinds of killings," Wilder said. But Wilder capitalized on two recent rulings of the U. S. Supreme Court, *Escobedo* and *Miranda*, which extended defendants' rights, and won a hung jury in the first of several trials in which he represented one of the brothers. Eventually, however, they got their due—long prison sentences.

When Henrico Circuit Judge Samuel Binn appointed Wilder as one of the defense attorneys he told him, "This case will either make you or break you" as a criminal lawyer. The judge was right. "It catapulted me into a trial lawyer," said Wilder.

In 1975, Wilder was hired to defend a young black man who killed a judge and wounded the sheriff and one of his deputies in a courtroom melee.

Twenty-three-year old Curtis Darnell Poindexter did not deny that he killed Louisa County General District Court Judge Stewart A. Cunningham in his courtroom on February 13, 1975. Poindexter, who had appeared before Judge Cunningham a couple of weeks earlier on a traffic offense, walked into the courtroom, pulled a sawed-off shotgun from beneath his raincoat and fired two blasts at the sixty-five-year old judge. Sheriff Henry Kennon and a deputy were wounded as Poindexter fled the courtroom. He was arrested later that afternoon after an exchange of gunfire. Sheriff Kennon, who had known Poindexter since he was a child, testified at the trial that he didn't think Poindexter would have shot him had he not been in the path out of the courtroom.

The first trial was held in Louisa County, on December 16, 1975, under heavy security. Twenty-five to thirty police officers ringed the courtroom, and a machine gun was mounted on the courthouse roof. Poindexter, a member of a prominent family in the black community of Louisa County, pleaded not guilty by reason of insanity, and the case ended in a hung jury.

The second trial, in May 1976, was moved to Staunton, in Augusta County, before an all-white jury of seven women and five men, to which Wilder objected as not being composed of a cross-section of the community. "I don't think you can duck the fact you've got a black-white issue," Wilder said.

The jury deliberated ninety minutes before returning a guilty verdict. Poindexter was sentenced to life in prison. Wilder denounced the verdict as the work of a "hanging jury" and said his client's fate had been sealed "when the jury was empaneled."

Thanks to the sensationalized coverage in The Afro, the handsome, immaculately dressed Wilder soon became a familiar figure on Church Hill, a reputation that he enhanced by driving around in a top-down Mercedes-Benz

The Lawyer

sports car.

"All I ever drove were little (sports) cars," Wilder said. Eunice hauled the children around in bigger, family cars, a succession of sedans by which Wilder's financial growth can be tracked.

After the used Buicks of law school days, he bought a 1949 Dodge when he began his practice. Next came a used 1957 DeSoto, which he recalls with the blurred reverie reserved for first loves and first cars. "It was black with nice chrome, a beautiful car, absolutely no trouble with it, none. But I wanted a new car. I had never had a new car." So he bought a Chrysler New Yorker, followed, in almost annual succession, by a Chrysler Imperial, then another Imperial, a Cadillac and finally a Mercedes sedan.

His first Mercedes sports car (he has had one ever since) was a 1960 model that he bought used in 1963. In 1966, he bought a new one, which he still has, having replaced the engine a few years ago after it threw a rod on a trip to Tappahannock.

"When I rode around in that little car with the top down, everyone would call, 'Doug, Doug,'" he said. His law office "got to be like a doctor's office. Packed. That's what gave me the idea I could run for office."

Wilder became one of five charter members of the Richmond Criminal Trial Lawyers Association, and as his reputation spread, physicians and other acquaintances began referring personal injury clients, who were more lucrative than criminals.

By the mid-1970s, Wilder's reputation was such that he was one of four lawyers featured in a magazine article, "The Toughest Trial Lawyers in Town." Wilder, who by then had been elected to the legislature, said his first commitment was to be a lawyer, rather than a politician. His political activity, he said, was "a bridge between Church Hill and Capitol Hill" (Richmond's capitol, like the federal one in Washington, sits atop a hill).

As Wilder's fame spread, so too did the first indication of a proclivity that would haunt him throughout his legal and political career, a seeming inability or refusal to allow anyone to share the load. "I never turned anybody down," Wilder said. Many of his colleagues told him he took on too much, had more clients than he could handle. "That's half true," he said of the criticism. "I had enough work for ten lawyers, and didn't know it. I didn't know how to departmentalize the work." He had a partner, Arthur Samuel, but his specialty was real estate and title examination and that didn't help reduce the load that Wilder was accepting.

Wilder also gained a reputation as a troublemaker with more conservative members of the bar. He refused to sit on the side of the segregated courtrooms reserved for black lawyers, and he often argued with judges when he thought he, or his clients, were not getting a fair shake. His clashes with one particular police court judge, Harold Maurice, occasionally resulted in contempt warnings, and more headlines.

Wilder represented Ford T. Johnson Jr., a black man who sued the city of Richmond after he was arrested for sitting in the section of the courtroom reserved for white spectators. Johnson lost the case in Hustings Court, but appealed. While Wilder's name remained on the briefs, the appeal was turned over to veteran civil rights attorney Sam Tucker, a partner of Oliver Hill (and Henry Marsh). The decision was reversed by the U. S. Supreme Court, ending segregated seating in a number of different settings. Wilder also sued the city on behalf of a black golfer who was barred from playing on a public links.

In a commentary on how times had changed, several lawyers said that after Wilder entered politics, the judges often kowtowed to him because of his growing influence.

"As a lawyer, he was arrogant; a rat," said one attorney who crossed swords with him a couple times. "He'd show up late for a hearing, and then strut into the courtroom. Instead of being chastised, the judge would greet him with open arms. 'Oh, Senator Wilder, how good to see you.'"

16. Taking the Plunge

Wilder got into politics on a hunch. He announced his plans to run to fill a vacancy in the state Senate even before a vacancy existed. He was betting that state Senator J. Sargeant Reynolds would be elected lieutenant governor in the November, 1969, general election, thereby creating the need to call a special election to pick his replacement.

Wilder also believed it might be the first and last time, for a long time, that a black could be elected. Although no black had been elected to the Virginia Senate in the Twentieth Century, in 1967, one had come close.

But the city was preparing to annex territory from adjoining Chesterfield County that would add about forty-five thousand new residents, nearly all of them white. The new voters would dilute black voting strength, as it approached majority status, and prevent blacks from taking over the city government. The annexation also would lessen the chances of a black winning a special election for the Senate seat.

If any black were going to be elected citywide, he had better move quickly. Wilder did. On August 27, 1969, two and one-half months before it could be known if there would be an election, Wilder announced his candidacy.

There was something less than a groundswell for Wilder's candidacy. None of the three more likely candidates—Henry Marsh, who was by then on the City Council; Delegate William Ferguson "Fergie" Reid and William "Doc" Thornton, the head of the Crusade for Voters, the city's largest black political organization—expressed an interest.

Wilder admitted, "none of them was saying, 'we want you.'" Thornton recalled that "Doug was the only one wanting to run."

Councilman Marsh, who over the years was involved in an unspoken competition with his one-time roommate as the city's most prominent black politician, had a somewhat different recollection of how Wilder became the front-runner. He thought Wilder had strong-armed Thornton out of the contest, telling Thornton he had had his chance and muffed it.

Nevertheless, "once that was decided, once Doug decided to run, all of us settled on Doug, and we all supported him," Marsh said.

Doc Thornton had run for the seat in 1967, and the lesson of his defeat was that if a black were to be elected citywide in Richmond, he would need significant white support. As a lawyer, Wilder had an entree to the white establishment that Thornton, a podiatrist, lacked. During the nine years he had been practicing law, Wilder had become friendly with several white attorneys with whom he regularly exchanged pleasantries at the courthouse.

Chief among them were Robert Gillam Butcher Jr., and brothers James Watson Morris III and Philip B. Morris (they were not related to the tobacco company). Butcher and the Morris brothers were courtroom lawyers who often saw Wilder in action.

"We met Doug individually in traffic court," said Jimmy Morris, and "one by one we discovered his undeniable charm and his great ability to enchant." Jimmy Morris, a short, flushed, full-faced Irishman, was fond of quoting a line from *The Rubaiyat of Omar Khayyam*, "take the cash and let the credit go," and joking that it was a good motto for a lawyer. He often cited it around the courthouse, and asked friends to guess its origins. "They'd guess everything from the Mortgage Bankers Manual to Shakespeare," he said. One day he saw Wilder on the fourth floor of City Hall, and quizzed him about it. "Not only did he know the source, he gave me another three or four lines," said the nonplused Morris.

"Oh yes," said Wilder, reminded of the incident years later. "We used to engage in repartee. That one starts off, 'Some for the gold of this world, others for the prophet's life to come; take the cash, and let the credit go, nor heed the rumble of the distant drum.'"

Jimmy Morris, whose reputation as a defendant's advocate earned him the presidency of the 14,000-member National Defense Research Institute and Trial Lawyers Association in 1988, described himself and his partners in the 1960s as "the establishment firm for black defendants; liberals by the standards of Virginia. It was common for blacks to come to a white firm, thinking we might offer them an entree with white judges," he said. On the other hand, whites didn't hire the few blacks who were lawyers, because there was no advantage, as the judges and jurors all were white.

"Doug was a really good lawyer, damned good. He was one of most articulate people on the scene," said Phil Morris, who became president of the Virginia Bar Association in 1989, the year that Wilder ran for governor.

Butcher's interest in politics grew out of his friendship with Sarge Reynolds, whom he had met on the Virginia equivalent of the playing fields of Eton. Reynolds went to St. Christopher's arch-rival, Woodberry Forest, and they competed against each other in sports.

When Reynolds, the scion of the Reynolds Metals fortune, and also related to the R. J. Reynolds Tobacco company family, decided to go into politics, "Sarge was looking for people like me because I was not a flaming liberal, more in the mainstream," Butcher said. Butcher, who later founded a bank and became a pillar—a rotund one with a walrus-sized moustache—of the city's Main Street financial establishment, said, "For a guy like me to get on his bandwagon, not that I was a dyed-in-wool conservative, helped legitimize him."

Like his other pals, Jimmy Morris grew up in the Jim Crow era and, as U.S. Supreme Court Justice Lewis F. Powell, a Richmonder, admitted, lived through the period without protesting. "How could I have done that?" Jimmy Morris later wondered. "I only thought of blacks when I occasionally looked at a domestic in our home and said to myself, 'boy are you lucky to have been born white.'"

Butcher and the Morrises were not social friends of Wilder's; they seldom saw him outside of a professional context, but for several years running, they had a standard exchange with him about politics, urging him to run for one office or another, for the House of Delegates or City Council.

"Doug was an impressive guy, a nice guy and we got to be friends," said Jimmy Morris, who said they were almost always on different sides, because he represented insurance carriers—a defendant's lawyer—while Wilder was a plaintiff's lawyer. With no more than twenty blacks practicing law in Richmond, Wilder stood out, and not just because of his stylish clothes, handsome manner and quick tongue.

The Morrises also agreed on another trait—a failing—that was to cause Wilder trouble over the years. "He always seemed to have too much to do," said Phil Morris. "He could articulate legal positions pretty well, but I'm not sure he spent a hell of a lot of time in the law library. He should have had some people in there with him. Then he would have been a great lawyer. But he kept a hectic pace, and I'm not so sure he had the time to make sure all the i's were dotted and t's crossed." Added Jimmy Morris, "Doug was quite effective in the courtroom, but he never surrounded himself with a lot of help. And he attracted more business than he could handle."

Wilder also had a maverick streak—illustrated by his sparring with the Crusade for Voters over tactics—that the Morrises and Butcher liked.

They had taken advantage of Wilder's independence in 1968, when Butcher ran the legislative campaign of Henry J. "Pete" Streat Jr., a Henrico County insurance agent. Streat, who was white, had failed to get the endorsement of the Crusade, so Butcher asked for Wilder's help. Wilder agreed, and played host to a beer party for Streat at a black night club on the city's near North Side, which was paid for by the Streat campaign. Wilder introduced Streat and told the crowd he supported him. Among the interested onlookers were several leaders of the Crusade, who were infuriated, and the editor of The Afro newspaper, which later criticized Wilder for lending his name to Streat. "I don't think he cared that much about Streat," said Phil Morris. "I think he just bucked the Crusade for the hell of it."

Wilder's timing also was fortuitous when he asked Butcher and the Morrises for help. It was shortly after the 1969 Democratic gubernatorial primary and they were not otherwise committed because they had backed Lieutenant Governor Fred Pollard in the three-way race for the gubernatorial nomination. Pollard, a Richmond attorney and family friend of both Butcher and the Morrises, finished last, even though he had been swept into statewide office four years earlier on the coattails of Governor Mills E. Godwin and was considered the heir to the Byrd mantle. Had Pollard finished even second, he would have been involved in a runoff, and Jimmy Morris, who had served as his Richmond campaign manager, would not have been available to help Wilder. (Wilder had backed the winner, Charlottesville attorney William Battle in the primary, although most blacks had supported state Senator Henry E. Howell of Norfolk, the darling of the state's hardy but outnumbered liberals.)

With Pollard on the sidelines, Butcher and the Morrises were available, and anxious to help Wilder.

Butcher said that as conservative as he has always been about business and free enterprise, he had "very strong feelings that it was only fair that in a city that was fifty per cent black, one of its two state senators should be black," especially when one of its white representatives, Edward E. Willey, was "the most conservative man that God ever created."

When Butcher made it clear that he was going to back Wilder, he discovered that there was "all kinds of jealousy over there in the black community—I guess there still is. Dr. Fergie Reid, Henry Marsh and Doug." But Butcher was convinced that "Doug was clearly the best available candidate—smart, articulate, smooth, attractive," and he liked him personally.

"When I got involved in it, I got really involved," said Butcher, whose highly visible role in the Wilder campaign resulted in a lot of raised eyebrows among the gray bankers and lawyers of Main Street, and less polite racial harangues down the street at the Commonwealth Club.

"I'm competitive by nature, and the more people criticized me for it, the more competitive I got," said Butcher, who, in an understatement, laughed, "when I did what I did, it was not stylish in this town, I can tell you that."

Another early recruit, McLain T. O'Ferrall Jr., a financial planner, agreed that "it was a very unpopular thing to do. We weren't trying to upset the establishment, because we thought we were part of it," said O'Ferrall, whose great-grandfather, Charles T. O'Ferrall, had been governor from 1894 to 1898.

Thinking back, O'Ferrall said he isn't sure what motivated him to stick his neck out. "Maybe it was Vietnam," said O'Ferrall, who was twenty-nine at the time. "I'm not saying we were long-haired, because we were young business-men. We liked Doug, but I think it was ninety-nine per cent that we thought Bobby Butcher was great, and Butcher was the one who was pushing it."

"We were not social crusaders," said Phil Morris. "I guess you could say we were moderates on racial issues. We just thought he was a natural. He was a good guy, a natural. We just thought it was important to have someone that good involved in politics" and that the coming open seat represented "a chance to get a black elected."

Wilder was picking up white backers on his own too. Other friends in the legal community arranged for about seventy white lawyers to meet him at a Holiday Inn. "It was not a fundraiser, but just an event that said, 'we are behind you,'" Wilder said. He came away from that gathering convinced he could win if the election were held "in the small city" before annexation.

Meanwhile, Butcher, O'Ferrall and the Morrisses mailed a letter to all the registered voters in the white, West End precincts, touting Wilder's candidacy. "That's when it really hit the fan," said Butcher. "I got phone calls at home: 'Your father would turn over in his grave.' There were no actual threats, just nasty stuff." Butcher was young and idealistic and rather enjoyed the notoriety. And what little positive response they got to the letter and other activities convinced them that Wilder could pull it off. "With such a large black vote," Butcher said, "all you had to do was get the guy some reasonable white support."

But not even Butcher would have put his head on the block for Wilder had he known what was going to happen next.

17. The Art of Compromise

Wilder was right about Sarge Reynolds. He won easily even though voters split their tickets, also choosing A. Linwood Holton as the first Virginia governor elected as a Republican, and Democrat Andrew P. Miller as attorney general.

A few days after the general election, Wilder opened his campaign headquarters in a downtown office building that he co-owned with Dr. Charles Sutton, in space that had just been vacated by another temporary tenant, the Holton for Governor campaign.

Wilder's decision to put his headquarters in the white section of downtown caused a stir among the Crusade's leaders because black candidates—the few there had been—traditionally worked out of the Slaughters Hotel on Second Street in the "colored section" of near-downtown. Furthermore, Curtis Holt, a black activist whose law suits had been responsible for dividing the city into wards and led to the election of black members of council, insisted that Wilder needed an office in Church Hill.

But Wilder was not running a traditional black candidate's campaign. He was running citywide, and he was running to get white support. So he kept his headquarters downtown, but obliged the Crusade and Holt by opening satellite campaign offices both on Second Street and in Church Hill. Even so, the Crusade didn't endorse Wilder until the Saturday after Thanksgiving, just three days before the election.

Although the weekly Richmond Afro had dutifully reported the maturation of Wilder over the years, the story in the afternoon News Leader announcing Wilder's candidacy apparently was the first time the daily newspapers in Richmond had mentioned Wilder. The article did not identify Wilder as black, but mentioned his race inferentially. It quoted Wilder as saying, "there is a need for representation in all aspects of our government." With Fergie Reid in the House of Delegates and Henry Marsh on the City Council, "a voice is likewise needed in the Senate," the newspaper said.

As campaign co-chairman with Butcher, Wilder chose Benjamin J. Lambert III, an optometrist and member of a respected black family known to many in the white community because of its successful catering business.

The thorniest problem for Wilder—other than the seminal challenge of trying to convince whites it was safe to vote for a black—was whether the special election should be held before or after the scheduled January 1 annexation of land and voters from Chesterfield County. The annexation, according to The Afro, was "the white power structure's frantic drive to gulp up more land and more white population" in a city that had become majority black. City officials had backed off a more ambitious plan that would have annexed 72,000 residents, but even the lesser proposal would materially dilute black voter strength, which had grown to almost sixty percent.

Wilder's dilemma was that if he pushed for an election before the annexation, he might be accused of being unwilling to face all of the voters in the district he sought to represent in the legislature. If he asked that the election be delayed until after the annexation, the new voters, who were overwhelmingly white, could be the difference between victory and defeat.

The city Democratic party chairman, lawyer George C. Freeman Jr., favored a January 6 election, which would allow the newly annexed voters to participate and still be in time for the winner to be seated for the legislative session that began January 14. But whether the annexation would even occur was in doubt. The Virginia Supreme Court had scheduled a November 24 hearing to hear arguments by opponents of annexation, who were appealing the July 12 trial court ruling that authorized it.

Wilder found a compromise, as he would do throughout his career. He eased white angst by announcing his support for the proposed annexation, but urged Governor Godwin to set the date for the election before it took effect. To ease black concerns, he said any annexations should be accompanied by adoption of one-man, one-vote legislative districts, a concept that had not yet penetrated the Virginia General Assembly. He also opposed a proposed amendment to the state constitution that would empower the legislature to expand the city's boundaries every ten years.

The Times-Dispatch called Wilder's support of the annexation a "bold new move for a Richmond Negro politician," and its political writer, James Latimer, said later in an interview that it showed that Wilder was "distinctly above the typical black politician" of the day.

Governor Godwin set December 1 as the date for the election, with the Democrats and Republicans expected to select their nominees at caucuses. Although the names of half a dozen white Democrats had been mentioned as possible candidates, Wilder's only announced opponent was former Mayor Morrill M. Crowe, a Republican.

The city Democratic party engaged in a desperate search for a viable white candidate. The party's leaders literally advertised for a candidate in the daily newspapers. It was the kind of an anyone-but-Wilder mentality that was to plague Wilder, and stir his ire, in later years, when he sought statewide office. Nonetheless, Wilder welcomed a field crowded with white contenders, who could divide the white vote.

What none of Wilder's white supporters were prepared for was the belated decision by Lieutenant Governor Pollard to get into the race. After his defeat in the gubernatorial primary, there had been speculation that Pollard might be interested in Reynolds's seat—in what would have amounted to swapping jobs with Reynolds—but Pollard would not confirm it.

As Pollard procrastinated, Wilder made his pitch to Butcher, O'Ferrall and the Morrises. Had Pollard made his intentions known earlier, Wilder would not have gotten their support, but to Wilder's white knights, a deal was a deal. They stuck with Wilder.

Pollard, who had represented Richmond in the House of Delegates from 1950 until he was elected lieutenant governor in 1965, "was brilliant and acerbic, and although he had no platform skills, he may have been the most effective legislator, and he would have been a superb senator," Jimmy Morris said.

"I respected that," Wilder said, "but I wanted to run. I thought I could bring a new dynamic to the Senate."

When Pollard entered the race, on November 10, he made no mention of Wilder's candidacy, saying only that "again I ask for your help so that, together, we can work to ensure the bright hopes of all of us, for the future of our home, the city of Richmond."

The Art of Compromise

While Pollard's candidacy seemed to be an answer to the call for white opposition to Wilder, it also created a problem for party officials. The city Democratic committee called a special meeting for November 19 at Mary Mumford Elementary School, in the Caucasian-friendly West End, to select its nominee.

City Republicans planned to meet the day before to anoint former Mayor Crowe as their nominee. Clarence Townes Jr., a black who was assistant to the chairman of the national Republican party, scotched reports that he might run, saying "it would be heresy for me to bring confusion to a race that could bring about the election of a black man to the Senate."

A week before the Democrats' meeting, a move was begun to circumvent choosing between Pollard and Wilder, to avoid an intra-party fight that might allow the Republicans to capture the seat. A survey by The Times-Dispatch indicated that Pollard had the votes to get the official endorsement at the meeting, but party leaders feared Wilder would not withdraw his candidacy. He might run as an independent, or even bolt to the Republicans if he were denied his party's nomination.

Because Wilder had vowed to run regardless of whether the party endorsed him, the idea of resurrecting a party loyalty oath blossomed as a way to deny him the nomination. City Democratic Chairman Freeman announced that in addition to candidates who previously had signed up, nominations could be made from the floor, providing that the candidate was present and agreed to sign a party loyalty oath. "Persons considered must have taken the oath to support the party candidate; those are the rules and we have to go by them; we have no choice unless the committee should vote to suspend the rules," Freeman said.

About that time, Lieutenant Governor-elect Reynolds, the new titular head of the party, proposed a plan whereby both Wilder and Pollard could be "certified as good Democrats" and neither proclaimed as the official party nominee. It would avoid a split that only could aid the GOP, Reynolds said.

Richard S. "Major" Reynolds III said later that his brother took no public role in the election to pick his successor because of his newly won position, but that in private he was "quietly supportive of Doug, he spoke favorably of his candidacy."

The party accepted Reynolds's idea of neutrality, and the election became a three-way event.

(Sarge Reynolds, who with his charm and money was a Virginia version of President John F. Kennedy, was elected to the House of Delegates in 1965, at the age of 29. Two years later, he moved up to the Senate. As a legislator, Reynolds called for action against slumlords and sponsored Virginia's first housing act. Upon his election as lieutenant governor, his admirers began looking beyond what they already were counting as the Reynolds governorship, from 1974 to 1978, toward national office. "The Kennedys would take a back seat to Sarge in charisma," said Jimmy Morris, who along with other friends were only partly joking when they talked about "President Reynolds." Butcher kidded that he already had staked his claim to be attorney general in the Reynolds administration. But in a tragedy of Kennedyesque proportion, Reynolds was stricken with a brain tumor less than a year into his term as lieutenant governor. On the day the disease was diagnosed, Reynolds said his prayer for his fellow

WILDER: HOLD FAST TO DREAMS

Virginians was, "may we settle our petty differences of color and background and go on with the challenge of achieving the highest form of human dignity for people everywhere. We need all the help we can get, but each of us can do our little part." He died on June 13, 1971, two weeks before his 35th birthday. "Virginia has lost more than she presently realizes," said Wilder. He said Reynolds "held out a hope for people who had not yet begun to participate in the affairs of state, and he served as a unifying element for young and old, black and white, rich and poor.")

Before Pollard's entry into the race, Wilder's white backers were divided about his chances.

Jimmy Morris thought there was "no question Crowe would have won in a two-way race." He had been an effective mayor, and he was a respected, white-haired gentleman who looked the part of a public official.

"Doug would have never beaten Crowe one-on-one," said O'Ferrall. "I'm not sure Doug saw it that way, but if Fred hadn't got into the race, Doug would have lost. Fred did the biggest favor in the world to Doug. If Fred had said right after the primary election that he was going to run, we would have supported him. But afterwards, we weren't going to change. It just made us mad."

O'Ferrall said that "frankly, Fred, made a lot of people sort of mad," including many who were opposed to Wilder. "He did not do well [with them] because they were concerned about diluting the [white] vote." In the end, thanks to Pollard, "Doug didn't need any help, as such," O'Ferrall said. "But Doug does not win that election if Pollard stays out. I don't know how the lines were drawn, but they weren't in his favor."

Phil Morris was a bit more optimistic, saying "it would have taken an upset" for Wilder to have won in a two-way race. But after Pollard got in, "there was no question about it," Wilder would win.

Butcher also believed that Wilder "had a shot" against Crowe because the former mayor "was not a very dynamic guy. But it was going to be a lot tougher" than it turned out to be. Butcher, shaking his head in wonderment, pointed out that he ended up being Wilder's campaign manager against the mayor and the former lieutenant governor, the latter a close family friend. "You can imagine what people thought of what I was doing," Butcher said. "But by then, we had them in a three-way race, and we were going to nail them. Pollard's entry "changed the math of the thing. It was a two-handed layup," especially because Pollard ran "sort of a half-assed, whipped-dog campaign. With such a big black vote, all you had to do was get the guy some reasonable white support."

The candidacy of the thirty-eight-year-old, crew-cut Wilder also benefited from that the fact that he was not threatening to white voters, either in appearance or rhetoric. Some whites "expressed concerns about his lack of technical experience in politics, but no one was publicly rattling white sheets," Jimmy Morris said. "We had gotten beyond that. But there was some moaning about the whites knocking each other off."

The number of white votes that Butcher, O'Ferrall and the Morrises swung to Wilder was not proportionate to "the amount of work we put in to get them," O'Ferrall said. He recalls delivering Wilder's campaign literature door-to-door "and then running to the next house. That was a heckuva long time ago,"

The Art of Compromise

O'Ferrall said later, and "the thinking hadn't changed like it has today."

"We got some white votes; not a helluva lot, but some," said Butcher, who told Wilder on election day, "we're going to stand in the biggest precinct in Windsor Farms [the city's most exclusive white neighborhood]."

The campaign was short and virtually free of racial overtones so far as the candidates were concerned.

Crowe pledged to work in behalf of separate legislative districts in the House of Delegates for the city, which then shared its delegates with adjacent Henrico County. Pollard proposed a plan to relieve the city's financial plight that was such that he said "one good snowfall will put us in the red." Wilder too said the "state must revise its formulas for distributing various forms of financial aid to allocate more revenues to ease the urban crisis and ease the burden on city taxpayers."

On the Sunday before the election, Wilder rode in a convertible in a parade organized by the Reindeers Social Club, and visited nine black churches. Crowe was busy too, and visited two black churches. Crowe and Pollard also attended a reception marking the fiftieth anniversary of the Virginia League of Women Voters.

18. The Journey Begins

$\mathbf{W}$ilder and his supporters gathered at his headquarters on December 1, 1969, to watch the returns. Among those crowded into the room were more than a dozen relatives. In addition to his wife and three young children, his mother, several sisters and their spouses and children were there to cheer the results, as they were posted on a large blackboard.

At mid-evening the local television stations showed up, a reliable harbinger of impending triumph, and it was clear that the favorable mathematics of two whites versus one black was going to produce a historic victory for Wilder. It was vindication of another theorem appreciated by savvy campaign managers, but seldom acknowledged by candidates, that in politics, it's more important to be lucky than to be good. It was the first of half a dozen consecutive election notches that Wilder was to record on his belt, and the last time he would have an opponent until he ran for lieutenant governor in 1985.

Wilder polled nearly as many votes as his opponents combined. The final tally showed Wilder with 15,844; Republican Morrill M. Crowe with 10,318, and Lieutenant Governor Pollard, who failed to carry a single one of the city's 69 precincts, with 6,015.

A jubilant Wilder said he was "both happy and humble that the people have chosen me. I am very conscious that my margin of victory is a plurality (rather than a majority) and that the bulk of my support came from black citizens....However, the returns indicate that I also received a gratifying number of white votes. I particularly appreciate this support and look forward to the time when all men can run as candidates on their qualifications, and not as a 'Negro' candidate or a 'white' candidate."

Thirty-one-year-old Eunice Wilder, wearing a black knit coat and dress ensemble, black boots and large, gold earrings, arrived at campaign headquarters with the couple's three children about nine o'clock, after previous stops at the Crusade for Voters headquarters and the John Marshall Hotel.

Laughing, Mrs. Wilder told a television reporter, "Now I can say it: I have been expecting it all the time." She admitted to encountering election-day jitters, however, so she "went knocking on doors," encouraging residents to go to the polls, continuing a practice she had begun during the campaign.

As it became apparent that Wilder had won, the frail Miss Beulah was encouraged to go to the platform, where she told the head-nodding crowd how much her son's victory meant to her, and to the people of Church Hill.

Bob Butcher, who was among the minority of whites in the assemblage, could barely hold back the tears as Miss Beulah spoke. It was "one of the most satisfying moments of my life," he said. "I really felt rewarded."

Wilder, who still carries in his wallet a yellowing newspaper clipping of that first victory, said later that "it meant a lot to me to win in the citywide race. I got some white support, and I also got a lot of whites who were not vocal or open, but were good enough not to go to the polls."

The next morning's Times-Dispatch picked up on that later observation. A congratulatory editorial suggested that the fact that many eligible whites did not vote was an indication that racial prejudice was on the wane, and that whites were not alarmed by the possibility of a Wilder victory.

Wilder spent about $23,000 on the campaign, but had raised only about

$8,000, "so I had to eat about $15,000." Even in victory he complained about the Crusade, however, saying that "I had to pay for the entire Crusade operation—that cost me about $8,000—every poll worker, every piece of literature."

Despite its tardy endorsement, the Crusade was quick to take credit for Wilder's victory. Doc Thornton said "it shows what black people can do when we stick together. We've been talking about solidarity in the Crusade for Voters for years, but this time we really did it. I think it proves if we had been this solid in the past, we might have more blacks in office now."

Wilder piled up huge majorities in black neighborhoods—in one East End precinct he got all but 37 of the 1,147 votes cast—and, according to calculations by the Times-Dispatch, he got between 2,000 and 2,500 white votes, the higher number amounting to about 18 percent of the white turnout.

The banner headline in The Afro rejoiced, "Wilder Wins: He Integrates State Senate."

The Times-Dispatch, under a four-column, front-page headline, announced, "Wilder Succeeds in His First Try." The story described the senator-elect as a "busy lawyer and 'new breed' politician." Although the newspaper did not mention Wilder's race, it noted that "in many ways, Wilder is like his good friend (Reid), the first Negro elected to the General Assembly in this centruy. He (Wilder) talks softly, smiles frequently and has a relaxed, pleasant personality."

Howard Carwile, a loquacious white lawyer, broadcaster and Afro columnist who served on city council, hailed Wilder's victory as "history that this city can reflect on with great pride for many long years to come."

Carwile, who subsequently served in the House of Delegates until he was beaten in 1975 by a future governor, Gerald L. Baliles, said he was confident that Wilder "will perform his senatorial duties in a manner totally free of racial bias. I also know that behind that contagious smile there is political guts and crusading courage. He is not prejudiced against any people or race, but by the same token he is not possessed with any Uncle Tomish proclivities."

The day after the election, Wilder and his soon-to-be colleague in the state Senate, Edward E. Willey, pledged to work together in behalf of legislation that would benefit the capitol city.

On January 14, 1970, at five minutes after noon, as the first official act of the newly convened state Senate, Lawrence Douglas Wilder took the oath of office as the first black member of that body since Nathaniel M. Griggs represented the town of Farmville and Amelia and Cumberland counties from 1887 to 1890. His victory raised to three the number of blacks in the 140-member legislature in the twentieth century, all of whom were then in office.

Nationally, Wilder joined a select group of 168 black legislators, according to a survey compiled by the Voter Education Project of the Southern Regional Council.

In the balcony of the Senate chamber that day, a dozen members of Wilder's family craned their necks to see his investiture. His mother had arrived early to get a good seat and was not recognized as the new senator's mother.

"Mother was not very light skinned, but she was light," said Wilder's sister, Jean, "and when she walked in, the other people made room for her—they thought she was a white lady. Then we all showed up, and it got a little testy."

WILDER: HOLD FAST TO DREAMS

When someone attempted to squeeze in front of them, explaining that they wanted to photograph the historic event, Jean said her mother pulled herself up straight and said, "'Yes, I know, MY SON is becoming A SEN-A-TOR.' I thought, Mother, you're going to get us all in trouble."

Until his swearing-in, three days before his thirty-ninth birthday, Wilder had been inside the Capitol only once or twice, including the time he took the bar exam there. He was so unfamiliar with the building that he had to be directed to the west side of the building, where the Senate chamber was located.

His introduction was applauded warmly by his new colleagues, and Richmond's senior legislator, the crusty conservative Ed Willey, welcomed his colleague as "a highly respected lawyer, a gentleman in every regard."

Among the first to shake Wilder's hand was Pollard, who was still presiding over the Senate as the outgoing lieutenant governor. Also in the chamber was Lieutenant Governor-elect Reynolds, who was to be inaugurated on the coming Saturday.

The first social crisis arising from the involuntary induction of Wilder into the exclusive club that was the state Senate was the question of where he would be seated on the chamber floor. Rules assure returning senators that their desk assignments cannot be changed without their accession. Desk assignments are important because much of the business of the body is conducted on the floor, especially during the closing weeks of the legislative sessions. Because the desks are arranged in pairs, seatmates are likely to depend on each other for advice on a particular topic, or for parliamentary guidance, and—even though it is against the rules—to push the appropriate "yea" or "nay" button on a vote, when one of them is momentarily out of his seat.

Because Wilder had been chosen in a special election, the only empty seat was the one vacated by his predecessor, Sarge Reynolds. It was next to William V. Rawlings, who represented Southampton County and adjoining counties in the heart of Southside Virginia, where support for segregation had been, and to a large extent remained, adamant.

Before the ceremony, Ben Lacy, the Senate clerk, approached Rawlings apologetically, saying, "we just don't know where we're going to put him (Wilder). It looks like the only place is next to you." Instead of a there-goes-the-neighborhood reaction, Rawlings told Lacy, "'Are you trying to tell me that Wilder is going to be my seatmate? Great, I love it.'"

Another senator, William B. Hopkins of Roanoke, said Rawlings later regaled in telling the story. "Bill was a fellow who believed in human rights," added Hopkins.

When Wilder learned of the quandary precipitated by where he would sit, he realized "I was going to need friends in the assembly."

And Rawlings, a hog farmer from the land of the rednecks, became the best of them. "He never allowed me to make a mistake," said Wilder. "He would say, 'I know you like me and I like you, but you can't vote the same way as I do. If you vote the way I vote on some of these measures, we're both going to be in trouble.'"

Rawlings also made sure that Wilder was not ostracized by other senators, on either business or social occasions. "He included me, right away." If a group of senators made plans to meet in one of their offices to talk about a particular bill, or if they gathered at a desk after the session to decide where to go for a drink, Rawlings was there, making sure his friend was included. "He'd say, 'Wait a minute, let me get Wilder.'"

Hopkins's first recollection of Wilder was that of "a fellow who wanted to get along. And he was rather articulate, a gentleman. But it was his first session, and he didn't make a lot of noise. He was not a firebrand."

Now that her husband was elected, Eunice, the dutiful wife, pledged, "I'll do whatever he tells me to," which she said she hoped would include time for watching the Senate in session. "His sincere desire to achieve what he feels is necessary reaches the people," she told an interviewer for the News Leader. "I have the utmost confidence in what he sets out to do, and know he'll go about it in the best way he can." Mrs. Wilder added that although she had a degree in economics, and had worked in a local bank for two years, "my interests haven't extended very far beyond home because I've had the children to care for." Her current jobs were primarily chauffeuring their three children, housecleaning, and cooking for her husband, who was a "meat and potatoes" man. Now that all three children were in school for the first time, she said, "I definitely want to become involved in civic or school affairs, any type of volunteer work. This is something I can do being at home as a housewife, whereas someone else can't."   As for getting caught up in the political whirl, she said, "I don't expect the change to alter our home life as such, but then, maybe I'm naive about this."

Many blacks viewed Wilder's election as "a phenomenon, it was history," his sister Olga observed. "People would ask mother, 'what did you do for him?' and she would always say, 'I did the same for him as I did for all of the rest of them.' There was never any jealousy or distinction. We were all Wilders."

Even though he was not a member, Wilder was honored, along with Fergie Reid and Henry Marsh, as a distinguished member of the Fourth Baptist, the church across the street from the homestead. The Astoria Beneficial Club named him a "Citizen of the Year."

His sister Jean remembers going shopping with her mother shortly after the election. Jean's young son had wet his pants and was fussing to get home. But every time Beulah Wilder used her charge card to buy something, the clerk recognized the name and said something about how proud she must be of her son.

"Mother had this little spiel," Jean smiled in recollection. "She'd say, 'I am proud of all my kids. There is Naomi, and she is a teacher, and this is my daughter, Jean, and ....'

"By the time we went into the third store, I said, Mom, 'don't show that card. Pay cash. I've got to get home.'"

19. Carry Me Back

The junior representative from Richmond had been a member of the Senate less than a month when, on February 10, 1970, he made his maiden speech. It was one of those magic moments—like Jackie Robinson's first steal of home plate—that many who weren't there claimed years later to have witnessed.

He rose, he explained, to speak on a point of personal privilege. His remarks began innocently enough. He explained that he and his wife had attended a reception the previous night at the John Marshall Hotel, hosted by the Virginia Food Dealers Association.

"The hosts were gracious, as it is customary," he said, momentarily lulling his colleagues into recollections of one of the many pleasant evenings they spend during their sessions at the trough of special-interest groups. The receptions allow members of the sponsoring organization to rub elbows, and tip elbows, with senators and delegates, and perhaps put a bug in their ears about their group's agenda. The occasions are especially popular with out-of-town legislators, who can get enough to eat and drink so that they can pocket their per diem expense for that day.

"I should have hoped," Wilder said, "that my time in so rising could have been spent for much more a deserving and needed mutual cause, and really, by this time in our lives, there would be no necessity for what I have to say." A hush fell over the chamber, as if the often inattentive senators sensed a dark cloud rising on their horizon. They swiveled their leather chairs in the direction of the young black man standing in the corner, his oratorical skills having brought them to attention.

"However," he said, his voice rising, "at the end of the event, the guests were asked to stand and join in the singing by the two entertainers, who proceeded forthwith to lead us in the singing of `Carry Me Back To Old Virginny.'

"I was obligated to touch Mrs. Wilder and ask her to listen along with me," Wilder went on, in tones dulcet enough for any gentleman of the Old South, "to determine if this was to be a repeat performance." He pointed out that "we were afforded similar entertainment," and there was no disguising his sarcasm, when the legislators had been on a recent tour of Northern Virginia. "On that occasion," he recalled, "the 'Old Guard,' a singing group, launched into that tune, which obviously by history bears heavily nostalgic upon some. As the lyrics proceeded, I wondered whether we would be spared the part, `that's where this ole darkie's heart am longed to go.' I didn't have long to wonder, as the words burned in my ear.

"Mrs. Wilder and I left, as we did last evening, so as not to dignify the occasion."

As his colleagues shifted uncomfortably in their chairs, the immaculately dressed grandson of slaves plunged on, quietly assuring the squirming descendants of the landed gentry, "I wish to make one thing crystal clear: I am not saying that any member of this body has ever offered me the slightest impertinence. Quite the contrary. I have enjoyed the gentlemanly and courteous forbearing of this group of men, and have otherwise given utterance of same. Nor am I saying that any of the persons on last evening or in Northern Virginia, ever

Carry Me Back

evinced any design to be insulting.

"I should imagine the singing of this song has been traditional," he said, pausing to foreshadow the idea that a new day was dawning, "and yet, I know personally that there are so many of you who are not of a persuasion"—voice rising again—"to epithetically downgrade and make mockery of a race of people."

He pointed out that it was the beginning of "Negro History Week," which the new governor had officially recognized. At such a time, he said, "We can ill afford the luxury of coining into song, phrase or what have you, words which, by their very construction, recall the memories of our shameful history. Those of us in attendance at these events who join in so revering the memory of that horrid past are as guilty as the actual perpetrators of the deed."

Then, in an exhibition of his near photographic memory, Wilder pointed out that the state's officials—governor, lieutenant governor, attorney general and members of the General Assembly—"have sworn to uphold, among other things, the following," whereupon he recited from the state constitution: "that all men are by nature equally free and independent and have certain inherent rights, of which, when they enter into a state of society, by any compact, deprive or divest their posterity...That no man, or set of men, is entitled to exclusive or separate emoluments or privileges...

"Gentleman," he concluded, "I urge that we collectively aspire to the full implementation of the words of our Constitution, by deeds as well as by words."

With that, he sat down. Not to applause, but to a silence that bespoke a tribute to his eloquence, if not his message.

That afternoon, the News Leader reported, under the headline "Wilder Protests 'Old Virginny,'" that "the Negro senator rose on the floor of the Senate today to protest the singing of the song at functions held for the General Assembly." The next edition of the Afro bannered the speech, which it reprinted, with the headline, "Wilder Jolts Senate With Protest."

Even Wilder's staunch supporter, Bob Butcher, was upset by his speech. "Raising hell about 'Carry Me Back' was the most disappointing moment" of Wilder's first year, said Butcher, who called Wilder and asked, incredulously, "How could you, as your first official act, when the most important thing for you to do is to establish good will, and try to get those guys on your side, go down and take on something like that?" Wilder told Butcher that hearing the song at the John Marshall, where he had waited tables, "got under my skin so bad that I just couldn't resist it." Butcher still couldn't believe it. He told Wilder, "you're too smart for that."

Some whites, attempting to defend the lyrics, pointed out that the song was written by a black, James Bland, in 1875. It was one of more than seven hundred ballads composed by Bland, who apparently had never been to Virginia. The word "Virginny" was changed to "Virginia" when the legislature officially adopted it as the state song in 1940. It was sung, along with "Dixie," at semi-official events.

Nonetheless, a week later, Wilder introduced Senate Bill 425, which would have repealed the state song. It garnered no co-sponsors, and died without a hearing. But its message has echoed on for decades, and was a factor in Wilder's election as lieutenant governor fifteen years later.

Delegate William P. Robinson Sr., of Norfolk, one of the two blacks in the House in 1970, was one of the few legislators who agreed with Wilder. "Our slave heritage is a historical fact that you can't change," he said, but "in so-called polite society, there is no reason why intelligent people should persist in such nostalgia." He said blacks feel about the song as whites would feel about "whitey or honky."

A decade later, Wilder told an interviewer that "when I denounced [the song], I touched a nerve no one knew was there. The spirit of the song was that 'the old slave wants to go to heaven and join the old master to live in perpetual slavery.'" That first year, Wilder said, some of his colleagues "didn't really think I should be here, but they were gentlemen about it and kept it to themselves." Nonetheless, their insensitivity to black issues "sometimes made me so angry that I couldn't talk."

Wilder never made another effort to change the song, although others annually attempt to repeal it or sponsor contests to find a new state song. "Carry Me Back" remains the official state song, but Wilder notes wryly, "they never sing it anymore."

20. Holton: Courage and Conviction

W ilder and Abner Linwood Holton came to the Capitol together in 1970 as, respectively, the first black state senator in eighty years and the first governor ever elected as a Republican. If they did not become fast friends, they quickly became allies in a mutual cause—ending discrimination.

In his inaugural address, Holton sought "the help of all Virginians...no matter where they live, what they might do, what age or race they might be, or what political philosophy they might hold." Paraphrasing Lincoln, Holton said, "Let our goal in Virginia be an aristocracy of ability, regardless of race, creed or color. Here in Virginia we must see that no citizen...is excluded from full participation in both the blessings and responsibilities of our society because of his race. We will have a government based on a partnership of all Virginians, a government in which there will be neither partisanship nor prejudice of any kind. As Virginia has been a model for so much else in America in the past, let us now endeavor to make today's Virginia a model of race relations."

Wilder was so pleased with Holton's inaugural address that he sent a telegram to the Republican governor pledging his support. "I am impressed," Wilder said, "with your implementing your campaign promises by deed."

Holton not only preached equal opportunity, he practiced it.

"I will not tolerate, nor will any state official tolerate, racial or ethnic prejudice in the hiring or promotion" of state employees, he pledged in signing his first executive order. Candidates for state jobs, Holton said, should be examined "solely on the basis of his qualifications and his potential." That order outlawing racial discrimination in state employment subsequently became de rigueur as Executive Order Number One for his Democratic successors.

A few hours after Holton's announcement, Wilder and two white liberal senators from Norfolk, Henry E. Howell, who had retained his seat despite losing the gubernatorial nomination the preceding summer, and Peter K. Babalas, a self-educated millionaire son of Greek immigrants who was to become one of Wilder's closest friends and supporters in the legislature, expanded on Holton's order by co-sponsoring a bill that would prohibit discrimination in jobs and housing in the state.

While the symbolism was important, there also was substance in the new administration's commitment "to have an open government in which all people will participate." Holton named William B. Robertson of Roanoke as his special assistant for consumer protection and business development, the highest appointive post ever held by a black in the state. The thirty-six-year-old Robertson, who later fashioned a career with the U. S. State Department, had switched from the Democratic party the previous April. Holton also integrated the state police and the capitol police and named a black to chair the Richmond city election board.

More than anything that Holton said or did as governor, however, was how he and his wife, Jinx, lived their lives. When the Holtons arrived in the capital city, in January of 1970, the Richmond schools, like most in Virginia, were still far from integrated. Many whites had opted to send their children to private schools—either to all-white academies established for the specific purpose of abrogating the law, or in the more sophisticated, middle-class neighborhoods, to historically private, often church-operated college preparatory schools. For those who wanted to keep their children in the public schools, the city instituted a freedom of choice plan, which had the effect of allowing white parents to keep their children in neighborhood schools, while allowing blacks who chose—as did the Wilders—to send their children to any school that had room for them. But U. S. District Court Judge Robert Merhige found that the freedom-of-choice plan placed all the burden for integration on blacks, so he signed a decree that required crosstown busing of pupils in Richmond, which rippled the tranquility of life in Richmond like a rock skipping across the pool at the Country Club of Virginia.

A city school official assured the Holtons that Merhige's order need not apply to them, however, because the governor's mansion was a state enclave that was not a party to the suit. But the Holtons wanted to set an example, to provide leadership, so their children were bused to the assigned schools. A photograph taken of the arrival of their oldest child, Tayloe, at Kennedy High, accompanied only by her father and a plainclothes state policeman, was published in newspapers across the country. Holton displays the picture on the wall of his Washington law office, next to one that shows Alabama Governor George Wallace standing in a schoolhouse door, flanked by armed and uniformed officers, barring the entrance of blacks to a school. Framed with Tayloe's picture is a letter from one of Holton's predecessors, Democrat Gov. Colgate W. Darden Jr., who wrote that it depicts "the most significant happening in this commonwealth during my lifetime."

Despite the tone and good intentions set by the new governor, across the street from the Capitol in the Lyric Barber Shop, blacks were unable to get a shoe shine. One of the two black members of the House of Delegates, William P. Robinson Sr., a Ph.D. professor of political science at Norfolk State University, was turned away by George W. Whitby, owner of the shop, who made no secret of his whites-only policy. Wilder said turning away Robinson "clearly underscores the need" for the anti-discrimination legislation that he, Babalas and Howell had introduced. The bill, mirroring federal law, would outlaw racial discrimination in most areas of public accommodation, but it would not cover barber shops. But the anti-Jim Crow proposal got little support in the Senate. Holton joined in the criticism of the shop's policy at his first press conference and said he expected that none of his staff would patronize the shop. Not everyone shared the governor's sentiments. Chief Justice Harold Fleming Snead of the Virginia Supreme Court of Appeals, who had sworn in Holton, said he had patronized the shop for years and had no intention of stopping.

Holton, faced with a better than seven-to-one Democratic legislature, understood the value of coalitions and Wilder was one of the first he turned to for help. Holton had proposed a reorganization of the top ranks of state government, seeking to install a cabinet system similar to that of the federal government. The idea was anathema to the Democratic leadership because it would consolidate the power of the governor in half a dozen appointees, whereas the existing system perpetuated Byrd loyalists at the helm of scores of agencies, regardless of who occupied the governor's office.

Holton realized that he had to deal with the Democrats and that he had to divide them. It was clear from the beginning that he could not count on either majority leader—especially Bill Hopkins in the Senate, who was a political rival from Roanoke. So he started in the House, where he picked up the support of the chairman of the appropriations committee, and then of the speaker, John Warren Cooke. With their help, the bill squeaked through by the barest majority of fifty-one votes, on a last-minute conversion by Delegate Owen Pickett of Virginia Beach.

When the bill reached the Senate, Holton went to Wilder, among others, for help. But the governor realized that the freshman senator did not want to offend his party's leadership. "And why in the hell should he?" Holton acknowledged. Finally, though, after a number of meetings in Holton's office, Wilder indicated that "if my vote is necessary, you'll get it."

And it was. When the bill came up for final passage in the Senate, opponents attached an amendment that would have required a conference with the House, which, because they already had managed to delay its consideration until the final day of the session, meant such an action would doom the measure. Nonetheless, Wilder voted for the killing amendment, which passed by a single vote. At that point, Wilder delivered on his promise, calling for a second vote, on which he changed position, allowing the original bill to pass.

Holton said Wilder never asked for a favor in return. "That's one of the things that shows his great character, never asked me for a thing." Wilder got nothing out of it, majority leader Hopkins said bitterly, "and neither did the state."

The first significant test of Wilder's legislative ability came on a fair-housing bill that Delegate Robinson had sponsored in the House. There was less than overwhelming support in the House for the idea, which prohibited racial discrimination in the sale or rental of property, but it was allowed to pass, after being loaded up with amendments to make it unacceptable to the Senate. But the tactic backfired on Robinson's fair-housing bill.

"We got together and passed it," Wilder said. Its enactment, and subsequent signing by Holton, made Virginia one of the first states—the first in the South—to enact a fair-housing law. That success opened Wilder's eyes to the possibilities of success for a legislator who was able to build a coalition—which is the statesman's way of expressing deal cutting and vote swapping. "I was very impressed with the people who stuck with us on that. If we can do that, why can't we do some other things," Wilder reasoned.

One of Wilder's allies in that fight was William E. Fears from Accomack County on the Eastern Shore of Virginia. Fears, a self-described country lawyer—whose Arkansas accent masked an engineering degree from Yale—was elected to the Senate two years before Wilder. Fears gravitated to Wilder because "he got the same damn treatment I got when I got here." Fears was not readily admitted into the club because he had defeated a twelve-year veteran, "an old Byrd guy. That crowd gave me the old cold shoulder; put me over in the corner, the same place that Doug was put." Fears said he and Wilder formed an alliance: "He voted for my bills and I voted for his."

Wilder's legislative agenda that first year was modest—he introduced five bills, but only one of them was passed, and it was vetoed by Holton. It related to his erstwhile career as a toxicologist: It would have permitted chemical analysis to be admissible as evidence in trials if the information were provided to defense attorneys twenty-four hours in advance. The bill also marked the first collaboration of what became Richmond's Odd Couple in the Senate—it was co-sponsored by Ed Willey and Wilder's seatmate, Bill Rawlings.

Delegate Albert Lee Philpott of Bassett, who subsequently became Speaker of the House, recalled that except for the protest of the state song, Wilder was "a typical lawyer-legislator. He was a trial lawyer, and he was interested in bills like most trial lawyers. He very much was the average lawyer who came into the legislature, trying to correct what he could see were inadequacies in the law that related to his practice."

A classic example of that was Wilder's objections to a proposed revision of the state law governing human organ transplants. The bill would have excused hospital officials from notifying the next-of-kin of a potential donor for a human heart transplant. Two years earlier, after the second heart transplant in America was performed at the Medical College of Virginia in Richmond, the donor's family complained they had not been notified before the transplant, and they hired Wilder as their attorney to sue the hospital.

Although Philpott said that by 1970, "most of the racially related legislation had already been passed, and it was in a pretty smooth period so far as civil rights legislation," Wilder found plenty of room for improvement.

One of his proposals that first year had its genesis in those middle-of-the-night telephone calls from the jail: He sought to reduce what he considered extreme penalties for a number of minor offenses. Wilder's bill, which attracted no co-sponsors, would have reduced from three years to twelve months the minimum time a judge could sentence someone convicted of prostitution, keeping, living in or frequenting a bawdy place (which would have caused problems for Wilder's war buddy Watson), soliciting, vagrancy or contributing to delinquency.

He also proposed that counties and cities be required to initiate food stamp or commodity distribution programs. But again he found no co-sponsors and the bill died in committee.

Wilder "more or less played on the team," Philpott noted. "He paid attention, did his homework. It wasn't too long before Doug was showing some leadership ability in the Senate, and as time went on he became much more influential. He did this by not being just a black, but by being just another senator. That was my experience with him. A knowledgeable legislator who you could sit down and talk to, and explain your legislation, and get an attentive ear."

21. Is He Black Enough?

Wilder's activism has been divided between changing laws and changing minds. As a legislator, he often found Virginia's laws protecting minorities and assuring equality as barren as the Southwest Virginia mountain tops that had been stripped bald by coal mining. But he also found unplowed ground, as fertile as the rolling tobacco fields of Southside: The need to pass good new laws was nearly as vital as repealing bad old ones.

Whether he was dealing with the Good Ol' Boys in the state Senate, or the electorate at large, Wilder seldom was pessimistic about the chances of change, exhibiting what many viewed as a naivete about the possibilities of right triumphing over wrong.

One reason for his success is that he never put all the burden for change on his opponents. He was constantly poking and jabbing at a lethargic black electorate. The difficulty was that he did not know what his constituents wanted. For example, he was disappointed to discover that many black people were not aroused by his complaint about the lyrics of the state song. "They thought there were more important things to do, not realizing that you can't get the social pie until you cut the crust."

Less than six months after being elected to the Senate, his dichotomous relationship with the Crusade for Voters resurfaced. Wilder risked alienating support in the black community when, one day after the Crusade announced its slate of candidates in the upcoming May, 1970, city council election, Wilder made his own endorsements, including two candidates backed by a rival political group that had evolved from the political organization that had been a symbol of the white Establishment for many years.

Although Wilder's announcement included praise and endorsement of two black candidates—law school roommate Henry Marsh, who was an incumbent, and Walter Kenney, a young lawyer, who would "provide a voice for people whose voices have gone unheard too long"—his endorsement of two white nominees that had been bypassed by the Crusade, Phil Morris, his longtime friend and early supporter for the Senate, and William V. Daniel, was interpreted as a criticism of the Crusade. Wilder urged voters to "reject the idea that this particular group is good or that particular group is bad....We should consider each candidate individually—judging him not only by what he says, but by what he has done."

At the same time, he could be militantly black. To a predominantly black audience of the Eastern Star in Roanoke, he urged, "lift your voices to assert the right of the individual in a free society. We are free. Only others keep us from being free. I'm tired of apologizing for being black. I'm black, and I'm tired of being reminded of it. And this is what we must remind ourselves." He was fed up with blacks who merely wait for change to occur. "Militancy has brought us to where we are now." He said it is time for America to "take its place in a world where whites are, in fact, a numerical minority." But he added that just because "black is beautiful doesn't mean white is ugly."

In a speech to black health workers, Wilder said blacks must involve themselves without "fear of reprisal, incrimination and discrimination." He called the Voting Rights and Civil Rights acts of the 1960s the "second reconstruction," and said "the time is past when self-appointed people can speak for the masses of black people. Politics is not an exercise in colonialism."

He called for reform of the jury selection process. The 1970 census showed that the city was 42 percent black, yet Wilder said he had recently appeared before an all-white, middle-class, middle-aged jury. He also complained that in murder cases, prosecutors used peremptory challenges to get rid of blacks, because they felt they might be sympathetic toward a black defendant. "It's so absurd," Wilder said.

In a 1976 interview with the editors of The Afro, he talked about the special responsibilities that went with being the only black in the Senate, and one of only two in the assembly: "You are called upon to be sensitized to issues as they relate to black, poor and disadvantaged people. It is an awesome responsibility in that you might miss something....The real problem is not hearing enough from black people as to what they really want done....They don't write their legislators, don't attend hearings, don't come to committee meetings, don't visit in the galleries...don't make themselves visible."

Such apathy resulted in a lack of accountability, a free ride, to white legislators whose constituents included large numbers of blacks. "The voting records of people elected by black people for the most part go unnoticed....The accountability is very, very poor," Wilder said.

Wilder never was one to complain about being left out and then refuse to go in when invited. He and Delegate Robinson integrated one of the state's foremost symbols of white racism that year when they attended the twenty-eighth annual shad planking sponsored by the Wakefield Ruritan Club. They decided to attend the event, although without enthusiasm, because, as Wilder explained, "If you raise a lot of hell about something because you are excluded, you don't stay away when you're invited. I felt conscience-bound to go." Nonetheless, Wilder considered it tokenism that only two blacks were invited. James W. Renney, who had been master of ceremonies seventeen years, said only the eighty members of the club could extend invitations, which went to about three thousand men. Delegate Ray Ashworth (D-Wakefield) invited all male members of the assembly, but said he believed the legislature's seven female members would feel out of place. The sponsors pleaded lack of sanitation facilities and the amount of liquor consumed as reasons for excluding women. "I think this is a reason why women should be invited," responded Wilder. "Then maybe it'll be cause for Virginia gentlemen to conduct themselves as Virginia gentlemen."

Wilder also integrated a Richmond country club, when he accepted an invitation in 1977 to become the first black member of Jefferson-Lakeside Country Club.

Wilder's neighbor, James E. Sheffield, became the first black judge of a court of record in the state, in 1975. The failure to have more, Wilder said, showed how important it was for blacks to be involved in the political process, "to exert pressure when needed," because in Virginia, judges are elected by the General Assembly. Wilder followed his own advice, and frequently spoke out, with his targets as likely to be blacks as whites, Democrats as Republicans.

Wilder usually stuck to local matters, but that same month, in a guest column in the Richmond News Leader, he made the connection between black concerns—unemployment, dropouts, cities deteriorating, lack of voter registration, the widening gap between rich and poor—and world concerns—revolution in Nicaragua, uprising in Iran, unrest in Rhodesia, oppression in South Africa, nearing peace in the Middle East. "We must address them collectively," he said.

As a legislator, he succeeded in restoring compulsory school attendance, which had been repealed as part of the state's massive resistance to integration. As a result, there was no way to control truancy. About 25,000 children under sixteen were being taught at home, mostly by parents who were taking advantage of a provision in the law that said they did not need to send their children to school if they feared for their safety. Opponents said Wilder's bill would eliminate home instruction, an option zealously defended by some ultra-conservative religious groups, including the Amish. But Wilder said the courts already had recognized that home teaching was permitted on religious grounds. His bill was aimed at eliminating "essentially political, sociological or philo-sophical views, or merely a personal moral code," as the basis for permitting home teaching. "The constitution was founded on a system of public education," he said. "In the absence of a commitment to it, you don't have it."

He introduced dozens of proposals to prohibit discrimination in both the public and private sectors, in hiring, training, housing, education, purchasing and advertising. He supported minority set-aside programs, and obtained non-discriminatory pledges from contractors who did business with the state, and nonprofit organizations that got tax exemptions, and established a sickle-cell anemia detection program. Although not all of his proposals were enacted, the thrust behind many of them came into being, either voluntarily or by other legislation, at the federal, state and local levels. For example, he attempted to bar segregated employment advertisements in newspapers, which at the time speci-fied colored or white, men and women. It was, he said, "a perfect example of the law not passing, but the thought does."

After the 1976 legislature passed a bill that allowed merchants to detain persons suspected of shoplifting, Wilder complained that such laws are "an encroachment on our individual freedom" and were passed only because "we're struck with a paralysis of fear" about crime, he said. During debate on the issue during the session, Wilder and his senior Richmond colleague, Ed Willey, had one of their famous exchanges. Wilder had offered an amendment providing immunity to the merchant who detained a suspected shoplifter "provided he used no unreasonable force to detain the suspect." Without that, Wilder said, the shopkeeper could go to any lengths to keep the suspect in the store. Interjected Willey, "We're not dealing with lily whites here." As other senators, including Wilder, laughed, Willey, oblivious, continued, "these merchants aren't going to beat these people black and blue." Wilder, with a mischievous grin, turned to Willey and said, "I must say, my distinguished colleague certainly knows how to call a spade a spade." That brought down the house. Lieutenant Governor John N. Dalton made no move to suppress the applause and laughter.

Despite the laughter, the debate was a serious matter, with Wilder at one point dramatically recounting how two of his own children had been falsely accused of shoplifting on the same day. Neither, he said, got the courtesy of an apology. Wilder's reasonable force amendment failed, but he succeeded, by a vote of twenty-to-nineteen, in lowering the time a merchant could detain a suspect from two hours to one.

WILDER: HOLD FAST TO DREAMS

Wilder repeatedly clashed with state attorney general Andrew P. Miller in the mid-seventies, accusing Miller, a liberal elected with strong black support, of having "a negative attitude." When Miller said he needed proof of discrimination before he could bring state law to bear, Wilder snapped that "all he need do is look at his own office." When Miller announced his candidacy for the United States Senate in 1978, Wilder and Delegate Robinson, who after nearly a decade still were the only blacks in the assembly, called on blacks to withhold support from Miller because of his vacillation about the Voting Rights Act. They urged black voters to remain uncommitted until the June nominating convention, where they could examine the eight contenders and make a choice "on the spot, eye-to-eye, under one roof, where our impact can best be felt and utilized." Miller won the nomination anyway, but lost in the general election to former Navy secretary John W. Warner, who campaigned with his then-wife, actress Elizabeth Taylor.

Warner and Miller were battling to succeed the retiring Republican senator, William L. Scott, who had been the target of Wilder's wrath in 1974 after a Fort Worth newspaper reported that Scott and nineteen other members of Congress discriminated in hiring their staffs in Washington, specifying "white only" in job requests to the Congressional Office of Placement and Office Management. Wilder called for a federal investigation, and also urged a look at hiring on the state level, to determine why there are "so few minorities in all branches of state government." He denounced Scott's whites only employment practice, saying "the king of dumb has struck again." (Scott had been voted "dumbest" member of the Senate by a radical magazine.)

Wilder practiced what he preached when, as the new chairman of the Senate Committee on Rehabilitation and Social Services in 1976, his initial action was to name the assembly's first black clerk, Jean Boone, and its first black staff attorney, Melvin Black.

In the 1977 statewide election, Wilder attracted criticism from some blacks when he backed the Democratic candidate for attorney general, Delegate Edward Lane, a former Byrd lieutenant and segregationist. Lane's opponent was State Senator J. Marshall Coleman, a moderate Republican, who had criticized Lane for his support of massive resistance.

Wilder said, however, that supporting the Democratic ticket was "more important than any one candidate's record in another era." But two months after endorsing Lane, Wilder startled a Democratic rally in Capitol Square by calling on Lane to recant publicly his segregationist record. Wilder said that while Lane had made "an earnest effort to end forever" the controversy, he was not satisfied by a statement Lane made in a meeting with about forty blacks in which Lane said "it is clear now that segregation in public schools and governmental activities is wrong. It's wrong legally, it's wrong morally, it's wrong in every way you want to put it." But he added that "I have no apologies for my position during that time. I did what I felt at that time was right." Wilder, a co-chairman of the state ticket, said a candidate ought to "stand up to that error and say, 'I was wrong.'" Lane's statement, he said, was like saying a person shot the wrong man, but was sincerely motivated when he did it. Although Wilder stuck with Lane, he suggested that the Crusade for Voters might throw its support to Coleman. Although the Crusade did not endorse Coleman, The Afro did, calling him "a young, enlightened man who has an unblemished civil rights record," while Lane was "a staunch conservative who has an endless record of supporting anti-black causes." Coleman was elected attorney general that year, with the help of about thirty per cent of the black vote. (After losing the gubernatorial election in 1981, Coleman was the GOP nominee again in 1989, running against Wilder for governor and refusing to write off the black vote.)

In that same election, Democrat Charles S. Robb, a political neophyte whose claim to fame was that had married Lynda Bird Johnson, a daughter of former President Lyndon B. Johnson, was elected lieutenant governor, and John N. Dalton moved up from lieutenant governor to governor, giving the Republicans three consecutive terms in the governor's mansion. Governor-elect Dalton, who received 16 percent of the black vote, selected Dr. Jean L. Harris, Wilder's former playmate, to be secretary of human resources, the first woman and first black to serve in a high-level, policy-making position in state government history. Harris, a professor of medicine at Virginia Commonwealth University, had been introduced to Dalton only four days earlier. "I have chosen Dr. Harris because of her qualifications, not because of her race," said Dalton, in the first payoff of a campaign promise that blacks would be "policy makers, not a lot of special assistants serving as ambassador to the black community."

Wilder's activism may have resulted in the burning of a cross on the lawn of his house in mid-May 1983. Richmond police said the cross and a burning flare were discovered shortly before midnight by neighbors, who extinguished the blaze. Wilder, who was not at home at the time, said he could give no reason for the incident.

"It was meant to strike and draw fear, but I slept like a log," Wilder said. He said the incident supported his contention that racism has "never been really stamped down and out."

22. Lynn, Larry and Loren

Doug and Eunice moved out of his family's house in 1961, and lived in a rental house on Hildreth Street on Church Hill for a year, before buying a brick-and-frame Cape Cod in Battery Park, a mostly black middle-class neighborhood on the North Side of Richmond.

The move occurred shortly after the birth of their second child, and only son, Lawrence Douglas Jr. on February 17, 1962. There was no prohibition on nicknames in this generation of Wilders, and the son was called Larry. Their younger daughter, Loren Deane, was born on November 5, 1963. With his oldest child named Lynn Diana, Wilder had stamped all of his children with his initials, an egocentric trait that he shared with former President Lyndon B. Johnson.

The Wilders lived in the house at 2800 Hawthorne Avenue twelve years, and it is the house and neighborhood that the children think of as home. The house was on a corner lot on a one-way street, right across from Battery Park.

Most of the residents of the neighborhood were older than Doug and Eunice, including a few white families, who eventually left as more blacks moved in. For a while, the Wilders were the only family on the block with young children. Shortly thereafter, another young couple, James E. and Patricia Allen Sheffield, moved into a house across the street, and they soon became friends. Jim Sheffield also was a lawyer, and Pat had known some of Doug's sisters growing up in the East End.

The Wilders and Sheffields celebrated holidays in each other's homes, and Pat Sheffield had baby showers for Eunice when Larry and Loren were born.

Eunice joined the Richmond chapter of two national black organizations, the Links, a social club, and Jack and Jill, for mothers of young children, and Planned Parenthood, which helped her acceptance in a tight-knit community in which some considered her an outsider, and a Northern one at that.

She developed a reputation as a gracious and talented hostess. Janet Jones (Ballard), Doug's fellow newspaper carrier from childhood, said Eunice's flair for design was evident at parties at the Wilder house. One Christmas, for example, the house was decorated throughout in brown and silver, even to the candles on the mantle. "Eunice was creative, an idea person," Ballard said.

Eunice responded to compliments about her decorating skills saying, "I don't think I'll ever get the house decorated just the way I want it."

Lynn Wilder, who became a professional artist, said her mother is "a very creative woman" who pays attention to details and was given to grand gestures as a hostess. "Mom can literally create an environment," said Lynn, recalling a birthday party for her at which her mother carried out a carnival theme, complete with ticket booths and cages.

Carolyn J. Moss, who later became a cabinet secretary in the administration of Gov. Gerald L. Baliles, and her husband Al went to Richmond from their home in Washington a couple times of year for social events, at which they saw the Wilders, occasionally at their home. She and her husband met the Wilders standing around the pool at the home a prominent black real estate broker. She recalled that Eunice was "the kind of person, man or woman, you would focus on in a crowd. She had one of the best figures of any woman I knew."

Pat Sheffield concurred. She said that because of her height and looks, Eunice always stood out at social gatherings. She recalled a cocktail party at the

Lynn, Larry and Loren

Wilders' house before a Christmas dance, at which Eunice wore a Kelly green dress and black fur boa. "She was striking," Pat Sheffield said.

After Wilder entered politics, their friends commented that Eunice was a perfect spouse for a public figure. She was intelligent, attractive and loved to entertain. Eunice loved to cook, and when Doug was elected to the state Senate, The Afro printed her recipe for lobster, shrimp and crabmeat casserole, which she liked to served to guests and at club meetings. Her husband's favorites dishes, she said, were steak and rib roast.

"I always believed he would aspire to some political office since he's always been interested in politics," she said. Her children were "tickled to death about their father" and Larry Jr., because of his name, was telling his friends at school that he now would be a "junior senator."

Eunice recognized and nurtured Lynn's artistic talents early, even before it manifested itself in the drawings that her parents stuck on the refrigerator door with magnets. She noticed that Lynn insisted on wearing certain colors and that she arranged the toys in her room with an eye to design.

All of the children were creative, Lynn said. Her brother wrote such witty compositions that she laughed aloud while reading them, and Loren created "outrageously gorgeous, immaculately prepared" gift wrappings.

Growing up, Lynn said, "We never thought of anything as impossible." The confidence came from both of their parents, "in a realistical to a fantastical way...from being governor to painting a ceiling purple."

The city recreation department integrated its swimming pools a couple of years after the Wilders moved in, in time for Lynn, Larry and Loren to use the pool across the street and become accomplished swimmers. Their father, who had learned to swim after confidently plunging into the pool at the Y as a boy, seldom found time to join them, however. "Those were the things I regretted," he admits.

When Lynn and Larry were old enough to go to school, they walked across the park to Albert V. Norrel elementary school. By the time Larry was ready for first grade and Lynn was entering fourth, the city's school board initiated its freedom-of-choice plan by which parents could send their children to any school they chose, provided it had room. The Wilders took advantage of the plan to send Larry and Lynn, and later Loren, to Mary Mumford, an elementary school in the nearly all-white West End, one of the wealthiest areas of Richmond. Eunice became an active member of the Parent-Teacher Association at Mary Mumford.

Until they went to Mumford, the Wilder children were naive about race, and had little notion that some people might treat them differently because of their skin color. But at Mumford, they became aware that race was an issue, sometimes a hotly contested one. But there were few isolated racial encounters at Mumford, an occasional teasing, and once or twice shouts of "hey nigger." They did not experience prejudice from the teachers, and the majority of their classmates thought as little of race as they did. "Some kids didn't know what I was," laughed Larry. "They thought I was Indian."

Racial mystique was a two-way street. When a boy of Greek extraction came home with Larry after school, his black playmates did a double take. "What is that?" they asked. "He was just someone they were not used to seeing," Larry said.

WILDER: HOLD FAST TO DREAMS

The message the Wilder children got from their parents was that color was not a handicap. "I truly did not know what the big deal was, my being black," Larry said. When a problem concerning race arose, their father called a conference around the dinner table. Invariably, his advice was, "don't respond. You are who you are. Don't engage in it, go your course." And certainly don't respond physically. He wasn't advising them to run away, but merely not to respond to confrontations. "They're trying to bait you," he told them. "Don't fall prey to that."

Full-scale busing came to Richmond in 1970, when the children were in the seventh, fourth and second grades, respectively. The first year of the court-ordered integration, the Wilder children didn't know what school they would attend until a few days before the school year began. Larry recalls asking, "Where is that?" when told that he and the other fourth and fifth graders in Battery Park would be bused across town to Westhampton Elementary. Each year, it seemed, they attended a different school, but all without major incidents.

All of the Wilder children were good students. "They never gave us any trouble," said their father, adding that the credit goes to his wife's guidance. "She was there for them, no question," he said. "She was a good mother to them. She spent a lot of time with them when they were young" while he was busy working long hours, building a practice. Wilder kept late office hours, staying until the outer office was cleared of clients, many of whom just showed up without appointments. Eunice waited dinner for him so the family could eat together. After the meal, however, Wilder often retreated to his den to work on briefs, and prepare for the next day. He seldom promised the children that he would make it to after-school activities, to avoid disappointment if he didn't make it, so when he did manage to break away, they were pleased to see him, pointing out to their friends that their mother *and* father were in the audience. "You made it," they would say proudly afterwards.

Despite his busy schedule, Wilder felt he was there when his children needed him, although not as much as he would have liked. "I don't believe in 'quality time.' Time is time," their father said. Wilder regularly took them to a farm in Henrico County, where they boarded a pony they owned—the pony that Wilder yearned for as a child. "Eunice didn't care to deal with the pony," Wilder said, so a familiar refrain on weekends was, "Dad, can we go out and ride the pony today?" It was a request Wilder couldn't refuse. While the children took turns riding their pony, he would ride one of the horses, an activity he still relishes.

In 1974, after a dozen years at 2800 Hawthorne, the Wilders moved up the street to a two-story Georgian brick home at 3215 Hawthorne. Although the houses were only a few blocks apart, about the only thing they had in common was that the both had an address on Hawthorne Avenue. They were in very different neighborhoods. The former was in Battery Park, a mostly black middle-class neighborhood; the latter was in perhaps the finest block of Ginter Park, a predominantly white upper middle-class neighborhood. As if to emphasize the two-different-worlds of Hawthorne Avenue, the street even changed direction, from running east and west in Battery Park to north and south in Ginter Park.

Wilder remembers the day in late 1973 when Eunice excitedly called him

Lynn, Larry and Loren

at the office and said she had found their dream house. They often had driven by the beautiful homes in the 3200 block, expressing the desire to someday be able to afford to live there. Their two favorites were the Georgian bricks on the east side of the block, the first and second ones from the corner of Westwood Avenue. When Eunice spotted the advertisement in that morning's newspaper, she knew exactly which house it was. So did her husband. She called the real estate agent, who arranged a quick tour of the house. As soon as she stepped through the front door into the marbled hallway, she knew she wanted it. She breathlessly called Doug from the house. He asked which one it was. "The second one from the corner," she said. (Although they didn't know it at the time, the corner house was owned by Congressman David E. Satterfield III.) "You like it, right?" Wilder asked Eunice, knowing the answer. "Then get it. Do it." He agreed to the purchase even before asking the price, which was $65,000.

Before they moved in, early in 1974, they had the floors refinished, and carpeting installed, and over the years, they spent more money on remodeling than they paid for it, adding a sauna, jacuzzi and landscaping. It was a good investment. By 1989, comparable houses were selling for more than $300,000, which was in the upper brackets for Richmond residences.

The Wilders were the first blacks on the block, although they didn't know it at the time, and it was not a consideration. But no matter how much they loved the house, it wasn't enough to save their marriage.

After living in the new house less than two years, and most of that time under stressful conditions, Eunice and the children moved out early in 1976, to an apartment in Monroe Towers, at the edge of the campus of Virginia Commonwealth University. Their father remained alone in the big house on Hawthorne Avenue. "It was a strange time," Larry recalled, especially because his parents continued to live in the same house for six months after they had decided to get a divorce.

At the time, Lynn was a junior at Thomas Jefferson High School, Larry was in eighth grade and Loren in sixth. Lynn remained at Jefferson High, graduating in the class of 1977, and went on to study architecture at Howard. Larry and Loren left the public schools in favor of Collegiate, one of Richmond's premier private schools. Their father paid all the bills. Larry attended Collegiate for part of the eighth grade and all four high school years, graduating in 1980, and Loren went there six years, graduating in 1982.

After their parents' separation, the children continued to see their father often, although not on a regular schedule. He sometimes took them to school or picked them up afterwards. Larry lived with his father a couple of summers when he was home from college. Loren saw her father more often than Lynn, who remained in Washington year-round after her first year of college.

When it came time for the two younger children to go to college, both Larry and Loren opted for the University of Virginia, even though so many of Larry's classmates at Collegiate were going to UVa that he initially balked, worrying that it would be "like the thirteenth, fourteenth, fifteenth and sixteenth grades." But when he asked his father for advice, he suggested UVa. However, he never said anything about wanting them to go to college in Charlottesville because he had not been allowed to enroll there. Larry thinks his father recommended UVa primarily because it was cheaper than the out-of-state schools. He was paying a lot of tuition: A total of ten years for Larry and Loren at Collegiate, four for Lynn at Howard, and eventually another thirteen for Larry and Loren's college years (Larry took a law degree and Loren got a masters of business administration). And thanks to Wilder's successful law practice, nearly all of the tuition was paid in cash. "We didn't take a lot of student loans," said Larry. Their father said of student loans, "all you do is pay it back, maybe at a lower rate of interest" than normal. So in the finest Virginia tradition, it was pay-as-you-go for the Wilders.

In 1986, their father, then the lieutenant governor, delivered the commencement address to Loren's graduating class. Larry was also in the audience on The Lawn at UVa, having completed his second year of law school.

Lynn graduated from Howard in 1981 with a major in architecture and a minor in fine arts. She worked five years for an architectural firm in Washington. During that time, she specialized in examining patented art and designs, prompting the firm to ask her to become a patent attorney. With the company picking up the tab, she attended George Washington University law school. But she quit after a year, having decided she wanted to devote fulltime to the fine arts. She studied in Washington and Paris, and made her professional debut with a show at the Amber Gallery in Richmond in January, 1987. Subsequently she had one-woman shows in Washington, Baltimore and Richmond. She moved to New York City in mid-1989, to continue her career as a painter.

It speaks of the closeness of the family that when Larry is asked to name his best friends in college, his sister Loren is among the first he names, and when Lynn had an opening at a Richmond art gallery early in 1989, it was a family affair.

After graduating from UVa, Loren got a master of business administration degree at the University of Michigan in 1988, after which she moved to Washington, where she became a management trainee for the U. S. Postal Service. She frequently is her dad's escort at dinners and other formal functions, and he said during the gubernatorial campaign that if he is elected governor, he may ask Loren and Lynn to function as official hostesses for events at the Governor's Mansion. Loren is vivacious and outgoing, as illustrated by her posing, wearing a waist-length strapless, red bandeau, for a calendar called "Exceptional '88," produced by UVa students.

Larry compared the differences between his sisters to "left-brain and right-brain" functions. Free-spirited Lynn "wants to explore a thousand things," and is more laid back and patient than the more strait-laced Loren, who is numbers-crunching serious and can be brutally frank.

Asked to distinguish between his parents, Larry said his father is quite introspective. "There was not much babbling about emotions and private concerns." It was always easier to talk to his mother; however Larry said that may have been just from being around her a lot more.

23. Divorce

On July 25, 1975, Eunice Wilder filed for divorce, charging her husband of nearly seventeen years with "cruelty and reasonable apprehension of bodily harm."

But because Eunice and Doug and the children continued to share the house after the divorce was filed, word of the breakup did not become public for nearly six months, until Eunice moved out, on February 2, 1976.

It is not a pretty picture that is painted in court documents filed over the next five years, as Eunice attempted to reach a property settlement.

Five days after Eunice moved out, their separation was front-page news in The Afro, under the headline, "Marriage on Rocks, Wilders in Court." The story was accompanied by one of those in-happier-days photographs.

"For nearly a year now," began the article, "the grapevine has been bristling with gossip about a marital strain between State Senator L. Douglas Wilder and his wife, Eunice. The rumors reached a peak last summer when there were widely-circulated reports that linked the senator with an alleged shooting incident that involved a married woman and her husband. But the rumor mill subsided after Mr. and Mrs. Wilder appeared together and gave the impression that their lives were no more hectic than that of any other married couple. At the affair at the Hotel John Marshall honoring the senator last June, Wilder himself referred to the shooting reports and dismissed them, saying he wished he knew how they got started. At the same affair, Mrs. Wilder took the rostrum and spoke of their sixteen-year marriage in proud terms. `There's been a lot of fun and sometimes things were not easy—but it was always an honor,' she said.

"More rumors floated over the recent holiday season when the Wilders, one of the Richmond area's most socially prominent couples, became conspicuous by their absence at traditional social functions, which in the past almost never ended without the Wilders. Now the rift is official," the paper said.

It said papers filed in Richmond Circuit Court revealed Eunice Wilder, thirty-seven, charged that Doug Wilder, forty-five, had cursed her, physically abused her, locked her out of her home and made her car inaccessible to her. He had withdrawn support to the extent that she could not "keep food in the house," the suit alleged. She also charged that her husband had been involved in "affairs," but did not identify a co-respondent.

Three days after filing for divorce, Eunice had hand-delivered to the court a letter asking that the divorce action be stopped. It could not be learned if a reconciliation was under consideration. But the request was withdrawn two and one-half months later, on October 8, however, and the divorce action resumed. The next day, Eunice's attorney, Charles A. Blanton 2d, told the court that his client had been "induced and coerced" into asking that the divorce be stopped.

At a hearing two weeks later, Wilder, who represented himself throughout the ordeal, denied all the allegations and demanded that his wife provide "strict proof" of the accusations. He said he had been "a faithful and dutiful" husband and had provided "the sole support" of his wife and children. He asked that the suit be dismissed.

On December 9, 1975, even though Eunice and Doug were living under the same roof, Judge Alex H. Sands Jr. ordered them not to molest or interfere with each other. At another hearing, on December 17, two of their children testified, along with a physician, after which Judge Sands ordered Wilder to pay $1,200 a month support for Eunice and the children. Sands turned down Eunice's request that Doug be ordered to vacate their house.

Six weeks later, Eunice gave up the battle for the house, and with the children, moved into an apartment. In addition to paying child support, Wilder paid the costs of sending Larry and Loren to Collegiate and Lynn's expenses at Howard.

On September, 27, 1977, with the divorce still pending, Wilder reported to Richmond police the theft of $1,800 in silverware and $3,500 in cash from his home, which some acquaintances said may have been related to their squabble.

It was nearly twenty months before the hearing was held, on November 25, 1977, in the chambers of Judge Sands. By then the original charges of "cruelty and reasonable apprehension of bodily harm" had been dropped in favor of the innocuous fact that they simply had lived apart for more than one year.

Two and one-half years after Eunice initiated the divorce preceding, the decree was granted, on January 25, 1978. The judge found that Eunice was not entitled to spousal support because she had "not proved that when she deserted the premises...that she did so for cause." Because Lynn had turned eighteen and was no longer eligible for support, the judge reduced the support payments to $200 a week, $100 each for Larry, who was almost sixteen, and Loren, who was fourteen.

Wilder not only did not have to pay alimony, but he was permitted to keep the house on Hawthorne, where he continues to live, and he did not have to share any of the substantial property holdings that he had acquired during their more than nineteen years of marriage.

The divorce was made final and the judge ordered the record of the proceedings sealed "to prevent an indiscriminate perusal of the record of the divorce proceeding, which was conducted in chambers." (A longtime employee of the clerk's office said that conducting a divorce hearing in chambers and then sealing the record was not uncommon, especially when one of the parties was well known.)

But the trouble wasn't over. The acrimony surely was escalated by her decision to change attorneys and employ Sa'ad El-Amin, a brilliant, radical black attorney who was constantly criticizing Wilder, in a column in The Afro and elsewhere, for "selling out" to the white establishment in return for political gain. In April, 1979, El-Amin filed what was described at the time as a novel law suit, in that it cited no legal precedent, seeking one-half interest in all the real estate Wilder held an interest in during their marriage.

Wilder responded that their divorce "extinguished any property interests of either spouse in property of the other."

On May 9, 1979, El-Amin asked the court to unseal the divorce file, saying it was necessary for him to become familiar with what had transpired in the divorce case to prepare the new action.

Wilder resisted, complaining that throughout the proceedings, Eunice had "tried to sensationalize...[and] engaged...in a highly successful effort to bring public attention to a very private matter." The attempt to unseal the divorce record was "purposefully brought to the direct attention of the news media, who abundantly aired the contents of the pleadings repeatedly. Nothing in the sealed file could have the remotest connection to the case at bar," Wilder argued. He added that Eunice was privy to the entire proceeding and could furnish her counsel whatever information she chose to.

Wilder won that battle, but Eunice was undeterred. In July of 1979, she filed a new lawsuit, asking for half of all his property holdings. She said that at Doug's insistence she had "provided and cared for all the necessities of their household and children, making all appropriate appearances with [him], whenever and wherever he requested, to promote his social, political and professional image." El-Amin added that Eunice and Doug had "maintained a confidential relationship in which [he] was the dominant party and [she] was the subservient party. [Wilder] breached this confidential relationship and has been unjustly enriched at [Eunice's] expense." Fairness demands that the court make Wilder share the wealth, El-Amin argued.

El-Amin pointed out that Eunice received a bachelor's degree while eight months pregnant and never held professional employment during the marriage. Wilder never allowed her to have or use a bank account, "and by virtue of her completely domestic role, had no exposure to the world of business, finance, and investments." On the other hand, Wilder "has a law degree, and is a highly successful attorney, politician, and business entrepreneur who is well versed in financial matters."

During the first two years of the marriage, when Wilder's law practice was producing only minimum income, Eunice worked as a bank teller. Also, during the first five years of their marriage, she maintained her husband's accounts and filled in at his office when clerical help was needed. But when the law practice began to flourish, and he no longer needed her services, Wilder would not allow her "to be in any way knowledgeable or involved in any of his business ventures," requiring her "to maintain the household and children and to assume the traditional female role in their marriage," the court documents said.

From time to time when Eunice sought to buy items for the house, Wilder told her of their need to be frugal, in light of the heavy obligations they faced in acquiring investment properties. Meanwhile, Wilder imposed a frugal life style on her so he could acquire various income-producing properties. He mandated that he would be the breadwinner and that her contribution to their partnership would be to perform the domestic chores, to free him to handle the purely business aspects of their partnership.

All along, according to her court complaint, Wilder required his wife to support his professional, political, economic and social endeavors in a manner consistent with his station. He refused to allow her to accept outside employment or otherwise develop herself as a person. She resigned herself to these restrictions because she believed it was her duty as wife and mother and that she would ultimately benefit from their overall partnership activities.

Eunice complained that she wound up in a subservient position, with three children and no professional work experience, forced to rely upon her husband's representations that she would share with him in the fruits of their combined labor.

Meanwhile, Wilder acquired a number of properties, including the downtown office building he owned in partnership with a physician-friend, Charles Sutton, which they leased to the Richmond Chamber of Commerce;

adjoining townhouses on Church Hill, which he had remodeled to serve as offices for his expanding law firm; a restaurant building rented to a Korean family, and several rental houses. He never put Eunice's name on any of the deeds.

The one piece of property that was in both of their names was not mentioned in the divorce papers—an oceanview lot that they purchased in 1973 on the Outer Banks in North Carolina, with plans to build a beach house. Those plans were sidetracked because of their marital difficulties, however, and the lot was vacant until 1988, when Wilder, having bought out Eunice's half-interest for $1, built a vacation beach house.

The court complaint said Wilder gave Eunice only enough money to run the house. She was led to believe, however, that their relationship was a partnership, and that in return for foregoing economic involvement outside of the household, and by supporting his professional and economic endeavors, she would share equally in the real estate acquisitions he was amassing. She argued that she did not provide her services to the partnership gratuitously, particularly in light of his insistence that she refrain from employment outside of the home.

Because he refused to share the profits, Eunice contended that the court should award her one-half interest in the properties from which Wilder had been "unjustly enriched" at her expense.

A deal is a deal, attorney Wilder responded. A contract such as Eunice suggested, Wilder told the judge, "completely dehors the marriage relationship...`if we marry, and if you promise to convey to me, I'll cook your breakfast; if you promise that you will give me one half of whatever you may ever accumulate in life, I'll wash your clothes, I may even have a child or two'..."

Wilder said he was not contesting the truth or falsity of her allegations. He merely contended that nothing in a marriage contract automatically gives one partner the right to claim one-half in the other's property interest. "This was never statutorily contemplated. It is not statute in Virginia," he said. "Where is the law that says that must be done?"

As for her suggestion that she did not provide her services gratuitously, Wilder responded that Eunice "is saying that the only way that the marriage took place and the services, whichever services they were in the allegations...were services based upon a contract, if there was a contract...There isn't any contract here....This is a situation in which for eighteen years two parties lived together, exchanged whatever, do whatever, and then all of a sudden there is a divorce....There is no allegation that there is any contract...any [such] understanding....And then, lo and behold, the plaintiff, after the divorce is entered, after it's filed, after that which by law in Virginia divests the other of an interest in the property of the other, then the plaintiff comes in and says, notwithstanding the finality of that, notwithstanding the law which says that a final decree of divorce in Virginia completely dissolves the property interest of one spouse from another, and says, 'Give me some property, because I feel I should have gotten a bit more somewhere along the line.'"

Judge Marvin F. Cole dismissed Eunice's lawsuit in December, 1979, agreeing with Wilder that no basis in law existed for the action.

Wilder and his ex-wife reached an agreement, dated February 22, 1980, that gave her $52,237.54 in return for giving him full title to their house on

Divorce

Hawthorne Avenue and a small house on Church Hill that later was to cause problems for Wilder.

Several acquaintances pointed out that Eunice put on weight during the long ordeal, and that as concerned as Wilder always has been about looks, might have accelerated their breakup. "I'm sure she was heavier than the ones he was running around with," said one lawyer who knew the couple.

Wilder's good friends Petey and Alyce Paige never understood why Doug and Eunice broke up. "Nothing I could say that made sense," said Petey. "I do think, unfortunately, that they separated because she was misled by a lot of people [telling stories about him that were untrue]. Maybe they could be telling something about him that could have been true, but what they were telling her to do....Mistakes were made. Bad advice....He is the type of person, you're not going to tell him what to do, especially when he is meeting his obligations [to his children and to his creditors]." Wilder didn't understand what Eunice had to complain about, Petey added. "He gave her a good house, clothes. Lots of people were jealous of her. 'You should get him to do this and that,' they told her. I really think that if it had not been for those other people, they would have had there little ups and downs, but they would still be there together."

A possible point of friction in their marriage, several other friends suggested, was that Wilder hasn't made a habit of surrounding himself with intellectual peers, and that Eunice may have been a threat to his cerebral aloofness. She graduated from Howard with a degree in economics, and after their divorce, became a certified public accountant.

Alyce Paige does not believe they broke up because of another woman. "If he was [playing around], that was not the reason Eunice left. Knowing her, she would not leave. She came out on the short end by pulling out like that. She should have told him what was on her mind, and stayed right there. Right today, she knows that she made a mistake." Wilder refused to give her anything other than child support because "he was mad that she left. He couldn't get over her leaving him. That's the whole thing," Alyce said. Petey "had to talk him [Wilder] into finally agreeing to a settlement. That was stubbornness. That's all it was."

Did Petey have to convince Wilder it was the right thing to do? "Nah," laughed Petey, "He already knew that."

Alyce and Petey pointed out that despite Wilder's stubbornness over settling with his ex-wife, he never shortchanged his children. "Nobody had to get him to help the kids," Petey said. "Everything was for the children, that I do know. He sent them to any school they wanted to go."

Shortly before Wilder's nomination as lieutenant governor in 1985, reporter Dave Miller aired a story on radio station WRVA in Richmond saying the divorce could be the subject of a whisper campaign. Miller said Wilder "could be vulnerable if and when the full details of his divorce papers and charges of spouse abuse are ever made public again." Both Wilder and his ex-wife told reporters that their divorce was a private matter, and refused to discuss it, and except for casual mentions in profile stories about Wilder, the issue did not surface during the campaign.

Although Wilder insists that he and Eunice have maintained a good relationship since their divorce, he rarely refers to her by name. Instead, she is almost exclusively "my ex-wife," as in, "I met my ex-wife my freshman year," and "my ex-wife then gave birth to our second child" and even "my ex-wife and I were married on..." In refusing to utter her name, Wilder has plunged Eunice to the deep cellar of a small, exclusive club of former friends whose names he will not speak. At the very bottom is El-Amin. "He does not exist," Wilder says with the finality of a monarch dismissing a former subject.

In a 1988 interview, Wilder compared Eunice's request to share in his holdings with the palimony action brought against actor Lee Marvin. "I was really shocked" when she filed the law suit "after I was divorced a couple years." He suggested that "no one in the United States" had ever been forced to give up property to a former spouse, after a divorce decree had been signed. "It's a palimony thing," he said.

When he was asked why he didn't just give Eunice half in the first place, Wilder became defensive and ill-at-ease, pacing the floor of the lieutenant governor's office. "How do you know that I didn't?" he snapped. When the court documents were cited, he explained that the divorce was granted before a property settlement was agreed upon. "So many of those particulars you don't know, and you don't know why. You don't know what ever else was shared in the process. So how are you to know what the record shows?"

During his campaign for lieutenant governor, when his divorce was the subject of rumors, Wilder indicated that he didn't object to the unsealing of the documents, but that they had been sealed at his ex-wife's request. As his campaign for governor approached, he amended that view, saying, "the question [of whether to unseal] was determined by the court, rather than by me."

Finally, Wilder was asked to characterize what happened to the marriage, a topic that Eunice declines to discuss. After a pause, he responded, "It was dissolved," laughing uproariously, obviously pleased with his answer.

He added, "I've always respected my ex-wife. Although a lot of people would like to believe it, we are not enemies, at each other's throats....I've never said anything other than that she's a very fine woman, a wonderful mother to our children."

24. The King Holiday Bill

If there is one word that best describes Wilder's legislative career it is perseverance. And there is no better example of that than his long, successful fight to get a state holiday honoring Dr. Martin Luther King Jr.

As a candidate for governor in 1989, Wilder preferred to be remembered as the author of a wide range of legislation—for issues that showed he had been a hard-liner on crime and drugs, worked (albeit unsuccessfully) to repeal the sales tax on food and over-the-counter medicine, and to increase aid to education—but he acknowledged that "people do associate me nationally" with the King holiday bill. "They say, 'That guy was able to get the Martin Luther King bill passed.' The King bill had its moments, its crowning moments."

When Wilder talks about the odyssey that led to its eventual passage—it was nine years from his introduction of the original bill in 1975 until Governor Charles S. Robb signed it into law in 1984—he reveals an unmistakable pride and optimism about his native state and its residents.

"People look at it now and think it was passed because of some great change of heart. And I keep telling them, that Virginians had already, through their elected representatives, committed themselves to it. If anybody was behind, it was people who vetoed the bill (two Republican governors) or those who didn't understand that the people of Virginia were ready for it. I knew that the King bill would have its day. Lack of understanding has been one of the biggest problems we've had in Virginia, legislative and otherwise. People didn't know hunger existed; they didn't know about sub-standard housing, didn't know how people felt about the need to have someone they could rally behind."

Despite almost yearly setbacks for nearly a decade, Wilder seldom lashed out at his opponents. He explained his attitude: "People say you don't get mad, you get even. They say that, but they don't usually practice that. You don't get mad, you get smart. And after you get smart, you use it, and try to move ahead. The more you refrain from displaying your anger, the better your chances of success. Because those who were not with you the year before, you might pick up a vote or two, and those votes often are so narrow. The perceptions, as portrayed in the press, can either kill something the next time around or not."

He also said he realized that "there would be other mountains to climb," and he did not want to risk permanently alienating colleagues over one bill.

There was irony in Wilder's long effort to memorialize King, because he had never been a big fan of the civil rights leader. When King marched on Washington in 1963, Wilder stayed home. Although Wilder had abandoned his war-inspired plots to overthrow the government by force, he did not believe that King's non-violent tactics would make a difference. Also, Wilder's ego is such that he cannot bring himself to rave over the accomplishments of his contemporaries, whether it is King, who was two years older than Wilder, or Jesse Jackson or Henry Marsh.

His effort in behalf of a King holiday began in 1975, when he introduced a resolution to designate January 15 in King's memory and permit jurisdictions to observe it "in such manner as they choose to commemorate that day." It did not pass. It culminated on April 9, 1984, when Governor Robb signed legislation that established the third Monday in January as Lee-Jackson-King Day, an official state holiday in Virginia. In retrospect, to Wilder the denouement

107

was "totally anti-climatic. I knew it eventually would pass and be signed into law."

The first effort, in 1975, even though it was just a resolution—merely an expression of sentiment that wouldn't carry the weight of law—it didn't rate the courtesy of a discussion by a committee, much less a hearing where the public could express its views.

Wilder didn't try again in 1976, but in 1977 he came back, calling for a law to designate January 15 to be Martin Luther King Jr. Day, a state holiday. On that approach, he got full-blown hearings in both houses.

"You should have seen them," Wilder said of the protesters who packed the hearing rooms when the bill was considered, first in the Senate and later in the House. Little old ladies, representing the Daughters of the Confederacy, got "misty-eyed" as they talked about the state's two special holidays, Lee-Jackson Day, on the third Monday in January, and Confederate Memorial Day, on the fourth Monday in May. "Those women were very respectful," Wilder said, unable to suppress a grin. "They'd say things like, 'the Chinese people, they're good people, and they're not after their own holiday.' And they'd go on down the list (of nationalities who didn't have a state holiday). Finally, they'd lapse off, and say, 'Let 'em work for what they want.'"

After the hearings, the Senate amended Wilder's proposal to observe King's birthday on New Year's Day. That version passed the Senate unanimously, and although it barely got out of the House General Laws Committee, by a vote of nine to seven, it was approved by the full House on a vote of sixty-seven to twelve. Wilder had suggested the date change when he saw that his original bill was not going to be approved that year. He wanted to avoid an argument about how much an extra holiday would cost; honoring the slain civil rights leader on New Year's Day would not impose additional costs on employers, public or private.

Besides, getting the legislature to agree to honor King on January 1 was something of a private joke by Wilder on whites who were unaware of the special significance that New Year's Day has for many blacks. It was on January 1, 1863 that President Abraham Lincoln signed the Emancipation Proclamation, declaring that blacks were free. In many black households, including Wilder's as a child, New Year's Day also was called Emancipation Day, and was observed with solemnity and joy. The Wilder family Bible has a copy of the proclamation in it.

After the bill had cleared both houses, it went to Governor Mills E. Godwin for his approval or rejection. Wilder met with Robert McIlwaine, a top aide to Godwin, who as a legislator had been a leader of the massive resistance movement, and explained the details. Godwin, who had switched parties and had become the first person ever elected governor twice by a vote of the people, the second time as a Republican, didn't know anything about the special significance of January 1 but he vetoed the bill anyway. Godwin noted that there were no formal holidays to honor Thomas Jefferson and other distinguished Virginians. In response to a reporter's question, Godwin said, "there would be absolutely no basis for such an implication [of racism] to be placed upon it. Dr. King was certainly a great leader and he accomplished much during his lifetime."

But Wilder charged racism. At a news conference at the Capitol on

The King Holiday Bill

April 4, the ninth anniversary of King's assassination, he said, "I think the governor has emerged from a cocoon...a racist. There was a mellowing...supposed to be occurring during this four-year (term). I'm saying (the veto) would indicate that he hasn't completely erased his previous image." Godwin's reasons for vetoing the bill "suggest that blacks cannot hope ever to have a legal holiday for a black person...I've lived a long time with Lee-Jackson Day," said Wilder, referring to a January holiday that honored two of the South's Civil War generals. A reporter said Godwin had received calls from people who said King was a communist. "People are continually trying to smear the name of Dr. King," Wilder answered.

Wilder noted that the bill passed the Senate unanimously and drew only a dozen nay votes in the hundred-member House. "I'm very shocked the governor paid no attention to the General Assembly by saying `I know what's best for the people of Virginia.'...That is authoritarianism, not democracy."

Wilder joined several hundred others in a protest at the Capitol. He told the crowd that the holiday "would have meant both the beginning of a new year and a day set aside for black aspirations." He vowed to reintroduce the bill in 1978 when "hopefully...we will have a Democratic governor."

The Democrats did not elect a governor the next year, but the Republican victor, John N. Dalton, was more like former Governor Holton, a mountain-valley moderate, than in the mold of Godwin, a segregationist Democrat-turned-Republican.

Wilder didn't try for a separate King holiday in 1978. Instead, he reintroduced the bill that Godwin had vetoed, and it sailed through both chambers, passing the Senate 38 to 0 and the House 78 to 10. And on March 2, 1978, Dalton signed into law a bill designating January 1 as Martin Luther King Jr.

On the Senate floor, Wilder thanked Dalton, acknowledging that the Republican governor "was under a great deal of stress and pressure" not to sign the bill. Wilder noted that the bill had passed the Senate in each of the last two sessions with no negative votes and said that blacks across Virginia and the nation were gratified at its enactment. As happened throughout his legislative career, however, while some whites were upset with Wilder for doing too much, some blacks were accusing him of doing too little.

But those who questioned why he had settled for something less than King's birthday "were persons who would not have observed the Emancipation Proclamation on the first," Wilder said. "They also were not aware that in politics, like in a lot of other things, you get the camel's head in the tent." Wilder was confident that if he could get his legislative colleagues committed to the principle of honoring King, on whatever date, "that we had crossed a Rubican far wider than they could envision." While they were saying to him, "all right, we'll give you January 1," in his mind he knew that they had agreed to honor the man. Once that occurred, Wilder said, he was confident that eventually he would get the date changed to King's birthday.

Wilder was back in 1981 with a revised plan, to change the date of the observation to January 15. Again, he was the lone sponsor in the Senate. The Senate General Laws Committee amended that proposal in favor of making a single holiday, honoring King and the two Virginia Civil War heroes, Robert E.

Lee and Stonewall Jackson, on the third Monday in January, which already was a state holiday, known as Lee-Jackson Day. That version was approved by the Senate 30 to 8, but it produced a torrent of protests from both the Sons of the Confederacy and the National Association for the Advancement of Colored People, neither of which was anxious to share a holiday.

One of the loudest criticisms came from Sa'ad El-Amin, the black activist attorney and Wilder nemesis who had represented Eunice in her efforts to win a property settlement. El-Amin ranted at a hearing about the proposed compromise until Wilder silenced him by pointing out that El-Amin's reasoning matched that of the United Daughters of the Confederacy.

Wilder's office was deluged with calls from people who wanted to be involved, but he always discouraged them from bombarding other legislators for fear their zeal would alienate prospective supporters. "I never needed anyone—never—to get it through the Senate," said Wilder, seemingly oblivious to the idea that many of the volunteers simply wanted to be part of the process as a way of honoring King. He urged supporters who showed up at hearings not to speak. He knew he had the votes in the Senate, for any version of the plan.

He even had the vote of his conservative Richmond colleague, Ed Willey, who may have taken as much grief for his position over the years as Wilder did. Willey was under tremendous pressure from his conservative cronies to oppose the measure. They pounded on him during nightly sessions around the card table in the basement grill room of the Commonwealth Club. "Ed was very much against the King bill, in any form," said his seatmate, Bill Hopkins of Roanoke. "Ed was pretty much the man who was for whatever came out of West End Richmond. He didn't want to deviate from what the club out there wanted. That's what he said, vocally, but when it came time to vote, he knew that Doug, who sat right behind him, was looking over his shoulder. And he couldn't do it." Willey's loyalty to his Richmond colleague was not appreciated at the Commonwealth Club. "'Ed, you told us you'd never vote for anything like that,'" he heard following his votes for the King bill over the years. Willey tried to hedge, once even denying he had voted for it: He pleaded that had been in the cloak room and his deskmate, Hopkins, had flipped his button for him. Hopkins laughed. "Ed told that so many times that I think he actually got to the point that he believed it."

When the Lee-Jackson-King bill got to the House, Wilder employed what Times-Dispatch columnist Shelley Rolfe called "the classic military theory that the best defense is a surprising offense." In response to criticism that the state could not afford to grant its workers another paid holiday, he asked the General Laws Committee to amend the bill again, to eliminate Election Day as a state holiday. That compromise passed both chambers, in the House 56 to 25, with 18 members not voting, and in the Senate by 24 to 16.

"You have no idea what this means for Virginia's image nationally," said an elated Wilder, anticipating its signing by Governor Dalton. "It would show that Virginia does have a concern for minority interests. This holiday would reflect the true diversity of Virginia. It really is diverse when you consider you have a state which honors Confederate generals on the one hand, and on the other hand honors a man who worked for civil rights—a prince of peace, so to speak."

The King Holiday Bill

But there was a question about whether Dalton would sign it, and the doubts had more to do with politics than his attitude about King. After all, Dalton already had signed one King bill. But Dalton was what Republican state Senator Wiley F. Mitchell Jr. called "a virulent partisan," and with his term expiring at the end of the year, he wanted to do whatever was necessary to elect a fourth consecutive Republican to the governor's office. A number of party leaders had faulted Governor Holton at the end of his term for allowing Godwin and other former Byrd Democrats to capture the party reins, and some of them blamed that on Holton's willingness to kowtow to Democrats in general and blacks in particular. Signing the King bill might send conservatives back to the Democratic side in the upcoming gubernatorial election. That fear was compounded by what looked to be the likely matchup in the fall: The popular, young Democratic lieutenant governor, Charles S. Robb, already was wooing conservatives, while the putative Republican nominee, attorney general J. Marshall Coleman, was perhaps more moderate-to-liberal than Robb, whose main claim to fame was that he was the son-in-law of former president Lyndon B. Johnson.

During the time that Dalton was pondering his decision, Wilder violated one of his political tenets, and may have committed a rare tactical error in the process, by allowing non-Virginians to get involved in one of his political battles. Although Wilder insists that he didn't seek outside help, King's widow, Coretta Scott King, wrote to Wilder and congratulated him on passage of the bill, and to Dalton urging him to sign it. At the time, only Massachusetts, Michigan and the District of Columbia observed King's birthday as a holiday. Wilder responded to Mrs. King with an invitation to attend a ceremony and reception upon signing of the bill. "I will inform you the time that the governor signs the measure, as there have been many persons like yourself who have expressed an interest in the ceremony and what would follow," Wilder wrote. Wilder sent copies of Mrs. King's letter, along with his invitation to her, to Dalton, with a note requesting advance notice of when the governor might sign the bill.

Although Wilder denies that he was trying to put pressure on Dalton, it was clear that he was playing two sides of the street. Without telling Dalton, Wilder sent copies of that package of correspondence to a number of others, including Doc Thornton at the Crusade; Michael Brown, the state lobbyist for the NAACP, (who is Wilder's nephew, his sister Doris' son); the four other black members of the legislature; selected colleagues in the Senate, and to the Senate clerk. J. T. Shropshire.

Dalton vetoed the bill, saying "it would be much more appropriate to honor an outstanding Virginian such as Thomas Jefferson, who authored the Declaration of Independence, was governor of Virginia, president of the United States and founder of the University of Virginia." Dalton pointed out that seven other Virginians who served as president were not honored with a state holiday, nor are "many other great Virginians, such as Booker T. Washington, a Virginian whose contributed greatly to the benefit of mankind, and Patrick Henry, our first governor." The governor also argued that state employees preferred to retain Election Day as a holiday, rather than have three holidays in January.

A disillusioned Wilder predicted that the veto would "help make the fuzziness disappear" between Robb and Coleman, which may have been what Dalton desired. The two candidates immediately came under pressure to take a stand on the idea. Robb responded by saying he would have signed the bill, calling it "symbolically of great importance to a large number of Virginians," adding that Dalton had "missed a real opportunity" by not signing it. Coleman supported the veto, saying "substituting this for Election Day is a mistake....Election Day should be a state holiday. It is and will forever be the most important day of the year in any democracy."

Wilder said the veto meant the GOP was appealing to elitism. "I would rather use that word than racism," he said. Later, Wilder said "everyone had expected I would rail a great deal about the veto. I recall saying I wasn't angry about it, that I would get it passed. I couldn't understand it, but I didn't say anything. I never asked Dalton, I never asked anyone" about why he took that action.

Robb won the election in 1981, with the strong support of blacks, but how much effect the King veto had to do with the outcome is unknown.

Yet the arrival of a Democrat in the governor's office, after a twelve-year hiatus, didn't help the King bill. Far from it. In the 1982 session of the assembly, Wilder offered two versions of the bill, and both failed. The first, to establish January 15 as a holiday in King's honor and to eliminate election day as a holiday, passed the Senate, but by only 25 to 14, and then died in the House Committee on General Laws. The second version also would have designated January 15 as King Day, and would have given state employees the choice of taking off any three of four holidays: January 15 for King; January 19 for Lee-Jackson; the third Monday in February for George Washington, and the second Monday in October for Columbus. Wilder admitted the latter proposal wasn't well-thought -out. Someone else had suggested it and he introduced it as a hedge, but he didn't push for its passage. It was killed in the Senate Committee on General Laws.

At that point, in the first of an enduring series of jibes that Wilder would aim at Robb over the years, Wilder said, "a lot of people were questioning the commitment of the (Robb) administration" to the black community. Robb was obviously upset with such accusations, Wilder said. "I made it clear that I had not asked for his help or support." Failure of the King bill in the first term of the new Democratic governor "gave the perception, I think erroneously, that Robb was not cooperating....But I think he owed some responsibility in getting things done. You'll have to ask him why it didn't happen." Wilder said 1982 "was a bad year. And there was a great deal of resentment expressed around the state, by blacks and other people" who felt more would be accomplished in Robb's first year as governor.

In 1983, after thirteen years as the only black in the Senate in nearly a hundred years, Robert C. Scott, a Harvard-educated lawyer from Newport News, moved over from the House to join Wilder as the second black in the Senate. Also that year, the legislature for the first time permitted co-sponsorship of legislation by members from both houses. As a result of those changes, the King bill picked up its first co-sponsors, Scott in the Senate and the four black members of the House of Delegates. Wilder told his colleagues in what amounted to the assembly's first black caucus, "I want you guys involved. It's just as much your bill as mine." But the added help wasn't enough. The 1983 proposal, which would have substituted King's birthday for election day as a state holiday, struggled through the Senate 26 to 11 but again was scuttled in the House General Laws Committee.

Looking back, Wilder said he couldn't understand why the bill was rejected again. He took another slap at Governor Robb, saying that he hadn't asked for the help of the Robb administration "and to my knowledge, they didn't."

Finally, in 1984, in the tenth legislative session since it originally was proposed by Wilder, a bill honoring Dr. Martin Luther King Jr. made it all the way into law.

A key to its final adoption was the switch of Republican Robert S. Bloxom, an Eastern Shore auto supply dealer, whose support allowed the bill to get out of the House General Laws Committee on a vote of eleven to nine. It passed the full House 67 to 27, after having again won nearly unanimous support in the Senate, where the vote was 36 to 4.

The final measure, Senate Bill 112, established the third Monday in January as Lee-Jackson-King Day, an official state holiday. It was co-sponsored by the seven black members of the General Assembly: Senators Wilder and Scott, and Richmond Delegates Roland D. (Duke) Ealey and Benjamin J. Lambert III, who had been Wilder's campaign manager in his first race; Norfolk Delegates William P. Robinson Jr., who had succeeded his father in 1981, and Yvonne B. Miller, the assembly's first black woman member, and Newport News Delegate W. Henry Maxwell. It was signed into law by Governor Robb on April 9, 1984, which, in a bit of unplanned irony, was the 119th anniversary of Lee's surrender of Confederate forces at Appomattox, Virginia, which ended the Civil War.

Taking a cue from his famous father-in-law, President Lyndon B. Johnson, who in the mid-1960s had signed a major civil rights law at the Statue of Liberty, Robb moved the ceremony from his office at the Statehouse to the nearby campus of Virginia Union University, where Wilder had graduated thirty-three years earlier. Robb signed the bill before an audience of two hundred in Henderson Hall that included all but one of the black legislators, veterans in the civil rights movement, college officials and students, and Richmond's black mayor, Roy A. West, who praised Wilder for "laboring relentlessly" in behalf of the legislation.

In his remarks, Governor Robb, who was living up to a campaign promise to sign the measure if it got to his desk, said he was "pleased to help bring into focus the dream King helped to symbolize for so many in our society. This has not been an easy day to come to. It was not easy to confront an issue not seen in the same light by all Virginians," Robb added, acknowledging that up until the last moment he was being urged by opponents not to sign the bill. "We can't call this the end of the story, or even the end of chapter," Robb said. "But it certainly is the end of a paragraph."

25. Wisteria

Lawrence Douglas Wilder, who has made a career out of starting at the bottom, and Charles Spittal Robb, who has made a career out of starting at the top, had a symbiotic relationship from the beginning. Their careers intertwined, in the metaphor of Guy Friddell of the Norfolk Virginian-Pilot, like Southern wisteria vines.

Wilder, the one-time lab technician, recognized that symbiosis, the term in biology for two dissimilar organisms living together in close association, especially where it is advantageous to both, was possible, perhaps even necessary, in his dealings with Chuck Robb. Robb did also, though he may not have thought of it in scientific terms.

When Robb considered running for lieutenant governor in early 1976, he thought it was likely that he would have two opponents, Delegates Richard S. (Major) Reynolds of Richmond, brother of the late lieutenant governor, and Ira M. Lechner of Arlington, and possibly two more, state Senators Hunter B. Andrews of Hampton and Wilder. Robb believed he could beat either Reynolds or Lechner, but if Andrews or Wilder were to become a candidate, Robb would not. "I didn't think I could put a campaign together that could prevail against either one of them," said Robb, who had absolutely no experience in government. Thus he wasn't prepared to challenge Andrews, the most brilliant and acerbic member of the legislature, whose mastery of state government was unparalleled, or Wilder, who could be the key to tapping black votes, which was an integral part of Robb's plan.

Robb acknowledged that Wilder was "a force to be reckoned with," and understood that it was important to keep communications open with him "so if there were some misunderstanding [between them] down the road, it could not be interpreted in a racial context. I wanted to see Virginia move beyond that."

Robb was part of a new generation of Virginia politicians, "not burdened by having defended or being an architect of massive resistance." He was born in Arizona, spent his early years in Ohio and had not grown up in a race-conscious environment. He didn't have any of the baggage of his predecessors. Robb wasn't sanctimonious about it, however, recognizing the good fortune of "not having to grapple with it when I was younger. I didn't want to contend with it then, or since."

His family moved to the Washington area when he was a teenager and he attended a segregated high school, Mt. Vernon, near Alexandria, graduating in 1957. Like Justice Powell and Tom Wolfe, Robb felt segregation was wrong but never did anything about it. He recalls peering out the window of a school bus while riding through Gum Springs, a black enclave in Fairfax County, and wondering "where they went to school. It bothered me that I didn't don't know. I didn't do anything about it, though, I just remember thinking that it wasn't right."

Robb was pleased when both Wilder and Andrews assured him they were not going to enter the already crowded field for the nomination.

Robb announced his candidacy over the New Year's weekend of 1976, and although he did not have Wilder's public support, he did not face him as an opponent either. Robb didn't flat out ask Wilder for his support; he was grateful enough just not to have him as an opponent. "I probably said, 'I would like to have your support at some point, if it's convenient,'" he recalled. While Robb had high hopes of capturing black support in the general election against a Republican, he was clearly the most conservative of the three Democratic hopefuls. Reynolds was the brother of an icon who had helped energize and finance black voters early in the decade, and Lechner was a labor lawyer who may have been the most liberal candidate ever to run statewide in Virginia. So Robb was looking ahead to the general election when he went before the Crusade of Voters before the primary and suggested, "if the occasion arises... and you can be with me...." The Crusade endorsed Reynolds.

H. Benson Dendy III, who was a teenaged political junky when he became a volunteer for Robb, said he thought that Wilder remained neutral in the nominating process, which was the best Robb could have hoped for, considering the strong attachment so many blacks felt for Reynolds. Dendy sensed that all three of the candidates were dissatisfied with Wilder as a result, "but it was probably the best thing for him to do."

Robb's failure to get the Crusade's endorsement in the primary wasn't all bad news, as he was trying to perform the balancing act of being the voice of moderation while at the same time wooing Old Guard conservatives back to the party from the Republicans. Not being the candidate of the Crusade helped. Robb won the June, 1977, primary with 39 percent of the vote; Reynolds got 33 percent and Lechner 28 percent.

Once Robb secured the nomination, Dendy said Wilder "very actively helped us get the endorsement in the fall," which was far from automatic, because a number of black leaders were dissatisfied with the Democrats' candidate for attorney general, Delegate Ed Lane, who lost the Black Caucus endorsement, in addition to that of The Afro, to Republican Marshall Coleman.

For the fall campaign, Robb found himself sandwiched between a liberal, populist gubernatorial candidate, former Lieutenant Governor Henry E. Howell and former segregationist Lane for attorney general.

Howell had won the nomination, squeaking by Attorney General Andrew P. Miller 51 percent to 49 percent, while Lane topped the four-way field for attorney general with 35 percent. After Howell got the nomination, he dumped his campaign manager, Paul Goldman, an eccentric New Yorker who eight years later would be the architect of Wilder's unconventional campaign for lieutenant governor. Howell, in turn, was dumped by a number of regular Democrats, including a third of his former colleagues in the state Senate, who either outright endorsed the GOP nominee, Lieutenant Governor John N. Dalton, or practiced the Golden Silence that the Byrd organization routinely employed in presidential elections, which freed its supporters to vote for the Republican nominee. The diversity of the ticket was too much for others also. Even Delegate Alson H. Smith Jr. of Winchester, a Howell fundraiser, declined to endorse the ticket until the dust settled.

The Crusade endorsed Howell, Robb and Coleman at a closed meeting in Richmond on September 11, 1977, although Wilder and his former roommate, Henry Marsh, who by then was the mayor of Richmond, urged support of Lane. Wilder had written a letter to The Afro urging support for Lane and suggesting that Lane apologize for his support of massive resistance. Marsh was booed when he pleaded for an endorsement for Lane. Wilder did not attend the meeting, citing a previous meeting of a legislative study commission in Charlottesville. The Howell endorsement was lopsided, Robb's was unanimous and Coleman beat Lane by a margin of two-to-one.

Robb credited his endorsement to his speech to the Crusade before the nomination. Robb said "it apparently impressed some people that I didn't stiff arm them." Robb went on to develop an independent relationship with some blacks, so he was not totally dependent upon Wilder for his contacts. Wilder has always been an important element of that relationship, Robb said, "but it never was a sole dependency."

Robb's Republican opponent was state Senator A. Joe Canada Jr. of Virginia Beach, who had few differences with Robb philosophically or physically—both were tall, handsome thirty-eight year-old Boy Scouts-turned-lawyers. So Canada, a former Democrat who got the nomination at the GOP convention over the opposition of the head of the ticket, Dalton, pounded at Robb as an outsider and dilettante. About the only issue on which they differed was the ERA, with Robb in favor and Canada having cast the deciding vote against it in the Senate the previous year. Robb was being touted as a future candidate for president even before he beat Canada by eight percentage points. Robb's standing within the party was further enhanced because he was the only Democrat to win statewide office: Dalton thumped Howell, getting 56 percent of the vote, and Coleman easily beat Lane, polling 54 percent.

Robb broke with tradition and became the first lieutenant governor to treat the office as a fulltime job, even if he got only part-time pay for it. His predecessors had usually come to the capitol only for the one- or two-month legislative sessions, and then returned home, performing an occasional out-of-session chore while working at their private employment. Instead, Robb remained on unpaid leave he had taken during the campaign from his Washington law firm. His family stayed at home in McLean and Robb rented an apartment in a renovated coffee warehouse in Richmond's historic Shockoe Slip section and walked up the hill each day to work. At first, his daily presence around the Statehouse created a problem, if not an embarrassment, for the administration of Governor Dalton. Not only did Robb have nothing to do, he had no place to do it. There was no office space assigned to the lieutenant governor other than a windowless cubby-hole off the Senate floor that was used during the sessions. Dalton didn't consider Robb part of his administration and didn't want him in the Capitol, and the leaders of the General Assembly, jealous of the balance of power between the executive and legislative branches, didn't want him in the General Assembly Building. Finally, space was found for him in a room atop the two-and one-half story antebellum Bell Tower, a free-standing structure in the middle of the lawn, half down the hill from the Capitol. First, though, maintenance workers had to remove the fertilizer and groundskeeping equipment that had been stored in the narrow brick edifice, which had served as a lookout for Yankee invaders during the Civil War. Once installed, Robb climbed the stairs to his perch each morning and worked on the only task that faced him, planning his 1981 campaign for governor. Except for the location of the office—space was found in the Supreme Court building for the next lieutenant governor—Robb's pattern served as a blueprint for his successor, Wilder.

Wilder and Robb got to know each other over the next four years, although

Wisteria

Robb said "we were never intimates, but we were friendly. Little things would cause separations in our closeness. Occasionally offense would be taken at a word that was quoted. Usually, something I had said," Robb acknowledged.

Robb worked closely with the Senate's new majority leader, Adelard "Abe" Brault of Fairfax, who had been installed in an off-session coup that deposed Ed Willey. Four years later, Brault was ousted by Senator Hunter B. Andrews of Hampton. The difference in perception between Robb and Wilder is illustrated in their respective views of the role Wilder played in those back-to-back coups. Wilder considers himself a major player. Robb said "Doug was never particularly a critical player in that. He had been on both sides of the equation at the right time." Robb said Wilder and his friend Senator Pete Babalas of Norfolk delighted in being the swing vote. "They enjoyed the notoriety of being part of the change," according to Robb.

Whatever Wilder's role, most observers concede that through all of those changes, his power increased.

Halfway through his term as lieutenant governor, Robb began planning his campaign for governor, assembling a group of advisers that came to be known as his core group. His opponent, Coleman, established a similar team known as the Quiet Committee. The core group's first task was to raise money to pay off the debt from Robb's 1977 campaign. The original participants were two legislators, Delegates Alson H. Smith Jr. of Winchester and Alan A. Diamonstein of Newport News, Lain O'Ferrall, the investment counselor who had worked in Wilder's 1969 campaign, and William G. Thomas, an Alexandria attorney and former state party chairman. They were all friends, but they didn't come as a package; each had his own strengths and circle of associates. The core group met regularly over the next four years, expanding and contracting like an accordion to fit the need. As the 1981 campaign approached, other frequent participants included David G. McCloud, Robb's chief of staff in the lieutenant governor's office; David Doak, Robb's campaign manager; W. Roy Smith, a former Byrd legislator and advertising executive, and Wilder.

In a contest between liberals and moderates at the 1980 state Democratic convention in Richmond, Wilder sided with Robb and the moderates. He criticized former Lieutenant Governor Howell for threatening to form a third party in the 1981 governor's race if the state's liberal national committee members George C. Rawlings of Fairfax and Ruth Harvey Charity of Danville were replaced by moderates. Rawlings and Charity were supporting the presidential bid of Senator Edward M. Kennedy of Massachussets against President Jimmy Carter. In an argument that in retrospect seemed disingenuous in light of his own actions two years later, Wilder argued that the party needed leaders who would not threaten to "move on" when they didn't get their way. When Howell protested, Wilder told the party's twice-defeated gubernatorial candidate, "In the 1980s, there is no reason to have the people who will speak for us in the future be the same people who spoke for us in the past." The moderates prevailed, and when state party chairman, liberal Richard J. Davis, resigned later that year to run for lieutenant governor, Delegate Owen W. Pickett of Virginia Beach, a moderate-conservative, was named Davis' successor.

The Democratic party had a big stake in Robb—Virginia was the only state in the country in which the Democrats had not elected either a senator or governor in a decade—but some party regulars were upset with Robb's palsy-walsy reluctance to criticize Governor Dalton and stake out an alternative view. By late 1979, a few party leaders were having second thoughts about handing the 1981 nomination to Robb without a challenge.

When Robb finally took a stand, over federal judgeships, which are among the most prized of political plums, he made everybody mad. The federal judiciary was expanding, and President Carter hoped to use the added positions to expand minority and female representation on the federal bench. Virginia was to get four new judges. Although senior Senator Harry F. Byrd Jr. had abandoned the Democratic party and won election in 1970 and again in 1976 as an independent, he still helped the Democrats organize the Senate, and as such was accorded the courtesy of selecting the panelists who would recommend the names of prospective judges to the Justice Department: To no one's surprise, Byrd's appointees suggested ten white men. The list was unacceptable to the Carter administration, which threatened to leave the judgeships unfilled unless Byrd agreed to add names to the list. Byrd refused, saying he already had done what the president had asked, at which point Robb, the state's senior elected Democrat, waded in—on Byrd's side.

While the White House and Byrd parried, the state's black leaders came up with a candidate to rally behind, Richmond Circuit Court Judge James E. Sheffield, whose earlier appointment as the first black judge in a court of record in the state had been championed in the legislature by Wilder, his former neighbor. In August, 1978, the White House leaked the word that Sheffield would be Carter's fourth nominee, three men from Byrd's list having been selected earlier. Republicans, sensing they might be able to pick their own judge if they could delay the hearing until after the 1980 presidential election, leaked stories about a run-in Sheffield had with the Internal Revenue Service over an unspecified matter, which reportedly had been resolved, and that he once had been delinquent in paying $1,071 in local real estate taxes. On the day of his hearing in August, 1979, as Republican Senator Orrin G. Hatch of Utah began broaching material in Sheffield's IRS file, Sheffield asked that his name be withdrawn from consideration. It was never revealed what the file contained.

In a final, desperate move, the Carter administration, through Robb, made an offer of a judgeship to Henry Marsh, who by then was the mayor of Richmond. He turned it down. Eventually, as the Republicans had hoped, the vacancy was filled by the administration of President Ronald Reagan.

"Regrettably," Robb admitted at the end of the fiasco that had dragged out nearly three years, it was "mishandled from start to finish." Wilder concurred. Warming to what was become a favorite pastime—criticism of Robb—Wilder said, "Chuck wasn't totally helpful. He sort of helped set this thing in concrete when he indicated he supported Harry Byrd."

Robb's actions, Wilder said, were "deplorable, compromising and not in the best interest of all the people of the Commonwealth." In the upcoming governor's race, Wilder said, "blacks have other places to go. Hell, we can go fishing."

26. The Robb Era Begins

W ilder didn't go fishing, but he didn't show up for Robb's official announcement of his gubernatorial campaign at the John Marshall Hotel on March 19, 1981. Wilder emphasized that his absence, along with that of several other black leaders, "was not by accident. We've got a number of questions and concerns that still need answers and frankly the appearance of unity when there is no unity would be foolish." He said he personally planned to support Robb, but other black leaders were still "smoldering" over Robb's role in the black judge debacle.

On the other end of the spectrum, letters of endorsement for Robb were read from William M. Tuck, a segregationist governor from the late 1940s, and from Colgate W. Darden, a moderate who served as governor from 1942 to 1946. Robb was introduced by another reluctant supporter, state Senator Hunter B. Andrews, who had publicly derided him as "Chuckie Bird."

There was still considerable uneasiness among blacks about Robb as the convention, or coronation, as cynics called it, approached, especially because of his indecision on whether he supported efforts to get Virginia exempted from some confines of the federal Voting Rights Act, which was up for renewal in Congress.

As a condition for supporting extension of the 1965 act, which otherwise would expire in August, 1982, some members of Congress, led by Republican Representative Henry Hyde of Illinois, were seeking modifications that liberals, including Wilder, the NAACP and the American Civil Liberties Union, said would weaken it. The original act required Virginia and the other states of the Old Confederacy to submit in advance to the Justice Department any proposed changes in election procedures. One of the modifications would allow exemptions to that pre-clearance provision if it could be shown that the change was not designed to hurt blacks. The existing law required proof that the changes would not result in harm, regardless of intent. Wilder said, for example, that while redistricting of the state Senate was accomplished with public hearings, and pre-notification of the NAACP, "many of the crucial decisions (about redistricting of the House of Delegates) were made in the Commonwealth Club, to which blacks do not belong."

The day before he was to be nominated in Virginia Beach, Robb dispatched his press secretary, George M. Stoddart, to meet with Wilder, to see how much trouble Robb might expect. Wilder was cordial and confident, assuring Stoddart that he would calm fears. And he did, meeting that night with about two hundred black delegates in the theater of the Virginia Beach Pavilion. Wilder fielded questions about Robb's views on a number of issues, including the Voting Rights Act. Wilder made a soothing speech, assuring the delegates, "I am in communication with Chuck. Trust me." Looking back, Wilder said, "to their credit, the delegates never backed away from Chuck. Wilder came out of the meeting and said, "I have no problem supporting Chuck Robb. I am doing it enthusiastically." But as always in their relationship, there was a caveat: "I can well sympathize with the frustration of many people in not having a more delineating choice." As he campaigned for Robb that fall, Wilder said, "everywhere I went I ran into the question. People said, 'we can trust you, but can we trust Chuck?'"

Stoddart said Robb may not have appreciated the sacrifice Wilder was making by going out on a limb for him. Stoddart said Robb did not realize that Wilder was taking pot-shots from other blacks for his loyalty to Robb, and that such instances of insensitivity played a part in their frequent clashes. On the other hand, Stoddart was urging Robb to expand his reach into the black community beyond Wilder, warning that he was committing a classic mistake of a white Anglo-Saxon politician by beknighting a black spokesman, or a Jewish spokesman. Blacks are not monolithic, advised Stoddart, offering an observation that Wilder often invokes.

In another pre-convention move, Wilder helped state party chairman Richard J. Davis win the nomination for lieutenant governor over Arlington Delegate Ira M. Lechner, who was making another try. "When Ira was hitting hard from left, Doug came out early for Dick and took care of that problem," said Robert "Bobby" Watson, who directed Davis' campaign. Eva S. Teig, who had worked for Davis when he was mayor of Portsmouth and came to Richmond to help in the campaign, added, "I asked his (Wilder's) advice on issues, who to call, and it was not always just black issues, it went beyond that."

How much help Wilder was to Robb in that campaign is a matter of debate. Robb didn't consider Wilder a key player in his campaign, although he said "his embrace just before the convention helped alleviate some unrest in the black community." He doesn't recall asking much of Wilder, or of him offering much. "Doug would always say, 'let me know, I'll help out,' but I don't recall him volunteering for anything specific, but he may have. It would not have been a significant factor either way, asking or volunteering. But I was never aware of him not being supportive, I don't mean that."

Wilder said that as he campaigned for Robb that fall, "everywhere I went I ran into the question. They were asking, 'what's the difference?' between Robb and Coleman. Marshall was relying on what he did in 1977, when he got the Crusade's endorsement, without doing anything more. People'd say, 'we like you, respect you, but we're not voting for you.' I ran into a great deal of resistance. But we turned it around. We got most people on board."

The discomfort with Robb among blacks peaked in Southside, heart of the state's black belt, and of the most conservative white voters, where a write-in campaign was begun for an independent black ticket, headed by Cora Tucker, a Halifax County black activist and housewife. "There is a lack of enthusiasm in the black community...even among those who support one or the other of the candidates," said the Rev. Curtis Harris, head of the Virginia branch of the Southern Christian Leadership Conference. Wilder discouraged the write-in campaign, which was being boosted by the black Fifth Congressional District Voters League. "This is not the time...to go out the door. We shouldn't walk out, but stake our ground and work for more involvement." Mrs. Tucker was unconvinced. "A few black leaders have gotten a few crumbs for themselves and their families." And she added an observation with which Wilder could hardly disagree: "They're part of the power structure. They'd commit political suicide if they broke off and worked with radicals." Robb only vaguely recollects that movement, which he didn't view as a serious threat to his election, saying, "oh yes, Cora Tucker...I don't think I asked Doug to help there."

Bill Thomas, a member of Robb's core group, said Wilder "was a full participant in Robb's strategy for capturing black votes, but he added that Robb didn't have to be sold to the black community. He noted that Robb's mother-in-law, Lady Bird Johnson, campaigned with him in a number of black churches around the state and "nobody ever had to sell her." Nevertheless, Thomas said "attracting a large black turnout was critical to Robb, and Wilder was the point person in communicating with the black community. Thomas added, however, that "there was an awful lot of effort to communicate with the black community other than just through Doug. The black community is not monolithic. I didn't think then, and don't think now, that we wouldn't have gotten essentially most of those black votes, maybe all of them, if Doug had been sitting on the sidelines. But it was also important to have symbolism."

To show solidarity for Robb, Wilder, under the letterhead of the Democratic Black Caucus of Virginia, a nascent organization that he ran out of his home, composed a letter which the Robb campaign mailed to four thousand, five hundred black voters around the state, quoting Wilder as saying that Robb's election "will make a difference." It said the "conservative tone of the campaign gives cause for concern, and it forced me to make a more determined effort to know where Chuck stands. I want to share with you what I know." Wilder spoke of Robb in glowing terms, more so than at any time before or after. "I trust the man," he wrote. "He has not lied to me. He has been consistent. We have taken opposite sides on many issues, but he has always dealt from the top of the deck." The four-page letter went on to outline Robb's support of a number of issues of concern to blacks: affirmative action, minority contractor set-asides, Martin Luther King holiday, voting rights for the District of Columbia, extension of the federal Voting Rights Act, voter registration by mail...."

Voter registration by mail? Robb's strategists went crazy at the idea that Robb would endorse such a liberal proposal. They knew the Republicans would seize on it.

At the next meeting of the core group, at Robb's house in McLean, Al Smith brought a copy of the letter, which none of the other regulars yet knew about. Smith moaned that it would send conservatives rushing to Coleman. Campaign treasurer Lain O'Ferrall said Smith and Bill Thomas "started in on Robb," who despite what outsiders thought, made a lot of decisions on his own. But Robb said he didn't know anything about the letter. They tried to figure out who had approved it. "Nobody Ok'd it," O'Ferrall said they concluded. "It was devastating. We were sitting there wondering if the whole empire had caved in. Al (Smith) was furious; he thought it was the end of the campaign. Al ran out to the car, he was leaving, and Chuck ran out and got him. It was a great scene."

Robb doesn't recall that Smith reacted that emotionally. "The most Al would do, typically, was just shake his head. He wouldn't walk out. With Al, you could see it in his face. The color drains." Nonetheless, Robb admits, "I was livid."

Thomas said he did not think the Wilder letter would have a major impact. Others, however, say Thomas had a delayed reaction. He reportedly began boiling about it after leaving Robb's house, and by five o'clock the next morning, was on the telephone to David Doak, the campaign manager, screaming that the election had been lost.

It turned out that Robb had approved the letter, but after he had signed off on it, a couple of paragraphs had been inserted without his knowledge, apparently with the approval of Art Murphy, a member of a prominent black Baltimore family who had been hired by Robb to co-ordinate the get-out-the-vote effort in black precincts. Wilder said Robb let him know that he would have preferred no mention of what he called "issues that are divisive," in the letter, but Wilder added, "He never said I misquoted him or distorted his positions."

Fortunately for the Democrats, the letter snafu was overshadowed by an even bigger gaffe it prompted in the Coleman campaign. Again the perpetrator was someone other than the candidate, this time former Governor Mills Godwin, no friend of Coleman's to begin with. Godwin was importuned by party regulars to make a pitch to the conservatives. Godwin chose an auspicious occasion, an appearance by President Reagan—who had carried Virginia by 230,000 votes the year before—at a Coleman fundraiser in Richmond, just a week before the election. He quoted excerpts from the Wilder letter, zeroing in on postcard registration and voting representation for the majority-black city of Washington, using "code words" that reminded listeners of Godwin's role as a leader of the state's massive resistance to integration.

"Godwin's words galvanized blacks," according to Wilder. Between Wilder's letter, and Godwin's response to it, blacks turned out in record numbers to vote for Robb, who defeated Coleman by about one hundred thousand votes.

"Chuck might have won without that letter," O'Ferrall said, "but if there was one thing in the campaign that helped Chuck the most, it was the letter from Doug."

For those who were keeping score—and Wilder always did—Robb owed Wilder at that point.

One measure of the importance Robb gave to Wilder's role in his election was the prominence Wilder got in the inauguration, and the clout he got during the transition from twelve years of Republican domination of the Statehouse to the Democratic sweep of the three elective statewide offices.

Yet again, Robb and Wilder look into the same prism, but the light refracts differently for them. Robb saw himself doing a favor to Wilder, and Wilder saw it as payment for services delivered.

Robb believes that Wilder "was given credit probably for more of my rapport with the black community than is accurate, yet it served both of our interests to let that perception remain. Because of the symbolism involved, his embrace at the appropriate time, particularly when I was running for governor, was important, no question about it." Wilder's support, however, "was not based on a long-term, personal relationship," said Robb, in an observation with which not even Wilder would quarrel.

While there were a lot of things that Robb disagreed with Wilder about, he was always impressed with Wilder's political skills. "He had an ability to communicate effectively and could be articulate spokesman for whatever case may be," Robb said. He couldn't resist adding, however, that Wilder "clearly identified more with his own constituency than with a statewide constituency."

Robb said Wilder is "a little like [New York Governor] Mario Cuomo, in that anything that doesn't sound like it's one hundred percent supportive gets a reaction. There were bumps in the road. But for the most part, it was friendly.

The Robb Era Begins

We exchanged some confidences. There was a time when I thought I pretty well could rely on Doug, but that changed from time to time. That's like all political alliances, there are very few true-blue, lasting relationships. It's because of the kind of work we do."

Wilder was a co-chairman of Robb's inaugural, which Al Smith, who was chairman of the inauguration, said was a position reserved for those who played a key role in the campaign. "Doug was very active," Smith recalled. "In campaigns, very few people do more than they are asked. Very few volunteer. If he hadn't been very active in the campaign, I can assure you he never would have been vice chairman of the inaugural."

Robb downplayed that, however. "I probably put a black and a woman and whatever in co-chairman roles, that's probably what it amounted to. That's being honest. I tried to give him an opportunity to comment on potential black job applicants and appointees, and I did that pretty routinely, as a courtesy. I think that gave him a certain stature in the black community."

Robb's press secretary, George Stoddart, said Wilder had "a great deal of input and influence on black appointments," specifically to the governor's staff, cabinet, agency heads and on the board and commission levels. He cited seven important appointments where Wilder's candidates were selected, or cleared through him, including blacks who were named as secretary of public safety, head of the office of personnel and training, a commissioner of the Alcoholic Beverage Commission and the state board of elections. One of the people who worked in the transition office was Judy Anderson, who was very close to Wilder.

Laurie Naismith, who as Robb's secretary of the commonwealth was in charge of filling a thousand patronage jobs, said at the time, "we probably call Doug Wilder's office a minimum of two or three times a day."

"There isn't any question, whether it was an express agreement or a tacit understanding," Bill Thomas said, that "Doug provided a tremendous number of suggestions for people from the black community for jobs in the administration. My sense is that his recommendation was sufficient" to be hired.

Whether Wilder's influence went so far as to have veto power over hiring, as some of his friends suggest, is not so clear.

Richard Dickerson, who was the only black assistant to the governor, said "Doug was the gatekeeper. No blacks were appointed that were not run by Doug." Dickerson said Wilder also suggested blacks for appointments to boards and commissions, and that Robb relied on Wilder's recommendations. "It was a very happy marriage," Dickerson said. "Doug was King Black, King Negro, whatever you want to call it. He got his juice from being King Black. And Robb was appointing black folks. So everybody benefited."

Robb disagrees with the assertion by Dickerson, and others, that without a nod from Wilder, a black could not get a job in the Robb administration.

"He didn't have veto power by any means," Robb said, "but he did have a good deal to say. I don't recall him ever talking me out of anyone, but I would get his comments before I went into the final decision-making process, and I think it's fair to say that if it was an arch-enemy of Doug's, they probably would not come to my attention." Because Wilder was consulted more often than other blacks, Robb said he was "certain that gave him a sense of power in the black community, where he could let them know, although we never really talked about that." While Wilder was the only black that Robb checked with routinely, he also talked to the black members of the General Assembly and with "other black leaders that I did not go through Doug to talk to," including Wilder's former roommate, Richmond mayor Henry Marsh.

Robb said it was not his goal to increase Wilder's status, but "I accorded to him the stature of being the senior black elected official" in the commonwealth. Nevertheless, some blacks were appointed without Wilder's imprimatur. Robb said, for example, that Wilder "probably wasn't crazy about" his naming Frank White as the cabinet secretary in charge of corrections, or Richmond lawyer John Charles Thomas to be the first black on the Virginia Supreme Court. "So it was not exclusive. It's fair to say his recommendations carried significant weight with me, but on the highest level, with people he didn't know, that wasn't necessarily so."

Wilder's influence was being validated by the Richmond newspapers, whose conservative editorialists empowered him in a manner they reserve for influential figures they oppose—through sarcasm and ridicule. In one instance, the News Leader chided Robb's selection of Thomas to the Supreme Court, calling it an appointment "by Governor Wilder—oops, Governor Robb" (obviously unaware that Robb points to Thomas' selection as an example of picking a black Wilder was not enthused about).

Robb's chief-of-staff, David McCloud, observed that "Chuck and Doug had a strong relationship. When Doug had somebody he wanted appointed, and Chuck didn't appoint them, he got teed off, just like Bill Thomas and Al Smith got teed off. But it was all within the normal range, never any blow up or animosity." McCloud said Wilder often dropped by the governor's office, unannounced, in the afternoon or night, and chatted with Robb in his office. They didn't talk every week, but there was a dialogue that went on. So much so, said McCloud, that some of the other black leaders around the state felt Robb listened too much to Wilder.

Carolyn J. Moss, who was director of the department of minority business enterprise in the Robb administration, doesn't know if Wilder played a part in her appointment—she had met Lynda Robb and Lady Bird Johnson during the campaign—but once she was part of the administration, as the highest ranking black woman in the executive branch, she learned of Wilder's influence. She said Wilder was a chief adviser to Robb, not just on minority issues, but on major issues in general. "Robb relied on him a great deal in dealing with the General Assembly." So much so, Moss said, that it incensed some other black legislators, who did not enjoy equal access.

Moss's department was under Secretary of Human Resources Betty Diener, who shortly after Moss's appointment told her she wanted to merge her agency with the department of economic development, under the Secretary of Agriculture. Moss didn't like the idea because she thought it would play down the importance of the office and be a disservice to Robb, so she went to Wilder for help. Wilder, whose legislation had created the department, said he would "take care of it."

The next thing Moss knew, the conservative Secretary of Agriculture told Diener that he didn't want the minority business office merged with economic development. When she asked Wilder if he had spoken to him, Wilder merely winked.

27. The Pickett Affair

If there was any doubt about how much clout Wilder had during the Robb administration, it was put to rest after the selection of the party's nominee for the United States Senate in 1982.

Even before the selection process began, pundits were saying the first test of whether Chuck Robb had the star-quality that could someday boost him into the White House was whether his coattails would be long enough for the party to gain the Senate seat that came up less than ten months after his inaugural.

(Because of the peculiarity of their election calendars, only Virginia and New Jersey elect governors in the off-year following the presidential election. There is an important statewide election three of every four years, for president, senator or governor.)

The Senate seat up for grabs in 1982 had been held either by the incumbent, Harry F. Byrd Jr., or his father, since 1933. "Young Harry" announced shortly after Robb's victory that he would not seek re-election. If he had not, he likely would have had opposition from both the Republicans and Democrats. Paul S. Trible Jr., a brash, young three-term Republican congressman from the First District, wasn't going to wait for Byrd's decision: He was going to enter the race, regardless. Byrd had abandoned the party in 1970, saying he could no longer support the liberal drift of the national Democratic party or swear to its loyalty oath, but he went on to win re-election twice as an independent, largely on the strength of the family name. Even though he retained a place in the Senate Democratic caucus for purposes of organization, in his later years he was largely ignored by most of his colleagues on both sides of the aisle.

With that seat opening up, the pressure was on Robb and his backers to demonstrate that the 1981 sweep was not a fluke—that this newly reconstituted party—they liked to call themselves "Virginia Democrats," connoting an amalgam of fiscal conservatism and social moderation—that welcomed both the "yellow dog" Democrats who had stuck with the party despite differences with its presidential nominees and the increasing number of new residents of Virginia, many of them from the East and Midwest, who were settling largely in the booming suburbs of Washington—in a state-of-mind known as Northern Virginia—or in the Hampton Roads area, where the nation's largest shipyard at Newport News and navy base at Norfolk combined to guarantee prosperity.

The problem was, the Democrats had no obvious candidates. Their best three vote-getters—Robb, Lieutenant Governor Richard J. Davis, and Attorney General Gerald L. Baliles, had run and won the year before. Republicans held nine of the ten seats in the Virginia delegation in the House of Representatives and the only Democrat, W. C. "Dan" Daniel, was so conservative that he was constantly being confused with another Virginia congressman, Bob Daniel, who was a Republican.

Most often mentioned early in the year as potential candidates were Hunter B. Andrews, the arrogant and aristocratic Senate majority leader; Bill Thomas, the Alexandria attorney who was a founding father of the Robb "core group;" former state attorney general Andy Miller, who had lost the 1978 Senate race to Republican John Warner; and Delegate Owen B. Pickett of Virginia Beach, who had succeeded Davis as state party chairman the year before.

None of them was clearly superior, but they were all qualified on the basis of experience and political skills and could handle the job. Robb's goal was to avoid a divisive nominating contest in which so much of the party's resources would be expended that it would not have enough left for the general election. In an attempt to be more democratic than what he soon would learn was smart for a would-be kingmaker, Robb convened a series of private meetings, including some chats in the governor's office, during January to discuss the pros and cons of various potential nominees and to see if a consensus could be reached. Among those who regularly attended were David Doak, Robb's campaign manager, David McCloud, Robb's chief of staff, and Wilder.

Bobby Watson, the impish, red-haired chief aide to Lieutenant Governor Davis, recalled that at one of the meetings, in a conference room on the fourteenth floor of the John Marshall Hotel, Wilder said the only prospective candidate that he could not support was Miller, because of Miller's stance as attorney general in support of weakening the federal Voting Rights Act. Having lost the 1978 Senate race, Miller already was damaged goods and got little support from the fifteen or twenty people in that meeting. Watson was leaning toward Pickett but remained silent because he was there representing Davis, who was neutral. Watson didn't necessarily believe that Pickett was the strongest possible candidate but he was the best one available. Watson left the meeting believing that there had been a consensus, if not an enthusiasm, expressed for Pickett.

Doak, at Robb's direction, contacted party leaders around the state and floated the various names. Doak set up an informal chart that awarded points on a variety of categories and then recorded comments next to each name. Although Robb was a little uneasy with the process, the four contestants seemed to be willing to go through it. And to nearly everyone's surprise, Pickett came out ahead, by virtue of being the first choice of a few and the second choice of many.

"I think very clearly nobody ever thought Owen would come out as person selected," said one of the regular participants at the meetings. "Everybody thought it would be one of two—Hunter Andrews or Bill Thomas. I never have figured out how Owen got the nomination. I won't say it was his (Robb's) finest hour. Politically, some of these things can get away from you."

The fifty-one-year-old Pickett, who had represented Virginia Beach in the House of Delegates since 1972, was neither the old school or the new, but rather a bland mixture who managed to please neither constituency. He had begun thinking about running for the Senate in mid-1981, when he was the state party chairman.

"No one was certain what Harry Byrd was going to do, so I went up (to Washington) and chatted with him," Pickett said. Although he did not get a definitive answer, Pickett came home and began exploring his chances. As state chairman, Pickett was cognizant of the importance of the black vote, so he put the word out to Wilder and several other black leaders—he's not sure if he sat down with them face-to-face—but he remembers seeing no warning flags hoisted.

Robb had agreed to be bound by the consensus, "but in my heart," he later acknowledged, "Owen wasn't really my candidate. He's a man of incredible— he's hard-headed like I am—tenacity. When he believes he's right on something, there is nothing that will move him, nothing. Although I had tremendous respect for him, still do, I didn't think he was flexible enough to be a successful statewide candidate. But I kept that to myself."

One person who didn't keep it to himself was Paul Goldman, the young New Yorker who had maintained his ties in Virginia since he ran Henry Howell's successful campaign for the nomination for governor in 1977. Goldman was not overjoyed with Pickett and said so. The year before, Goldman, operating as an independent activist, had forced a review by the Justice Department, under provisions of the federal Voting Rights Act, of the delegate selection plan that Pickett had designed for the state convention, which Wilder and other blacks contended discriminated against blacks. Party officials reluctantly submitted data to the Justice Department, while saying it wasn't required, and got the plan approved. Along the way, Wilder accused Pickett and others of asking people around the state to write letters to the Justice Department indicating their approval of the plan. "If it is your desire to continue this method of diluting and circumventing black leadership and not to resolve these matters, then no further negotiations are necessary," Wilder wrote to Pickett. Eventually, party officials agreed that black delegates would be elected in numbers roughly equivalent to the black voting strength in general elections.

"I never thought Pickett would be a good candidate," said Goldman, who by then had become a friend of Wilder's. "I didn't like the process, going from a primary to the convention, and I thought he was chosen the wrong way, by just six people in a room. It's not my kind of politics. I didn't think Pickett had any experience. He was picked for all the wrong reasons. You go out and earn it."

When Pickett got the word in February that he had won the contest, he made plans to declare his candidacy at the end of the legislative session in mid-March. Robb indicated he would support him, although Pickett admits that "It wasn't anything ironclad or written in blood, but implicit in what was going on was whoever came out of this as the consensus would have the support."

It may have been because of heightened expectations brought about by the election of the first Democratic governor in a dozen years, but for whatever reasons, the 1982 legislative session had not been a good one for blacks in general and Wilder in particular. "It was not a good year for relationships. Period," said Wilder. "Any number of persons were livid, terribly upset, not only with others they felt were not out there pushing, not helping, but also with me—they said, 'we went all the way out for you'" in supporting Robb.

Wilder had had one of his worst years, as far as a batting average, of his career in the assembly. Six of his eight bills were killed. In addition to killing two versions of the King holiday bill, legislators rejected measures that would have eliminated tax deductions for contributions to schools that discriminated on the basis of race; established a human rights commission with subpoena power and penalties for discrimination in employment, housing and public accommodations, and a voluntary plan for the state to make at least ten percent of its purchases from minority businesses. And—despite that controversial campaign letter's statement—nothing was done about postcard registration or other proposals to expand voter participation.

Wilder was particularly upset, and being criticized by some blacks, for the defeat of the bill that would have revoked the tax-exempt status of the whites-only academies that were a remnant of massive resistance. His nemesis, Sa'ad El-Amin, said Wilder was "guilty of political treason. The failure of the senator to obtain Robb's support raises a serious question of whether Senator Wilder sold out the black community."

Wilder knew Robb was not at fault—the governor had intervened the last night of the session and attempted to revive the bill—but he did blame House Speaker A. L. Philpott, who had stacked the twenty-member committee that considered the King bill with a record nine Republicans (they seldom got more than half a dozen seats on a committee) along with several conservative Democrats. "I'm not sure he (Robb) could have done anything" after that, Wilder conceded.

Wilder was angry, however, over Robb's suggestion at a post-session press conference that he had limited his involvement on the King holiday bill because he gave priority to budget and tax measures. Neither Robb nor Philpott pushed on the King holiday bill, which was the litmus-test issues for blacks. "It all gave the perception, I think erroneously, that Robb was not cooperating," Wilder said. He had not specifically asked the governor to help with his legislative agenda, but on the other hand, Wilder said, "I think he owed some responsibility in getting things done [without being asked]."

Pickett announced his candidacy on March 18 in his home district of Virginia Beach. In his kickoff speech, he invoked the name and spirit of Harry Byrd, whom he hoped to succeed in the Senate, saying that he too was a fiscal conservative. Pickett didn't consider himself a Byrd Democrat as such—he had little more than a nodding acquaintance with Young Harry—but he was a protege of Sydney Kellam, the Virginia Beach Democratic boss, who was a Byrd lieutenant, and he shared generally shared the Byrd philosophy. The next day, along with a story about his formal campaign debut, Pickett read that Wilder had expressed some concern about his invocation of the Byrd name, which was anathema to many blacks as the symbol of racism in the state.

Pickett's campaign manger, Tim Ridley, hastily arranged a meeting with Wilder, with whom he had cordial relations during their years together in the assembly, though they were hardly bosom buddies. Pickett interrupted his initial campaign swing and went to Wilder's law office on Church Hill, where Wilder told him his references to Byrd had presented a problem because of the perception that his constituents had about the senator.

"He didn't ask me to renounce the statement," Pickett said. "But he said things were happening that weren't acceptable, or he didn't find satisfactory. He felt that some of his legislation had been dealt with unfairly—not by me—and he had to use the means that were at his hand to try to resolve them." Pickett left, uncertain what Wilder would do, and returned to the campaign trail.

The next day, back on the campaign trail in the university town of Blacksburg, Pickett told an audience that he "probably could have used other names" instead of Byrd's to make his point. "It was just an example of legislators working their way to Congress, just as (former Senator William) Spong is an example," he explained.

Wilder's expressed concern about Pickett's statement initially was dismissed as an overreaction. "I don't think anybody paid attention," said Governor Robb, who didn't see anything wrong with Pickett's use of Byrd's name. Wilder's lawschool roommate, Richmond Mayor Henry Marsh, said Pickett "hadn't done any more than anyone else did. When Robb and the other people ran for office, they saluted Byrd to try to pick up those votes. It was a universal gesture that was understood; it was something you did." Marsh said he understood that Pickett had been selected "by some sort of caucus and people had agreed he would be the candidate, and that Doug was part of that process. Therefore, I was surprised when Doug used that excuse to torpedo him."

Former Lieutenant Governor Howell, who had set the standard for liberalism for some Virginians in the 1970s, also found Pickett's remarks inoffensive. Howell had examined Pickett's voting record and "it wasn't apparent to me that he was all that conservative, and neither was he a racist. I never saw why Doug got so upset." Howell detected the hand of Goldman, his former campaign manager, in Wilder's maneuvering. "Paul is a tactician," Howell noted, and may have convinced Wilder that "he had to establish himself as a leader, as much as one can lead a group of black citizens of Virginia, and they were a significant voting bloc from the Democratic standpoint."

Goldman, who became Wilder's closest adviser in the 1985 campaign for lieutenant governor, didn't know Wilder well at that time, and said he had not discussed the matter with him. But Goldman agreed with Wilder that "Pickett's choice of words was a big mistake—I don't know who advised him on it, but I thought it showed he wasn't ready" for statewide office.

Within a few days of Pickett's announcement, Wilder broached the possibility of running for the Senate as an independent, against Pickett and the presumed Republican nominee, Congressman Trible.

In the midst of all of his involvement with state and national politics, Wilder also found time in 1982 to take an interest in local affairs.

Richmond's patrician white business establishment, which had dominated the capital of the Confederacy since the War Between the States, realized its days of unchallenged rule were numbered in the 1960s, as the civil rights movement came into full bloom. So like a retreating army, it bobbytrapped the territory before surrendering it: Fearful that a revisionist black government might explode its own bombs, the city fathers turned over to the state the authority to protect the stone and brass tributes to Robert E. Lee, Stonewall Jackson, J. E. B. Stuart, Jefferson Davis and other dead heroes whose statues give a name and glory to the city's grand boulevard, Monument Avenue; and the departing leaders temporarily shored up the sagging white population by annexing 40,000 suburbanites from adjoining Chesterfield County. But time, and justice, was against them. A legal challenge of the annexation prompted the U. S. Supreme Court to freeze in place the existing elected council—allowing Thomas J. Bliley Jr., an undertaker, to serve uncontested as mayor from 1970 to 1977—until it could be determined, as charged, that the annexation violated the 1965 Voting Rights Act, by diluting black voter strength. During the seven years it took to get an answer, the seven whites and two blacks on Council were perpetuated in office by the absence of an election. And when the answer came, agreeing with the complainants that the annexation had violated the law, a federal court ordered that a ward system be instituted before a new election was held. As drawn, the boundaries should have produced a five-four white majority—a slight majority of the city's 250,000 residents was white—but the voters didn't know that, and elected a council that had a five-four black majority, thus making Richmond the first Southern city to elect a black majority to its council.

The five black council members in turned appointed one of them, Henry Marsh, Wilder's former law school roommate, as mayor. Marsh was first elected to the council in 1966, initially as the lone black, and until Wilder came to statewide prominence—which arguably could be set as 1982—Marsh was considered the leading black politician in the state, and thanks to a close relationship with President Jimmy Carter, was known nationally. As a result, the natural rivalry between the old friends was exacerbated.

The first five years of black majority rule on the council were often tumultuous, with Marsh and his black colleagues generally shaking up the long-ruling white establishment. School busing was blamed for a steady erosion of the population, which despite the 1970 annexation decreased about 30,000 by the end of the decade, and when the council fired the white city manager—who subsequently was elected to council—the Times-Dispatch accused it of "raw racism," comparing its majority to "a band of black Bilbos," a reference to the late Mississippi Senator Theodore G. Bilbo, a white supremacist. The more strident afternoon News Leader compared the council's black majority as "monkey-see, money-do leaders of a banana Republic."

Wilder said of the white complaints, "There's always been a feeling that, 'let's not rock the boat.' And I wouldn't want to rock the boat either if it had been going along for me the way it has for them."

The white civic and business leaders "treated us like window washers," complained Councilwoman Claudette B. McDaniel. "Well, I don't wash their windows."

The first breach of the black solidarity on the Council occurred in 1982, when Roy A. West, a black school principal, successfully challenged one of the black incumbents, Willie J. Dell. Marsh had heard that his old friend Wilder was helping West in the campaign, but Marsh said, "I wasn't overly concerned, because West said he was going to be part of the team." Once West was elected, however, the four white council members encouraged him to join with them in forming a new majority. West went to Wilder for advice, who told him that "he shouldn't come away from the situation with nothing." When Wilder heard that West had decided to vote for himself, "I didn't discourage him."

On the day he was sworn in, West's first act was to team up with the white members and dethrone Marsh as mayor, installing himself as his successor.

With that as the extent of his involvement, Wilder was enraged when a national black magazine, Jet, suggested that he had taken West's side against his long-time friend Marsh out of jealousy, because he had run second to Marsh in prominence in the black community. Wilder sued the magazine for ten million dollars, charging that he had been defamed by the suggestion that he had abandoned Marsh. Wilder reportedly accepted a settlement before the case came to trial.

Marsh said he and Wilder have been friends more than rivals over the years. "I never perceived (a rivalry) although some people thought that. I was working in one area, local government, and he was in state politics. I also was involved in a lot of national politics, and Doug wasn't involved in that at all. I never thought of competition. I was working in one sphere and he another, and I was supportive of what he was doing."

WILDER: HOLD FAST TO DREAMS

Marsh said he didn't know why Wilder supported West, who was not well known in political circles, but Marsh said it didn't change his relations with Wilder. "In the struggle that we are in," Marsh said, "we can't let personal feelings interfere with the cause. I would support Doug for governor, even if the rumors had been true. That wouldn't stop me, because I think it is important for blacks to be in those positions. And if he has an opportunity to do it, I'm going to support him."

28. An Independent Threat

Wilder's threatened entry into the 1982 Senate race provoked the most soul-searching and potentially divisive test of Virginia's "new" Democratic party.

As soon as the news broke, Robb summoned Wilder and Pickett to his office, to see if he could resolve the dilemma. But throughout a forty-five minute discussion, "we couldn't seem to get to the specifics" of Wilder's concern, Robb said, although by then the governor appreciated that "you might conclude that it had been impolitic" for Pickett to have invoked Byrd's legacy. It was not an angry meeting, no voices were raised, but nothing was settled. Wilder just repeated that he was "going to have to do what was necessary." Afterwards, the governor emerged grimly and acknowledged that Wilder was "giving very serious consideration" to challenging Pickett. "I think there's simply no resolution of the question at this point," Robb added.

"I haven't backed out of it," Wilder emphasized.

As Wilder stepped up his criticism, Robb and his advisers became concerned that "the Pickett thing," as McCloud called it, "was going backward in terms of the progress the state had made in race relations. It seemed to us there was going to be some sort of Armageddon if this thing didn't get resolved. Robb thought he had to exert some moral leadership, to bring a potentially volatile and disruptive situation back into line."

McCloud said Robb had a number of conversations with Pickett and, despite the governor's public pronouncements, "basically told Owen he wasn't going to be able to endorse him. He told him it would be self-destructive to him and to the party, to what had been built over the past few years in improving race relations in the state. The whole thing would unravel, and that Owen would not want that to be something he would be lastingly remembered for."

It wasn't so much a belief that Wilder was justified in his complaint, McCloud said. A number of Robb's associates "felt Doug had overreacted, that he had gotten himself way out there, but there was pretty widespread agreement that we had a significant problem we had to deal with," McCloud said. "Doug can be a very volatile person, and what we saw was something that started on impulse, in reaction to something that was said, and escalated from there. Maybe I'm naive, but I don't think there was any great Machiavellian scheme. That's not to take anything away from Doug, for he is one of the shrewdest politicians in the state. No question about that."

Cora Tucker, the black activist who ran at the head of a write-in ticket the previous year that Wilder had derided as "a bunch of kamikaze pilots," couldn't resist saying, "maybe Doug's seen the light."

The Republicans, of course, greeted the intra-party blood-letting with glee.

Wilder's saber rattling was prompting even his staunchest white supporters to question his judgment. State Senator Stanley C. Walker of Norfolk said, "Democrats I've talked to think Doug's gone too far this time. He likes the conflict and the contest." Senator Dudley J. (Buzz) Emick Jr., a quick-witted backbencher from rural Botetourt County (pronounced Bot-a-tot), who usually admired Wilder's dramas, said, "Doug's blaming the wrong people here. The real blame should be with the House leadership, not with Robb and Pickett."

Emick worried that Wilder could throw away twelve years of seniority in the Senate.

Not so sympathetic was Senator Abe Brault of Fairfax, who was still smarting from Wilder's role in the coup that had removed him as majority leader two years earlier. "Governor Robb has really gone the last mile in supporting the blacks," Brault said. "It just goes to show, you give somebody an inch and they want two miles. Wilder has been given a mile and now he wants ten miles."

Meanwhile, Pickett's friends were astonished at the level of criticism of their mild-mannered friend, who had posted a moderate voting record and had enjoyed good relations with blacks during his decade in Richmond. "Owen is kind of a victim of some circumstances no one could have foreseen," said his friend and law partner, Glenn R. Croshaw. Pickett's campaign manager, Tim Ridley, complained that the Senate race had become "an occasion for some historic tension in the Democratic party to erupt." Yes, Pickett had voted against a proposed constitutional amendment that would give the District of Columbia full voting representation in Congress—but that was an issue that was going nowhere anyway—and he had cast a deciding vote against a bill, proposed by Delegate Robert C. Scott, a black from Newport News, that would have provided prenatal care for welfare mothers. But those were blemishes on an otherwise progressive record—he favored voter registration by mail, the King holiday bill, extension of the voting rights act, and eliminating tax breaks for all-white private schools, which was more than Robb wanted.

Wilder was unmoved. "Each day that passes gives me more reason to believe that the need for a third party in this race is necessary," he said. He denied that his trial balloon was designed to quell criticism of him by other blacks, and said he was developing "a hit list" of potential contributors. The Afro found support for the idea among its readers and noted that one of Pickett's first actions upon becoming state party chairman had been to abolish the office of minority coordinator. By March 22, Wilder was distributing petitions to get his name on the ballot, saying "this time the numbers may be right" for a liberal to run between two conservatives. And he showed up at the founding meeting of the Congress of Virginia Action, Inc., sporting a pale pink "vote Wilder for U. S. Senate" button. He emerged buoyed from a meeting with former Lieutenant Governor Howell, after which Howell said he was convinced Wilder would become an independent candidate. Wilder also met briefly with the new state party chairman, Alan A. Diamonstein, a Robb core group member who had replaced Pickett.

Robb attempted to downplay the seriousness of Wilder's threat. Although Wilder "would make an excellent United States Senator" and would be "a formidable candidate with party backing," Robb said, because he is "a very practical politician and a very savvy legislator, I don't think Doug Wilder is going to become fully involved in a race that he doesn't think he's got a good chance of winning. And the major obstacle at this point in trying to win a statewide race without party backing." Robb said that while "Virginia is much more enlightened today than it was even a couple of decades ago...as a practical matter, it's still an uphill battle" for a black to win statewide office.

As an independent, Wilder suggested he could put together a coalition of labor, women, teachers and minorities. "If those constituent groups would speak with one voice, there is no way a person could not win."

Picking up on reports that Pickett's lackluster style on the stump was hurting his candidacy, Wilder briefly changed his tune slightly, and suggested that instead of making a third-party bid, he might seek to wrest the Democratic nomination from Pickett. "I'm terribly afraid, whether I run or not, Owen, if the nominee, might not be in position to win the Senate race," said Wilder, momentarily the party loyalist again. "My purpose is to be certain the Democratic Party fields its best candidate and that we go on record showing that the party leadership is not in tune with many of its supporters... maybe it is time for Owen Pickett to consider that he cannot win, and it is time for him to step aside for me." But when the deadline for filing a candidacy for the state convention arrived, Wilder ruled out a challenge for the nomination. "At this late stage," he said, "even though I sense this dissatisfaction with the delegate (Pickett), it would be awfully difficult to mount a serious challenge." However, he predicted that black participation at the convention would be minimal. "I don't think blacks are going to go down there to get hooked into working for a candidate they can't live with." Therefore, he was "more encouraged than ever before" about an independent bid.

With the approach of the mass meetings, which are community gatherings at which convention delegates are selected, a series of behind-the-scene confabs was called to see if the differences could be resolved. Robb, Wilder and Delegate Al Smith, the Robb core group member who was chairman of the House Democratic caucus, met in the governor's office. Wilder convened a summit of black legislators to talk to Philpott, but the Speaker ignored their request, choosing instead to sit in on a meeting of the state crime commission two floors away. "It was obvious he was giving us the back of his hand, that he doesn't have any time for us," said Wilder, adding that there no longer was room in Virginia politics for the likes of Philpott. And at Pickett's instigation, he and Wilder met again, amid speculation that Wilder would propose that they both drop plans to run. Wilder emphasized that he was not personally upset with Pickett, but said a number of blacks were displeased with his record, both in the legislature and as state chairman, and they especially wanted to know what he had in mind mentioning Harry Byrd.

In an effort to address one of Wilder's specific complaints from the recently concluded legislative session, Robb issued an executive order that eliminated the tax deductions for contributions to the segregated academies, accomplishing by fiat what the assembly had been unwilling to do. After announcing that conciliatory gesture, Robb met again with Wilder and tried to convince him to drop his plans for a third-party campaign, conceding that it would clearly cost Picket thousands of votes. But Wilder was steadfast.

George Bowles, a radio commentator and weekly newspaper columnist who saw no need to hide his allegiance to the Democratic party in his writings— his wife, Nancy, was the Goochland County Democratic chairman—wrote that many Democrats were asking, "what does Doug want," a question many white politicos would ask in 1984 and 1988 of Jesse Jackson's presidential aspirations. Bowles suggested that one answer might include better committee assignments for blacks in the legislature, so that the King holiday bill would not be forever sabotaged. But Bowles also said that Wilder's motivation might simply be to win the election—that his campaign was serious—and that continued insensitivity to black aspirations could harm the party. Privately, Bowles also was among the first to tell Robb that Pickett's campaign was a flop. Bowles seldom shied away from offering advice to Robb, be it political or personal—he periodically informed the governor of rumors that Robb and Lynda Bird were on the verge of a divorce, or other untrue tales that were cultivated and circulated by wishful-thinking Robb detractors.

Another columnist, Shelley Rolfe of the Times-Dispatch, observed that Wilder saw himself as a symbol, a voice, for the one-in-five Virginians who are black and that "it may be impossible for a white to appreciate the depth of his feelings."

Black support for Wilder was widespread. Doc Thornton, the co-founder of the Crusade for Voters, said he was prepared to back an independent bid by Wilder. "I think it's possible that he can win," said Thornton. "This is as good a time as any to test the waters." And Mayor Henry Marsh, without committing himself to Wilder, concurred that Wilder "didn't have anything to lose."

At the mid-April mass meetings, Pickett won 1,942 of the 3,500 delegates, 182 more than needed, but Wilder pointed to minimal black participation as further evidence of the lack of enthusiasm for Pickett. Fundraising by Pickett also was below expectations, with his campaign committee reporting only $40,000 at the first deadline, most of that from hometown friends. Paul Goldman, who was becoming more of a player, launched a move for an open convention. "We're on a collision course that is threatening to destroy everything we built up with the Robb victory. There are hundreds of thousands of Democrats out there who want an alternative," Goldman said.

Meanwhile, the unopposed Republican candidate, Congressman Trible, was picking up financial support from defecting Democrats, such as stockbroker S. Buford Scott. But Delegate Bobby Scott said he was not worried about electing Trible over Pickett: "I'd rather have Ronald Reagan than Harry Byrd."

But with more than enough pledged delegates in his pocket to assure his nomination, Pickett set off on a campaign swing. He attempted to address the conservative tag by criticizing President Reagan's economic policies in an appearance before at the Reston Democratic Club. But Pickett's speeches remained wooden, and his reception was lukewarm, to be kind. "I wouldn't characterize him as a boy orator," said Arlington County board member John Milliken after hearing Pickett speak to the Arlington Democrats. A story in The Virginian-Pilot, Pickett's hometown newspaper, damned him with faint praise, as "something less than Gerald Ford on the stump."

As these reports drifted in from the hustings, along with Bowles' observation, Robb for the first time began to view Wilder's minacious challenge as an opportunity rather an obstacle. Perhaps he could use it as a way to ease Pickett out of the nomination, in favor of someone more dynamic, although the governor didn't know who that might be. Wilder would fit that bill—but even if he thought that was a good idea, and he didn't, Robb couldn't afford to appear to be caving in to pressure. Wilder would have to be satisfied with exhibiting that he had the clout to get rid of a candidate.

By late April, with the convention less than six weeks off, Robb gave the first hint that he might back down from his pledge to support Picket "no matter what." In answer to a question at a news conference about the depth of his support for Pickett, the governor said, "I'll have more to say next week," adding, "I'm going to have to seek the advice of Owen Pickett before I make any statement regarding that equation."

On April 28, after Pickett had breakfast with Robb at the mansion, and consulted with party chairman Diamonstein, Seventh District chairman George H. Gilliam and political consultant David Doak, who had been Robb's campaign manager the year before, he announced that he was releasing his delegates from a pledge to support him on the first ballot, setting the stage for an open convention. "I'm inviting any Democrat who has been disillusioned or disappointed with the course of the party to seize this opportunity, challenge me on the issues and challenge the party on its record," Pickett said.

Wilder dismissed Pickett's maneuver as "an empty gesture." The emancipated delegates were established Pickett supporters, Wilder said, and Pickett retained the backing of Robb. "I find it incomprehensible that he would expect me to come to a convention that's stacked like that."

Though derided by Wilder, Pickett's move was praised by Robb, state party chairman Diamonstein, and Goldman, who had just launched his campaign to force an open convention. Goldman denied the committee he planned to form was designed to bring Wilder into the race.

That same day, Wilder also met briefly with Diamonstein, and then huddled for an hour with former Lieutenant Governor Henry Howell, after which a smiling Wilder said, "suffice it to say that I was buoyed." Howell came away convinced that Wilder planned to enter the race as an independent.

29. Lunch at the Club

At the height of concern that Wilder might make a third-party bid for the Senate, Robb contacted Jay Shropshire, the Senate clerk, and asked him to set up a lunch among Wilder and the two legislators who were Robb's closest allies, Delegates Al Smith and Alan A. Diamonstein (Al and Alan, as Robb called them). Diamonstein by then had taken over as state party chairman. The idea was to see if they couldn't resolve the problem before the convention. Shropshire, who is a master of playing more than one side of the street, was viewed by both Robb and Wilder as a trusted ally, and was expected to attend the lunch also.

It was late afternoon when Shropshire was summoned up the two flights of steps from his office to the governor's suite. One of Shropshire's many political skills is knowing where people are at any given moment, or how to find them. He knew that Wilder was at that moment having a drink at the Tobacco Company restaurant, a favorite touristy watering hole in the city's historic Shockhoe Slip district, with Ken Bode, the national political correspondent for NBC, who had made the hundred-mile trek down Interstate 95 from Washington to chat with Wilder about his potential Senate bid. Shropshire raced down the terraced steps of Capitol Square to the restaurant and broke the news to Wilder, who greeted the idea with laughter. If there is anyone in Richmond who loves political intrigue more than Shropshire, or who is better at it, it is Wilder. Bode was given a quick fill in and then Wilder, in an inspired response, said, "sure, tell Chuck I'll do it—but it's got to be at the Commonwealth Club."

They all broke into laughter and ordered another round of drinks. Even an outsider like Bode knew of the reputation of the Commonwealth Club, that bastion of nineteenth-century conservatism that defined waspishness and racism in Richmond. A luncheon there would present a double dilemma for the governor's men, as the club had neither any black or Jewish members, although both Wilder and Diamonstein had dined there in the past as guests of members. Shropshire couldn't wait to finish his drink so he could dart back up the hill, literally skipping up the wide, terraced steps in excitement, to break the news to the governor. It was a warm spring day and Robb was working in his shirt sleeves when Shropshire bounded in with his report. "Mission accomplished," beamed Shropshire, before adding the caveat about the meeting site. "That 'Little Douglas' is something," roared Robb, employing a term of endearment for Wilder he had picked up from Shropshire. "I'll have to talk to Al about this," he added, his laughter spilling out the open window.

Al Smith is a self-made millionaire, "the Tastee-Freez king," whose ice creams stands dot the towns that are sprinkled along the Shenandoah Valley between West Virginia and North Carolina. Shortly after he was elected to the House of Delegates in 1973, Smith learned he had a talent not only for making money, but for raising it—by the time Robb became governor, he was the Democratic party's premiere fund-raiser, whose pockets perpetually bulged with checks and memos about persons to call for a check. Smith is largely self-educated—as one of the few non-college graduates in the assembly he takes great pride in being the legislator responsible for appropriating funds for college construction in Virginia—who enjoys the trappings that money can buy, including membership in the Commonwealth Club. But while he was a member, he was hardly a regular. Smith lacked the cachet: He had only recently become a player in Richmond, with the election of Robb. Before that he was a rural legislator who chewed toothpicks, occasionally used poor grammar and confided that he never cheated on his wife for fear it might be like how he felt after he missed his first Rotary meeting—once he had done it, perfect attendance no longer seemed so important.

When Robb called Smith in Winchester to tell him of Wilder's proviso, Smith didn't blanch. He had been at the Commonwealth Club before with Wilder, in one of the small, private dining rooms on the second floor that offered just the privacy that the topic, and the guest, warranted. But when Smith called in the morning to make the reservation, none of the private rooms was available, having all previously been booked. But there was no time to make other plans, he had to hop on the private plane that was taking him to Richmond.

Wilder had asked Shropshire to tell his hosts he would pick them up at the Capitol and drive them the fourteen blocks to the club. Shortly before noon, Wilder met Shropshire outside the Capitol, and was told that Smith and Diamonstein were at the governor's mansion, which is located at the eastern edge of the Capitol Square complex. Smith had walked over there to discuss the progress of the commission that was raising private funds to refurbish the 170-year-old executive residence. Wilder pulled his 1973 Mercedes-Benz sedan into the circular driveway and Smith and Diamonstein got in the back seat.

After exchanging greetings, Wilder drove west on Grace Street through downtown toward the club. "Where are we going?" asked Smith. "I thought we were going to the Commonwealth Club," said Wilder. "Oh, no," explained Smith, "I couldn't get us a room." About then, Wilder was turning his car left turn onto Monroe Street, and the club was just one block away, on Franklin Street. "Well, we won't have a problem, with all the people we both know we'll be able to get a room," Wilder assured the others. He knew the club well: Not only had he been there as a guest a couple times, but he had worked there as a waiter and his friend Bobby Dandridge was the bartender in the lower level grill room. "No problem," Wilder continued. Shropshire, sitting next to Wilder, glimpsed the trace of a grin sneak across Wilder's face. Neither Diamonstein nor Shropshire said a word, as Wilder slowed to pull his car into the club's parking lot.

"We can't do this," said Smith.

"Do what?" answered Wilder, adding, "we can always get a table" in the men's grill, which didn't require reservations.

"No, I am not going to do that," blurted out Smith, who had never eaten in the informal, paneled grill room on the lower level, an inner-sanctum in which he was not comfortable. Furthermore, he understood that blacks were not admitted there. "I'm not going to spend the rest of my life apologizing to my friends for carrying you all in there."

"OK, forget it," snapped Wilder, jamming his foot hard on the accelerator. "We'll go to *my* club." He swung the big Mercedes right onto Main Street, made another right turn onto Belvidere Street, and sped north toward the Jefferson-Lakeside Country Club. No one spoke about the incident during the fifteen-minute trip to the club, just north of the city in Henrico County. Instead, they engaged in idle chatter, and listened to Wilder explain that he had joined the traditionally Jewish club about three years earlier, as its first black member.

As they entered the nearly empty dining room, they encountered Sydney and Frances Lewis, wealthy benefactors of the arts and politics (he founded the Best Products discount stores) who were regulars at the club. The four politicians chatted briefly with the Lewises, and Smith and Diamonstein listened anxiously as Wilder said he was still considering a candidacy, and that he would make a final decision Wednesday, after conferring over the weekend with black leaders around the state. Wilder, Smith, Diamonstein and Shropshire then ate lunch, during which they continued a general discussion of Wilder's plans, and how Smith and Diamonstein thought it would hurt the party. But no one mentioned the incident at the club.

Robb learned about it from Diamonstein and Shropshire, who called him that night from Roanoke, where they had gone for a meeting immediately after Wilder dropped them off at the Capitol after lunch. Diamonstein placed the call, which interrupted a family dinner with Lady Bird Johnson, but when Robb came on the line, Diamonstein was so flustered that he handed the phone to Shropshire, telling the governor, "Jay will tell you what happened."

The next day, the story was all over town, with News Leader political writer Tyler Whitley recounting it under the headline, "Lunch With Wilder Backfires Over Club Incident." It quoted Wilder as saying Smith "still feels blacks are an embarrassment. It is ironic that Smith says it is in the best interests of the party for me not to run, when he clearly is exemplifying what he stands for."

Apprised of Wilder's comments, Smith responded, "this is awful. I told Doug yesterday it looked like he was trying to make a campaign of blacks against whites....Blacks and whites have been getting along exceedingly well in Virginia. It hurts me to see him doing this to the commonwealth of Virginia." Smith admitted that he refused to take Wilder to the grill room, saying "there are rules and regulations, and it's a private club." A club spokesman confirmed that all of the private rooms were booked that day, but said there was no rule prohibiting blacks from eating in the basement grill.

The feud escalated the next day, with Wilder saying he was hurt and disappointed at Smith's refusal to take him to the club, and Smith angrily firing back, accusing Wilder of setting up the incident to help solidify black and liberal support. "He wants to make it an issue and he's made it an issue," said Smith, who was feeling "about as low as I've ever been" by what he said was Wilder's attempt to use him. "He ought to apologize to me," Smith said. "The people that he's hurting the most," Smith went on, "are the governor and himself." Smith said Robb had done more than any governor to appoint blacks to jobs at all levels of state government and to support legislation of importance to blacks. "The governor's bent over backwards...and Doug Wilder's slapping him in the face," Smith said.

Robb said Smith "felt betrayed. He was badly shaken. He felt he was used. Set up and used, and you don't do that to Al without destroying a relationship. I thought Al over-reacted. But he felt he was set up. I could probably agree that it may not have been a set up, but he felt it to his core."

Robb agreed with Smith's premise that "it would have caused comment within the grill. Al felt he was losing face to be put in that situation. Al is an honest man. You don't have to agree with him or with his priorities, but he has a fundamental value system, and he was being pushed against his will. Al was acting according to his own instincts, and he didn't think he could do it. If it's not right in here (pointing to his gut) with Al, he has trouble doing it." But even if Wilder were "doing a little mischief," Robb said, "I was disappointed with the way Al took it."

Wilder agreed with Robb that Smith overreacted, "and in the process, he had to reach into himself to find what he is, and what he was, and to be confronted with that. That's the difficulty even now."

Sa'ad El-Amin jumped into the fray, twitting Wilder that blacks "have issues that are much more topical and important to us" than admission to an all-white club.

Wilder said the incident did not affect his decision about the Senate race, although "it underscored all that I've been saying all along." If anything, however, "it emboldened me. It said, 'go ahead.' It had nothing to do with the future. I say this to so many young people who are interested in going to politics. Those jobs are not yours forever. You do what you can to while you are there. I had no thought about what would happen to me, with reference to the party, with reference to my career in politics, or anything else. It wasn't important. The important thing was for me to do what I had to do on that occasion. When the thing is right, the time is right," he said, invoking a favorite expression.

By then, he said, the only thing that could stop him from running was if Pickett got out, although he insisted that he wasn't trying to cut a deal.

Both Wilder and Smith remain bitter about the incident.

Wilder resented the accusation that he wanted to embarrass Smith, and when he thinks about it, the conversation turns ugly. Had he had wanted to set Smith up, Wilder rambled, "the little bit of embarrassment associated with this would be nothing compared to the recompense I would demand....Because I believe it should be total. If I was going to set up...(laughing). This isn't any payback or anything. It bothered me on so many occasions when people said, 'Al Smith is still angry with you about what you've done with him.' I have never lifted a finger at him. Had I lifted that finger, it wasn't going to stay in the air forever. It was going to fall. I am not a hipshooter as such. I don't miss the mark. He hasn't done anything to me. When he said what he said, I felt he didn't say you, he said you all, he didn't want 'us' (Wilder and Diamonstein) to be there with him for his friends to see us. He disserved himself, no question about it. It's a clear illustration that times never change, people do."

Since then, Wilder said, Smith has attempted to make amends, and volunteered to raise money for Wilder in the 1989 campaign. Wilder said Smith even offered to take him to lunch at the Commonwealth Club "and we'll sit anywhere you want." They have not gotten together at the club, Wilder said, because Smith has never set up a specific date. If they do, Wilder said, "it will have to be genuine, rather than artificial, rather than to say, 'hey, press, guess what we're going to do.'"

"The Commonwealth Club is behind us," Smith said. "I'm for Doug Wilder being a member of the Commonwealth Club. That would be a wonderful thing. I would never in my life, never, ever....That to me is over. Past."

After Wilder was elected lieutenant governor, several members of the Commonwealth Club approached him about joining, saying they would sponsor him, even though the club did not yet have any black members. (The club accepted its first black member, a Republican dentist, in late 1988.)

Wilder said he would not foreclose the possibility. "You don't turn anything down out of hand," he said. "You just don't say 'no' for the heck of it." But his busy schedule had prevented him from "using the minimum" at Jefferson-Lakeside. In the meantime, he became a fairly regular guest at the club, lunching there a couple times a month with his chief aide, Joel Harris, who is a member.

If he waits long enough, he points out with a smile, he might not have to be invited: the club traditionally offers membership to the governor.

30. Pickett's Retreat

Governor Robb, who had said little publicly about the incident at the Commonwealth Club, used the occasion of a commencement speech at Virginia Union University, with Wilder on the podium at his alma mater, to send a message to whites: "The persistence of old attitudes among those who still hold them should prompt serious introspection," the governor said, adding that "the well-publicized events of the last two weeks are of deep personal concern to me. The anger and frustration of those who are understandably and acutely sensitive to the injustices of the past are responses at once legitimate and alarming."

Embracing the state's long history of segregation threatens to "reverse the course of progress" and "damage irreparably" the pattern his administration was attempting to establish, Robb said. All people should be judged on "merit and ability, not on race and heritage," the governor told the audience of 400, who gave him a standing ovation.

In addition to the incident at the club, Robb was referring to House Speaker A. L. Philpott's reference to four black delegates as "boys" the week before. The delegates had met with Philpott to express concern that the Democratic leadership in the House was insensitive to black concerns. Later that day, at the annual shad planking in Wakefield, Philpott said he had assuaged their concerns. "I've never had any problems with those boys. They understand the system," Philpott said.

While tempers flared over the remark, Wilder downplayed its significance, accepting the explanation that Philpott often referred to members of the House, white and black, as "boys." Although Philpott may have been misunderstood, Wilder said, "the difficulty was that he said there was ab-so-lutee-ly no problem, and that they (the black delegates) understood the system. In other words, that they were almost eunuchs. They weren't going to cause any trouble and there wasn't going to be any trouble." What rankled Wilder was the idea that the black legislators should "sit there, not abused at all by what has gone on."

The weekend of Robb's graduation speech was also the beginning of the end for Owen Pickett's campaign for the Senate, as Pickett's aides acknowledged for the first time that the party was looking for an alternative candidate.

One name being floated was that of Lieutenant Governor Richard Davis, who Wilder said "could pull together the people I've talked to." But Davis' aide, Bobby Watson, said, "under no circumstances is Dick interested in running for the U. S. Senate. He has endorsed Owen Pickett and continues to support him wholeheartedly," which turned out to be the Virginia equivalent of presidential candidate George McGovern's pledges of one thousand percent support for Senator Thomas Eagleton of Missouri for vice president a decade earlier.

As Picket wavered, he and Sydney Kellam, his Virginia Beach political mentor, met with Robb for a final time at the governor's mansion, in a grim, forty-minute session during which Robb told Pickett that if he decided to stay in race, he would stick with him. But it was clear that Robb also would welcome a withdrawal. "The numbers just don't work out," in a three-way race, Robb told Pickett. Kellam said Robb added, "If you get out, I don't believe that he (Wilder) will run as an independent." Wilder and Delegate Benny Lambert also met with Robb at the mansion over the weekend, after which Wilder announced that he would reveal his decision two days later.

But Pickett pre-empted that by quitting the next day, May 4, abruptly issuing a press release that said, "There may be others more able to unify the Democratic party and reassemble the coalition that contributed so mightily to last year's success." With that, Pickett went fishing. "Swamped in a storm of Democratic infighting," wrote Times-Dispatch political writer Dale Eisman, Pickett "went sailing on calmer waters in the Atlantic," ending a campaign by a quiet, lackluster legislator that had been implausible from the beginning. "Unless you are completely heartless," opined Eisman, "it is hard not to feel a bit sorry" for Pickett, whose crime, in addition to being about as inept a speaker as Robb, was refusing to apologize for saying, not that he would vote as Byrd did, or stand for what Byrd stood for, but only he would follow his example of independent thought and action, and "not walk in lockstep with any administration, be it Democrat or Republican."

"Owen was the victim of a very irrational attack," complained his law partner, Glenn R. Croshaw. "What Wilder has done is to take out the most electable candidate the party has. I don't plan to get angry, but to get even with him (Wilder)."

Within hours of what editorialists around the state inevitably dubbed "Pickett's Retreat," Wilder called reporters to the Capitol and announced that he would not run as an independent, but the man who had held the party hostage with threats for weeks announced he would be available if the party wanted him as its nominee.

"My concern is presently with the Republican nominee," said the suddenly partisan Wilder. Nonetheless, Wilder called for the formation of a campaign "war chest" for progressive candidates at congressional and legislative levels in that year's and future elections, and suggested that blacks convene a statewide, nonpartisan convention to "explore not only the issues that affect us, but also the establishment of permanent measures to meet the financial needs and obligations of black statewide congressional candidates."

He praised Pickett's courage for withdrawing and Robb for cutting "the Gordian knot" and reaffirming "his personal commitment" to issues of concern to blacks. Wilder took credit for brokering a new, decisive role for blacks in the party. "I am certain that our cause will no longer be pooh-poohed and ignored the way they were before...the myth has been exploded" that the party can automatically count on black votes. While some warned he had destroyed the successful coalition that had brought Robb to office, Wilder said, "coalitions change," recalling that "disgruntled Democrats, labor and blacks" had helped elect Republican governors Holton and Godwin.

Wilder said later that some people thought he was bluffing, but that they didn't know him. He said Robb knew him "and he knew that I wasn't bluffing." Had Pickett not withdrawn, "there would have been three of us running. There was no theoretical consideration. When I tell you something, I'm going to do it. The worst thing you can do is not follow through on our word. That's why I don't believe in threats. I was prepared to run. I wasn't flexing muscle."

As for suggestions that his candidacy would have wrecked the party's chance that year, Wilder said, "I was trying to bring about an understanding that what we were going to put together was a winning combination, not for just one six-year term, or for another six-year term, but for a long time to come. And I think we've seen that development.

Later in the day, in a speech before his fellow Prince Hall masons, Wilder said blacks "are not seen and seldom heard from" and "that's not the way democracy should work. If you wait for the lights and similar colors to meet, that time may not come. Things that have gone on before" in the history of blacks "have been lost because we threw up our hands and said, all is well. I don't care how you look at it, things will change because we'll make them change. Our star is on the horizon, and we've got to believe that and seize the time. We have to deal with the mechanism to make things happens." After the Supreme Court decision in 1954, "we thought that was the end of our problem. That was twenty-eight years ago...and all that deliberate speed is still being deliberate. We thought to get a black man in robes and put him on the Supreme Court, our problem would be over." Justice Thurgood Marshall "is a giant in our time," but he is "a lonely figure" on the bench.

Robb issued a statement praising Pickett's withdrawal as "an unparalleled act of political courage." And he paid tribute to Wilder as "one of the brightest and ablest members of the General Assembly" who has "proven again, as he had repeatedly throughout his distinguished career in public service, that he is a loyal Democrat who places principle above personal ambition....He has used his talents (as orator) to raise the public consciousness."

Wilder and Pickett both insisted that no deal had been cut, but Wilder made it clear that Robb had a hand in Pickett's withdrawal, which in turn led to his own. In their private session, Robb temporarily abandoned his Sunday school vocabulary and asked Wilder if he would "quit all this bullshit" if Pickett stepped down, to which Wilder answered, "absolutely."

As for the convention a month away, Wilder conceded it would be cynical to offer himself as a candidate, considering the role he had played. But if party leaders came to him, he might consider. Wilder discounted suggestions that his actions already had assured that droves of white voters would switch to the Republicans in the fall.

He was still open to a draft, he said, but "I have never known persons, should I say of my 'persuasion,' to be drafted for anything" in politics, he laughed. But he remained optimistic, quoting George Bernard Shaw, "You see things and you say why? But I dream things that never were, and I say why not?"

Whether Wilder won or lost in the long run was problematic, but there was little disagreement that he had demonstrated power never before exhibited by a black in Virginia politics.

Law professor and federal judge-to-be J. Harvie Wilkinson observed, "It is the first time ever in Virginia's Twentieth century history that a prominent black official has altered the entire course of one of Virginia's major parties." Wilkinson pointed out that under pressure from Wilder, Robb had issued pronouncements unheard since Holton's days as governor. At the shad planking, Robb warned of a "long, hot summer" from prolonged unemployment of black youth; he had signed an emergency order denying tax exemptions to all-white academies; and at Virginia Union deplored "the persistence of old attitudes" on race.

Wilder had "achieved something Harry Byrd never did; he stopped a political party from naming its candidate. He was at the pinnacle of his power," said Senate clerk Jay Shropshire.

"He danced through the hoop with the fire going again, and came out without a hair singed on his Afro," said an admiring Senator Buzz Emick, who thought the entire episode had been "a stimulant for the party."

His power was such, said Lain O'Ferrall, that "if I was going to run for governor in four years, I'd be taking Doug to lunch once a week in the basement of the Commonwealth Club." The selection process certainly will be changed. "I don't think we're going to have a handpicked candidate again."

At the moment Pickett withdrew, said W. Roy Smith, "Doug Wilder reached a pinnacle of power that very few people ever have in state politics. He completely changed the course of a political party." Smith, the conservative former delegate from Petersburg who had gotten along so well with Wilder the year before, when they both were backing Robb, expressed sorrow that "one faction of the Democratic Party got what amounts to veto power over the party's nominee for the U. S. Senate." Smith, who was particularly angry about the governor's comments about "the persistence of old attitudes" in his speech at Virginia Union, also thought Robb "has been damaged in the eyes of many people."

Wilder's victory, if that's what it was, was not without cost. He infuriated many, such as Roy Smith, forever, and perhaps also Al Smith and Alan Diamonstein. And he sacrificed a decent man, Pickett, for his own political end. Even Benny Lambert conceded, Pickett was "a victim of circumstance." "People up here who tend to be very concerned with black rights think Wilder's been hurt," said Mary Cahill of the Tenth District. "What a shaft," said another district chairman.

While Wilder's ploy established him as a real power in the party, because he had clearly manipulated black voters, it tended to reinforce the view that he was a black power. There also was the view among whites, and particularly those who supported Pickett, that Wilder could not be trusted, because he had been involved in the selection of Pickett, and then doublecrossed him when it was to his advantage.

Richmond Mayor Henry Marsh was not sure if he would have backed Wilder. "It wouldn't have been automatic. It probably would have depended on whether he had a reasonable chance of winning. I wouldn't have supported him just because he was running. Because it was important that we keep that seat in the liberal or moderate column."

Paul Goldman said if he had been in a position to make a recommendation—and he insists he was not yet that close to Wilder—he would have discouraged his candidacy. "I didn't think Doug could win a three-way race. Unfortunately, he would have been labeled the black candidate. He would have a better chance in a two-way race. But I wasn't suggesting that either. That isn't to say if he went into that race, I wouldn't have supported him."

Certainly, Goldman liked what he saw of Wilder that year. "He always stood up. He didn't blink first," which is important because "so much of politics is perception, what people think you may do."

After both Pickett and Wilder withdrew, a reflective Robb said he came out of it all "battered and bruised, yes; defeated, no....The real danger was not so much that the Democratic party would lose an election because, regrettably, we've lost elections before and we've survived and put things back together. The concern was that we were about to divide along essentially racial lines in a way that would have set the Commonwealth of Virginia back decades in terms of the relatively good race relations that have been developed and the progress that has been made."

Wilder objected to the governor's suggestion that a campaign among himself, a white Democrat and a white Republican would have polarized voters along racial lines and given the state a black eye beyond its borders. "I think people in Virginia resent that attitude," Wilder said. "The people I've had contact with say that I could have won a three-way race" and would have had substantial white support. Robb's comments were "a put-down of black aspirations." Wilder said it was "almost like saying, 'little brown brother, I'll let you know your time.' I'm damn tired of being talked to like that."

Despite the rhetoric, Robb didn't think the flap hurt his relations with Wilder. On the contrary, "because he got credit for running Owen out of the race, I think that strengthened our relationship. That was the first time he was getting credit for showing muscle." Robb was irritated about Wilder's threat to bolt from the party, but he was not inclined to push that, once the matter was resolved.

By mid-summer, Republicans were whispering that Wilder was virtually running state government, according to a George Bowles column. They attempted to plant the idea that the Democratic party had "surrendered to liberal—read black—domination," Bowles wrote. "The fact is," Bowles concluded, "that Wilder's awesome power exists only in the minds of those who, to paraphrase a sentiment from a bygone day, believe that one drop of black influence equals black domination."

Wilder's muscle-flexing caught notice beyond Virginia. His antics were front-page news in The Baltimore Sun that summer, where the headline described him as a "black heavyweight" and power broker. Reporter Fred Barnes wrote that Wilder "is the most influential black politician in Virginia—ever. And he may be the most influential black politician in the entire South." Wilder got there, the newspaper pointed out, "by helping elect a governor, vetoing a Senate candidate, helping oust a mayor—his friend Henry Marsh—and getting dozens of top jobs for blacks. And he is talking about statewide office in 1985."

State Senator Joseph V. Gartlan Jr. of Fairfax, however, found it unlikely Wilder could win. "The reality is that a black, especially in a two-person race, would have a very difficult time."

Wilder was upbeat. "Virginia has changed," he told Barnes. "I'm optimistic that it will change more. I've found that if you just persevered and never lost sight of your goal, you picked up allies. The change has come because more and more whites have helped. Any black who says change has been made by themselves isn't right."

While he felt compelled to express his outrage as a black, about the incident at the club, and Speaker Philpott's use of the word "boys," it was also time to rise above being black, he said.

In a reflective interview with Margie Fisher of the Roanoke Times and World-News, he launched into the kind of soliloquy that had awed his contemporaries in the Senate. "Life is like land. You either plow new ground or you watch the weeds grow. I would like to believe if ever you had the opportunity to get the type of exposure you needed to bring in a direct confrontation with the people, that you could dispel some of the fears, the false fears" that all blacks are "great liberals, give-away spenders."

Thinking of his childhood, he said, "we were poor, but ours was a gentle poverty. There's not a soul in my family who's ever known what a welfare check was—not that I disdain that—but we were poor people. I wasn't reared in an atmosphere of affluence, of giving, of waste. The family was geared to a basic conservatism and a lot of it has rubbed off on me. I don't believe in wasting money. I don't believe in giving money away. And I don't cotton to the theory that you're a liberal because you vote for social issues."

One of his major gripes about Pickett was that he thought he had to "wrap himself in the Byrd mystique" to prove that he was conservative. "Little" Harry Byrd is "one of the most gentlemanly persons you've ever known. His gentlemanly forbearance is almost overwhelming." Yet because of his association with massive resistance, "I don't know a name that evokes more evil" for blacks.

"This magnolia mentality has got to be broken. Too many minds are just closed to accepting that a black might win." It's not just whites, he said. He also faulted blacks who think they can't win. "We can't wait until we have twenty percent or twenty-five percent or forty percent of the voters before black candidates are elected." While there were some "under the table and behind closed door" assumptions that he couldn't win, "I submit to you that is not true. You're going to have a certain amount of people who are racist, who are not going to vote for a black. Period. However, that is not as large a group of persons in Virginia as some would like to believe."

He carried with him a letter that he had received from a white jail inmate, written on toilet paper, warning him to stay in his place. But he gets more letters of encouragement, "from persons who are not black, who are not liberal, and in some instances, who are not Democrats. These people felt of three persons they saw at the time—that I would provide the better representation in Washington. That I wouldn't pander to what was popular at the time, but rather, would speak their convictions. So it makes you believe it's possible.

"I know that it's somewhat anathema in conservative Virginia for a black person to even consider that he could represent a state" with an overwhelming white, conservative population. "But I really believe that the time is past when the hue and color of a person's skin should be considered. Unfortunately, people must be made to recognize the qualifications and capabilities and the merits of individuals, short of color, religion, race. It is necessary to open the minds of people to the high possibility of the individual, the development of it. And it's never going to be developed if it's short-changed by self-imposed or falsely imposed restrictions in terms of race, sex and age."

He hearkened back to his first election, saying people said it was futile. and to his attack on the state song. "They say, 'he done it now, he dared to talk about singing that song. We don't do that in Virginia. We don't trample on them things, boy.'"

He complained about "phony restrictions" placed on certain groups of people. "They still say blacks don't do this, women don't do this. Catholics don't do this, Jews don't do this. We have to get away from this foolishness."

Pickett's Retreat

To replace Pickett, the Democrats nominated a reluctant Lieutenant Governor Davis. It was hardly a united party that left the convention to do battle with Trible. With no campaign organization in place, Davis raised money for his filing fee by passing the hat among delegates as they left the convention. By the end of June, Trible had about a million dollars for the campaign and Davis had five thousand.

On the campaign trail, Davis encountered a lot of anti-black sentiment, including remarks about "the nigger." He walked out of a meeting with a potentially large contributor because of his repeated use of the word. But the comments usually were anti-black in general rather than anti-Wilder, said his aide, Bobby Watson. Davis lost to Trible by about thirty-five thousand votes, or two percentage points, and when it was over, Davis felt he had wasted six months of his life. He had gone from the being the party's most likely nominee for governor in 1985 to a loser, an also-ran.

Campaigning for Davis in the fall, Wilder spoke to blacks about the need for them to increase their participation in elective politics. With newly established single-member legislative districts, he challenged, "I'd like to see young blacks standing in line like shark's teeth; when we lose one, someone else would fall in line. We need to establish the discipline....It would be a beautiful thing to see." Blacks are not monolithic, however. "We have a mutual respect...but we don't sign any oaths in blood that we are not going to disagree."

Speaking to a predominantly black congregation in Roanoke, he said that while blacks "have come a long way, we yet we have not turned the corner." He longs for the day, he said, when "the color of your skin is no more important than the color of your shoes, and your religion is no more important than what you had for breakfast in the morning....Equal opportunity is all I ask for," he said to the gathering, which included some white politicians. "If you can't give me that, stay out of my way." Cherish the past, he said, noting that he had met a young man who didn't know what a poll tax was. "Remind them that what we have was not won so easily. We fought for it, and some of us died for it."

31. Welcome to the Club

People started taking Wilder seriously after the Pickett affair, and the Senate debacle. He was, in the words of Davis' aide, Bobby Watson, "one of the most powerful politicians in Virginia, without a doubt," a full member of the ruling political club.

After being the only black in the Senate for more than a dozen years, Wilder was joined in 1983 by Bobby Scott, who moved over from the House. Scott eked out a victory in a special election, called to replace Republican Herbert H. Bateman, who had been elected to Congress from the First Congressional District, filling the seat vacated by the new United States Senator, Paul Trible. Scott's election signaled more than just the arrival of the second black to the Senate. It marked the first time that a black had been elected to the Virginia General Assembly in a predominantly white district. As political scientist Larry Sabato pointed out, Scott's victory was "exceptional, not just for Virginia, but pretty important for Southern politics," and it was accomplished by "an exceptional candidate." Scott, a physician's son who was educated at Groton and Harvard, beat a white city councilman by 2,600 votes in a district that was 70 percent white.

Scott provided the blueprint for Wilder, or any black candidate, who hoped to succeed with a majority white electorate: He campaigned hardest and longest in white precincts, confident that black voters would turn out for him in large numbers and that they would be understanding if he didn't spent a lot of time wooing them. "There's no way in 1983 or 1984 that you can suggest to people that race ought to be an issue and not have it backfire," Scott said. "Unless the district has a seventy-five percent black population, you've got to run a credible campaign across the city."

In April of 1983, Wilder announced he would seek a fourth four-year term in the state Senate and he used the occasion to discuss the political gains he and other blacks had made in state government. He was then chairman of the Senate Transportation Committee and widely recognized as part of the chamber's leadership, a role that he said he had achieved through a combination of forming coalitions and seniority. He admitted that when he was elected in 1969, "I was perhaps as naive as anyone could be. I thought you went to committee meetings and voted on bills and that was it." But he quickly learned of "the intrigues, the factions—things they don't give classes in....There is nothing like preparation. You need to know who's going to be on whose side before you get into a battle." Over the years, he found that "resistance to change is not as cast in concrete as it one was....(but) like quicksand, you can take a step forward, but you have to take the next one. By no means can we back up."

Wilder was ambivalent about the Robb administration. He praised the governor for appointing black judges "from the lowest level to the highest" and for naming blacks from Cabinet level to boards and commissions, "where none has previously served." Speaking at a predominantly black business fair, he said "we have blacks in on the running of the third floor (the governor's office) like never before." Yet he was "flabbergasted, dumbfounded" by the choice of former delegate W. Roy Smith, a Byrd loyalist, to serve on Robb's budget steering committee, although it should have come as no surprise, given Smith's fundraising role in Robb's campaign. It was "an offense to blacks," Wilder said, and proof that Robb believed he "had to be good to the old fellows."

Wilder's intuitive political radar was busy scanning the horizon for potential opponents, should he decide to seek statewide office in 1985, and one of the bleeps that came on his screen was emitted by Mary Sue Terry, who was elected to the House of Delegates in 1977 one of two women lawyers elected that year, the other being Elise Heinz of Arlington, whose shrill demands for passage of the Equal Rights Amendment and other feminist causes may have helped the soft-spoken Terry be more acceptable to the overwhelmingly white, male legislature.

In her first try for office, the thirty-year-old Terry led a ticket that included House majority leader A. L. Philpott, a lawyer from Bassett who had been representing the district since 1957. She led the ticket again when she was re-elected in 1979 and even in 1981, after Philpott had been elevated by his peers to Speaker of the House.

Terry was one of three overachieving daughters of Nate and Nannie Ruth Terry, who operated the Southern States co-operative in Critz, a crossroads town in Patrick County. Their proud parents placed plaques on the bedroom doors identifying the girls' respective rooms: Mary Sue Terry, attorney general, slept here; Ruth Terry, CPA, slept here, and Sally Ann Terry, Ph.D slept here. Mary Sue practiced law and was the assistant commonwealth's attorney in the two-lawyer prosecutor's office in Patrick County before she ran for the legislative seat, which was vacant as the result of a retirement.

Terry quickly established herself as a solid conservative. In her first term, she was in the minority in voting against Medicaid funding for abortions, providing state funds for administrative aid to local welfare boards, identifying the party affiliation of candidates on the ballot, allowing voters in Northern Virginia to decide if they wanted to impose a regional sales tax to help build Washington's subway system, and allowing voters statewide to decide whether they wanted parimutuel betting. That same year, Wilder voted on the opposite side of all those issues.

In 1979, the Carter administration, reportedly at the suggestion of Lieutenant Governor Robb, offered her the position of United States attorney for the western section of Virginia, but she turned it down.

By 1982, after the legislature had established single-member districts, the conservative Terry, like the liberal Wilder, was looking ahead to statewide office, and had begun to moderate her views. She began supporting the Equal Rights Amendment, and state funding of abortions for victims or rape and incest, saying she switched positions after a survey showed her constituents favored those issues.

The first rumbling that Terry might run for attorney general in a couple years was heard shortly after she was elected to the legislature. "It didn't emanate from me, and it didn't emanate directly from Chuck (Robb)," she said, "but there was speculation during my first term that I might run at the time that Jerry Baliles ran," in 1981. One of the things she had going for her was that she had been a law school classmate of Governor Robb's at the University of Virginia in the early seventies.

As if to validate Terry's potential, by the summer of 1983, Wilder was firing pot shots at her. Robb had appointed her chairman of a thirty-three member

Governor's Task Force to Combat Drunk Driving, whose recommendations included raising the age for buying beer from nineteen to twenty-one, which already was the minimum age for wine and liquor purchases, and setting a blood alcohol content of one-tenth of one percent as automatic proof of guilt of driving under the influence of alcohol (DUI). During the 1983 legislative session, he opposed the DUI bill, saying that as a criminal defense attorney, he thought it "smacks of unconstitutionality. I can't think of another circumstance in the law" in which a defendant is not able to rebut charges. "There is no need to have a trial. The commission is saying we will be judge and jury." He dismissed the entire task force as "political puffery" and added that "to the governor's credit, he didn't endorse this hogwash." He also abetted opponents of Terry's bill to raise the drinking age when it came before the Rehabilitation and Social Services Committee, which he chaired.

By the summer of 1983, Wilder was back in a familiar pose, talking about running for statewide office, for the United States Senate again, this time against Republican John W. Warner in 1984. That might be "a very good time (for a black) to test the water," he said. "I'd love to be in the U. S. Senate. No question about it, the place was tailor-made for me," he said mischievously. "If I'm not going to run soon, why should I stay in politics and play the Pied Piper?" Wilder told one of his favorite sounding boards, Margie Fisher of the Roanoke Times and World-News.

It should have come as no surprise when Wilder finally decided to run for statewide office. For a dozen years, he had talked about quitting the state Senate and running for virtually every other public office in the state. And it wasn't all self promotion: As early as 1972, he was being mentioned in print as a possible candidate for lieutenant governor.

In July, 1975, in a wide-ranging interview with Bill Baskerville of the Associated Press, Wilder said that although he was not actively thinking about it, he could envision running for governor in 1977. He also hinted that he might run for the United States Senate in 1978 against William L. Scott.

The congressional seat from the third district, which included Richmond and its suburbs and was then occupied by his next-door neighbor, Democrat David Satterfield, "in my judgment, cannot be won by a black," Wilder said. "It would be an exercise in futility. I have consigned the district to being so racist that you could just not do it. There are people who just don't believe blacks have any business living, much less aspiring to high office."

He had no interest at all in running for attorney general. "None. It's not my cup of tea. I don't consider the attorney general's office a stepping stone, as others might find it. I just don't want to be attorney general."

As for lieutenant governor, it is "a rather vacuous position. You just rap the gavel and do what a page for the most part could do."

In response to a question about whether he might someday run for governor, he said, "there are so many deep-seated prejudices that we're not going to get over. Let's not kid ourselves." Nonetheless, he was pleased that the question had come up. He told Baskerville that it was the first time anyone had ever asked him about running for the number one spot. "It's always been put to me for lieutenant governor. Why stop there? If people will elect you lieutenant

WILDER

L. Douglas Wilder acknowledges cheers upon his
nomination for governor at the Democratic state convention in Richmond in June, 1989

Douglas and his sister, Agnes, in front of their house on Church Hill; playing with piglets in the back yard, and senior class picture, Armstrong High, class of 1947

Singing with the band at
Camp Breckinridge,
Kentucky; at the front in
Korea, and Bronze Star
citation

Douglas and his mother "Miss Beulah" Wilder, at the family homestead on Church Hill

With wife Eunice and children Larry, Loren and Lynn, and at the state Capitol

Senators J. D. Hagood of Clover and M. M. Long of Wise greet their newest colleague (above) and with Republican Governor A. Linwood Holton

An early black caucus, with Dr. William Ferguson Reid, first black member of the House of Delegates since Reconstruction (left), and expressing mutual vexation with Delegate A. L. Philpott during a Democratic state central committee meeting in 1977

The Dude

Top: Delegate Alan Diamonstein, who also was the state Democratic chairman, and Wilder emerge from meeting in governor's office at the time of Wilder's threatened independent candidacy for United States Senate in 1982. At left, with Jesse Jackson in 1983. Above, law school roommate and former Richmond Mayor Henry Marsh

A newspaper poll in 1985 ranked Wilder fifth most effective senator, and his Richmond colleague Ed Willey number one.

After dethroning Owen Pickett, the Democratic leaders' choice for the United States Senate

The winning 1985 Democratic ticket, nominees Wilder, Gerald L. Baliles and Mary Sue Terry, was called "too cute by one," and "too much of a rainbow." Left, Wilder's opponent, state Senator John H. Chichester. Right, Campaign sticker

I'M WILD ABOUT
WILDER
LT. GOV. '85

Rundown rowhouse on Church Hill owned by candidate Wilder was subject of complaints by neighbors and city officials

A statewide auto tour, with stops at country stores and small towns, was credited with breaking down racial barriers in 1985 campaign

Closest advisers are Senate clerk J. T. Shropshire (left), chief of staff Joel Harris (right) and campaign consultant Paul Goldman (below)

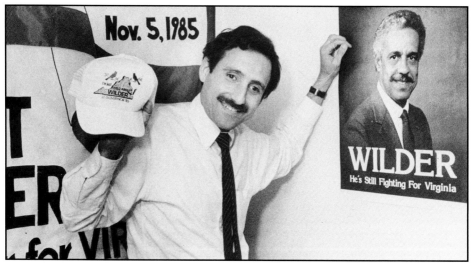

Attorney Jackie Epps (center), grassroots fundraiser and sometimes companion, and a potential donor, Carol Wellons of Thor, Virginia

The 1986 inauguration, with state Supreme Court Justice A. Christian Compton swearing in the new lieutenant governor, as his children, Larry, Loren and Lynn look on with House Speaker A. L. Philpott

The new administration of Attorney General Terry, Lieutenant Governor Wilder and Governor Gerald L. Baliles, with First Lady Jeanne Baliles behind him

The new lieutenant governor presides over the state Senate for the first time, on January 14, 1986

Firing a broadside at the governor's transportation program (left) and with United States Senator and sometimes pal Chuck Robb

With his Republican rival for governor, J. Marshall Coleman, at their first debate of the 1989 campaign, at the Greenbrier resort in West Virginia

DOUG **WILDER** FOR GOVERNOR

governor, they'll elect you governor. I would think it would be an interesting test somewhere along the line for a black to run for one of those positions—attorney general, lieutenant governor or governor—so as to put prejudice right on the line. Say you can't vote for a guy because he's black. Say it."

Wilder said white politicians will cite that "they talked to the maid or to John down at the club, 'and he told me this or that.' All of a sudden, John takes on a certain mystique. He is the black voice, while those persons in the vanguard of black progress are invisible, as Ralph Ellison said, blacks are to whites."

Wilder indicated he may have missed his chance to run for statewide office in 1972. "The climate existed for it (then), and there has been a pendulum swing from that climate now. The McGovern movement, the composition of the conventions, the accent on youth and women comprising the delegate strength would give the potential for a black, woman or liberal to be nominated. I think retrenchment is taking place—it's a purge of liberals as such—allowing more conservative Democrats to come back into the party. I don't think the Republicans could ever do it. If it's done at all it would be done by the Democrats."

As for why his party had never nominated a black, Wilder said, "they tell you that the time is not now. The problem is convincing the psyche of blacks first to aspire, and then to almost be outraged when whites refuse them. There's no reason to deny someone public office because of color. The only excuse they can give is that a person is black."

Blacks at that time were "just about at the bottom. I don't know if blacks have any clout in terms of officeholding. This is why I'm so desperately interested in seeing more blacks in the General Assembly....We're the last state (in number of black elected officials) in the South. Virginia in 1968 was the highest. Now we're the lowest. Florida, Alabama, Mississippi, Georgia, South Carolina, North Carolina, Texas—all of them outrank us. Virginia is leading the way—backwards."

Why not more black candidates? "They've been taught that the time is not now by whites and they have parroted it to all blacks....The professional black who should be in the vanguard mollycoddles and mollifies and pacifies...He's so happy to have escaped the ghetto and the maze of poverty that all of us were in. It's a blanket indictment, and I mean it to be."

When he did run, it would not be as a black candidate, Wilder said. "You'd be surprised at the number of white people who have told me they will support me," he said.

Wilder got into a brief flap with the party over selection of delegates to the 1984 national convention, when he objected to a change in the party plan that would allow black members of the state central committee to decide which black should serve on the party's steering committee. Wilder wanted that choice to continue to be made by the Democratic Black Caucus, of which he was chairman. At one point during the negotiations, he threatened a walkout, snapping, "if you all don't want us, get to it." The committee dropped the change.

Testing out his national perspective, he said, "it is a time when we have been forced into the midst of a fierce struggle to maintain what we have achieved over the past decades," he said. He pointed out that while new federal legislation requires ten percent of the value of federal highway construction to go to minority firms, other federal programs for minorities were on the wane. "Federal support, always lackluster and inadequate, recently has faltered," he said, calling for a reversal of "these destructive federal policies" of the Reagan administration.

Wilder's newly earned establishment stature was confirmed by his perpetual critic, Sa'ad El-Amin, who said Wilder had "inserted himself into a narrow niche (between black and white officials) in which he appears to have more influence than he has, because he is the only game in town." El-Amin dismissed him as "an apparition. What you see is not what is." Wilder "has chosen to use power in too narrow and personal a vein," added El-Amin. "He is vain, power hungry and self-centered."

Wilder's appearance and dress exuded confidence—his gray hair was styled in a modified Afro fashion, his moustache meticulously trimmed, and he was at ease in suede suits and leather jackets among the dull double-breasted pinstripes of his seatmates—and he boasted of his insider status, saying, "there are not too many things that go on in the Senate that I'm not made aware of."

Former majority leader Abe Brault attributed his success to a different reason: "Wilder is a very flexible person. If he can be loyal to anyone, I guess his loyalties are to the present leadership." Other critics, unnamed, called Wilder "a showhorse rather than a workhouse," and another said he was "a colossal liar."

But most of the reviews were good. Larry J. Sabato, a University of Virginia political science professor who was establishing himself as the state's premier political pundit, credited Wilder's growing influence to being "willing to get out front, to be on TV, to be quoted. He exercises considerable influence in the black community. There are one million blacks in Virginia and I would guess 80 percent of them have heard of him." G. C. Morse, the executive director of Common Cause of Virginia, who later served as Governor Gerald L. Baliles' speechwriter, said Wilder "knows the Senate very well as an institution. He has a sense of place."

Before anyone had time to decide how serious Wilder was about the United States Senate bid, however, he switched gears and was looking to the 1985 state elections, saying "it's time for a black to be on the slate. No other constituency tends to be ignored this long, and I just don't feel we should be taken granted forever. It's time to get together and talk," he told party leaders, pointing out that blacks had been delivering thirty to forty percent of the Democratic vote. He had reached the point in his public career where "you either move up or out."

In assessing which office he might seek, he appreciated that not only were there already three strong Democrats being mentioned for governor, but because of what he called his "uniqueness," he admitted to himself that it would have been more difficult, perhaps too difficult, to have tried for governor directly. The same held true for Terry. "I don't believe she could have run for governor directly. Not just her, but any woman." Any black or woman "had to have shown, proven, proficiency at another level."

Having previously dismissed the office of lieutenant governor as primarily ceremonial, where he would "not gain anything in terms of influence," he briefly considered running for attorney general, an office that he said "might well be a stepping stone" toward governor. When fellow Democrats pointed out that Terry, with Robb's blessing, appeared to have the inside track for the nomination, Wilder bristled and said he wouldn't shy away from a confrontation. "Why not (challenge) Mary Sue? Because she's a woman?" he asked, suggesting that was not a good enough reason to back off. He then renewed his criticism of Terry for switching to support of the Equal Rights Amendment, which never got through the Virginia legislature. Later, when he was criticized for switching positions on issues such as capital punishment, he responded that he was responding to a different constituency.

Looking back, he said he never seriously considered running for attorney general. "I never wanted to rely on politics for a living. I knew if I ran for attorney general, I would have to give my up law practice, and I wasn't ready to do that." But it was more than financial considerations. "I just never really wanted to be attorney general, never wanted to do that. I always thought it was a good job, a position with great power, it's just that I never wanted to do that."

Through the process of elimination, he decided that if he were ever going to be a statewide office holder, the office of lieutenant governor offered the best entry level.

The challenge of seeking an office that "no one had served in who looked like me" was irresistible. "It won't mean the same thing in later years, because it won't be unique. It will be bland and almost blended in the passage of time." But just winning would not be enough, nor would be just doing a good job. Under ordinary circumstances, it would have been viewed as a "natural, arithmetic progression" for an experienced legislator to move up to lieutenant governor or attorney general. But because of his "uniqueness," Wilder believed it was important "how" he got elected—the kind of campaign he ran—and once in office, that he do a little more, which is why he committed himself to devote fulltime to the "vacuous, ceremonial" part-time position.

32. Favorite Son

The die was cast by December, 1983, nearly two years before the election. Wilder wanted to make the decision before the start of the 1984 legislative session so that none of the potential candidates for governor might decide to drop back to the vacant number two spot.

Lieutenant Governor Davis and Attorney General Baliles obviously were going to stay in the race, but Wilder was less certain about House Appropriations Committee Chairman Richard M. Bagley, a popular and powerful legislator whose supporters were floating generic "Bagley Statewide in '85" rumors. Also, Wilder was hearing that some of Terry's friends were encouraging her to go for it also. Near the end of the year, Wilder got the good news that Bagley was not going to step back, but make the run for governor.

Wilder talked over this plan with several members of the Senate, and with Senate clerk Jay Shropshire, who had become one of his principal sounding boards.

But in advance of his announcement, he commissioned no poll, consulted no campaign professionals, hired no staff, and raised no money.

"It was intentional," he said. "'I am going to run, to seek the nomination,'" he told himself. Too much advice-seeking and planning could be a mistake. He had seen potentially good candidates thwarted because people told them, "'I don't think you are ready.' They would ask, 'have you done polling, sampling, fundraising?'" Well, he didn't need that kind of help.

He had run into the naysayers in 1969, friends with the best of intentions, telling him he couldn't win, that it was too big a barrier to break. They said, "It's still Virginia." Friends from childhood, schoolmates, told him, "I'll vote for you but you can't win." Wilder's response was the same then as now, "Just vote for me, and don't worry about it."

After fourteen years in the Senate, he was confident that his experience made him as credible as anyone. Certainly he was prepared to be in charge of the affairs of the Senate, which was the only official duty of the lieutenant governor.

He sought no commitments from, nor did he offer any to, any of the three gubernatorial contenders. He told them, and nearly anyone else, of his plans, and made a special point of notifying Governor Robb before the official announcement. When he informed Robb, Wilder said the governor, "in his typical amusing fashion, said 'interesting.'"

Was he looking for advice from Robb? "Yea, on how to win."

The first public notice of his intentions came in a interview on January 4, just before the opening of the 1984 session of the General Assembly. Wilder told a reporter for WXEX-TV, Channel 8 in Richmond, "I have thought of it very seriously and I've thought about it very candidly. I may, this time, offer for lieutenant governor. I haven't heretofore made that public."

The legislative session that followed may have been Wilder's best, providing a big boost to a statewide campaign. As a result of his seniority—only five of his thirty-nine colleagues had served longer—he moved up to chairman of the Senate Committee on Privileges and Elections, and was second-ranking on his two other committees, Transportation, and Rehabilitation and Social Services, both of which he previously had chaired.

His legislative agenda was broad and successful—thirteen of sixteen proposals enacted—and showed little inclination to back away from so-called black issues in hopes of luring future white support.

At long last, the King holiday bill was enacted and signed into law by Governor Robb, as were proposals that allowed the state's office of minority business to supply the names of minority businesses to whom bid proposals should be sent, and required the state Real Estate Commission to investigate and conduct hearings on complaints of discrimination against licensed agents and agencies. Wilder also secured passage of a resolution that asked the legislature to make a final report in 1985 on the proposed constitutional amendment that would have given the District of Columbia full voting representation in Congress.

But he failed, even with the help of Ed Willey as the co-sponsor, to win approval of a law-and-order bill, sought by the Richmond city government, that would have allowed municipalities to regulate the possession of firearms in public places.

Near the end of the session, Wilder sent a letter to his fellow Democrats in the General Assembly that was seen as attempting to head off possible competition for his 1985 race. "It is no secret that I have expressed interest in running for lieutenant governor in 1985," he wrote. "I know that it is too early for commitments, but I would appreciate your support in that regard." Wilder wrote the letter after he got a similar one from Delegate Bagley of Hampton, who was lining up support for his prospective run for governor. Many Democrats thought Bagley lacked the support to capture the top position on the ticket but would be a strong candidate for the number two spot, perhaps in competition with Wilder.

Wilder was not taking sides in the gubernatorial race—" I have committed myself to myself for statewide office next year," he said when asked about a preference—but supporters of Attorney General Jerry Baliles weren't convinced. They complained when Wilder asked Baliles to appear before the Privileges and Elections Committee to explain the lengthy history of the interstate compact of the Washington area's Metro rail system. The committee was considering legislation, which Baliles had endorsed, that would make the state's right-to-work law apply to Virginia employees of the rail system. When Baliles showed up, the hearing room was packed with union members opposed to the bill. Wilder denied that he had set up Baliles at the expense of Lieutenant Governor Davis, who opposed the bill and was considered a friend of labor.

Wilder wasn't beyond keeping other options open. In March, when the party was searching for a candidate to run against Republican U. S. Senator John Warner in the fall, and the Rev. Curtis Harris, a black civil rights activist and perennial candidate announced that he was considering the race, Wilder was non-committal on Harris' bid, and refused to rule himself out when his own name was mentioned as a possibility.

But he had decided to run for lieutenant governor. In June, Wilder invited about ten prominent Richmond Democrats to his house to map strategy and discuss fundraising. Among those attending were Lain O'Ferrall, the investment broker who since working in Wilder's first Senate campaign had been a key fundraiser in several statewide campaigns, including Robb's successful race for governor; Ben Dendy, by then an aide to Robb; Senate clerk Shropshire; Coy J. Eaves, a longtime party activist, and Delegate Benny Lambert, who had been

Wilder's first campaign manager. When word of the meeting leaked out, Dendy made sure everyone knew that he had not attended at the behest of the governor. "I consider Senator Wilder a very close, personal friend," said Dendy, who never met a Democratic politician he considered otherwise.

The year 1984 marked the twenty-fifth anniversary of school integration in Virginia, a milestone that had been achieved reluctantly, after having been denounced by legislators variously as "an evil," "a cancer," and "a sickness in the heart." Massive resistance had been abandoned by a few votes in 1959, after which twenty-one timid black children edged their way back into public schools—seventeen in Norfolk and four in Arlington—over which their small bodies had cast such giant shadows that the thought of them being there had frightened grown men and women half a decade earlier.

But while the law had been changed, many hearts had not. "It's not true integration, it's co-existence," scoffed House Speaker Philpott, who had been a staunch defender of segregation as a young delegate from rural Henry County. "Co-existence," mused Wilder upon being told of Philpott's term. "Co-existence," he repeated. "He's absolutely right, tragically so."

"Lots of things have changed here," Dr. James Bates, a school board member and community leader in rural Halifax County, told The Washington Post. "But as far as visiting on Sundays, or going to church together, that has not happened. In desegregation, you have to desegregate the heart. And that hasn't happened yet."

Wilder, who was in his fifteenth annual legislative session, said massive resistance "has been replaced with a more subtle form of discrimination, a chipping away at the moorings of what we thought was secured."

But there were acknowledgments of change, and its acceptance, everywhere.

James J. Kilpatrick, the caustic former editor of the Richmond News Leader, who had become a syndicated columnist in Washington, had softened his rhetoric. "In the old days," he told The Post, "blacks and whites saw each other through a glass barrier; we never really touched. I know integration has been a good thing in terms of human relations and the basic dignity of people. You will see black and white families that are actually friends now. That's a good thing."

Even former Governor Mills Godwin, who as a legislator was one of the more outspoken opponents of integration, conceded, in language similar to that later employed by Jesse Jackson, "we have moved on to higher ground."

It was from that higher elevation that Wilder surveyed the political landscape and determined—unilaterally, as he does most important decisions— to follow the lead of those black children a quarter of a century earlier, and walk where no black before had trod.

A favorite Wilder dictum is, "when the thing is right, the time is right," and Wilder decided that the right time for his right thing—a formal declaration of candidacy—was July 3, 1984. He gambled that because the next day was a holiday, it would be an otherwise slow news day, enhancing the publicity given to his announcement.

33. In the Shadow of Byrd

Wilder was right about the timing. His announcement was front page news all over the state, although given its historic nature, it probably would have been so no matter what day he had selected. He calculated that the way his announcement was treated would give him a handle on how his candidacy would be accepted, both by the public and the media.

He made the announcement on the second floor of the Capitol, in the Old Senate Chamber, positioning himself so that he would be photographed in front of the portrait of the late Harry F. Byrd Sr., the symbol of Virginia's segregationist past.

"A record of accountability and concern is what I bring, and a unity of variety and abundance is what I seek," he told the overflow crowd. "I believe in coalition politics, and coalition politics doesn't just mean that we all vote together for a certain candidate, but that we all share the pie." He said he believed that the state had changed enough since the passing of the Byrd era .

He said that he did not intend "to spend a lot of time telling you that I'm black." Pulling at his face with both hands, he said, "There's nothing that could change the color of my skin."

While insisting that he was running to win, he also admitted that he wanted to see "just how far the horizon has stretched."

Asked why he picked the ornate chamber, an historic reminder of the state's past, for his announcement, Wilder unconvincingly asserted that he selected it for its size rather than for its symbolism. I've been in this room on a number of occasions," adding coyly "and the picture and I get along well." Turning serious, he added, "we must not languish in our past glories and bright stars, because this commonwealth's star is yet in ascendancy."

He announced early, he explained, because he wanted to prove he was serious. He admitted that in the past, "I've been crying wolf."

Even the conservative Richmond News Leader concluded that Wilder could win. "People in Virginia, like other places, are prepared to elect persons based on their record and accountability."

Wilder was not the first black to seek statewide office in the Old Dominion—the trail had been blazed, however dimly, by John Mitchell Jr., the editor of the Richmond Planet, and banker Maggie Walker who, respectively, ran for governor and superintendent of public instruction in 1921 on the mockingly named Lily Black Republican ticket, in protest of the Lily White Republican ticket of that year; by Moses Riddick of Suffolk, a little-known candidate who made a weak bid for the Democratic nomination for lieutenant governor in 1959; and by Cora Tucker, the Halifax housewife-activist, and her write-in running mates in 1981—but Wilder was the first black to run as a potentially electable candidate.

Wilder went to the Democratic state convention later that month as an uncommitted delegate, wanting to stay out of the intra-party fights between supporters of Vice President Mondale and Jesse Jackson. He was elected a delegate to the national convention in San Francisco, garnering more voters than any other uncommitted delegate. That told me something," Wilder said, "that if I could get that kind of support, being uncommitted, then all I needed to do was to continue to nurture it."

159

Blacks had been so successful in sending delegates to the state convention, where their disproportionate number permitted Jackson to get twenty-two of the seventy-eight delegates to the national convention, that there was some talk by those unhappy at the prospect of Wilder's nomination about returning to a primary for the 1985 nominating process, but Wilder said he was prepared to run, and win, under either method of selection.

Lain O'Ferrall said "there are people saying it might be a no-win situation to run against Doug—how much of a chance would you stand in the general election if you alienated blacks" in the nominating process.

Given his early start and solid support among blacks, who made up about one-fifth of the state's population and traditionally account for nearly one-third of the participants in mass meetings and state conventions, not many doubted that Wilder could get the nomination. But there was open concern about whether he could win in the general election, and more importantly, whether his candidacy would drag the other two Democrats on the ticket to defeat with him.

"I think the Democratic party is ready for a black, statewide candidate; I don't think the general electorate is," said Professor Sabato. Thomas R. Morris at the University of Richmond said "it would be an adventuresome candidacy for the Democratic party, and not in keeping with their safe ticket" of three years earlier, which featured the usual three white males. Wilder "will have to prove himself a lot better than other candidates," said James Carvile, who managed Lieutenant Governor Davis' unsuccessful race for the Senate in 1982. "I don't agree with that," said Carvile, a Louisianian, "but that's the way it is."

When the question of racial prejudice was posed to Wilder, he expressed an almost childlike faith in the electorate, and suggested that "prejudices are not so much with people as with some people who speak of them." He said blacks have helped elect whites over the years and "turnabout is fair play."

The most vivid example, of course, was Robb's win three years earlier, when he got more than 190,000 of the 200,000 votes cast by blacks, enough to make the difference. Other examples in recent Virginia history included the repeated election in predominantly white Roanoke of Noel Taylor, a black Republican preacher, as mayor, and Bobby Scott's elevation to the Senate in a predominantly white district by voters in Newport News.

In a convoluted expansion on that theme, Wilder told Margie Fisher of the Roanoke Times and World-News how he planned to overcome the prejudice of the "magnolia mentality" he had complained about in the past. "There are always times when first things bring about first things. When I first ran in 1969, I was told it was impossible that I'd be elected. Fortunately, we have had examples when cognitive judgment has taught us that people are prepared to make these types of changes....I don't intend to spend a lot of time telling you I'm black," he said, vowing that his campaign would concentrate on discussing issues.

Two weeks after his announcement, Wilder took "a button or two" to the national convention in San Francisco, where he cornered the Virginia delegates, pinning his button on them and seeking commitments of support. State Senator J. Granger Macfarlane of Roanoke, and his wife, Ann, took him to dinner and pledged their support. Marie Ridder, a McLean neighbor of Governor Robb's, whose husband was the principal owner of the Knight-Ridder chain of newspapers, introduced Wilder to her circle of friends on the national scene, including the chronicler of presidents, Theodore White.

Lieutenant Governor Davis and Attorney General Baliles also were working the delegates in San Francisco, and everytime Wilder was seen talking to one of them, the other's supporters reported back that a deal was in the making. "It was a thin line to walk," said Wilder, who had no intention of aligning himself with any gubernatorial candidate, at least not that early in the game.

Meanwhile, under pressure to support Jackson's impending nomination, Wilder allowed himself to be counted as a Jackson supporter, backed all the amendments to the platform resolutions that Jackson sought and then breathed a sigh of relief because Jackson's name was not placed in nomination.

When Wilder got back to Virginia, he contacted a number of people who had encouraged him in California, but he shied away from follow-up contacts with some out-of-state residents who were ready and anxious to support him. "I knew I didn't want to have an other-than-Virginia campaign," he explained.

He made no secret that, if successful, he would run for governor four years later. "In politics," he said, "you either move up after a period of time, or you watch the weeds grow."

Wilder's perpetual critic in the black community, Sa'ad El-Amin, weighed in with a column in The Afro that ridiculed Wilder's candidacy. El-Amin said he was "puzzled why anyone would run for an office that has no real power...why anyone would spend almost a million dollars to wage a statewide campaign" for an office "whose only function is to break an occasional tie vote. Why should black folk become excited, or even committed to helping him obtain a position which is in essence meaningless. It is indeed ironic that we have spent blood, sweat and tears just trying to get the right to vote, and then turn around and spend a million to put a man in an office which prohibits him from voting."

El-Amin said recent elections in states far more politically liberal than Virginia "have proven that white voters could not bring themselves to vote for a black candidate running for statewide office," saying Mayor Tom Bradley of Los Angeles "found this out the hard way" when he ran for governor of California. "He lost even though everyone conceded he was the better qualified candidate.

"Virginia is still in the stone age. The fact that we have no blacks in the federal judicial positions, nor do we have a single black elected to statewide or federal office is sufficient evidence to carry my point. I an not, however, suggesting that the present status quo should deter a black from running for statewide or federal office. On the contrary, I believe that we should go for the roses, but not a rose that is without stem or petals." El-Amin said Wilder should have run for the third district congressional seat, "or if this local challenge does not appeal to his ambitious nature, he should campaign for governor, a position that does have power. Really, if one is going to lose, why not campaign for a position which is significant. Wilder should take a page from Jesse Jackson's political notebook."

As much as El-Amin's ranting pleased racist whites, who enjoyed the sight of blacks fighting among themselves, he was, of course, dead wrong about the strategy. The last thing Wilder wanted to do was imitate Jesse Jackson. As Wilder explained to those who questioned whether he might have lost support among blacks for failing to endorse the failed presidential bid of his fraternity friend,

WILDER: HOLD FAST TO DREAMS

"Jesse Jackson understands me and I understand him. He runs to strike the conscience of the country; I'm running to be elected."

34. This Time It's for Real

Wilder held his first major strategy meeting in the fall of 1984, at a Sheraton resort hotel on the edge of Fredericksburg. Among about a dozen people invited were Lain O'Ferrall; Dottie Schick, the head of the party in Fairfax County, Edward M. Holland, a state senator from Arlington, and Delegate Benny Lambert.

Noticeable by their absences were others who, with O'Ferrall, had played key roles in Robb's campaign four years earlier, such as attorney-lobbyist Bill Thomas and Delegate Al Smith.

Although it was apparent that Wilder had already made up his mind about running, he extended to the group the courtesy of asking them if they thought his candidacy were a good idea. Several expressed doubts or asked questions, the same kind that would be asked throughout the campaign, such as, "Do you think a black can be elected statewide in Virginia?" Another had been hearing "all sorts of things," such as that he used drugs (not true) and dated white women (occasionally), the kinds of stories that the poker players in the basement of the Commonwealth Club liked to think were true.

"I'm going to be up front with you," confronted O'Ferrall. "It's probably because of the color of your skin, but there's a lot of talk out there about you, about skeletons in the closet. In this day and time, they're going to come out and grab you." Wilder answered that whatever skeletons were in his closet already were known to, and had been thoroughly investigated by, the press. The most potentially juicy story involved his divorce, and Wilder knew that whatever Eunice might have felt about him personally, publicly she was behind him. O'Ferrall was comforted by the belief that the divorce had not resulted from Wilder's involvement with another woman, the proof of which, to him, was that not only hadn't Wilder remarried (neither had Eunice) but that he did not appear to have any steady relationship. As far as dating white women, O'Ferrall said, "I guess that could irritate some people—but times had changed."

Another person at the Fredericksburg meeting was David Temple, a school principal in Fairfax County, and the son of The Afro columnist who had so dutifully recorded Wilder's social career as a child. Temple recruited a number of Democratic activists in Northern Virginia.

From the other end of state came Kenneth R. Melvin, a young black lawyer who had been a roommate of Wilder's nephew, Keith (his brother Bob's younger son) at Colby College in Maine, and who was going to run for the House of Delegates from Portsmouth in 1985. Wilder accepted Melvin's offer to make space in his law office as a campaign headquarters in the Hampton Roads area.

The success of the meeting in Fredericksburg had a snowball effect, with the participants organizing similar, larger meetings in their various home-towns.

Shortly after Wilder's announcement, Paul Goldman called from New York and expressed an interest in working in the campaign. He could be available in December. Wilder was interested. He needed help. Contributions were starting to dribble in, enough so that Wilder didn't have to take anything out of his own pocket, but the fundraising had to be accelerated. The word was getting out in the black community, thanks largely to the editor of the Afro, John

Templeton, who was working as volunteer, writing news releases and advertising copy.

One of Goldman's attractions was that he came cheap—he mentioned on the phone that he could get by on between two thousand and twenty-five hundred dollars a month—and as all of his campaigns illustrated, Wilder puts a premium on frugality. Anyone accusing Wilder of being a free-spending liberal couldn't be talking about his personal pecuniary proclivities.

Wilder bought a computer software system and five terminals, installed it in a basement office of his law building, and Goldman found someone to operate it. As a practical matter, his participation in the law firm had ended at the end of the 1984 legislative session.

He completed his paid staff by hiring his nephew, Michael Brown, one of his sister Doris' sons, who had been a field representative with the NAACP. His law office secretary and the receptionist, Laverne Robinson and Ruth Jones, were pressed into service; Laverne did the typing and Ruth "worked herself to death," serving as the campaign administrator.

Another nephew, Chuck Nicholson, Agnes' son, an accountant, took care of the filing requirements, reporting Wilder's contributors. "He never missed a deadline," his uncle said with satisfaction.

Over the Christmas holidays, Wilder spent a lot of time calling the Democratic party's city and council chairmen around the state. His pitch was to say Merry Christmas, ask for their support, and add, "'I don't know of anybody else running, but if there is, I understand your concern. But right now I want it.' I got a lot people to commit. They were surprised that I would call."

Before the opening of the 1985 General Assembly, Wilder asked Ed Holland to serve as treasurer of his campaign. Near the end of the assembly session, Holland, a wealthy banker, decided on his own to put together a list of Senate colleagues to endorse Wilder. With little effort, Holland got ten names, nearly one-third of the Democrats in the chamber. "That encouraged me a great deal," said Wilder, especially because it still wasn't clear who else might get into the race.

The ten senators signed an open letter to fellow Democrats, included in the state party's March newsletter, that foreshadowed the themes of the Wilder campaign. Wilder is "a Virginia success story," it said, "based on hard work. He wasn't handed anything....He hasn't sat back and waited. He's campaigned for our support—and got it." Although the leaders of the Senate were absent from the list, the signatories pointed out that they represented "a broad geographic and philosophic cross-section." Four were from Northern Virginia—Clive L. DuVal II and Joseph L. Gartlan Jr. of Fairfax County, Charles L. Waddell of Loudoun County, and Holland; three were from western and southwestern Virginia—Virgil H. Goode Jr. of Franklin County, James P. Jones of Washington County and J. Granger Macfarlane of the city of Roanoke; from central Virginia was Thomas J. Michie Jr. of Charlottesville; from Tidewater, Robert C. Scott of Newport News, and from the Eastern Shore, William E. Fears of Accomack. Philosophically, DuVal, Gartlan, Holland, Scott and Waddell were moderate-to-liberal; Jones, Macfarlane, Michie and Fears moderate-to-conservative, and Goode conservative.

Although none but Holland signed up for a role in the campaign, his old tennis partner Fears said he would raise money for him. "I think Doug's got an uphill fight. I told him that," Fears said. "If he wins, it will be no surprise for me."

Senator Charles J. Colgan of Prince William County was one of the few senators to explain why he refused to sign. He said he did not think Wilder could win in the fall, and therefore was hoping to convince Bagley to accept a draft. Senator Madison E. Marye of rural Montgomery County, who later was to be a strong supporter, said, "I have no problems supporting Senator Wilder," but said it was too early to make an endorsement.

Goldman was elated by the endorsements. "Two months before," added Goldman, "there were those who said he couldn't get any of his colleagues. Those voices of gloom and doom were misdirected."

Wilder's last session as a member of the General Assembly was a quiet one. He introduced only two bills, and only one of them passed. But it was a major coup, because it was a tough-on-crime bill that, in the wake of the largest death-row prison escape in American history, eliminated the possibility of parole for inmates serving life sentences who escape, and increased the penalties for all escapes. His other proposal, which had been carried over from the previous year, would have doubled, from six months to a year, the time allowed to file a complaint of discriminatory housing practice. It was killed in a House committee.

Those who suggested he was moderating his positions in preparation for a statewide race "haven't looked at my record," he said, but one of his votes that year raised a few eyebrows. In previous years, Wilder had been one of the strongest supporters of comparative negligence, a legal doctrine, barred by existing Virginia law, that allows partial recovery in law suits, even when the plaintiff is at fault. But in 1985, he cast a deciding vote against a milder version of the idea, which would have applied only to automobile accidents. He had supported the proposal the year before. His switch was interpreted by lobbyists on both sides of the issue as an attempt by Wilder to win the favor of insurance companies and corporations that opposed the bill. Wilder defended his change of position, saying that he had concerns about the constitutionality of the measure, as the result of a court ruling in a South Carolina case.

During much of the spring of 1985, Wilder's candidacy took a back seat to the divisive battle for the gubernatorial nomination between Lieutenant Governor Davis and Attorney General Baliles, which was a not altogether bad situation for Wilder.

Baliles claimed the nomination on the basis of a hundred-delegate margin at mass meetings on March 30 and April 1, but Davis supporters filed dozens of credentials challenges involving about seven hundred of the thirty-five hundred delegates to the state convention in Richmond June 7 and 8.

By late April, Robb, who was on a trip to Israel, was drawn into the fray by long distance. After conferring with both Davis and Baliles, and making "an objective analysis" of the caucus voting, Robb said "it is clear to me" that the challenges would not change the outcome. He then convinced Davis to withdraw his challenges and once again accept the post of state party chairman.

Wilder praised Davis's withdrawal as "a noble and unselfish act." What he didn't say was that it also was an enormous boost to his own chances of victory in November.

Davis blamed Wilder for his defeat, believing he had sided with Baliles so that the ticket would not so liberal. But Davis got over his bitterness, and in 1988, was among the first of the party leaders to endorse Wilder for governor.

"Baliles's candidacy is not going to be greeted with any great joy by Republicans," noted Republican state senator Wiley F. Mitchell Jr. of Alexandria, because it kept alive the coalition of conservatives, liberals and blacks who elected Robb. Ed DeBolt, a veteran Republican political consultant who was directing Wyatt B. Durrette's attempt to win the GOP gubernatorial nomination, agreed that Baliles "has tried very hard to emulate Robb," while adding that Baliles lacked "the charisma, the aura or personal magnetism" of Robb.

David Doak, the Washington political consultant who had managed Robb's campaign and was the chief consultant to Baliles, said "Virginia Democrats learned how to win in 1981 and they liked it."

"You can't win" became a familiar refrain to Wilder in the early part of the year. Speaking in Waynesboro in March at a banquet of the National Association for the Advancement of Colored People, he recalled that he had heard that song before, in 1969, when he announced his candidacy for the legislature. "I didn't argue with those who said it couldn't be done," he said confidently. "We went about to do what we had to do....I think the naysayers usually are the politicos. The people are not saying that it cannot happen," he said at a news conference preceding the banquet.

As he moved around the state, testing the waters, he stressed his experience, noting that "I have more experience in the senate than the five previous lieutenant governors combined."

He was running as a true Virginian: "I'm proud to be a Virginian and proud to be in a position to have represented it heretofore...I have come to understand the diversity of Virginia and its people, and the enormity of the state and its beauty."

Right after the session, at Goldman's suggestion, Wilder made a foray to Southwest Virginia, to establish a connection with rural Virginia, and to make himself known to the region of the state that had the fewest minorities. It would be a chance to get a realistic perception of how his candidacy might play in a statewide race.

Wilder was accompanied on various portions of the trip by local legislators, Senators Madison E. Marye, Virgil   Goode and James P. Jones and former delegate Edgar Bacon. It was not a formal campaign tour. Each place they stopped, the legislators introduced Wilder and gave people a chance to look him over, size him up.

The full campaign staff came along: Wilder and his nephew Michael Brown did most of the driving, while Goldman sat in the back seat. "Paul doesn't drive at night, and he shouldn't," said Wilder, citing an idiosyncrasy of Goldman's, who has enough quirks to be a character in a Woody Allen story. Although it was spring, at one point it began snowing as they drove, with flakes so big that Wilder had to open the door on the passenger side and warn Michael when he got too close to the berm.

Wilder and Goldman enjoyed the experience of following the serpentine roads from mining town to railroad yard to forestry stations—hardly familiar territory for the either of them.

After they returned to Richmond, Goldman suggested that Wilder return to the Southwest for a longer stay. "I think we'll need at least two months," said Goldman, introducing an idea that was to become a key ingredient—some called it a gimmick—of the campaign, an exhaustive, circuitous tour that took them, literally, into every one of the state's cities and counties.

The idea of the tour appealed to Wilder. "It was letting people know you were not shy about campaigning—anywhere, that you would go anywhere, anytime." Wilder liked "the lightness associated with it. No heralding, no calling up anybody to form a phalanx or vanguard to proceed us."

He wrote to the local Democratic chairmen, outlining his plan, and concluded that the only time to do the tour was in the summer, after the state convention, and before the demands of the fall campaign made it impractical.

35. Goldman

To understand Doug Wilder, it is necessary to understand Paul Goldman, who met Wilder early in 1977 at a meeting of the legislative black caucus in Richmond, to which Goldman had gone to drum up support for the gubernatorial campagin of Henry Howell.

Goldman, an ascetic vegetarian who has the frazzled look of a mad scientist—if not an Einstein, then the genius professor in the mid-80s movie "Back to the Future,"—likes to say that he is "a native Southerner," because he was born in Palm Beach, Florida, where his New Yorker parents were visiting. He grew up in Brooklyn, the older of two sons of second-generation Russian Jews whose parents had fled the Czar. "That's me," he says sheepishly after joking about his "Southern" heritage.

Other than a now deceased relative who had gone to medical school in Virginia before returning to New York to practice, Goldman's only connection to the Old Dominion was as a student of history and politics. He recalled reading about massive resistance, the Byrd organization, liberal George Rawling's defeat of Judge Howard Smith for the House of Representatives in the mid-sixties and historian V. O. Key's description of the state as "a political museum piece."

Goldman first visited Virginia in 1976, when a friend who was preparing to work in Howell's campaign invited him to come down and meet Howell, saying, "you'd really like this guy." Goldman was getting ready to go to Florida "to see where I was born" and take a rest—characteristically, he was traveling by bus—so he got off in Norfolk. In their first meeting, Howell, a shrill-voiced populist lawyer, reminisced about his 1973 gubernatorial campaign, when he ran as an independent and lost a bitter and close race—by seven-tenths of one percent—to former Democratic Governor Mills E. Godwin, who was running as a Republican. Howell had been elected lieutenant governor in 1971, to fill the vacancy created by the death of Sarge Reynolds. Goldman liked Howell immediately. He liked his enthusiasm and, listening to him complain that Frank McGhee of NBC had misrepresented his position on busing in the 1973 campaign, his willingness to nurse a grudge.

After a few days in the Norfolk area, Goldman went on to Florida, but the visit with Howell had sparked his interest in his upcoming campaign. When he got back to Princeton, where he was working in the legal department of the New Jersey Commission of Consumer Affairs, he came across an article Howell had written on consumer affairs several years earlier, for the William and Mary law review. Goldman dropped him a complimentary note about it, and he kept in touch with one of Howell's nephews, Joe Waldo, who invited him to his home in Virginia Beach—Goldman doesn't spend his money on hotels any more than he does on airplanes. During those periodic visits, Goldman ran on the beach—jog is too *au courant* to describe any Goldman activity—and talked politics. On one of his beach jaunts, he met an equally serious-minded young political science professor from the University of Virginia, Larry J. Sabato, with whom he was to work with, and against, in future campaigns.

Goldman had gotten his first taste of working in a political campaign in 1972, in the gubernatorial campaign of Dan Walker in Illinois. Goldman, who was in law school at Syracuse at the time, was assigned to be the advance man for the slow summer months preceding the Democratic primary. Walker, a urban-smooth, buttoned-down executive from suburban Chicago, knew that if he were to have a chance of defeating Lt. Gov. Paul Simon, the future presidential candidate who had, after earning his spurs as a reformer, become the candidate of Chicago Mayor Richard Daley's machine. Walker needed to pile up huge majorities in the lightly populated downstate areas, whose residents felt that except for visits to the outpost capital city of Springfield, most politicians thought that Illinois stopped at the Cook County line.

Goldman came up with the idea of a tour of Southern Illinois by jeep, which permitted Walker to accumulate a little dust and dirt on his shoes (he replaced his wingtips with cowboy boots, purchased especially for the tour at Abercrombie and Fitch), and some down-home knowledge of local customs and oddities, such as knowing that Cairo, in the region known as Little Egypt, was pronounced Kay-row, like the syrup. That steamy summer, while the political pros sat in their air conditioned Chicago offices and had a good yuk, Goldman, who knew even less about rural life than Walker, dragged his candidate into towns that are speckled like gritty mirages across plains as flat as a losing candidate's movement in the polls, stopping at every five-hundred-watt AM radio station and county-seat weekly newspaper.

"We created a guy who got elected because he knew the state better than any other Democrat," said Goldman, who filed away that successful experience. Never mind that Walker later when to jail. "That was after he was elected," Goldman said.

Goldman returned to Syracuse and finished his law degree, but before he got around to taking the bar exam, politics called again. He was was off to New Jersey, as a volunteer in the 1973 gubernatorial campaign of Brendan Byrne. Goldman thought Byrne was the perfect kind of candidate—he had the good sense to be in the right place at the right time and emitted the image of someone who couldn't be bought, when the public was immersed in the Watergate scandal. His opponent was Congressman Charles Sandman, who later would be remembered as the last defender of President Richard M. Nixon on the House Watergate Committee. Goldman followed the Illinois precedent, and moved Byrne around the state in the summer, hitting the small town festivals and beach concerts, and when the staff expanded in the fall, he was put on the payroll, where he came into contact with some of the big names in political campaigns, including the New York media consultant, David Garth.

After the election, his reward was a position on the legal staff (although he still had not taken the bar exam) with the state's office of consumer affairs, but what he was really supposed to do, because of his reputation from the campaign, was get publicity for the agency's activities, and its boss, Virginia Long, a crusading consumer advocate who later was rewarded with a judgeship.

In July, 1976, Howell contacted Goldman and asked him to be his campaign manager. At the time, Goldman, whose undergraduate and law degrees were from Syracuse University, had applied to graduate school at Syracuse, where he was planning to get a doctorate in political science. But he decided he could learn more about politics by running Howell's campaign than sitting in a classroom.

"We agreed on a salary," said Goldman, "but of course it got slashed" because of a shortage of funds. To help offset the financial pinch, Goldman convinced Howell to employ a strategy that focused on telephone banks staffed by volunteer callers and free media, a tactic that required Howell to regularly schedule press conferences that would be reported on the evening news.

Goldman depicted Howell as the underdog, which wasn't difficult because the polls showed him badly trailing his opponent, state attorney general Andrew P. Miller, and being outspent. After a Norfolk newspaper wrote that hardly anyone had shown up for a Howell rally, Goldman mystified the campaign workers by showing up at headquarters with a smile on his face, waving the paper around and declaring it a "great story." When a staffer complained that the story suggested that Howell couldn't win, Goldman exclaimed, "Exactly right, so no one will be mad at us." He explained his belief that the voters being polled weren't so much pro-Miller as they were anti-Howell. Thus, "the worse we look, the less Miller will attack us, because he wants our votes in the fall." Howell had a hard-core of supporters—Goldman figured Howell could expect a maximum of two hundred and seventy-five thousand, most of whom would turn out "come hell or high water"—a Miller victory depended on energizing a large turnout of anti-Howell voters, which was less likely to occur if Miller didn't keep up his attacks on Howell.

Although the campaign was going well, money was still a problem, so when Howell got a $25,000 contributions from Richmonder Sydney Lewis, the staff was ecstatic. Lewis, the founder of Best Products discount stores was a benefactor of liberal and artistic causes who had personally bankrolled Howell's unsuccessful gubernatorial campaign in 1973 with a then-unheard of contribution of contribution of $300,000. But instead of being grateful for Lewis's latest donation, Howell was devastated because he learned that Lewis also had contributed $10,000 to Miller. "Henry kept saying, 'he thinks I'm only two and one-half times better than Miller,'" recalled Goldman, and Howell finally got so frenzied that he announced he was going to return Lewis's donation.

"We were broke, and the people wanted to get paid," said Goldman, who urged Howell not to do anything rash. But Howell was adamant about giving the money back and telling the world why. He reserved a room at the state Capitol for a press conference and prepared a press release, writing it in longhand on yellow legal paper. He told Goldman he would stop at Lewis's house enroute to the press conference, to inform him. Goldman tipped off Lewis to the impending development. Lewis was understanding and sympathetic. "He said, 'I don't understand this, but I'll see him at eleven.'" Howell met Lewis, explained his intentions and read the press release, and then, inexplicably, changed his mind, telling Lewis he could not go through with it.

By election day, although the published polls still showed Howell trailing by double-digits, in-house polls taken for Howell by Patrick Caddell, President Carter's cigar-smoking pollster, indicated it was a tossup, although, in keeping with the strategy of trying to keep the turnout low, no one in the Howell camp challenged the public polls. "They played into our hand," Goldman said.

The hoped-for low turnout prevailed and Howell won by attracting 253,000 loyal voters, about six thousand more than Miller. But on election night, amid the cheers of victory, Howell fired Goldman as campaign manager. Howell said Goldman was not interested in the complexities of campaign structure. "He was thinking all the time. He'd come up with these brilliant ideas, but he didn't communicate with me a lot." Howell acknowledged that Goldman was "a great strategist," and was willing to have him stay on as tactician, but Goldman declined. Goldman was philosophical. "As sometimes happens in politics, the campaign manager has to make some tough choices" that don't always sit well with the candidate. "But if you want to win without sacrificing your principles, you play hard and you play pragmatic." In retrospect, Goldman said, "there were people I probably rubbed the wrong way....Campaigning is an art form, your creative thing. It was easy for me. I was an outsider. I came in, I said, 'you've got to do this, Henry, you've got to do that, Henry. This is the strategy.' It was two people who had fairly strong wills."

Goldman stuck around for the general election, however, and worked for state Senator Ed Lane, the Democratic nominee for attorney general.

"It was a rainbow ticket, and we were the first to use the phrase, long before Jesse Jackson," Howell said of the varying philosophies of the Democratic team of Howell, a liberal and populist; Lane, an old-line Byrd conservative, and Charles S. Robb, the candidate for lieutenant governor, a novice whose philosophy went largely undetected amid the spotlight of being the son-in-law of former president Lyndon B. Johnson.

In the general election, the "Howell cannonball" fizzled, and he lost by one hundred and fifty-thousand votes to Republican John Dalton. Goldman ended up working for a loser too. Lane lost to a handsome, energetic young state senator from Staunton, J. Marshall Coleman, who became the first Republican in the twentieth century to serve as the state's top lawyer. The only Democratic winner was Robb, who defeated state Senator A. Joseph Canada, setting the stage for a showdown with Coleman four years later.

After the 1977 campaign, Goldman returned to New Jersey, intending to begin a law practice, having passed the bar in the meantime, and to play the stock market, which he has done no matter what else he was doing. Instead, he was offered a job as a lawyer with the New York state consumer affairs board in Albany. He commuted to Albany from Princeton, and kept in touch with political developments in Virginia. He wrote to the new lieutenant governor, Chuck Robb, whom he had met briefly in the campaign, and said he might be interested in working for him if he ran for governor in 1981.

In the summer of 1980, William Wiley, whom Goldman had met during the campaign, arranged for Goldman to meet Robb, who invited Goldman to dinner at his house in McLean. Goldman remembers the evening vividly, not because of any political discussion, but because a couple of incidents that occurred in connection with his visit. He stayed at Wiley's house in Alexandria, and borrowed Wiley's car to drive to Robb's house, which is in a swanky neighborhood overlooking the Potomac River.

"I turned into the wrong drive, drove over this little hump and people jumped out at me," Goldman laughed. He explained that he was looking for Robb's house, but the men said they didn't know where it was. "Then it dawned on me," Goldman said. "I must have hit Ted Kennedy's joint." (Robb lives next door to Senator Edward M. Kennedy, whose house is protected by private security guards.) Goldman also remembers that night "because I'm a vegetarian, and his wife (Lynda Bird Johnson Robb) had made meat loaf, and mashed potatoes with milk, and I couldn't eat it. I ate the green vegetables. It was just the three of us. I think the kids were upstairs. We just talked." Goldman said Robb didn't offer him a position with the campaign "and I wasn't seeking one. Not at all." But he left convinced that Robb would be a good candidate for governor. "I've always liked him. And it was obvious that he understood Virginia very well."

The curious thing about that story is that Robb has no recollection of it. In fact, he insists that Goldman has never been to his house, and that he has never had dinner with him.

"What can I tell you?" asked Goldman when told of Robb's reaction. "It happened."

In any event, Goldman wound up working briefly in Robb's campaign the next year. But it was in a peripheral role. Robb confidant Bill Thomas said "I have no recollection of Paul Goldman in the '81 campaign at all."

"I think they put Paul in a back room and gave him all these numbers and asked him what they meant," said Bernard Craighead, who managed Robb's 1988 campaign for the Senate. "He is very good at analysis. He'd say 'they mean this and that,' and they'd say, 'fine, Paul, don't leave the back room.'"

During the campaign, Goldman renewed his acquaintance with Wilder.

36. Anyone But Wilder

The search for alternative candidates for the 1985 Democratic ticket—white male ones—began in earnest right after the 1984 Republican landslide victories by President Reagan and Senator John Warner. The beating given the Democrat's Senate candidate, Edythe Harrison, was prompting or giving excuse for reassessment of a 1985 ticket that might include both a woman and a black.

"There are a lot of people in the party who just say that ticket (with Wilder and Terry) isn't going to win, and that's why I guess some of them started calling me," said Delegate Frank M. Slayton of Halifax, who said he was considering opposing Terry. Slayton said all three potential gubernatorial candidates—Attorney General Jerry Baliles, Lieutenant Governor Dick Davis and Hampton Delegate Richard M. Bagley, had encouraged him to run.

Supporters of each of the gubernatorial candidates admitted that their campaigns were more concerned about the effect of a Wilder candidacy than one by Terry.

Wilder attempted to downplay concerns about his candidacy as a natural reaction to the Democrats drubbing in the presidential election. If they want to remove all worries about 1985, he suggested, "they should bring in Ronald Reagan to run for governor. I guess he would get elected." As for those who harbored hope that he might withdraw, Wilder said, "I'm not testing the water, I'm in it."

But concerns about Wilder's candidacy would not be wished away. "For better or worse," said Governor Robb's press secretary, George Stoddart, "this is still Virginia. That makes it very difficult. Once you get beyond the state Senate or maybe a congressional district, it becomes very difficult for black candidates."

Wilder later pointed to that remark as part of his portfolio of proof that Robb was encouraging others to challenge him. But Stoddart was merely expressing the conventional wisdom of the day.

Another casual remark, by Lieutenant Governor Davis, who said he would love to see Baliles run for lieutenant governor, infuriated Wilder too. "Dick was just trying to move Jerry (Baliles) out of the way, to put a nail in his coffin," said Bobby Watson, Davis' campaign manager. Nonetheless, Watson acknowledged that "many in Dick's campaign did not feel the state would back a Catholic, especially a liberal one [Davis], a black and a woman, and at the beginning, I was one of them. So there was always that hope, in the back of our mind, that someone else would pop up there (and run for lieutenant governor) and the nightmare of Doug Wilder being on the ticket would go away."

Later, when Davis realized Wilder's candidacy was inevitable, he resigned himself to trying to make the best of a bad situation. "But a lot of others who raised money were adamant that they weren't going to waste their money if Dick was on the ticket with Doug," said Watson.

Many Democrats, especially those who had helped bring conservatives on board with Robb, didn't want Davis at the top of the ticket for partly the same reason they didn't want Wilder in the middle, because it would make it too liberal.

Eva S. Teig, the lieutenant governor's chief of staff, said that "every time he (Davis) asked someone for money, they would complain that Doug was going to drag the ticket down. Mr. Davis was shocked by what he heard said about Wilder. He truly thought he should have the opportunity to run, and he took great pains to protest, pointing to Doug's distinguished record and leadership skills."

At the same time, Goldman was deliberating fostering the perception that Davis was against Wilder, an action that Teig said "caused a rift between two people (Davis and Wilder) who genuinely liked and respected each other." Goldman's motive was similar to those who wanted neither Davis nor Baliles: He figured one liberal on the ticket was enough, especially when he was also black.

Bill Thomas, the Robb intimate, thought Wilder would have a very tough time winning, but he denied that he suggested that Bagley run for lieutenant governor, although he told him it was too big a jump to move from chairman of the House Appropriations Committee to governor. "If you ask, was I encouraging him (Bagley) to run (for lieutenant governor), no, but I was telling him what I thought was the real world. But I didn't spend time running around trying to get people to run against Doug Wilder. That was the only discussion I had with anyone."

Bagley withdrew from the governor's race in mid-December, and almost immediately there were signs that some Democrats were pressuring him to challenge Wilder for the number two spot. John "Butch" Davies of Culpeper, the Seventh District Democratic chairman, said, "I don't think it's a stop-Wilder thing" but rather a matter of facing political reality and doing what is best for the party. Bagley did not rule out the possibility that he would accept a draft. "No politician is going...to forever say that something couldn't happen down the road that might interest him," but he said his main interest continued to be the governorship, which he might seek again in 1989 (for reasons of health, he did not).

Meanwhile, Wilder was picking up support on his own. The state AFL-CIO unanimously endorsed him, along with Davis for governor, at its convention in Norfolk, where Wilder told the unionists, "the biggest problem I see is getting out to the people so they can see I'm not the monster that some have tried to depict me as."

Wilder was the beneficiary of fundraisers held on successive nights at two of the state's better known law firms. Forty to fifty people, most of them lawyers, paid $50 each for a reception at the Richmond firm of Allen, Allen, Allen and Allen, the city's largest plaintiff firm, and the next night, a similar event was held at Bill Thomas's law firm in Alexandria, although Thomas had not endorsed him. The host was Carl T. Rowan Jr., son of the syndicated columnist and a partner in Thomas's firm. The sponsors that night included state Senator Ed Holland of Arlington, who was Wilder's campaign treasurer; Alexandria mayor Charles Beatley; Alexandria Delegates Bernard S. Cohen and Marian Van Landinghaqm, and Arlington County Board member John Milliken. While such supporters illustrated that Wilder was making headway with the party's establishment, a remark of another sponsor of the event, state Senator Clive L. DuVal II of McLean, the liberal chairman of Northern Virginia legislative caucus, showed how far he still had to go. DuVal said he was attending only out of friendship and respect for his Senate colleague, but his presence "in no way connotes an endorsement."

But an upbeat Lain O'Ferrall, who was advising Wilder, told reporters, "there's nothing that's going to get him (Wilder) out of the race." The correct political reality, O'Ferrall said, was that the Democrats could not win in 1985 without getting 90 percent support from black voters, and Governor Robb and gubernatorial aspirants Davis and Baliles knew that, and would do nothing to risk antagonizing Wilder and his black supporters.

Larry J. Sabato, the brash University of Virginia political scientist who had been naysaying Wilder's chances from the start, disagreed. At a news conference he held at the Capitol to offer his analysis of the 1984 Senate and Presidential voting, he warned that unless the Democrats took steps to recapture white voters—no Democrat running statewide had polled a majority of the white votes in eighteen years—their party faced a dim future. Sabato went on to suggest that in 1985, the Democrats would be better off risking the defection of blacks than to appear to be catering to them. "There's no issue like the race issue in Virginia," said Sabato. The party might be in a stronger position, Sabato said, "were it seen to be standing up to some of its constituency group members—be it women, be it teachers, blacks. The party is seen as captured by these groups," he said, noting that its Senate candidate, Edythe Harrison, a liberal female delegate, got only 30 percent of the vote against Republican John Warner, who snared 83 percent of the white male vote and 79 percent of the total white vote. While the prospect that Delegate Mary Sue Terry might wind up as the Democrat's nominee for attorney general also was a problem, Sabato said that would be a "peripheral weakness" compared to a Wilder candidacy.

The best issue Wilder had, Sabato said, was "white guilt, and so let's face it, he's going to try and claim that anyone opposing him for any reason is guilty of racism." If Sabato hadn't dug himself in a deep enough hole with Wilder over those remarks, another observation would forever bury his credibility with Wilder: Sabato said that Wilder had only one chance in a hundred of being elected, and "the odds are much greater that he would sink the ticket" and damage the party for years to come.

The long odds assigned to Wilder by Sabato and the resulting publicity given to them enraged Wilder, who said Sabato ignored a poll taken for one of the gubernatorial candidates that showed he had a 46 percent favorable rating among those likely to go the convention, while only 6 percent gave him an unfavorable rating.

Wilder dismissed the thirty-one-year-old Sabato, noting "this savant was even unable to say who would win the Coleman-Robb race. When did he get to be an expert on that? He's not a prognosticator of the future. What he can do is analyze the past." Allowing Sabato to air his view without challenge sets "a dangerous precedent. And unless Democrats in positions of leadership counter the nonsense issued by the likes of that professor at UVa, it will do more damage than my candidacy or any future black candidacy could have. I have never known of a more blatant, direct, and open racist preachment that the Democrats should kick blacks in the behind."

After a meeting with Robb, Wilder asserted that he effectively had the governor's support. "I intend to be at the convention to get the nomination. He

(Robb) didn't discourage me. And not only that, but he said he had no intention of discouraging me." Press secretary Stoddart, however, said Robb "did not indicate support or opposition. Rather, he reiterated his neutrality."

At a news conference a few days later, Robb joined Wilder in criticizing Sabato. "I reject categorically the thought that for any reason that anyone who is black or a woman cannot or should not seek statewide office....[but] I think spirited contests for all of the statewide offices are healthy." Sabato should be called "Dial-A-Quote," said Robb, employing a Stoddart-inspired moniker that stuck with the young professor. Robb also chastised the correspondents who regularly reported on Virginia politics for constantly writing about the perils of nominating a black and a woman. "If you keep it up," lectured Robb, "we're going to have the whole electorate feeling they have to view this whole decision on the basis of race or gender or ethnicity. I don't want that to happen."

However, Robb agreed with Sabato, in a foreshadowing of his role with the Democratic Leadership Council, an embryonic association of moderate Southern and Western Democrats, that the party must start appealing again, statewide and nationally, to white, conservative males, and not just blacks, labor unions and other "special interest groups."

The governor also supported a plan offered by Senate majority leader Hunter B. Andrews of Hampton that would strengthen white representation at the 1985 nominating convention. Andrews proposal automatically would certify as delegates the eleven hundred Democrats, predominantly white males, who held state or local office, leaving fourteen hundred other delegates to be chosen by the localities. Further, Andrews wanted to require the locally chosen delegates to be elected at the precinct level, rather than in citywide mass meetings that had permitted black voters in the Hampton Roads area to seize control of the nominating process earlier in the year in behalf of Jesse Jackson's presidential candidacy. Andrews, who was touted briefly by his political ally, Senate Finance Committee Chairman Ed Willey, as a possible candidate for governor in 1985, vociferously denied that he was trying to limit black participation in the party. "If you interpret it that way, you are the racist," he said. "I'm trying to broaden the base of the party...In Mr. Jefferson's house, there are many rooms. There is a place inside for everyone."

Not everyone agreed with Andrews' interpretation. "Without disguise or qualification, it is designed to eliminate significant minority participation in the Democratic party," said Richard Taylor, director of the American Civil Liberties Union's voting rights project in the state.

"Ironically," said the Roanoke Times and World-News, "Andrews believes that by restricting the influence of minority interest groups he would be broadening the base of the party."

Wilder was less caustic, saying only that "the limiting aspects of it bothers me."

A version of Andrews's plan was adopted by the state party for the 1985 convention. It expanded representation on the central committee from fifteen to twenty members for each congressional district, but insisted that the representation reflect participation in the previous governor's race, rather than in the 1984 presidential contest.

Anyone But Wilder

Robb acknowledged that some Democratic members of the House of Delegates, who run for re-election at the same time as the candidates for governor, lieutenant governor and attorney general, "understandably get a little bit edgy," about the prospects of running with a black and a woman, but he said he would stay out of the shaping the ticket unless he became convinced it was headed in the wrong direction. Robb all but invited challengers, however, saying, "I'm not discouraging anyone. If somebody wants to get in, I'm saying go to it. I think anyone who suggests that a challenge to Doug Wilder is racist or that a challenge to Mary Sue Terry is sexist is just way off base. I'm saying don't be intimidated by all of these stories about race and gender. I'm saying have enough backbone to declare your candidacy against a black or a woman or anyone else."

In Wilder's case, Robb said, a challenge would be healthy "particularly given the doubts that have been raised." Robb reiterated his observation, made when Wilder announced, that he was "not certain that Wilder, or any black candidate, can command a majority, but I would hope we've come to the point in Virginia that that can happen."

Wilder said, "Certainly I don't believe that anyone who challenges me *ipso facto* is a racist." It would be just as wrong for him to dismiss any opponent as racist as it would for others to dismiss him because he is black, he said. However, Wilder added that some Robb surrogates, whom he would not identify, were suggesting he give up, but Wilder conceded that "they're not necessarily operating at the governor's direction, and I have to take him at his word."

Added Terry, "I certainly wouldn't view a challenge to my candidacy as sexist."

Nonetheless, Wilder insisted that much of the talk about opposition to his candidacy was "racially inspired. They're saying I shouldn't have announced. That's racially inspired. No one should welcome opposition (but) I'm prepared for it, should it come. I never thought that no one else would announce."

Owen Pickett, still smarting from the Senate nomination that was wrested from him two years before, couldn't resist expressing doubts about a ticket with Wilder on it. "Unfortunately," he said with apparent sincerity, "I sense racism creeping into voting patterns. And if my perception is correct, putting a black on the ticket would crystallize that feeling."

In 1988, in an interview a few months before he died of a brain tumor, at age thirty-eight, Stoddart recalled Wilder's vehement reaction to the suggestion that Robb was looking around for others to run. "I don't think there was any pressure from anyone, for anyone. Robb had no ulterior motives. If anyone should be blamed, it's me," for his "this is still Virginia" comment.

Stoddart recalled rumors were swirling that Bagley was going to challenge Wilder; another group wanted Ronald Carrier, the effusive president of James Madison University, to run. "But politics at eleventh hour doesn't work that way," Stoddart said. "It's pretty hard to manufacture a candidate. The idea that there are people out there orchestrating who should run for governor, a conservative, is absurd."

Robb was aware that many people thought Wilder couldn't win, Stoddart said, and they repeatedly cited Sabato's dire quotes. If anything, Stoddart said,

Robb probably did more to say to the doubters, "'Hey, wait a second, we can win this race.' At that time, Robb absolutely considered Wilder and Terry would be nominees. But he wanted to say to others, 'You don't have to feel that you are hostages, for racial or sexual reasons, if you want to run.'"

No sooner had Wilder dampened the fire sparked by Sabato's inflammatory advice when he was faced with what he interpreted as an even more formidable anyone-but-Wilder threat. In early December, State Democratic Party chairman Alan A. Diamonstein presided at a meeting of eighteen members of the House of Delegates, all of them white males, at which the main topic of discussion was the danger to the party of running a ticket headed by a perceived liberal, Lieutenant Governor Davis, and including a black and a woman. "Too much of a rainbow," was one way that ticket combination was described.

Diamonstein, the Newport News delegate who had been a nervous passenger the day that his pal, Delegate Al Smith, had refused to take Wilder to lunch at the Commonwealth Club, insisted that he had not intentionally excluded black and female delegates from the meeting, which was held in the office of House Speaker A. L. Philpott. He said it was not intended to be part of a "stop Wilder" effort, but admitted that the attendees talked about how a too-liberal Democratic statewide ticket might affect the re-election chances of the delegates. (The senators serve four year terms and are not elected the same year as the governor and delegates.)

"The consensus," one legislator who attended told Margie Fisher of the Roanoke Times and World-News, "was that with Wilder on the ticket, Democrats can't win next year. It was generally perceived to be a very serious problem." Wilder's candidacy might be so disastrous, one member said, that Republicans could gain control of the House of Delegates, a fear worth mentioning only because it illustrates how far the paranoia had spread—the Democrats outnumbered Republicans two-to-one, and in many districts the GOP didn't bother to nominate a challenger. Among the strategies considered at the meeting, according to the delegate, were asking Robb to intervene, and getting one of the gubernatorial hopefuls to drop back and pre-empt Wilder.

Another delegate at the meeting pointed out that Robb had been telling national Democratic party officials that they must end the perception that the party caters to special interest groups. "How is it going to look," the legislator asked, "for the governor that he's building a castle on sand in Virginia" that could collapse under a wave of anti-black sentiment. The governor must "determine whether he's going to be a political leader or not. If he wants to be taken seriously at the national level, he's got to practice what he preaches at the state level."

Robb said he was unaware of the gathering, which came to be known as the Diamonstein Eighteen, but defended it, saying "you are not going to stop political people from getting together and talking about...prospects." The campaigns of Davis, Baliles and Terry also said they had been unaware of the session.

Baliles issued a statement that said while "the freedom to confer is fundamental...open minds and open meetings more accurately reflect the

Democratic heritage. I will not participate in any effort to deny consideration to candidates on the basis of race or gender....Those who raise these issues do not understand" that every candidate should have "a fair and equal opportunity to rise and stand and to run." A Davis spokesman, Ken Storey, said it was unfortunate that a meeting to discuss the party's potential candidates had been called without invitations being issued to the candidates.

Wilder was livid. "If it wasn't a stop Doug Wilder meeting, what was it?...Let's get it out on the table now, let's not kid ourselves. The problem is that I'm black and that is just anathema to some people. Party leaders and the politicos are the ones who bring it up, not the John Does on the street. The John Does on the street say, 'Listen, I'm going to support you.'" He said he was not surprised, however, and took a shot at Diamonstein and the Commonwealth Club fiasco, saying, "You remember that some members of my own party didn't think well enough of me to even have lunch with me."

Wilder said fellow Democrats plead, "'It's not me, I have no prejudices at all. It's that redneck,' that nameless, faceless redneck" who is not ready for a black so close to the governorship. "Well," Wilder went on, "in moving around the state I haven't found that redneck they're talking about." It was the white legislators who are not ready for him, Wilder said. "I think the real crunch is (they feel),' my God, it may happen.' That's the frightening thing to them. These people who don't want to be quoted—I won't say they are cowards—but these people who say blacks can't win, they go back to their respective areas and ask blacks to vote for them."

The day after the Diamonstein gathering, Robb held an hour-long news conference, called partly to get the race issue "out in the open," and behind the party, saying it had been "blown out of proportion" by the media. But Robb said, "If there is anybody who thinks they (Wilder and Terry) ought to withdraw (they're) not being either realistic or fair. But at the same time, there is absolutely no reason why either of those individuals cannot be challenged for those positions."

Robb said it wouldn't be easy for Democrats to attract white men across the country, which it must. "But I'm telling you it's going to be virtually impossible if every story begins with a race line or a gender line. They're never going to be able to cross over that threshold." He blamed reporters, saying, "everybody's had their turn at writing the stories that relate to race and gender. I think that's been pretty fully explored. Now let's move on to other qualifications. The candidates themselves can't do it unless you let them." Campaign coverage should focus on qualifications, Robb said. "You know the power that you have," he told the reporters. "If you choose not to cover something, it didn't happen, for all practical purposes. And how you cover it is how it happened...All I'm trying got do is point out that you can keep it alive or you can choose to try to not take the easy stories. Take the tough stories."

Two weeks after disclosure of the meeting, the legislature's seven black members issued a statement calling on the Democratic Party and its candidates for statewide office to pledge "in unequivocal terms their strong disapproval of any such meetings....Those who truly believe in opportunity and equal justice for all must make their voices heard."

That same day, Wilder and Diamonstein met for forty-five minutes, during which Diamonstein told Wilder that he had tried to invite Delegate William P. Robinson Jr. of Norfolk, one of the five blacks in the House, to the meeting, but could not reach him. "Alan regrets that any such meeting like that ever came off," Wilder said afterwards, but "how could one be satisfied with a secret meeting, with one of exclusion. I would hope that enough opprobrium has been justifiably raised that such a meeting will never occur again."

Diamonstein said he owed no apology to Wilder. "Anybody who knows the true facts of the meeting will know that is a question that is not deserving of an answer."

Ironically, the Wilder-Diamonstein get-together may have done more to estrange Diamonstein, and to some extent other close associates of Governor Robb, from Wilder, than it did Wilder from them. Diamonstein told friends that Wilder privately had accepted his explanation, and that he had promised to make a public apology, but he never did. Others said Wilder had no intention of apologizing because it would deprive him of an issue, and perhaps cost him support among blacks, some of whom were demanding Diamonstein's resignation as state chairman.

Wilder's latter-day view was that he never thought that Diamonstein was promoting a stop-Wilder movement, but he told him that would be the perception, and "even if I said it wasn't that way, no one would believe it."

Meanwhile, the Republicans were queuing up for the chance to run because, as state party chairman Donald W. Huffman put it, Wilder's candidacy had put the Democrats "in a real box." Although Huffman said that Wilder would be a "competent, articulate candidate...realistically speaking, in the state of Virginia (the Democrats) may well have a problem" if he were nominated.

George Bowles, a radio reporter and weekly newspaper columnist, wrote in September, 1984, that with Wilder as the likely Democratic nominee, "the Republicans regard winning the nomination as very nearly tantamount to victory." Bowles, who also wore the hat of confidante of, and conduit of planned leaks from, Robb and other Democratic officials, added that GOP strategists "do not believe he (Wilder) has the remotest chance of winning a statewide election in conservative Virginia. This view is privately shared, in fact, by many of Wilder's Democratic friends."

A Republican member of the Fairfax County Board of Supervisors, Thomas M. Davis, who was supporting the gubernatorial bid of former Fairfax County Delegate Wyatt B. Durrette, said the lieutenant governor is "a safe race for the Republicans this year" because Wilder "is so liberal than he is not in tune with mainstream Virginia."

The laundry list of potential Republican opponents to Wilder included State Senators John H. Chichester of Fredericksburg and Wiley F. Mitchell Jr. of Alexandria; Delegates A. R. "Pete" Giesen of Waynesboro and Frank D. Hargrove of Hanover; Maurice Dawkins, who headed the Virginia Council of Black Republicans; John Alderson of Botetourt, co-chairman with former Governor Godwin of the 1984 Reagan-Bush re-election effort in the state; Richard A. Viguerie, the direct mail wizard of the New Right, who previously had confined his activities to helping others run for office, and former attorney

Anyone But Wilder

general Marshall Coleman.

Coleman, who had been raising money for another run for governor, announced in early December that he would instead seek the number two spot. "I have decided not to be part of a long, bitter, divisive and potentially destructive campaign for the top of the ticket with two men (Former Delegate Wyatt B. Durrette and Congressman Stan Parris) who share my philosophy and ideals of government," said Coleman, who had moved to Northern Virginia after his defeat, and was practicing law in Washington. "The fight I have chosen will be with the Democrats, not the Republicans."

Hatcher Crenshaw, a Richmond businessman who was the Third District Republican chairman, said "with Doug Wilder as the Democratic candidate, it seems like to me a lot of conservatives are not going to vote for Doug Wilder." Asked if that were because Wilder is black, Crenshaw, who later became a member of the General Assembly, acknowledged, "that has a lot to do with it, but it's his record too. It's just like Geraldine Ferraro being the first woman" to run for vice president (on the recently defeated 1984 Democratic ticket)."

John Alderson, who was co-chairman of Parris's gubernatorial campaign, said any of the Republican hopefuls would do well against Wilder. "It's not because he's black," said Alderson, "and it's not because he's from Richmond. It's because he's a liberal."

Wilder assailed the Republicans repeated description of him as a liberal, saying, "that's a code word for racism." Whatever they brand him, or offer him, Wilder said, "I'm in the race to stay and there is nothing that will stop it." He said one caller had offered to make a half million dollar campaign contribution if he dropped out and opted to run for Congress in 1986, and another said if he waited four years, he would raise money and support him.

However, Wilder said, most people emulated a man, "white, with a red neck, driving a pickup truck," who double-parked, blocking traffic, and called out, "'I don't like what's happening to you; it's not fair.'"

181

37. Nomination

The Republicans met a week before the Democrats, in Norfolk on June 1, and nominated a ticket designed to reunite the state's conservatives, some of whom had bolted to Robb and the Democrats four years earlier.

Wilder's opponent would be a quiet and unassuming two-term Senate colleague, John H. Chichester, a forty-seven-year old insurance executive who was little known outside of the Fredericksburg area, where he was a member of a prominent political family of Byrd Democrats-turned-Republican. Chichester won the hotly contested nomination when weary delegates gave him a majority on the fourth ballot over Coleman and Viguerie. Giesen and Dawkins had dropped out in early balloting. Heading the ticket was Wyatt Durrette, a former Fairfax County legislator and lawyer who had moved to a more conservative base in a Richmond suburb after his loss to Baliles in the attorney general's race in 1981. Rounding out the ticket was the GOP nominee for attorney general, Delegate W. R. "Buster" O'Brien of Virginia Beach, an affable lawyer and former football player.

The Republican lineup was considerably more conservative than the 1981 ticket that was swept by the Democrats, on which Durrette lost a close race to Baliles, but it lacked a moderate, mountain valley Republican, who once were the core of the party. At a unity breakfast following the Norfolk convention, former Governor Godwin predicted the Durrette-Chichester-O'Brien team would bring "a response from that great army of conservatives, independents and conservative Democrats...who have voted with us in the past....and are so vital."

Chichester had announced his intention to seek the Republican nomination for lieutenant governor on December 12, 1984. In what might have served as a blueprint for the presidential campaign of George Bush three years later, he made it clear he was going to run as a law-and-order conservative against his presumed Democratic opponent, a criminal-coddling liberal. Chichester denounced the "philosophy of leniency" that led to "coddling of criminals." Specifically, he criticized the state corrections department agreement with the American Civil Liberties Union over operation of the prison at Mecklenburg, saying Virginians want a government "that will not acquiesce to the ACLU and other pressure groups."

Republican state chairman Donald W. Huffman also took aim at Wilder, declaring that the GOP will "be able to make a liberal out of him...and I think he is..."

Chichester's announcement did not reflect a polished campaign apparatus—his prepared text was distributed on paper that had no letterhead, and it was peppered with misspelled words. He praised the Southern tradition, quoting Woodrow Wilson as saying "all Southerners seem to be born with an interest in politics," and invoking the "legacies of our nation's sons" from his area, including Washington, Monroe and "the great Lee family."

Chichester had compiled a solid conservative voting record during his six years in the Senate, but some party leaders worried that his reluctance to support transportation issues for Northern Virginia would hurt him—he had voted against funding for the Washington area subway system. He also was remembered for a legislative ploy on ratification of the Equal Rights Amendment, which effectively doomed its passage in Virginia. Chichester abstained from voting, offering the lame excuse that he had a potential conflict of interest in that female members of his family might derive personal gain should it be ratified. The final vote was 20 to 19 in favor of passage. The amendment, which required twenty-one votes for adoption, likely would have passed had Chichester voted either for or against it. If he had voted no, Lieutenant Governor Robb would have broken the tie, and as a avowed supporter of the measure, that would have produced the twenty-first vote.

Nonetheless, Chichester had the qualities that make for a safe candidate: He was pleasant and good natured, with wavy, gray hair; he wore glasses, was slender, and had an attractive young wife, Karen, and daughter, Holly. He had been a Jaycee, Big Brother, Rotarian, Mason, Shriner, Army reservist and was a graduate of Augusta Military Academy and Virginia Tech. Chichester was also a licensed pilot, and campaigned around state in his own airplane.

In the mass meetings leading up to the GOP convention, Chichester attacked Coleman with the fury underdogs reserve for frontrunners. Coleman, who had run a credible race for governor against Robb four years earlier, was hoping to use a victory as lieutenant governor to catapult him back in line for another try for governor in 1989. Chichester mailed a flier to prospective convention delegates citing endorsements from three of the state's six GOP congressmen, about three-fourths of the Republicans in the legislature and his seventy-six percent plurality in his most recent re-election campaign. "If Marshall Coleman helps the 1985 GOP ticket so much," Chichester asked, "how come only one Republican legislator supports his candidacy?" The mailer included a photograph of his legislative supporters standing on the steps of the state capitol: Twenty-three white men.

Chichester also benefited from an unofficial alliance with Durrette, who won the gubernatorial nomination over Parris.

The Democrats nominated Baliles, Wilder and Terry, what Governor Robb called "the ticket for Virginia," at their convention June 7-8 in Richmond. The party clearly was hoping to build on the momentum that had begun four years earlier when Robb broke the string of three consecutive Republican gubernatorial wins. The nominees attempted to wrap themselves in Robb's mantle: Baliles invoked his name seven times in a fifteen-minute speech and Wilder, with his usual reservations, said of Robb, "with slow, steady, workmanlike style, he has changed the face of Virginia." Even the Republicans were respectful of Robb's popularity. "I'm not running against him," said Durrette, "I'm running against Jerry Baliles."

In his acceptance speech, Wilder said he "asked for no special favors" and pledged that "this is one Virginian who never has and never will lose faith in Virginia."

Baliles ridiculed the Republicans as a party of "closed minds and closed doors" whose candidates offered "a narrow and negative vision which looks backward and to the far right." Therefore, Baliles said, "we shall invite the Republican refugees from the Mountain Valley and the suburbs into our party."

Despite an outward show of unity, many delegates questioned whether the ticket might be, in the words of University of Virginia pundit Larry Sabato, "too cute by one." And the one that most of them worried about was Wilder. Senator Joseph V. Gartlan Jr., a liberal Democrat from Mount Vernon, called it "a double-edged sword. It could cut into black support, and I don't think Baliles and Terry can afford to give any of that away."

Robb warned that the Republicans "are going to belt us and they're going to bash us."

"I don't think there's any question they (the Republicans) are going to attack the ticket by showing how liberal it is," said Wilder, adding, "I'm definitely the underdog....I don't think anyone will walk away from the other two [candidates]. If any walkaway occurs, it will be my spot on the ticket."

Wilder had good reason to think that, but even if he didn't, it fit in nicely with his strategy of being portrayed as the underfinanced underdog. He also had a cornball slogan that negated any suggestion of radicalism: "Pragmatism, individualism and effectiveness through old-fashioned hard work—PIE, three fundamental values as American and as Virginian as apple pie."

Poor mouthing was a key to Goldman's strategy, to win sympathy and contributions for Wilder, and to throw the opposition off guard. It was a technique he had learned playing chess and honed in the Howell campaign, and he outlined it in a memo to Wilder. And, Goldman said, paraphrasing Henry Kissinger, "it had the added advantage of being true." Or, at least partially true. Beginning shortly after the convention, "we spun the fact that we didn't have money," Goldman admitted later, and the idea was accepted "because it was what people wanted to think, so we didn't have to push them hard in that direction. People bought the story. A few caught on; they knew differently."

The no-frills Wilder campaign was operated out of a basement of Wilder's law office on Church Hill, albeit a nicely appointed one in a building restored to garden-tour elegance, with a campaign staff composed of the candidate's son, two nephews and Goldman, who required only subsistence support to function. "It was a great office," Goldman admitted later, but it created a bit of a stir when supporters found that Wilder didn't plan to open a visible campaign office, accessible to the public.

In early summer, Goldman spread the word that Wilder probably would not have enough money to air television commercials—any—in the fall. He let the word out in typical Goldman fashion, in a series of telephone calls to reporters, so that each thought that if it wasn't an exclusive story, his or her version at least benefited from answers elicited by their own incisive questioning. The truth, of course, was that each reporter got the same carefully scripted story from Goldman.

"We'll be outspent two-to-one," Goldman said. "That's a fact of life. He (Chichester) can raise one million dollars; we can't." The relative hard times at the Wilder campaign had nothing to do with race, Goldman said, cleverly planting the idea that it might. Rather, "the bulk of the reason" Chichester would have money, Goldman went on, was because of his strong support from conservatives such as former Governor Godwin, further raising the idea of racism without really saying so.

The first deadline for reporting campaign contributions was July 8. Chichester filed early and reported contributions of $238,000. Goldman made his pitch about money on July 5, after Chichester's report was in, but three days before Wilder's was filed, which showed that he also had raised almost as much as Chichester. The gambit worked. When Wilder announced a "Dollars for Doug" drive, the News Leader dutifully reported that Wilder had cut in half his original fund-raising goal of one million dollars and had been able to raise "only" $204,000.

Wilder had set the million-dollar goal the previous fall. But Goldman said he had been unable to tap "traditional Democratic sources. It's difficult when you are the underdog." Goldman singled out organized labor, which had endorsed Wilder, as an example of a group that had not contributed. That comment appeared to be another twist of the plot. If the unions provided a lot of the early money, Wilder might have had more trouble refuting the liberal tag that his opponent was trying to hang on him. The unions came through with their contributions in October, as expected, in time to help fund a closing advertising blitz.

Goldman chose to ignore the fact that Wilder had raised $42,000 the previous month from that most traditional of sources—forty-two Main Street lawyers, stock brokers and bankers, who paid one thousand dollars each to attend a party at Lain O'Ferrall's house.

Because of the lack of funds, Goldman said the campaign would rely largely on volunteers. There was no money for a manager or a press secretary, he said. "The three-member staff will be doing triple-duty," Goldman said, and relying on Democrats around the state for a field organization. "We'll just have to be a little bit shrewder," Goldman said. Which he was. The campaign never had any intention of hiring a manager other than Goldman, who served also served as press spokesman. (Years after the campaign, Goldman insisted on sticking with the story that he was not the campaign manager.)

"I'm not troubled. I'm extremely confident," added Goldman, as well he should have been. He was confident that the reporters would swallow the story and they did. Bill Byrd, a reporter for the Norfolk Virginian-Pilot, "called me back and said, 'they like this story, give me more,'" said a smug Goldman. The Pilot put it on the front page, and the Washington, Richmond and Roanoke papers all dutifully reported the woeful problem, The Roanoke Times and World-News under the headline, "Democratic wallets barely opening for Wilder." Nephew Michael Brown was adding fuel to the tale, telling The Afro, "we still have a major need for money," pointing out that a lot of the early contributions had been in-kind, rather than cash. Back at headquarters, Goldman was smiling. The gambit had paid off again. "Like with Howell," he said, "people were asking, 'how could you do this. It says your man can't raise any money.' I said, 'great.' The idea was to get people to think you are the underdog. We set it up. People wanted to see us a certain way. An underdog was consistent with that view. We aggressively adopted the banner of not having money, what we called the Poor Boy strategy. We aggressively spun that story. I never denied that (although he didn't volunteer it at the time). The reports were there for everybody to read."

It also was important not to give the perception that Wilder couldn't raise money. "It's a narrow line to walk," said Goldman. "But let Chichester be the million-dollar candidate."

WILDER: HOLD FAST TO DREAMS

Dennis Peterson, Chichester's campaign manager, wasn't buying the story, however. He said the million-dollar war chest being attributed to his candidate included joint campaign efforts with the rest of the ticket, and donated services. "It's a traditional Democratic approach to cast themselves as an underdog," said Peterson, who pointed out that Chichester was $98,000 in the red, while the Wilder report showed he had $131,000 on hand.

But few listened to Peterson's lament. It was too good of a story: The black guy, the underdog, rebuked by what Henry Howell calls the Big Boys, would turn to the little people.

As for all that money in the bank, Goldman said it merely showed that Wilder was frugal and conducting his campaign in "a sound, sensible manner. We believe that is one reason we have over fourteen hundred small donors; the middle-class taxpayers of Virginia know that we will spend their hard-earned dollars wisely." If that wasn't convincing enough, Wilder lowered the goal again, saying the campaign hoped to raise between $400,000 and $500,000.

Goldman added that he had confidence in his candidate, who was "a war hero, who has voted six times more effectively than our opponent and who has twice as much experience. I don't think we need a million dollars" to beat the lackluster Chichester, of whom one wag said, that even in Virginia "it's better to be black than gray."

It all played nicely into the next step of the scenario—the tour. If he couldn't afford to reach the people by television, Wilder would do it the old fashioned way—he would go to them directly, in their towns and homes, no matter how far off the beaten track. He might be able to afford that kind of a campaign, in a borrowed station wagon, if people would be good enough to feed him and give him a place to rest his weary head at night. He hoped to raise $34,000 along the way, in a "Dollars for Doug" drive, or $10 for each mile of the tour, to cover its costs. "We're hopeful there's more money out in them thar hills," said Goldman in a feeble New Yorker's imitation of hill talk. Wilder played the game too, saying at the start, "I like to think of it (the tour) as an effort to show that we care, even though we do not have the millions to do it on television."

38. On the Road

Wilder began his tour in the southwesternmost corner of the state, four hundred and fifty miles from Richmond, an area so isolated from most of Virginia that some towns are closer to the capitols of eight other states than to Richmond, and as a result, its college students are treated as in-state students by universities in nearby Tennessee.

To be ready for the kickoff on Monday, Wilder flew down on Sunday night. To get there by commercial airlines from Richmond, it is necessary to change planes in Charlotte, North Carolina, and land at the Tri-Cities Airport in Tennessee, from where it is an hour drive to Jonesville, where Wilder spent the night at the home of Edgar Bacon, a former delegate who had seconded Wilder's nomination at the convention.

Goldman and Wilder's nephew, Michael Brown, drove from Richmond to Lee County in the car they would use during the tour. In one of the many master strokes of the campaign, Goldman managed to convey the impression that Wilder was bumping around the state in a borrowed, beat-up station wagon. Nothing could have been further from the truth.

"It was a magnificent station wagon, just tremendous," a brand-new, full-sized, fully equipped Pontiac, grinned Wilder, who had left his two Mercedes Benzes at home, but hardly was sacrificing comfort. As for being borrowed, that was true in so far as it had been loaned to the campaign, an in-kind donation from a Richmond auto dealer.

It was a rainy Monday morning, August 1, 1985, when Wilder set off on a trek that would take him into three hundred cities and towns, traveling 3,400 miles over sixty days. The first couple days were critical to the public relations success of the tour, because a large section of the Richmond-based press corps had shown up for the kickoff, but would begin to fall off as the trip settled into a routine.

Day One began with a fundraising breakfast at a motel in Lee County, and Wilder was impressed that thirty-five or forty people squished through a heavy summer rain to have eggs with Bacon, and to meet Wilder.

Bacon, Wilder's guide on the first leg of the tour, whom Robb had named to the state highway commission, then led off a trek around the county, "doing everything he could to impress us about the lack of roads," Wilder recalled with a smile. The caravan of press vehicles trailing Wilder's station wagon wound its way over mountain roads to Cumberland Gap, where Wilder was photographed standing in the rain by a tablet that marks where Virginia, Kentucky and Tennessee intersect, and from where the pioneers cut through the mountains on their way west. Next the contingent snaked its way to whistlestop crossroads with the kinds of names that reporters love to use for datelines—Cudjo's Caverns, Ewing, Rose Hill, Ben Hur, Dryden, St. Charles and Pennington Gap.

At each stop, Wilder shook every hand offered, and a few that weren't. "We never bypassed a town," said Wilder, whose route followed the back roads because "that's the only way you can meet people. You can't meet people on the interstates—all you'll see is cars." At the Lee County courthouse, Wilder was greeted by one of eighty-nine black residents of the county of 26,000 people, and he was non-committal about Wilder's candidacy. "I'll have to weigh it," the man said.

Charles Calton, the Lee County circuit court clerk, told reporters that some folks in the area "might not vote for Wilder because of the color of his skin, just like some might not vote for a woman, but by and large that won't make a difference."

He stopped in medical clinics, auto garages, grocery stores, banks, and in the coal country, he exchanged his customary uniform of suit and tie for a miner's cap, boots and striped coveralls, an outfit that provided yet another carefully scripted "photo opportunity" that kept his tour in the news.

Wilder had decided not to campaign on Sundays, both out of respect for those people who observe the Sabbath, as many residents of the rural Bible Belt do, and to give him a chance to plan the next week's strategy. After a couple weeks on tour, he made occasional trips to Richmond on Sundays, but initially he stayed on the road.

The first Sunday he spent at the home of "a fellow named Bob Lambert, who had this giant Confederate flag on the flag pole in his yard." Lambert, whose historic home in the lovely town of Abingdon had been the residence of a former lieutenant governor, cooked fresh trout for Wilder, and as they chatted over dinner, Lambert "told me what the flag meant to him, and assured me that it had nothing to do with me. And," Wilder added, "he made a nice contribution to my campaign," before he left the next morning, for the second week of the tour. The chat with Lambert about the Stars-and-Bars reassured Wilder, who thereafter said he was not necessarily turned off, or offended, when he encountered people who proudly displayed various Confederate symbols.

"I've come to learn that the flag represents Virginia's heritage, its history, not activism for the cause," Wilder told reporter Nancy Cook of the Newport News Daily Press, who took a picture of Wilder standing in front of a Confederate flag at a general store in Boones Mill. The owner of the store told Wilder, "I really like what you're doing; I'm going to support your candidacy."

As with the Confederate symbols, Wilder adjusted to hearing men called "boy," a term that had so upset him three years before, when House Speaker A. L. Philpott had invoked it to refer to Wilder and other black legislators. It was a revelation that the word had a more benign meaning in the western part of the state, where The War Between the States was not the living legacy it was in Richmond and Southside. After a while, Wilder and his son, Larry, began to refer to each other as "boy," slapping each other on the back and calling out, "hey boy." Larry, who was between his first and second years of law school at the University of Virginia, replaced the candidate's nephew, Michael Brown, as the driver so Brown could return to Richmond and work at campaign headquarters.

While Wilder was willing to pose with relics of The Lost Cause, most of the time he refused to talk about race, except to acknowledge that he realized it was going to be a factor in the election. "I will not suggest that anyone who votes against me is racist," he said. "I don't want anyone to vote for or against me because of my race. It's not a political consideration. I ascribe it to irrelevancy."

On the Road

He made an exception to his guideline of not discussing race when the tour arrived in Appomattox, the town where, a sign boasts euphemistically, "the North and South were reunited." Near the spot where Lee surrendered to Grant, Wilder admitted, "sure, I've felt resentment at the racism myself and other blacks have had to suffer in Virginia. But I've never let it permanently scar or destroy me. I didn't let it turn me bitter as it has other blacks who didn't receive encouragement."

For that, he credited his parents, especially his mother. "Of course, they told me there's a double standard in judging blacks and white, but they said, 'don't dwell on it. Be the best, seek excellence so there's never any question you're qualified.'"

He assured anyone who asked, "This run is not symbolic for me. I'm in it to win—and I will, despite the naysayers and doomsayers. The tortoise will catch the hare. I've beaten longer odds in my life before."

He went to places no politician had gone before, and everywhere, people were waiting for him, in groups large and small. "Doug Wilder's my name. I'm running for lieutenant governor. Need all the help I can get," he repeated. "I never in my wildest dreams thought I'd see the energy and enthusiasm that was being devoted to my campaign."

In Wytheville, he met the father of Judy Peachee, a consultant in Wyatt Durrette's campaign for governor (and the manager of Paul Trible's unsuccessful campaign for the Republican nomination for governor in 1989), who told Wilder, "give me some literature. I told my daughter, you're the best man and I'm going to vote for you." Wilder recalls, "I was floored."

Throughout the tour, Goldman emphasized that the low-budget trip was necessary because Wilder didn't have money to conduct the usual television-oriented appeals, a ruse that lulled the Republicans into undue confidence. Goldman bolstered the pretense by appealing for money everywhere they went, "just hoping we can get enough money to cover the costs of the tour," he said. He collected as little as five or ten dollars at some stops, to more than one thousand dollars in Wise County. More importantly, the campaign was piling up that great equalizer of commercials known as free media—every weekly newspaper and local radio station they encountered interviewed Wilder.

Wilder did his share of poor-mouthing, calling the tour "an effort to show that we cared, even though we do not have the millions to do it on television." But he also genuinely believed that "people want to be able to see you and talk to you and touch you before they decide to vote for you. Television and media are not enough. This is a way of becoming more intensely aware of what's taking place in all parts of Virginia. And when I'm through, no one, not one group, will be able to say they were written off. I want to be a candidate that cared to come, to be a voice for all Virginians," he said in what was to be the standard rhetoric of the tour.

One of Wilder's favorite escorts on the tour was Madison E. Marye, a farmer-businessman who had served in the state Senate since 1973, representing the thirty-seventh senatorial district, which includes the area around Virginia Tech, the state's largest university. Marye lives on a farm near Shawsville, on land that has been in his family since the Revolution. Marye's daughter, Charlotte Hawes, an administrator at Tech who later served as the

189

legislative aide to Lieutenant Governor Wilder during the 1987 session, and her husband live next door, in a house whose log portions were built before 1800.

As he campaigned with Marye, Wilder spoke of their friendship, the grandson of slaves and the grandson of a Confederate officer. "Today," Wilder said proudly, "we serve together in the state Senate and are friends. Only in America could that happen."

At a Democratic picnic in Montgomery County, attended by both Wilder and gubernatorial nominee Baliles, the folksy Marye, who is one of the legislature's premiere storytellers, reminisced about his grandfather, who was buried nearby.

Shortly before his death, the old Confederate soldier's wife, "a very devout, stern lady," Marye said of his grandmother, asked if his grandfather were prepared for Judgment Day. "What's going to happen on Judgment Day?" his grandfather asked. "Gabriel will sound his horn, there will be soft music, everyone will stand up, they'll play 'The Old Rugged Cross' and 'Nearer My God to Thee,'" she explained. "Won't they play Dixie?" his grandfather inquired. No, his grandmother said, she didn't think that was part of the angels' repertoire. "Well, I'll be dad-burned if I'll stand up," vowed his grandfather. Such a breach of decorum so worried his grandmother that, as Judgment Day approached, she arranged for her husband's pallbearers to bury his casket vertically, so her husband would be standing, like it or not. "But my grandfather's best friend told him what she was up to, and grandfather made him swear to reverse the coffin as they carried it up the hill," Marye went on, his eyes twinkling. "So my grandfather, very strangely, is buried standing on his head. It's that little round mound," he said, pointing to a nearby knoll.

The entourage developed a routine as the tour progressed, and the warm July days turned into hotter ones in August. Wilder arose about six and tried to be on the road an hour later. When they arrived in a town, Wilder would bound from the car and start shaking hands. Occasionally a formal event had been planned, but more often, he just walked the streets, and stuck his head in doors. A few times he was asked to leave a business establishment, but invariably it was a nervous employee unsure of the owner's policy about campaigning on the premises, rather than a statement about his candidacy.

Wilder tried to avoid campaigning in beer halls, realizing "they're not the most healthy places." Yet on occasion, around dusk, someone would urge him to greet the men—he might even call them the boys—in a village tavern or American Legion club. In such spots, his campaign card on which his Bronze Star citation was reprinted was well received. "The fact that he had served earned him great respect in Southwest Virginia," said Marye, a retired career army major. In addition to "the Korea card," as he called the reprint of his Bronze Star citation, Wilder distributed postcards with a map of his tour and a picture of him standing in front of the Main Street Grill, a blue grass bar in Richmond. The photograph, taken by a nephew, Albert Brown, (Michael's brother) was a subtle jab at The Establishment. "We were trying to show we really did represent Main Street," the short-hand term for Richmond's business and financial community, Wilder said.

He was careful about what he ate and drank. "You had to," he chuckled, "or people would feed you to death." He tried to eat a big breakfast, usually grabbed a sandwich in a convenience store for lunch, and then ate dinner with his host family, or at the pot-luck suppers that occasionally were planned for him. A favorite treat was the fresh lake mountain trout that he was served in the mountains.

"Paul doesn't eat," Wilder said of his vegetarian campaign manager, "so he never planned any meal stops in the schedule." As a result, Wilder neither gained nor lost weight during the tour. He "tightened up, lost some fat," and maintained his normal weight, between one hundred sixty and one hundred sixty-five pounds, just right for his size forty-regular suits. "It was great exercise, especially for the leg muscles."

No one in the group smoked—Wilder had given up his two-pack-a-day cigarette habit years before—which helped keep the air in the car clear, and he decided in advance to keep his alcohol consumption to a minimum. "I determined I would drink white wine only, and then just one glass." In its absence, he drank sparkling water, with a twist of lemon when he could get it, or soft drinks. Beer and hard liquor were out. But Wilder's sophisticated palate would not allow him to pass up champagne, "if it's a place where you know what you're getting."

"A lot of people told me, 'I thought you were a taller man,'" said Wilder, who stands five feet, nine inches. He explained that "people look taller on television," especially when they learn, as he had, "to stand a little in front of the taller guy, so you don't look so short."

He had packed sparingly; two suits, a sports coat, several pairs of trousers, and plenty of shirts, because they were seldom in one place long enough to send out to a laundry.

When it was time to leave for the next town, Larry and his dad might have to track down Goldman, who often had squirreled himself away in a back room, making phone calls. Back on the road, Goldman hunkered down in the back seat, a road map on his lap, munching oats and nuts and plotting the next day's itinerary.

So many well-wishers greeted Wilder that the heel of his right palm became so tender that he wore a partial glove for protection when he wasn't shaking hands.

Sometimes, Wilder got a bit giddy while riding in the car. Nancy Cook, one of the reporters who took a turn riding in the car with Wilder, said that to break the monotony, Wilder told corny jokes, slapping his knee and roaring. He talked about watching Looney Tune cartoons and "wishing the cat would eat the dumb tweety bird," or puzzling about "why the coyote spent all that time chasing a worthless roadrunner." They got punchy and silly, and would laugh at anything. Wilder dreamed about soaking in a whirlpool with water up to his chin, just low enough to prevent him from drowning if he fell asleep.

Then, snapping out of it, he and Larry would chant a mocking campaign slogan, "Never fear, Underdog is here."

"We never got lost," Wilder said. "Paul was amazing." The station wagon was equipped with a cellular telephone, which Goldman used to apprise people along the route of their timetable. "He was going crazy between those mountains," when the phone wouldn't work, laughed Wilder. As a result of calling ahead, Goldman knew which roads were closed, and what detours to follow. "We only passed up a town or two and had to go back."

Just as Wilder was becoming sanguine that he had little to be concerned about in the hills and hollows of the region, where few blacks lived and fewer visited, Larry pointed out that a carload of men appeared to be following their station wagon.

"Pay them no mind," said Wilder, glancing over his shoulder, looking over Goldman, slouched down in the back seat, beneath his ever-present baseball cap, and out the rear window, where he saw that the speeding car was closing ground on them. "They're motioning to us," Larry reported warily, "they want us to pull over."

"OK," his father said. "Pull over. I'll take care of this."

Larry wheeled the station wagon onto the berm of the two-lane road, and several men jumped out of the pursuing car, and ran to Wilder's vehicle, smiling and waving.

"You missed our town," shouted one of them. "We've got half a dozen people back there waiting to see you."

Wilder beamed, and a relieved Larry made a u-turn, and they drove back to a two-gas station crossroads called Elk Creek, in Grayson County, where several carloads of people, having read of Wilder's route in the local newspaper, had gathered at the road junction to meet him.

He never delivered a written speech, and seldom mentioned his opponent other than to point out inferentially that "rather than fly all over the commonwealth," which was how Chichester, a licensed pilot, campaigned, "I choose to walk and meet the people." Wilder said later, "that's as ugly as I got. I thought that was a fair distinction." He crossed paths with Chichester just one time, in a mountain-valley town. "You must be heading to your airplane," Wilder said good naturedly. "We always had a pleasant relationship, one on one. We never said anything negative about each other, before or after the campaign."

As he travelled from the mountains to the shore, Wilder promised "to end regionalism. We need to get away from pitting region against region, area against area," he said, in what was to be a theme of the tour. Wilder credits the tour with shaping some of his views. As a result of first-hand knowledge, he concluded for example that voters would support bond issues if they knew their own areas would benefit. They might approve a billion dollar bond issue even if their home county only got a million of it, if they were sure a local road, or school, would be built by a certain time.

The emphasis on concerns varied by locality—in Northern Virginia transportation was the top gripe, while in the depressed areas of Southwest Virginia, where the 3Rs are jokingly called, "reading, writing and the road to Cincinnati," jobs was the number one subject.

But Wilder found that many problems were common to all: Crime and drugs were concerns of students and teachers in Staunton and other small towns as much as they were in inner-city Norfolk and Richmond; transportation and education were as critical to the economy of the coal fields as they are to the government contractors around Washington's beltway.

"People know that transportation brings jobs, and that without education, you can't keep a job," he said. On topics of such universal concern, "you don't need a position paper. People don't care about all that crap," he said, having watched subway riders in Fairfax throw away his white-paper treatises as quickly as shipyard workers in Newport News.

He became convinced that voters would approve a lottery if it went to referendum (as it was in 1987) because "little old ladies came up to me and said, I'm against crime, but what's wrong with bingo?'"

The tour, which ended in September, "helped my campaign then, and it helps shape it now," Wilder said four years later, as he prepared for the governor's race, in which he repeated a condensed version of the tour. "I think I now know a little bit about what people think about taxes, crimes, transportation. But I had to hear it from the people. That's why I still travel a lot around the state."

Wilder compared the experience of traveling around the state as applying "coats of paint. You never really cover all the pores in the wood base with one coat, or two. You might think so, but that's why it pops after a couple years. So everytime I get a chance, I like to put on another coat of paint."

In politics, he said, "the more direct involvement you have with people, the better. You need to derive your strength from the people," and when that happens, "you don't need a poll" to learn what people are thinking.

"I've never had a more rewarding experience in my life," Wilder said at the conclusion of the tour. "You can't do what I'm doing as a celluloid media candidate. I met the people Norman Rockwell used to paint."

Near the end of the tour, campaigning on the Eastern Shore with Senator Bill Fears, Wilder was introduced by Fears as "the next lieutenant governor of Virginia. "The guy mumbles, 'oh he is, is he?'" recalled Wilder, who gave the skeptic one of his Korea cards. As he turned to leave, Wilder heard the man say to Fears, "they're letting all kinds of people run these days." After the election, Fears told Wilder the man confessed that "I voted for that guy" because "he came in here and asked for my vote. Never had that happen before. Not just because he's black. Never had anyone at the state level asked me." A pleased Wilder, noting that the man was not a Democrat, said, "my chances of running into him would never had occurred if I had not gone into the streets."

He never encountered a racial slur. "Never," he emphasized, adding, "and I guess less than ten people refused to shake hands. That's unbelievable. Not one incident. That's when I knew I could win."

39. Details

Doug Wilder has never been a detail man. From the start of his law practice, he always bit off more than he could chew. And it constantly caused trouble for him. Big trouble and minor trouble. Sooner or later, if he stayed in politics, it was bound to catch up with him.

It did, in the middle of the 1985 campaign, with a flurry of stories that suggested, at best, that he was sloppy in his legal practice and private business dealings. The charges were dredged up again in the 1989 campaign.

Wilder was sued twice by clients alleging malpractice (one suit was settled out of court, the other complaint was dismissed); a rundown house he owned was the subject of neighborhood complaints that led to a special grand jury investigation; he was late applying for his license to practice law the year he entered the legislature; he was late paying property taxes on his automobiles another year; an insurance company of which he was chairman of the board was investigated for misrepresentations in the sale of its stock, and the annual conflict of interest statements that public officials must file more than once contained errors that had to be corrected on amended returns.

The most serious problem, which resulted in an official reprimand by the Virginia Supreme Court, arose from Wilder's handling of a lawsuit, which was initiated before he was in politics, that he had filed in behalf of a New Jersey family who had been involved in an automobile accident in a Richmond suburb on August 15, 1966.

Cortess Wills Jr., his wife, three children and a nephew, all residents of East Orange, New Jersey, were injured in the crash in Chesterfield County, which appeared to have been caused by the driver of the other car, Anna Ruth Neal, who gave an address in Chesterfield County, where the accident occurred.

The Willses hired Wilder shortly after the accident, to recover damages from Neal, but he apparently did little for two years, other than to write a letter to . Wills on March 6, 1968, saying he was trying to negotiate a settlement for her immediate family, and that her nephew's case was going to be separate. On July 31, 1968, Wilder filed an action in U. S. District Court in Richmond. But the U. S. Marshal was not able to locate Neal. On February 13, 1969, time ran out on the action, and Wilder was so advised by the court, but he didn't notify the Wills family. On the contrary, Wilder wrote to Mrs. Wills six months later that "your case is proceeding as well as can be expected at the moment. I shall keep you apprised of any new developments," a letter that the Virginia Supreme Court later said "could obviously have had no effect other than to mislead his clients."

Another twenty months after sending that letter to Mrs. Wills, Wilder filed an affidavit with the state commissioner of motor vehicles alleging that Mrs. Neal was a nonresident of Virginia, and on May 20, 1971, he filed a new complaint in federal court on behalf of the Willses, under the state's uninsured motorist law. At that time, Mrs. Neal was located in Richmond and served with notices of the law suit, and because she didn't respond within the required twenty days, she was found to be in default.

On October 7, 1971, Wilder addressed a letter to "Motor Company of America," in Orange, New Jersey, enclosed a copy of his new suit in federal court, and inquired if it were the liability carrier for Cortess Wills' car at the time of the accident more than five years earlier. Five days later, an insurance agency in Orange, which was located at the address to which Wilder had written to the Motor Company of America, sent Wilder a copy of a letter it had written to the St. Paul Fire and Marine Insurance Co., indicating that St. Paul was the company that had insured the Wills' car. Another six months passed before Wilder wrote to Mrs. Wills saying he had received no response from the insurance company other than the copy of its letter to St. Paul.

Nonetheless, the next step by Wilder, taken almost another year later, on March 2, 1973, amended the federal complaint against Neal to add the Motor Club of America as a defendant. There was no mention of St. Paul. The Motor Company, or Motor Club, of America, promptly moved to be dismissed as a party to the case, and a U. S. District Court granted their motion. Wilder said he listed the Motor Company, or Motor Club, of America, because the Willses told him that's who held their auto insurance policy. A lawyer for the Motor Club later said one of the Wills took out a policy with the club after the accident.

Wilder next attempted to amend his complaint to add "the proper defendant," presumably St. Paul's, to the complaint but the judge denied the motion. Wilder then voluntarily dropped the suit, without consulting the Willses. That arbitrary decision had the effect of barring the Willses from seeking a default judgment against Neal under the uninsured motorist's law, because the statute of limitations then expired.

In October, 1975, three of the Willses filed malpractice suits in Richmond Circuit Court totaling two hundred and twenty-five thousand dollars against Wilder, accusing him of negligence. Wilder was even late in filing his answer to the charges, but then hired his old friend Robert G. Butcher, one of his earliest white supporters when he first ran for the state Senate in 1969, to defend him. Wilder denied that he had been negligent, and had the gall to ask the judge to rule that his former clients were barred from suing him because the statute of limitations had expired.

About the same time as the malpractice suits were filed, the third district committee of the Virginia State Bar association, which had been investigating Wilder's conduct in the case, asked the Richmond Circuit Court to reprimand him for negligence.

Wilder hired Samuel W. Tucker, the civil rights lawyer and senior partner of Henry Marsh to represent him. Tucker argued that it would have been meaningless for Wilder to have sought a default judgment from Neal, because the Willses would never have been able to collect from her, and thus, Wilder had saved the family money and trouble.

But Judge Alexander H. Sands Jr., who later presided at Wilder's divorce, said many people obtain default judgments in the hope that one day the person involved might be able to pay. He found Wilder guilty of "such procrastination...as to amount to neglect" in his handling of the Willses' case. Sands ruled that Wilder should be reprimanded for violating two disciplinary rules, which state: "a lawyer shall not neglect a legal matter entrusted to him" and "a lawyer shall not intentionally prejudice or damage his client during the course of the professional relationship."

Wilder, who was touring Europe with a group of legislators at the time, appealed the disciplinary action to the Virginia Supreme Court, contending that he didn't pursue the case because he believed his clients' chances of recovering damages were remote. On August 31, 1978, the Virginia Supreme Court upheld the circuit court, saying Wilder was guilty of "unexcused, unreasonable and inordinate procrastination" in behalf of his clients, which the court said "constitutes unprofessional conduct and warrants reprimand. "

The court found that Wilder's handling of the case did not "reflect on his character, nor upon his legal ethics," but it did find his conduct was unprofessional and said he had "neglected a legal matter...and that he prejudiced and damaged his clients...."

The Willses' case was "relatively simple," the justices observed. What Wilder needed to have done was "routine and required no extraordinary legal expertise, only diligence and promptness." Yet he "offered no valid excuse" for not pursuing the action. The court pointed out that nearly two years elapsed after Wilder took the case before he initiated any legal action, and then he allowed that to lapse. Another two years passed before he filed another complaint, the court noted.

The reprimand, which was the level of disciplinary action sought by the bar, is a formal slap-on-the-wrist, less severe than a suspension or disbarment.

The malpractice suits eventually were settled out of court, for an undisclosed amount.

The malpractice suits and the disciplinary action both came at a time when Wilder enjoyed a reputation as a flamboyant and top-notch criminal defense lawyer, who was in the middle of one of his more publicized cases, defending the man who had killed a judge in his courtroom.

Wilder had developed a reputation for a cockiness that bordered on arrogance. He wouldn't return phone calls, and he was awful about setting court dates. One lawyer recalled that after he repeatedly ignored her requests to file a response to a lawsuit in which they were involved on opposite sides, she sent her secretary to his office on Church Hill, posing as a prospective client. When she got in to see him, she said, "now, about setting the date for this hearing." Wilder was furious.

Wilder was sued for malpractice again in 1982. An elderly Hampton woman, Maggie Allen, had hired Wilder in 1972 to recover $51,523.19 in cash that police had seized in a numbers raid at her house. The gambling charge was dismissed on a mistrial. and a judge ruled that a second trial would constitute double jeopardy. But Wilder's suit to recover the money also was thrown out. When Allen attempted to appeal that decision, her new lawyer, Michael Morrissey, discovered that her right to appeal had been forfeited because Wilder had delayed signing the judge's decision for six months, an inaction that Morrissey contended was a crucial error. In 1977, state Senator Wilder introduced legislation to get the state to reimburse the money to Allen, but the bill was rejected by the Senate Finance Committee. Two years later, Delegate James F. Almand, an Arlington Democrat, introduced the bill in the House on Wilder's behalf, but again it was killed, amid complaints that Wilder had a conflict of interest. Wilder denied an ethical problem, however, saying her claim "doesn't matter a damn to me." Finally, Allen sued Wilder, alleging malpractice, and Wilder countersued her for harassment, but both cases were dismissed.

The Supreme Court's reprimand of Wilder was raised during the 1985 campaign, and his critics pointed out that the case, which had occurred nearly a decade earlier, was still being cited in a Virginia State Bar guidebook on professional responsibility that is given to all new lawyers who begin practice in the state. But William S. Francis Jr., the attorney who represented the Willses in the malpractice actions, said "Doug made an evaluation there was no way to collect the money; he thought the claim had no merit." Although Francis was upset with Wilder about the case, he supported Wilder in the election.

"I don't think it [the reprimand] had anything to do with my candidacy and still don't," said Wilder during the campaign, adding that "I accept the judgment of the court." Wilder said later that "the tolerance that might be allowed of others, if you are in the political field, is not allowed. So I've never complained."

"It was an unfortunate episode," said State Senator Ed Holland, who was Wilder's 1985 campaign treasurer. "Frankly, it's the kind of thing that every lawyer dreads." Other lawyers weren't so forgiving, and said privately that Wilder's handling of the case was bad enough that it called attention to his judgment, and they would not support him for public office.

Wilder invested wisely over the years, particularly in real estate, and by the time he ran for lieutenant governor, he had amassed more than a million dollars worth of property in Richmond. His most substantial properties included the downtown building he owned with a physician friend, Dr. Charles Sutton, which he had used as his campaign headquarters for his 1969 race for the state Senate. Their partnership, called S & W, leased the building, at up to $70,000 a year, to the Richmond Metro Chamber of Commerce, until the Chamber purchased it in the mid-eighties.

In September, Richmond Times-Dispatch reporter Michael Hardy pointed out that while Wilder was campaigning on a pledge to improve housing and landlord-tenant laws, part of his own real estate portfolio was the subject of a dispute. A number of property owners had been complaining for years about a boarded-up row house that Wilder owned on Church Hill.

The house had been vacant since Wilder had purchased it in 1975. In the summer of 1982, a couple who was renovating the adjoining attached property, one of ten in a row of handsome, three-story brick turn-of-the-century residences, wrote to Wilder, complaining about two-foot high weeds and grass, piles of rotted construction debris and was a haven for vagrants and rats. The couple, who were preparing to move into the adjoining house, warned that a stucco wall on a two-story addition to Wilder's house was "about to crash down" against their new addition. Also, the man said he had hired a roofer to repair Wilder's side of their common roof because it was leaking into his house, "but I cannot afford to continue doing so." Finally, he said, "your rear garage is caving in."

By the summer of 1983, with the property still in disrepair, eighteen neighbors signed a letter to the city building commissioner, asking that Wilder be forced to fix up the property. Wilder responded that a truck delivering material to the adjoining house had damaged his front porch and that the company had refused to repair the porch or pay for the damages. Then he added, "having contacted the news media as well as the building commissioner's office, you certainly are not doing anything to create the type of neighborly goodwill that one would expect."

By the next year, what had begun as a spat between adjoining property owners had escalated. An area association, Neighbors of Chimborazo Park, joined in the complaints, writing Wilder to say that vandals had set two fires in his vacant and unlocked house and had entered it to burglarize adjoining property. Wilder was ordered to appear in Richmond General District Court for violating the city's building code, at which time he assured the city he would make the necessary repairs. After getting two continuances, Wilder went to court on May 14, 1985, by which time the roof and doors had been removed from his garage, leaving two free-standing walls. That action temporarily forestalled further action by the city,

But the neighbors remained irate, and in the summer, they contacted Chichester, Governor Robb, Mayor West, newspaper reporters and anyone else who would listen. Wilder dismissed the complaints as politically inspired. "I can show you a whole lot of roofs around the city that are caved in, and it's not news," he said.

A month before the election, with the row house still in disrepair, eight of the neighboring property owners, invoking a seldom used section of the law, filed a petition that compelled a circuit court judge to empanel a special grand jury to determine whether Wilder should be indicted on a charge of maintaining a public nuisance. The nine special jurors, six of whom were required to be residents of the councilmanic district that includes Church Hill, trooped out to inspect Wilder's row house, and found there was not sufficient cause to indict Wilder.

In addition to the squabble with his neighbors, Wilder had failed to list about $100,000 of his properties on disclosure forms required to be filed with the state Senate, an omission that was a violation of the state's conflict-of-interest law. But failure of legislators to list all of their assets was a rarely enforced provision of the law, and Wilder was not penalized. Wilder subsequently filed an amended report listing the properties, which included four boarded up town houses on Church Hill.

Coming just a few weeks before the election, the investigation served as fodder for the Chichester campaign, which put together a commercial detailing Wilder's various problems. The ad, which Chichester initially resisted airing, cited the housing code citations, the Supreme Court reprimand and Wilder's late payment, just a few weeks before the election, on a bill due May 1, of $1,315 in personal property taxes on his two Mercedes automobiles. Also, a radio station reported that details of Wilder's divorce might be revealed by the rival campaign, but that did not occur.

Chichester's campaign manager, Dennis Peterson—who served as J. Marshall Coleman's press secretary in the 1989 gubernatorial campaign—said the late payment of taxes was part of a pattern that illustrated Wilder's "values and sense of his responsibility. The public has a legitimate interest in whether a person seeking to represent them or every other citizen pays his taxes on time," said Peterson, who produced city tax records that showed Wilder had paid his taxes late three years in a row.

Goldman sought to downplay yet another illustration of Wilder's failure to pay attention to details, dismissing it as an oversight by "his bookkeeper or accountant."

Wilder also contended that his properties were no worse than others in the area, which was in a generally renovated section of Church Hill in what had been the white section when Wilder was growing up. In recent years, that part of Church Hill had become an integrated, gentrified neighborhood, popular with young people who often could buy historically significant houses at bargain prices for restoration. "The plan I had was to fix them up and rent them out," he explained to Washington Post reporter Tom Sherwood. "I don't think when I buy them they should automatically be transformed into a Taj Mahal."

Neighboring property owners had a different view.

"I like him personally," said Evelyn Browne Fields, a family friend who said she "used to push him (Doug) in a baby carriage." But Fields, who lived two doors from the property that was the subject of the housing violations, said, "what he is doing to our neighborhood I sure don't like. It's an eyesore. We don't like having that boarded up property in our block."

Donald L. Reid, another neighbor, said, "I can't think of worse neighbor. The thought of a politician [allowing this]...a kid could wind up falling and getting hurt. He must be stupid."

Wilder said he never rented the house—no one ever suggested that he was a slum landlord—but held on to it because of its location, facing Chimborazo Park and overlooking the valley into Fulton, from where, as a boy, rival gangs of boys had climbed the hill to battle Wilder and his friends. He hoped that one day one of his children might live in it. But the publicity forced Wilder to sell the house.

Shortly after the election, he announced the house had been purchased by HLS Associates Trust, which was owned by Wilder's friend and business partner, architect H. Louis Salomonsky, who had contributed $7,000 to Wilder's campaign. However, no record of the sale showed up at the courthouse until six weeks later, on the afternoon before Wilder's inaugural, which also was, perhaps more to the point, one day after the issuance of a second summons by the city against the property, on a complaint that inspectors had reported on December 20. The deed indicated the sale, for $34,000, had occurred on November 29, 1986, but the year 1986 had been marked out and 1985 written in. There was no explanation for the forty-three day delay between the sale date, which had been notarized by a secretary in Wilder's law office, and recordation of the deed, and neither Wilder nor Salomonsky volunteered a reason. Several persons familiar with real estate transactions said delaying recordation is rare, because in the interim the buyer conceivably could lose the property to lien holders or to another purchaser, and because mortgage holders insist on an immediate filing to protect their investment. A cash transaction could obviate the later reason, however. As soon as the deed was recorded, Salomonsky requested a building permit to make repairs on the house, prompting the city to announce that the summons would not be served.

(In late 1986, owners of the house next to Wilder's sued the lieutenant governor, complaining that in the course of repairing the roof to Wilder's house, before he sold it to Salamonsky, workmen had damaged their roof. The suit, for $10,000 damages, was settled out of court in November, 1986, a year after the election.)

What Wilder and Salomonsky didn't say—in fact they went out of their way to say the opposite—was that the sole beneficiary of HLS Associates Trust was none other than Doug Wilder, which explained why there was no hurry filing the deed. For all practical purposes, Wilder remained the owner of the house until late 1986, when the trust finally sold the house.

News of the cover-up surfaced during the 1989 gubernatorial campaign, playing into Coleman's contention that Wilder couldn't be trusted.

With reporter Tom Heath of The Washington Post uncovering a string of embarrassing details about the trust, Coleman charged that Wilder had violated the state's conflict-of-interest law by failing to list the trust's assets in his financial disclosure statement. To counter the bad publicity, Wilder made details of the trust public. Its $380,000 assets included a twenty-seven and one-half acre plot of land in Louisa County that Wilder received, in lieu of a legal fee, from the family of Curtis Darnell Poindexter, who had killed the judge in his courtroom in 1975.

Wilder also had problems as the result of dabbling in the insurance business. In 1974, a Virginia Beach-based firm, Lincoln Group, Inc., of which Wilder was board chairman, voluntarily agreed to rescind the sale of $500,000 in stock after the State Corporation Commission began an investigation of its activities. Wilder said he had been advised that misrepresentations were being made in the sale of the stock and that the board unanimously agreed to stop the sales. Lincoln Group had been formed in 1973 and sold half a million shares of stock, at one dollar each, in an intrastate offering. Other directors included an official of the state AFL-CIO and one of Wilder's fellow legislators. A number of prominent black athletes were on the board of Lincoln Group, which concentrated its stock sales in the black community. Wilder was critical of the SCC handling of the case, saying implications that it had ordered Lincoln Group to rescind the stock offering were not true. "The SCC in my judgment is attempting to give the impression of looking out for the consumer," Wilder said. He said Lincoln Group's directors fully cooperated with the SCC and wrote a letter to subscribers explaining the decision before the SCC issued its order to the Bank of Virginia-Tidewater to release the $500,000 in funds.

As lieutenant governor, Wilder got back into the insurance business, as chairman of the board the Armitrage Holding Co. of Bridgeport, Pennsylvania. Wilder's 1988 financial disclosure statement erroneously reported that Wilder had earned more than $50,000 that year from the Interstate Guaranty Insurance Co. (IGIC) of Richmond. After a check of records at the SCC failed to reveal the existence of such a company, Wilder's press secretary said IGIC "might be a Georgia company." A check with the Georgia Secretary of State's office revealed that IGIC had been sold in March of 1988 to Armitrage. Anthony J. Witzak, the president of Armitrage, said he had met Wilder at a cocktail party in Richmond a few years earlier and had invited him to become one of a handful of investors in the company, which insurances high-risk businesses. Another investor was Joel W. Harris, Wilder's top aide in the lieutenant governor's office. Harris said Wilder listed IGIC instead of Armitrage "because we wanted to show the true nature of his investment." Harris also said the $50,000-plus figure represented Wilder's investment in the firm, rather than his profit.

Harris also was a business partner with Wilder's son, Larry, and Salomon-sky, in two large discount wine and beer stores in suburban Richmond.

If some of Wilder's problems arise from his failure to pay attention, other situations arise from a penchant to challenge authority, flashbacks to his younger days, when he challenged military activities in Korea and courtroom regulations in Richmond.

State Senator William E. Fears, Wilder's seatmate and one of his oldest friends in the legislature, recalled a trip the two of them took in the mid-1970s, to South America. They signed up for a package deal, about $600 for the trip and a week at one of the best hotels in Caracas, Venezuela, where they planned to play tennis and unwind from the recently ended assembly session. Their families stayed at home. Knowing Wilder's lackadaisical attitude, Fears told him, "you better damn sure have a passport. He mumbled, 'I'll get one.'"

On the day of departure, a Saturday, Fears picked Wilder up at his home and they drove to Washington, from where they flew to Kennedy Airport in New York and transferred to Viasa (Venezuelan International Airways). Enroute to Washington, Fears asked Wilder if he had his passport. "He said, 'I won't need one,'" Fears recalled incredulously. "He said, 'a visitor's card will be enough.' The hell it will," responded Fears, as they argued most of the way to New York.

They arrived at the Viasa ticket counter about two hours before their scheduled departure, where they were immediately asked to show their passports. After an I-told-you-so exchange, Wilder said, "I'll take care of it," and bolted off. As the time approached to board, Fears told the woman at the counter that he would wait for his friend. "You know," he explained, "he's the black guy with an Afro. He's a senator, a state senator from Virginia. He'll get a passport," said Fears, not believing it.

Wilder called his congressman and next-door neighbor, David Satter-field, and "unbelievably," said an incredulous Fears, within the next ninety minutes, managed to get a passport. "I don't know how he did it," said Fears, but about twenty minutes before flight time, Wilder waltzed up the counter, passport in hand.

Not only that, Fears went on, but "we're treated like celebrities. Talk about being biased, we're immediately ushered into a VIP lounge, served drinks and food" before being ushered onto the plane. At the gate, Fears said, the woman from the ticket counter gaped in disbelief.

Having pushed their luck with customs, the two continued their bluff throughout the week. According to a friend who heard about their escapades upon their return, when Wilder and Fears got to Caracas, they found that their hotel was playing host to participants in the Miss Universe pageant. And in a Virginia version of "I Spy," a popular television series of the day in which

WILDER: HOLD FAST TO DREAMS

American spies played by Bill Cosby and Robert Culp posed as touring tennis pros to cover their identity. In halting Spanish, the cheeky Fears introduced the svelte and stylish Wilder, who sported a huge Afro haircut, as a tennis professional. Fears, who is eleven years older than Wilder, could not pass for a player, so he told the women he was Wilder's coach.

While some of the challenges Wilder raised as a lawyer were to curb injustices, such as his habit of sitting at the white lawyers' table in Richmond's segregated courtrooms, other confrontations with authority had less noble purposes.

Former Delegate W. Roy Smith, a Petersburg advertising executive, said that on visits to the courthouse in that city, Wilder's Mercedes sports car, a trademark that contributed to his flamboyant image, often could be seen parked in spaces reserved for the judge and other court officials.

"The bailiffs would come in to the courtroom and ask him to move it," Smith said, and he'd just say, "sure, in a minute."

Wilder's mercurial temperament flared briefly at the 1988 Democratic national convention in Atlanta, when he insisted that a reporter who was accompanying him onto the convention floor did not need a pass. The reporter, who had a credential that permitted him into the Omni arena but not on to the floor, volunteered to meet Wilder later, after he could obtain a floor pass, which were rotated among the media.

But Wilder was adamant. "It'll be all right," he assured the reporter. But when they got to the head of the stairs, leading to the convention floor, a police officer stopped them to check their credentials.

Wilder pointed to his own credential, which identified him as a lieutenant governor, and permitted him to go anywhere in the arena, and explained to the officer of the credential-less reporter, "it's OK, he's with me."

The officer attempted to explain to Wilder that his word wasn't good enough, that no one was allowed onto to the floor without a credential. Wilder's eyes blazed. "It'll be all right," he said, and grabbed the reporter and shoved him along, ahead of him.

At the bottom of the steps, Wilder had another confrontation with a guard. Whether it was a flashback to the injustices of his youth, or a mere tantrum arising from an arrogance of power, Wilder nevertheless muscled past the guard, reporter in tow, and headed for the podium from which Jesse Jackson soon would speak.

At the podium, two guards, armed with walkie-talkies, wrenched the reporter from Wilder's clutches, boasting "we've got him" triumphantly into their radios. Suddenly the authority-bating Wilder was transformed, replaced by a playful one. As the embarrassed reporter was escorted from the hall, a grinning Wilder called out, "I'll see you later."

40. The Campaign of '85

By mid-July, the Chichester campaign was rolling, with the candidate, in a letter to thirty-thousand Virginians, saying, "It would be hard to find two candidates for the same office who differ more than my opponent and I." The fundraising letters said "He (Wilder) has been consistent—consistently wrong on such issues as post card registration for voters, meet and confer bargaining sessions for public employees, easy abortion laws and others. He favors these issues. I oppose them." Chichester added that he was "in tune with voters. I have been a consistent advocate of the death penalty. I've worked to make it easier to get drunk drivers off our highways." He criticized Wilder's support of "liberal" Democrats, including former President Carter and former Vice President Mondale. By comparison, Chichester invoked his support of Senators John Warner and Paul Trible, and former governors John Dalton and Mills Godwin. "These are great leaders Virginians know and trust."

Chichester's campaign hit a bump in the road in September when it was revealed that he had supported legislation favorable to the insurance industry. Specifically, during the 1984 session, he sponsored and won approval of a bill that effectively prevented state insurance authorities from fining insurance agents for the same offense for which his own company had been fined $250 a year and a half earlier. Chichester contended the legislation was merely an attempt to repeal a law that was "absolutely silly....I don't have a conflict-of-interest bone in my body."

Nonetheless, the disclosure damaged Chichester's reputation and "made it difficult for him to attack Wilder," campaign manager Peterson conceded. "He was no longer Caesar's wife." Not that Wilder was. It was just another irony in Chichester's star-crossed campaign. Like a timid poker player holding a full house who is bluffed by a wily pro who has nothing better than a pair of eights, Chichester was afraid to call Wilder for his multiple indiscretions because of one slipup on his own.

"To John's credit," said Peterson, "it troubled him to go on the offensive. He was frustrated running against him (Wilder). We knew we could not win without contrasting their records," but everyone in Chichester's camp worried that whatever they did or said in attacking Wilder's record might be interpreted as racist.

To make matters worse, Wilder used the legislative voting records of Chichester's running mates against him. Research by Governor Robb's staff revealed that Durrette and O'Brien often had voted with Wilder and against the more conservative Chichester. "Doug had it both ways, and skillfully used it," Peterson conceded. "His race was an asset.'

A watershed in the campaign was a joint appearance at St. Catherine's School in Richmond, which is *the* waspish West End preparatory school, where Wilder charmed and wowed the largely white, upper-class audience of teenaged girls, whose applause for his comments were widely interpreted as a sign that his race was not a disadvantage.

After that, Wilder and Chichester made another half dozen joint appearances, and "the more they did, the worse John got," said Peterson. Chichester canceled debate briefings and rehearsals and rejected written statements as "unmanly."

WILDER: HOLD FAST TO DREAMS

Wilder's campaign slogan, "From Korea to Richmond: He's still fighting for Virginia," and his distribution of 40,000 cards that reproduced his Bronze Star citation, caused a stir when a Chinese American group complained that emphasizing his Korean War record was contributing to social strife. James Tso, president of the Northern Virginia chapter of the Organization of Chinese Americans, in the organization's newsletter, wrote an open letter to Wilder that said, "while we are appreciative of your service to our country in Korea, we must, however, point out that such an overemphasis in your campaign literature may accentuate and bring out negative images of blacks fighting Asiatics. This issue, in light of current events, is particularly sensitive in Northern Virginia, where black American and Asian American relations are going through a period of suspicion, envy and sometimes outright contention," wrote Tso, citing "fights between black and Asian high school groups."

The complaint prompted a bipartisan rallying around the flag in behalf of Wilder. Republican Senator Warner wrote a letter to Tso, defending Wilder, while emphasizing that his defense of Wilder on the issue should not be interpreted as being soft on his overall support of Chichester. "There are times when one must rise above politics to defend the rights of veterans," Warner explained. Another Republican senator, Warren Rudman of New Hampshire, who had been an army infantry captain from 1952 to 1954, telephoned Wilder in sympathy. "The Chinese Communists were the enemy," Rudman told Wilder. "They were killing us and we were killing them." A Rudman aide said the senator knew nothing about Wilder's politics, but said imputing racism in citing his war record was "one of the most preposterous things he had ever heard in his life."

Nothing symbolized Wilder's ability to unite the worlds of the old and new dominions that shared power in late twentieth century Virginia—to cross the Rubicon, as Wilder is fond of saying—better than a breakfast held in his honor in mid-August near Martinsville.

The host was House of Delegates Speaker A. L. Philpott, a crusty conservative lawyer from the furniture town of Bassett, Virginia, deep in the heart of what had been the stronghold of segregationist sentiment. Philpott invited all the Democratic committeemen and other political leaders from Martinsville and adjoining Henry County, but "to be very honest, I didn't think we'd have more than ten or fifteen."

When about fifty people showed up, Philpott admitted, "I was shocked," not only at the turnout of the townfolks, but of the media, who showed up in full force to witness the laying on of hands of two longtime adversaries.

Philpott had a history of making racially insensitive remarks, the most recent having come just two months earlier, when he complained that blacks had voted for candidates by color rather than ability in helping defeat two incumbents and Philpott allies in the Democratic primary. One of the victors, Kenneth Melvin, a young black lawyer from Portsmouth, had been a roommate of one of Wilder's nephews (a son of his brother Robert) at Colby College. As a result of that Philpott remark, the National Association for the Advancement of Colored People called for his resignation, and in lieu of that, to work against his re-election in November, something that Wilder also had threatened to do after Philpott stacked a House committee in 1982 so that Wilder's pet project, the Martin Luther King holiday bill, once again failed. Later that year, Philpott offhandedly said of the legislature's black members, "I've never had any trouble with those boys. They understand the system."

What tension may have existed in the crowd dissipated when Jay Shropshire, the clerk of the Virginia Senate and a Martinsville native who can put on a good-ol'-boy act with the best of them, said in an introduction that he felt like "President Carter when he reached the Camp David accords" between Israel and Egypt. "I embrace A. L. Philpott and Senator Wilder and I'm ready to meet anyone at the O. K. Corral" he said to laughter.

On a more serious note, Shropshire added, "times have changed and philosophies have changed." Shropshire confronted the racial issue frontally, telling the predominantly white audience, "his (Wilder's) grandfather was a slave. He couldn't go to any college he wanted to. He couldn't get into any law school he wanted to. I'm not crying on your shoulder, but he couldn't." Wilder "won the Bronze Star in Korea and he came home to Richmond and he had to ride on the back of the bus." Shropshire concluded that "you're not going to agree with everything, but regardless, he tells you what he thinks."

Such courageous public remarks undoubtedly helped cement Wilder's friendship with Shropshire, who is one of less than a handful of associates that Wilder truly trusts.

In his brief remarks, Philpott spoke warmly of Wilder, calling him "a man of high intellect, ability and oratorical experience, and told the assembled Democrats that "you'll be better for it (a Democratic victory in November), and so will the state."

A serious Wilder delivered a twenty-minute speech, the longest and most formal of his tour, in which he said "Virginia is a unity, a variety, an abundance. We can, in fact, bring all the disparate elements of this state together. To those who said it never could be, we are gathered here today to march to victory."

Philpott, besieged by reporters after the breakfast to "tell us how you really feel," echoed Shropshire's observation. "These are changing times and changing environments. Doug Wilder is proof of that. You have to change with them if you're going to survive. What's past is past." He dismissed their past differences, saying, "if I were going to comment on every disagreement I've had with every politician in Richmond I would not be there. He's the Democratic nominee, and I support the nominee of the party."

Wilder gave Philpott his due. "There were moments when I had questioned the sincerity of his involvement with the full totality of Virginia," he conceded, "but I think that today that has been put to rest." A grateful Wilder confessed, "I've grown wiser," adding with a grin that Philpott's blessing "might be the wisdom coming to me right now."

In an interview in 1989, Philpott recalled that he entered politics when he got out of the army after World War II, in the heyday of the Byrd machine, and admitted that never in his wildest dream, or nightmare, did he expect to see a black run for, and win, statewide office, much less be part of the reason it happened.

Philpott thought that many of the black politicians "never went past the civil rights stage; they stayed within the parameters of the civil rights movement, never got on a broader scale. They were one-issue politicians." Did some of his white friends get stuck too? "Yes, they couldn't change." But Philpott did? "I supposed I changed to a degree. I never went along with them on the school closings, that sort of thing. Obviously, I was a segregationist, couldn't have been otherwise, coming from my background. But I thought there were limits (to segregation) and I wasn't willing to destroy the whole damned education system just over that issue (integration). Obviously, we were going to lose anyway. I tried to tell them."

Philpott attributes Wilder's success "to the fact that he was never a one-issue person. From the first, he was able to grasp the total. I don't think Doug ever forgot his background, where he came from, who he was, but he could also see the total picture, and how you had to deal with that rather than just a small segment."

Wilder said Philpott's public embrace was "most important because it sent a signal and a message that the election was about ability and the integrity."

The moment that Joe Adler, a barrel-chested, slow-talking lawman, lumbered out of his gray patrol car outside the courthouse in Lunenburg County, and walked over to Wilder and introduced himself, a star was born. And, perhaps, a campaign was won.

Goldman had picked the antebellum courthouse, in the heart of Southside Virginia, as the background for a television commercial designed to combat Republican contentions that Wilder was soft on crime. And when Goldman observed the chance meeting between the small-town southern police officer and the urban black politician, Goldman switched plans. He dismissed with thanks the sheriff's deputies he had been planning to use in the advertisement, threw away the prepared script, and seized upon Adler. Goldman had found his man.

Working in a ninety-five degree heat, Goldman slapped a yellow legal pad on the hood of the patrol car and scrawled some dialogue, which a willing, if perplexed Adler, recited, one line at a time, for the camera. After more than an hour, Adler had recited four lines, and Goldman had his commercial.

"I'm a working policeman," Adler twanged into the camera. "I put my life on the line every day. That's why we need people in public office we can trust. The Fraternal Order of Police endorses Doug Wilder for lieutenant governor."

The thirty-two-year-old Adler, one of four policeman in the town of Kenbridge, population twelve hundred, wasn't a member of the FOP, but this wasn't "To Tell The Truth," this was cinema verite, redneck style. He pronounced "loo-tenant" governor with the appropriate downhome accent, and he looked the part: a husky white man with a moustache, full neck and broad shoulders, wearing a trooper hat, open collar shirt with badge above the pocket, standing before an open farm field giving his approval to a black dude from the city.

Adler, whose only payment for the commercial was the notoriety he gained—which included he and his wife being invited by Wilder to the inaugural festivities—didn't seek permission to appear in the commercial, there was no time for that, although Jim Edmunds, the town attorney, wandered by during the filming "and said it was OK." After seeing the spot, Police Chief Jesse C. Carter said he figured "a little publicity can't hurt" the town, which is about 30 miles north of the North Carolina border. Sergeant Frank Whitlow, who frequently shares patrol duties with Adler, gave his partner's performance a "no comment" review.

Film critic Goldman had no such reservations. He could barely control his excitement as he and Wilder drove back to Richmond to process the film. The resulting thirty-second spot was the hit of the campaign. In addition to the original spot, a portion of it was included in an end-of-the-campaign commercial originally designed to feature only Governor Robb. But Goldman spliced Adler into a portion of the spot. In all, Adler appeared in about half of the $480,000 worth of TV time purchased by Wilder. The Adler commercial won raves from syndicated columnists Mark Shields and Carl Rowan, as well as from many politicians and campaign workers.

But no one was more enthusiastic, or appreciative, than Wilder. "It established an issue for me that the Republicans usually have going their way, strong on law and order. Adler was the image of a guy who was not supposed to be supportive of my candidacy. He destroyed the myth that the Joe Adlers wouldn't support me. He was mainstream-blue-collar and rural." The beauty of the ad, Wilder added, was that "it wasn't set up—and he came over that way—not as a slick politico."

Adler said that his TV role brought him a lot of good-natured teasing, and admiration from black residents, who were "tickled to death" by his support of Wilder, which was genuine. With the boost from Adler, Wilder carried Lunenburg County by three votes, 1,542 to 1,539. Adler said he voted for Wilder, but didn't know right away if he had won because "I went bear hunting right after I voted, and didn't get back until Sunday night."

The press had been stalking former Governor Mills E. Godwin like the nearly extinct species he was. Godwin was considered a trophy to the conservatives, the only person ever elected governor of Virginia twice, once as a Byrd Democrat and once as a Byrd Republican. But like many a creature out of his natural habitat—and Godwin's was the nineteen fifties and sixties, when he was a leader of the state's massive resistance to school integration—his reactions could be unpredictable and threatening. Republican gubernatorial candidate J. Marshall Coleman found that out in the 1981 election, when he wooed Godwin until he got him, only to later decide that Godwin's endorsement, cloaked in racial terms that permitted the Democrats to exploit his message, probably cost him votes. Four years later, the Republicans again accepted Godwin's blessing, but many in the GOP were wary of what they considered a potentially fatal combination—Godwin commenting on Wilder's candidacy.

So when Godwin ventured on to the stump in behalf of the Republican ticket in mid-October, the press corps tracked him as he roamed the friendly confines of Southside Virginia, the heart of the state's Black Belt, and of its least forgiving segregationists.

The hunt paid off, appropriately, in Prince Edward County, home of some of Virginia's most strident opponents of integration, and one of the four localities that prompted the historic *Brown versus Board of Education* decision by the United States Supreme Court in 1954, which signaled the end of segregated schools in America. More than thirty years after that decision the Prince Edward Academy, originally financed with taxpayers' money to insure that the county's white children would not have to go to school with blacks, was still a viable, and virtually all-white, private school.

Godwin appeared in Prince Edward County at historic Hampden-Sydney College, whose officials, by way of disassociating the all-male school with any lingering racism in the surrounding countryside, went out of their way to point out with pride that one of its black students recently had been honored as a Rhodes Scholar.

Nonetheless, the student body was so conservative that when Republican gubernatorial nominee Durrette was greeted at the airport by members of the college's chapter of the Young Republicans, the only sign of non-conformity was that two of the dozen students who lined the tarmac—in matching blue blazers, repp ties, khaki trousers and loafers—wore no socks. There is no Young Democrat club, one of the young men announced proudly, and explained that a recent poll that showed "only" eighty percent of the student body backing the GOP ticket had been distorted by liberal faculty members.

The locale for Godwin's speech could have passed for a movie set of the antebellum South: Black women in ankle-length white dresses fussed over the young children of college President Josiah K. Bunting, and other black women in white maids' uniforms poured iced tea with fresh mint, and served hors d'oeuvres on silver platters for the guests, who mingled on the back lawn of the president's house. It was the last stop in a grueling day, and Durrette and his aides left before Godwin spoke.

The governor's jowls wobbled as he spoke, seemingly increasing the resonance of his deep baritone voice. He began with what had evolved during the day as his standard stump speech, prompting the reporters, who had heard the talk half a dozen times, to begin typing their stories, sitting on the back porch of the president's house, within ear shot of Godwin, clicking away on their lap-top portable computers. Earlier in the day, at stops in Suffolk, South Boston and Danville, Godwin, badgered by reporters for his views about Wilder, said that the election "had nothing to do with race or color." Durrette is "one of us," he told a gathering of peanut farmers at A. W. Moore's farm, not far from Godwin's home in Chuckatuck. "I know a litle about the way people in Southside think. This is the heart of Virginia," where local government officials espouse "a philosophy and commitment to government almost precisely like Wyatt Durrette's."

He repeated those views at Hampden-Sydney, but then, with enough discernible difference in the pitch of his voice that the reporters stopped typing their stories to listen, the former governor ad libbed comments that were later reported in The Afro-American under the headline, "Godwin Does It Again."

Without mentioning Wilder by name, Godwin said, "I have a hard time seeing how Jerry Baliles could ask for and espouse the record of this man. Why," he said, his voice trembling with indignation, "he actually introduced a bill to repeal the state song. He wanted to repeal the song,' Carry Me Back to

Old Virginny,'" Godwin repeated.

There was an awkward silence, broken by reporters rushing into the house to call their editors to report that yes, Godwin indeed had done it again.

Under mounting pressure from conservative backers to employ negative advertising to attack Wilder, Chichester finally relented—three weeks before election day. With $60,000 pledged by Godwin and other financial backers, Peterson, who had a camera crew standing by, dispatched it to Church Hill, to film Wilder's boarded-up row house. The next morning, Peterson flew to Philadelphia and produced three commercials that attacked Wilder on the issues of the house, his failure to pay personal property taxes on his Mercedes-Benzes and the reprimand. "While I was in the studio," Peterson said, "John called. He had changed his mind—we could make one thirty-second commercial, but twenty seconds of it had to be something like him and (his wife) Karen walking, holding hands. The last ten seconds could be negative. But for every time we ran the negative spot, we'd have to run three positive ones."

Peterson ignored Chichester and produced the three negative spots, and the next day drove to Hampton to play them for Godwin, "who liked them, and said, 'we'll pay.'" But when Peterson told Chichester what he had done, the candidate was furious. "Keep him (Godwin) away from me," Chichester said. "I don't care how much money they have."

Peterson compared Chichester's refusal to approve the negative commercials to the "rope-a-dope" defense employed by former heavyweight boxing champion Muhammad Ali, who, when facing an opponent, covered his face with his hands and dared his opponent to hurt him. "Hit me, hit me—that's what John said, to Wilder, to The Washington Post (which had revealed the insurance legislation) to everyone who attacked him," said Peterson. "But he wasn't strong enough to take it. And he wouldn't counterpunch. It was a nonsense strategy."

Finally, five days before the election, with a Washington Post poll showing Chichester trailing by thirteen points, Chichester agreed to allow the negative commercials to be aired. But by then, Godwin and his associates were not willing to foot the bill, so there was only enough money for limited showings.

The Republican National Committee had no qualms about going negative. In early October, the RNC ran advertisements in several Virginia newspapers under the headline "why did Doug Wilder neglect the needs of battered wives?" It went on to ask, "Should a beaten wife have to flee her home to protect herself—and her children?" The ad went on to say that Wilder was one of two senators who voted against a bill in 1982 that would have allowed a court to order an abuser out of the house. Wilder responded that the ads were "nasty" and a distortion of his record. He had voted against two bills on the subject, but said he did so because they were poorly drafted. One of the bills would have broadened the power of juvenile court judges to issue injunctions against abusers, and the other would have given magistrates authority to order an abuser out of the house. Both bills passed the Senate but died in the House. In 1984, Wilder noted, he voted for a much stronger bill on the same topic. Chichester's campaign manager Peterson said, "I supplied the content...there's no mystery to it. We stand by the ad."

Democratic state party executive secretary Bobby Watson, the one-time aide to former Lieutenant Governor Dick Davis, denounced the ads, which bore the name of RNC chairman Frank Fahrenkopf Jr., as "scurrilous and the lowest form of politics" he had seen in a Virginia campaign. "It's starting to appear that the RNC is trying to rescue the GOP," Watson said. The half-page ad, which did not mention Chichester or the election, ran in the Norfolk newspapers, and with minor revisions ordered by newspapers in Roanoke, but were rejected by the two Richmond dailies upon the advise of their lawyers. The RNC did not try to place the ad in the Washington area. The RNC already had spent more than $200,000 on ads for the Durrette campaign, but this was its first negative broadside. William Greener, the RNC political director, defended the ad, saying it was "as airtight a case as any a campaign has ever witnessed." He said it was time the voters "have an opportunity to view the differences of the candidates on issues the voters feel to be important."

William Wood, editor of the Norfolk Virginian-Pilot, found it "remarkable that the RNC would run an ad" in a race "that was supposed to be a foregone conclusion. Whether the ad...is accurate or not, it obviously indicates Wilder has exceeded everyone's expectations. This is the guy that was supposed to get the hell beat out of him."

About a week later, the battered wife charge resurfaced in a flier that Chichester mailed, comparing his stand with Wilder on ten issues. The mailing also said Wilder opposed capital punishment, tougher laws against drunk drivers, parental consent for teenaged abortions and "laws to protect police officers." Wilder answered by saying Chichester had voted against legislation in 1980 that would have improved coordination of services for battered wives, and pointed to Wilder's endorsement by the Fraternal Order of Police as proof of his support of law enforcement. Wilder also aired a radio commercial that said that while he was being attacked, Chichester "is the only state legislator who has been fined for unfair business practices."

Peterson credited the last-minute flurry of negativism with cutting Wilder's victory margin to four percentage points, which was closer than either of the other Republican candidates came to their opponents.

Peterson, a party pro who found another horse to ride against Wilder in 1989, when he served as press secretary for Republican gubernatorial nominee Marshall Coleman, wound up as a target of Chichester's ire. But that was after the election. "It was like the fall of Saigon," Peterson said. "We couldn't get out fast enough."

The dilemma Chichester and his advisers faced—a challenge that Coleman faced again in 1989—was how to attack Wilder without being viewed as racist. "To John's credit," Peterson said, "he was troubled to go on the offensive. He was frustrated running against him. There was nothing to go on, but we knew we could not win without contrasting their records."

Whereas in 1988 when Republican presidential candidate George Bush successfully intimidated Democratic rival Michael Dukakis by labeling him a liberal, when Chichester, or any one, tried that on Wilder, they were accused of attempting to substitute the "L" word for the "R" word, racist. "Doug had it both ways, and skillfully used it," said Peterson. "His race was an asset."

The Campaign of '85

Not to everyone. At a Republican breakfast in Weber City, on the Tennessee line, George Daugherty, a retired tobacco farmer, confided that "if the colored boy wins, darkies all over the South will get the same idea."

In the closing weeks of the campaign, Wilder outspent Chichester more than three to one, including a $400,000 television barrage. For the closing days, Goldman patched together a commercial featuring Governor Robb and the cop.

As election day neared, the Democrats increasingly spoke of the historic nature of their ticket. At a Wilder rally in Newport News four days before the voting, a retired school teacher spoke with emotion about "a cause that surely will be written in the annals of history. Robb, who was introduced as a future president, predicted that the results of the election will "say once and for all" that Virginians "look to individual qualifications and merit" rather than race and gender in selecting public officials. The Democratic ticket, he said, was "a vision of Virginia's future; they are the future of Virginia." An ebullient Wilder, hearkening back to the acceptance of his statewide tour, added, "to those who say it cannot happen, they've not been there. They've not been to the people."

On the final weekend, both campaigns made the traditional trek to far Southwest Virginia, where their campaigns culminated with rival rallies in the mining town of Clintwood. A disconsolate Chichester, asked if he in retrospect he would do anything different, said, "It wouldn't make any difference. The results would be the same. I've been talking about his record for months, but I can't get it in print....his softness on crime, on capital punishment...It's like running against a brick wall." Wilder was the picture of controlled confidence. Sitting in the back of a van next to the stiff and serious Terry, enroute to the Democrat's rally at the local high school, a wisecracking Wilder patted Terry's hand and advised, "loosen up Mary Sue."

41. Destiny

On Tuesday, November 5, 1985, Virginia voters kept what Governor Robb had said was "a rendezvous with destiny" by electing the entire Democratic ticket.

Wilder beat Chichester by 48,634 votes, garnering 685,329 to Chichester's 636,695. In capturing 51.8 percent of the total vote, Wilder also snared 44 percent of the white vote, just two percent less than Robb got four years earlier. Although he trailed both of his ticket mates—Baliles won by ten percentage points and Terry by twenty-two, he declined to blame his race for the difference. Rather, he said he had spent less than either of them.

Marshall Coleman, observing the results from the sideline, said Wilder's win "shows the stereotype has been wrong all along. These things don't just happen of the moment. It's an accumulation of demographics, of the changing face of the electorate. If the state were all 71-year-old white men, Wilder wouldn't win. Wilder's and Terry's victories are to Virginia what John Kennedy's victory was to the nation. It's particularly significant that Virginia, the leader of the Confederacy, is the first state in the South to elect a black."

A resident scholar at the conservative American Enterprise Institute, Austin Ranney, said "Wilder and Terry are considerably less frightening to whites and men, respectively, and were considered much more on their records. They are the kinds of blacks and women who are going to get elected, who don't represent a narrow constituency." Ranney added that the Republicans "certainly kept their gloves on, partly because it might affect them [adversely] at the polls, but also because it would have offended them" to inject race into the campaign.

Eddie N. Williams, president of the black-oriented Joint Center for Political Studies in Washington, ticked off a laundry list of factors that he said boosted Wilder's campaign: "It was fairly low-key; he avoided overidentification with black voters; he controlled some of his instincts; he appeared as the tactful statesman; he avoided major gaffes; he didn't pursue themes that Virginians may remember him for—polarizing themes like civil rights—and he demonstrated he was a team player....Wilder symbolizes or personifies a new thrust in black political behavior among candidates who depend on majority white audiences to win."

The day after the election, the fifty-four-year-old Wilder, relaxing in an office at the state Capitol, took time out from talking about the election to reminisce about his childhood. The first black elected to statewide office in the South since Reconstruction pointed out that his father, who died the year before he entered politics, also believed in the system. "He paid his poll taxes and never told anyone how he voted. But he was a Republican until FDR (President Franklin Delano Roosevelt) and he revered the name of Lincoln."

Wilder related the story in the same restrained manner that was the hallmark of his campaign. He appeared to be neither bitter about the past nor boastful of the future.

He was asked whether his campaign might provide a blueprint for other would-be black officeholders, and if so, what was his advice: "Speak for more than just a narrow constituency," he said. While insisting that his record was that of a moderate, even conservative on fiscal matters, he didn't shy from pointing out his support of issues important to blacks. On equal housing, redistricting, sickle cell anemia and black colleges, "I was there," he said. He doesn't dwell on it, he added, because "if you've got to show it, you ain't got it," slipping into a rare use of street vernacular. In his early days in the legislature, he could have "pandered to constituents who wanted me to put in a bill to impeach" his conservative Richmond colleague, Senator Ed Willey, "and been a hero in the black community," he said. Likewise, he said he could have jumped on the presidential bandwagon "and blown Jesse Jackson's horn, but I knew his candidacy wasn't going to do it." Nevertheless, although he resisted the temptation to "restrict my sphere of influence to color," he acknowledged it took a long time to build a political resume. He hadn't set out to build a record on which to run for statewide office, but, "I don't mean to be esoteric—as Emerson said, 'events are in the saddle, and they ride mankind.'"

He thought Mills Godwin's attack on him had backfired. "That 'Carry Me Back' stuff," as he called it, "was meant to conjure up tremendous visions" of radical behavior. So too did Godwin's criticism of the King holiday bill. "They (Godwin and his allies) said everything they stood for I voted against. It was incredible, and impossible to document. They must have been talking about style and personality, not substance and record."

He credited his two-month tour with allowing him to carry seven of the state's ten congressional districts. "I thought I could win even before I went there, but I felt even more so when I returned. He said he had no history of being offensive, but he wanted people to "know that I was not just trash" and could reject negatives themes that his opponent raised. The turning point, he said, was the breakfast with House Speaker Philpott, who pledged to support him that day "and never wavered."

If people insist on making him a symbol, he hoped what they would see in his election was that "you can't give up, you can't believe that your origin, your birth status must be a detraction; that young people will see the value of staying in school, of directing their life away from the wastefulness of crime. I'm not suggesting that I'm a role model, but if there is any benefit (to his victory) it is to show that just because you are black doesn't mean you can't rise, notwithstanding obstacles placed in your path."

While Wilder was bombarded with requests for interviews from reporters all over the country, and beyond, praise also was being lavished on Robb. "It gives him national credibility; it shows he has coattails," said Bob Roberts, a political science professor at James Madison University. Added Merle Black, a University of North Carolina political scientist, "Robb is showing other Democrats in other places how you can still win in the South—balancing the ticket and running candidates who are not really threatening." Eddie Williams agreed: "It helps to have the blessing of Robb and the ineptness of the opposition."

Wilder too credited Robb, for "cutting a swath of cloth that hasn't been seen" before. "And don't pooh-pooh that talk of a New Dominion. Some people may get the wrong impression—that Virginia has gone liberal, bananas, crazy but the change is real."

WILDER: HOLD FAST TO DREAMS

"It was people like Jackie Epps who won it for Doug," said Goldman. Jackie Epps, whose previous political involvement had been limited to giving a little money and licking stamps for State Senator Bobby Scott's campaign for the state Senate a year earlier, volunteered to work in Wilder's campaign after she attended a fundraiser for him in November, 1984.

Epps, who is a lawyer, had come to Richmond from Newport News in 1982, to work in the office of newly elected attorney general Jerry Baliles. Her application got boosts from Scott and Judy Anderson, an aide to Wilder (who later married Scott), who was working in Governor Robb's transition office. Also, unbeknownst to her, Wilder, whom she met at the inauguration, was promoting her application, as part of his unofficial duty of recruiting talented blacks to the Robb-Davis-Baliles administration. Baliles offered her a job as one of three senior assistant attorneys general, a new level position between assistant and deputy, heading the criminal litigation section, with nine lawyers reporting to her.

Epps began her volunteer activities by asking David Baugh, a barrel-chested former Richmond prosecutor, to give a fundraiser for Wilder. Baugh said "'OK, if you'll help,'" Epps said. But Baugh was so busy with his law practice that she found herself doing the bulk of the work. So she called a few friends—Jean Cunningham, who would be elected to the legislature in 1986, Roger Gregory, one of Wilder's law partners, Bob Gray, a partner in the silk-stocking Richmond law firm of Mays, Valentine, and Jackie Fraser, who worked for the city of Richmond—and they decided to have a $100-a-person fundraiser at the Downtown Club, the private Richmond club that had the reputation of being the most open to blacks and women.

"We wondered, will people pay?" Epps said. She said black people were not used to giving money to political candidates. Politicians traditionally asked them for their vote, but not their money. "I don't know if they assumed we didn't have money, or what, but one hundred dollars is a lot of money when you haven't given before," said Epps, who considered it something of a big deal when she gave $50 to Scott's campaign. Epps and the other sponsors called their friends, most of whom were black professionals, and to their surprise and elation, fifty-four people agreed to serves as sponsors, and contribute a minimum of $100. With $6,000 to start with, they got another hundred people to attend, and ended up grossing about $15,000.

"It was a very encouraging experience," said Epps, who was pleased that she had held the expenses to about ten percent—she convinced a three-piece band to play for just the $50 it cost to get their equipment to the club.

"The next thing I know," Epps said, "Doug is sending me names of people who want to have fundraisers." Soon Epps not only was coordinating fundraisers, but acting as a surrogate at events Wilder was unable to attend. While she tried to make sure that every event was attended by a mix of blacks and whites, most of the hosts and guests were black, and as Epps had found with her friends in Richmond, they seemed to enjoy being asked to participate. Few of the events raised as much money as the initial party—"if anyone gave five hundred dollars or more, I'd go off the wall"—but some of the parties raised as much as $5,000. "It was a novel thing," Epps said. "We (blacks) were actually giving money" to help a black be elected to an important office.

Destiny

State Senator Thomas J. Michie offered to host a party at his home in Charlottesville, but Epps balked when she was told that local party officials insisted that the tab be just $10. Epps had set a minimum of $25 for the events, thinking it was "a waste of money and time" to ask for less. But Michie was adamant, so Epps made an exception. "It turned out to be a marvelous event. We raised about eight thousand dollars. So after that I shut up. When local people said, 'this is how we're going to do it,' I said, fine."

Wilder was tight with the dollar, Epps learned. "Nothing went out of there (the campaign treasury) without his approval." She followed his lead, insisting that the fundraising events be spartan. "Educated people know that fundraisers are not parties," she said in response to friends who teased her, calling her Wilder's "'Bag Lady.' You don't spent a lot on food and decorations. You eat before or after. You don't want to put money into people's stomachs. They want to see the candidate."

Epps estimated that between one-third and one-half of the $700,000 contributed to Wilder came from non-traditional sources, from both blacks and whites. "He didn't get the fat cats. They gave him less than others. To Doug, a thousand dollars was a major contribution."

The contributors' list was a microcosm of Wilder's life: His sisters and their husbands and children, and an aunt; the Armstrong High School Class of 1947; the Virginia Tech chapter of his fraternity, Omega Psi Phi; his Second Street social club, The 533; Doc Thornton, who founded the Crusade for Voters; lawyers Jimmy and Phil Morris and Bob Butcher, who liked the way Wilder could quote poetry; Arthur Ashe Jr., whom Wilder could no longer run off any tennis court; Shirley G. Merhige, whose husband, U. S. District Court Judge Robert Merhige, had been involved in so many civil rights decisions; Carol Witcher, one of Wilder's frequent dates; half a dozen members of the Congressional Black Caucus; the mayors of Washington and New Orleans; relatives of several men who had less than the best relations with Wilder—Delegate Alan Diamonstein's wife Beverly, (and Diamonstein himself, who was among two dozen or so of Wilder's legislative colleagues), lobbyist Bill Thomas's wife, Suzanne, The sons of Robb chief-of-staff David R. McCloud, Patrick and Jonathan; Henry E. Howell, the former lieutenant governor who had fired Goldman, and businessman Sydney Lewis, who gave $10,000, which Wilder, unlike Howell, never even considered asking Goldman to return.

Epps went after donations from political action committees (PACs), but wasn't always so successful. She said one group, which she did not want to identify, gave $25,000 to Baliles, $5,000 to Terry and $500 to Wilder. "I was furious," she said. "but I said, `thank you very much.' They just didn't think Doug could win."

But most of her experiences were positive. Typical was an event in October at a church in Culpeper. It was scheduled to begin at seven o'clock, and the crowd began arriving even before that. They packed the small sanctuary, and sat quietly, awaiting Wilder's arrival. At seven-thirty, he called from Northern Virginia and explained the obvious—that he was running late. Epps apologized to the crowd, which offered no complaint. Many of the folks had brought food for a post-rally dinner. "They sat and sweated," said Epps, who worried the food would go bad. "I was about to go nuts," she said. Wilder didn't arrive until twenty after nine, but as soon as he walked in, there was an air of excitement. He was uplifted by the mood, and talked longer than usual. Afterwards, people came forward and handed money to him. "One little boy handed him a crumbled up dollar bill," said Epps, and a few days later, a five-dollar bill came in the mail from an elderly woman who had attended. "Maybe you can buy some stamps," she wrote.

Wilder, who had campaigned as an underdog, a David against Goliath (although Chichester hardly fit the latter description), exuberantly announced a month after his victory that he was going to create an Underdog Fund, initially financed with about $50,000 in leftover campaign funds, to help Democrats across the country whose campaigns, like his, were given little chance of succeeding. The fund, organized under Virginia law as a political action committee (PAC), later was augmented with money raised at two lavish inaugural-eve parties, and other contributions that came in subsequently. Its first financial report showed it had about $45,000 in the bank, after having received contributions of $117,579 and spent $72,528, most of the latter on the two election-eve parties. The largest out-of-state contribution, $5,000, came from the Adolph Coors Brewing Co., which usually was not associated with benevolence to the Democratic party.

Goldman declared that Wilder's PAC was "innovative—there's nothing quite like it anywhere." It was designed to provide technical assistance "to experienced and qualified Democrats" whose campaigns "need a little boost." Because the help was to come largely in the form of Goldman's time, it was dubbed the Paul Goldman Full Employment Act, an assessment with which Wilder did not take issue.

"Selected underdog candidates will be offered a full range of campaign expertise," including advice on advertising and polling, but the fund would make no monetary awards, according to a statement filed with the Virginia Board of Elections.

"I thought it would not be a bad idea to aid people," Wilder said. "We were trying to provide services, and frankly it was Paul's idea to be that person that would help others around the country." Cash grants would not be made, Goldman said, because the money wouldn't go far enough, and in some states it might be against the law. Besides, Wilder noted that if he had spent $2 million and had done nothing else, he probably would not have won.

Awards would be made to assist candidates who, like Wilder, were "people with lots of experience, but who can't get started, or are told they can't win," Goldman explained. The fund would not single out minority candidates, he added. Later he amended that to say it would especially seek out qualified women and minorities, but would limit the grants to them.

The idea won immediate praise, with Congressman William Clay of St. Louis, in remarks on the floor of the U. S. House of Representatives, saying, "At last, a PAC that makes dog-gone good sense."

But after an initial flurry of positive publicity, it became apparent that the plan was flawed. The fund ran into problems largely because of the stipulations that Wilder had imposed on recipients. By the following August, the fund still had not found any takers. Goldman didn't get rich from the fund either. He drew about $4,000 in fees, in addition to spending between $5,000 and $10,000 travelling around the country seeking worthy recipients. As 1986 ended without any takers, Goldman announced that the fund was changing its focus and would concentrate on Virginia candidates.

"My guess is that this shift in emphasis to state politics is a recognition that he has a handy tool at his disposal to bolster his own position," said John McGlennon, a government professor at the College of William and Mary and a longtime Democratic activist. In an apparent effort to downplay that aspect of the fund, Wilder announced that he was divorcing himself from its operation and naming a five-member board to administer it. The board was headed by Epps. In another one of those missed details, The Underdog Dog fund failed to file its 1987 financial report on time. Epps said there had been a misunderstanding between the PAC and Wilder's office over who should file the interim report, and that articles of organization were not adopted until early May.

When the fund finally got around to making its initial grant, the recipient hardly fit the usual definition of an underdog. J. Jack Kennedy Jr., who received a check for $2,500, was a Democratic candidate for the General Assembly running in a traditionally Democratic district. Kennedy, a thirty-one-year-old white Norton lawyer with a famous name, was a full-fledged member of the party establishment who served as the Democratic chairman for the ninth congressional district and who himself had contributed $750 to the Underdog Fund. Kennedy received the grant after he already had proved his popularity by defeating the incumbent delegate in the primary. Although it had changed its original ground rules, the fund still was not just handing out cash, Epps said. The grant to Kennedy, and others that followed, was made for a specific purpose—in Kennedy's case, to finance a direct-mail plea to pay off Kennedy's $15,000 primary debt.

Kennedy's selection "significantly broadens the definition of the word underdog," scoffed the Norfolk Virginian-Pilot, pointing out that at the time of the grant, Kennedy had raised $42,000 while his opponent, a white Republican woman, had raised $5,000, in a contest for a seat that had never been won by either a Republican or a woman. "No wonder it took the people who run the Underdog Fund so long to find a recipient. Apparently they were looking for a very special type of underdog—one who seems certain of winning." Added Republican party spokesman Steve Haner, "if he's an underdog, it's only because he acted like a pit bull in the primary."

Wilder insisted that he was not involved in selecting Kennedy. Although Wilder conceded that Kennedy might not meet the classic definition of an underdog, he added, "An underdog takes on many flavors." Wilder pointed out that "I was the underdog (for his party's nomination in 1985) and I had no opposition."

Later, when Kennedy barely won in the general election, Wilder joked that the close call proved that Kennedy was an underdog. "People say the money was given to people in return for their support of me," said Wilder. But if that were the motive, he pointed out, it didn't work. In 1988, the ingrate Kennedy supported the short-lived campaign of State Senator Daniel W. Bird Jr. who challenged Wilder for the Democratic nomination for governor.

In all, the fund contributed $20,000 to nine Democratic candidates in the

1987 legislative elections. The recipients included three women, one of whom was black, and one incumbent.

After that, the fund lay dormant. In January, 1989, the fund, born barking three years before, died a whimpering, bequeathing its final $11,000 to that original underdog, Wilder, for use in his gubernatorial campaign.

A few days after the election, Governor Robb invited the three members of the winning ticket to Washington, to appear at a meeting of the Democratic Leadership Council (DLC). Governor-elect Gerald L. Baliles and Attorney General-elect Mary Sue Terry accepted quickly. But Wilder declined. He was going to take a vacation to a Caribbean island—with an unidentified date—and the trip to Washington would interfere. But it was clear to both Robb and Wilder that this wasn't a scheduling problem; it was a perception problem.

Robb, a founder of the DLC, a group of largely Southern and Western Democrats who were seeking to give the party a more moderate reputation, understandably wanted to show off his prizes, to clasp their hands and raise them above their heads in triumph, a pretty rainbow of a picture of what can happen when reason prevails in the party. But Wilder spoiled the picture. Deliberately. He wasn't going to give aid and comfort to Robb or the DLC or any other group that was going around saying that for the party to survive, it needed to woo back white Southerners.

"I didn't know much about the DLC." Wilder said, "but I had made it very clear, I told Robb, that I couldn't make it." Had he considered it important, he could have arranged it. But it wasn't important. "It wasn't my intention" to cause a fuss, Wilder said. "I don't know if I had stayed in town, if I had not planned to go out of town, if I would have gone." Then, mischievously, he added, "some people say people do what they really want to do. I had thought, and still think, that for the Democratic party to come together to win victories, all facets have to come on, and be involved, and there is no such question as one side is right and other side is wrong. I didn't think that my involvement was that important to them, not that necessary, and I still don't."

It was the first of a series of snubs and barbs that Wilder would aim at the organization. In a speech four months later, he emphasized that the DLC "had absolutely nothing to do" with his election, or that of Baliles and Terry, "and I think that ought to be said rather abundantly." In fact, Wilder said, had the DLC's philosophy prevailed, he never would have gotten the nomination. He pointed out that the Democratic party historically had relied on the votes of blacks, women and labor, and that when the DLC talks about breaking from special interest groups, it should say "who they want to abandon without being cloudy." In another speech, Wilder criticized the DLC as a divisive force in national politics, and lampooned its members as "me-tooists who put on Reagan masks."

Robb expressed surprise at Wilder's remarks, saying, "I don't want to do anything to jeopardize the effectiveness that Doug can have and the role that he can play." Robb acknowledged that "when it (the DLC) was first formed, there were a number of misunderstandings about it, but I think that's all in the past." After beginning as an organization of moderate-to-conservative white men from Southern and Western states, it expanded its geographic base, and by the spring of 1986 its membership of one hundred twelve included three blacks and ten women, including Mary Sue Terry.

Wilder refused to join the DLC because of what he viewed as its exclusionary philosophy. Its drive to give more control of the national party to elected officials "flies in the face" of the image of the Democrats as an umbrella organization that welcomes all individuals and views. Although at the time the party had lost three out of four presidential elections, Wilder said it "shouldn't fall into the trap of thinking that we have to create certain kinds of people in terms of perceived philosophy or regional balance to win in '88. I also don't believe we must abandon substance to win, and I don't believe we must continue to point fingers at some of our constituent groups of former candidates to prove to the public that somewhere, somehow, we have repented."

Wilder favored "free enterprise politics" in which anyone interested in the 1988 nomination should "go out and fight for it rather than complain in order to compete. No group, no region, no rule must deny the nomination to the best candidate, nor should any philosophy or any idea be ruled out. The Democrats of this country are just like the Democrats of Virginia. They are willing to listen, willing to learn, and willing to support the best qualified persons."

His own election illustrated that the concerns voiced by the DLC were unwarranted. "So now don't come to say that what took place in Virginia is the genesis of the kind of thing that the DLC stands for." The victory of the Baliles-Wilder-Terry ticket didn't occur because "a magic brew was concocted or a magic wand was waved" by Robb and the DLC.

Wilder's complaint got little sympathy.

Jerry Alley, writing in the Norfolk Ledger-Star, a newspaper usually sympathetic to Wilder, found nothing wrong with Robb feathering his own political nest over the Democratic success in Virginia. "It's how the political bird sings, and Doug Wilder knows it," wrote Alley. When Robb ran for governor in 1981, the state Democratic party "was in more pieces than Humpty-Dumpty. Mr. Robb put it together and pushed the Republicans off the wall." Alley pointed out that "you don't hear Governor Baliles or Attorney General Terry publicly moaning about Chuck Robb taking some credit for their success. If they feel resentment, it is being kept inside. There is good reason for this. Both plan to be in politics a long time. Both realize Chuck Robb's support is going to be an asset down the road."

In July, 1986, Wilder added a new target. In a speech to North Carolina Democrats in Raleigh, he took on Jesse Jackson's Rainbow Coalition, lumping it in with the DLC as a focus of criticism. "The aim of these groups seems geared at 1988," Wilder said, "but in maneuvering for 1988, I am fearful they are hurting our chances to win in 1986," when Democrats were seeking to retain an ample majority in the House of Representatives and regain control of the United States Senate. "The Rainbow Coalition doesn't think the Democratic Party is sufficiently committed to certain Americans," he said. "They believe the party is trying too hard for a 'too conservative' image. The DLC feels the Democratic Party is 'too liberal.' Some in the group have said the image of the Democratic Party is one of being too closely identified with blacks, women and labor, among others."

The message of the DLC and the Rainbow Coalition "hurt our image and chances for victory. I don't know about you," Wilder said, "but I'm tired of losing."

42. Lieutenant Governor

The night before his inauguration, Wilder celebrated with two fund-raising parties.

The first was a black-tie dinner in the rotunda of the Old City Hall, now restored as an office building, where Wilder once refused to sit on the side of the courtroom reserved for black lawyers, and where in the hallways he won the admiration of his fellow white lawyers by his quick wit, and ability to quote poetry. (Later, as a successful lawyer and investor, Wilder unsuccessfully made a bid to buy the building and convert into a luxury hotel.)

It was a vintage Virginia evening, late twentieth-century version. The guests paid $500 each to drink Virginia wine and champagne, eat Chincoteague oysters, Chesapeake Bay crabs and smoked rainbow trout, and listen to the Petersburg (Virginia) String Quartet. Robb, Baliles and Terry came by for the pre-dinner reception, but did not stay. Later that night, fifteen hundred people paid $25 each for a champagne breakfast with Wilder at the Sixth Street Marketplace.

The inauguration the next morning was preceded by an interfaith service across the street from the Capitol at Saint Paul's Episcopal Church, the "Cathedral of the Confederacy." A standing-room crowd, half black, half white, heard the black Harry Savage Chorale perform a spine-tingling rendition of "The Battle Hymn of the Republic," a song synonymous with Northern sympathies that must have stirred the souls, present and past, that have worshipped in the church of Jefferson Davis and Robert E. Lee. The Rev. Canon Robert G. Hetherington called it a benchmark in Virginia history, a new beginning of a "free, open and just society."

The lieutenant governor does not make a speech at the inaugural—that is the prerogative of the governor—but the message of Wilder's victory permeated the ceremony.

"This represents a very new day in Virginia and in the South," beamed Delegate Benny Lambert, who had run Wilder's first campaign, in 1969, and soon would succeed him in the state Senate.

In his inaugural address, the new governor, Gerald L. Baliles, acknowledged that his running mates were "more than our new lieutenant governor...more than our new attorney general. Their presence on this platform signifies and ratifies our long, sometimes painful, but morally imperative journey from the darkness of subjugation and discrimination into the sunlight of a fuller liberty."

After Wilder was sworn in by State Supreme Court Justice A. Christian Compton, he acknowledged the historic event, saying, "you play a part. It is humbling. Someone may not be aware that they are living a revolution. Some sleep through it." Of his victory, he said, "I always felt it was possible. I was constantly reaching for success." He recalled that his mother often said, "'You can do it.' I never lost hope and I never will." He did not run as a black candidate, and "to the extent that others do that (run on issues rather than race) they may find fertile ground. I never emphasized it (race) at all." His party simply had nominated "the best candidates, appealing to a broad spectrum." The result was an "uplifting of conscience in Virginia. "

Wilder said his election "cuts across every conceivable stage—the acci-

221

dent of birth, the consciousness of kind, you name it. A person of ordinary means and ordinary ability can be elected to a position others may have thought was reserved for person of a higher calling. If you dream you can do it and if you try to do it, it can be done. I hoped we could show (in winning) not the declining significance of race, I hoped we could show that racial differences will always be, but they should never be reasons for demarcation..." God intended men to be different, Wilder said, but "never intended to elevate one over the other."

The 1954 Supreme Court decision on desegregation of the schools "cut the biggest knot, the mental knot, the psyche." After that, Wilder added, "things started coming into place." He knew that he could aspire and achieve and that he could "eat and ride the same the public facilities and play golf on the same courses. I did not want to be a black candidate, and I don't intend to be a black lieutenant governor....Virginia has changed more than many Virginians think. Leaders are always behind the people. History is being thrust upon us."

Wilder's inauguration was almost as big news as his election. As the first black to win statewide office in the South since Reconstruction, photographs of him taking the oath ran on front pages across the country He told The New York Times that he realized that television was the most powerful force available to a candidate, and that "I had to use it to get people to look at me on the basis of class rather than race." That wasn't such an easy decision, he said, because "there weren't any people advising us to go on television. There was a concern that it could cause a white backlash against the ticket."

Goldman told The Times that "people were convinced that prejudice was based solely on the element of color. Our feeling was that that kind of prejudice was on the wane, and that the real prejudice that had to be overcome was based more on class. We put Doug on (television) long enough to establish his identity, but not long enough for his visual image to become the focus of the commercial. The idea was to use him in the lead-in, and then force people to look at his values and what he stood for."

Requests for interviews of Wilder were made via The United States Information Service from news agencies in eight nations on four continents. The USIS responded by distributing a videotape, timed for the birthday of Martin Luther King Jr., in which Wilder credited King with making his victory possible. He also was interviewed in Richmond by television crews from Sweden and Great Britain and his inaugural was covered by the Japanese press.

The USIS arranged for a satellite hookup so South African journalists could interview him on the first observance of the federal holiday marking King's birthday. Wilder's picture ran with a story the next day in The Johannesburg Star under a headline quoting him saying, "Blacks in SA Should Be Freed Immediately." Wilder said "the time to take the foot off the neck of the oppressed is now. I think that whatever brings an end to a system that enslaves people mentally and physically must be done. Sanctions properly imposed will have the effect of South African blacks saying they will suffer together to get rid of apartheid," a concept of shared suffering that was consistent with King's philosophy. He told the South African journalists that his own victory resulted from appealing to a broad spectrum of people who share common values. "We considered people to be different for too long."

Wilder also took time during the weekend's festivities to mend a political fence, unveiling a rapprochement with Delegate Owen W. Pickett at the black-tie dinner the night before the inaugural.

The man who just four years before had been viewed by Wilder as such a throwback to the days of the Byrd machine that he was compelled to personally block his nomination for the United States Senate, was seated, along with his wife, at the head table with Wilder.

The next month, at the Democratic party's annual Jefferson-Jackson day dinner, Wilder urged Pickett's election to the United States House of Representatives from Virginia's Second Congressional District. "Whatever comments I might have made about Owen four years ago are past," said a magnanimous Wilder. "I don't shrink from what I said, but Owen has changed. I have changed. People have changed."

Pickett downplayed their differences too, noting that Vice President George Bush had run a bitterly contested race against President Reagan in 1980, before becoming his running mate. "In the political process, this is nothing at all," said Pickett, who had worked for Wilder in his 1985 campaign. "I don't think it's making amends; there's nothing to amend. We never had any words, just a difference of opinion."

Among the congratulatory calls to Wilder was one from the Rev. Jesse L. Jackson. "He said he was proud and I thanked him," Wilder said succinctly, still anxious to maintain his distance from Jackson, who was still seen by many whites as, unlike Wilder, running on race rather than on issues. A few weeks earlier, a miffed Jackson, smarting from Wilder's refusal to aid his presidential campaign, said, "That's all right. Many people who will not shake the tree will pick up the apples." Now, in the flush of victory, Wilder was willing to concede that as a result of Jackson's efforts, "there may have been an uplifting of consciousness, of people believing that things were possible....When you win," he told Margaret Edds of the Norfolk Virginian-Pilot with a smile, "you can afford to be magnanimous." But he emphasized that "I owe my immediate allegiance to the people of Virginia, and they'll have it."

Several old friends offered suggestions to the new lieutenant governor. Arthur Ashe, who as a boy had been run off the tennis courts on Richmond's North Side by the teenaged Wilder, countenanced the new lieutenant governor to "Hold Fast To Dreams." Wilder's boyhood pal, John "Booty" Taylor, sent a card recalling Wilder's his first major league baseball game, when he saw Jackie Robinson and the Brooklyn Dodgers play the Cardinals, and his re-enactment of a key catch at the barber shop, calling out "I got it." He urged Wilder to use that phrase at his inauguration.

Even the Richmond Times-Dispatch was impressed. It noted that all three winners "came from modest backgrounds without the advantages of inherited wealth or privilege; all three had obstacles of one kind or another to surmount from childhood (Baliles was reared by his grandparents, in a family without a mother, and shipped off to military school); all three were voracious readers, eager students and diligent workers. Their lives offer eloquent testimony to the value of work and education ethics."

But Wilder's story "is the most amazing of all," the newspaper said, recounting how he his brothers and sisters "would beg their father to tell them again and again about how his parents, and even his older siblings, had been slaves. Today's white majority can only imagine the pathos behind those stories told on a paternal lap. But in overcoming a legacy of racial supremacy and discrimination to be elected lieutenant governor, Doug Wilder never acted as though the world owed him anything. Instead...he went out and earned it. He has credited his mother, Beulah...with instilling in him the drive to excel. If people want to take a message from his victory," Wilder told one interviewer, he hopes that it will be that " ' you can't give up, you can't believe that your origin, your birth status must be a detraction,' and that 'young people will see the value of staying in school, of directing their life away from the wastefulness of crime.'"

His election was the bearing of fruit planted by the seeds of the civil rights legislation of the 1960s, and as more blacks registered to vote, other blacks were preparing serious bids to be governor in Michigan and California, though both failed.

Many Democrats saw Wilder's election as "an example that a lot of black leaders would like to repeat on a national level," said Thomas Cavanagh, a scholar on black studies at the National Academy of Sciences.

Wilder was an instant folk hero.

For a while, the new lieutenant governor, whose staff included just four full-time employees, answered his own phone. When a surprised woman asked why, he said, "Well, I noticed it was ringing." But he soon realized he needed help, to answer the phone, and the invitations. Mail arrived at rate of a hundred letters a day, many of them with invitations to speak. To deal with the avalanche, Wilder sought and got from a friendly legislature a two-hundred-thousand-dollar increase, nearly fifty percent more than in the previous biennial budget for the lieutenant governor's office, which $390,000 previously had been allocated three for staff and office costs.

The acclaimed and the acclaiming competed for his attention. Senator Edward M. Kennedy sent a copy of a speech on South Africa, wanting to make sure Wilder had seen it. Senator Gary Hart, a presidential contender whom Wilder did not know well, sent a copy of his remarks on something or other, with a "Dear Douglas" note that caused Wilder, to repeat aloud, mockingly, "Dear Douglas."

Eight-year-old, Elizabeth Custer, a Chesterfield County third-grader, wrote, "you may not be a great man yet, but just in case you ever are, I would like to have your autograph." Another elementary pupil had no doubts. "To me," wrote Shawsishi Washington of Richmond, "you are more famous than Michael Jackson, and he's a hit."

On opening day of the 1986 session of the Virginia General Assembly, Lieutenant Governor Wilder told his former colleagues, "I intend to work with you, all of you. The people of Virginia have received a pledge from me in that regard. I assure you my office door is open on a regular basis to all of you. If I get out of line, I know that there are those of you who will let me know."

The most senior member, Wilder's Richmond colleague, Ed Willey, said: "We're mighty proud of him and wish him every success." But Willey cautioned Wilder to remember his mother's advice and not get a big head.

Lieutenant Governor

Wilder won praise from his former colleagues for the manner in which he presided over the state Senate. "He's doing a fine job, he knows the rules," said Majority Leader Hunter B. Andrews, one of only five members of the body who had more seniority than Wilder.

Wilder spent a lot of time explaining the arcane parliamentary proceedings to visitors, especially students, a habit that bored the senators but which won appreciation, and perhaps future votes, from those in the gallery. He offered visitors insight into the process with observations such as, "when I say the bill has been defeated, it doesn't mean a thing in the world," explaining that the matter could be brought up for reconsideration later. While some members grumbled that Wilder was showboating and grandstanding, Senator Howard P. Anderson of Halifax, one of the last of the Old Guard members, said, "it's good politics for him and it's good for our constituents."

Wilder urged the senators to explain their bills and urged participation in debate. Previously, many matters came up and were acted upon without discussion, lending mystery to the process, and centralizing power with the majority leader.

He trimmed the sails of Majority Leader Andrews, saying, "Nothing in the rules prescribes that the majority leader must make the motions." Though it was clear that Wilder and Andrews often disagreed, neither sought to push the differences. "I'm delighted," Andrews said of Wilder's forceful style of presiding. "I'm not trying to usurp his powers," Wilder answered. "We've been friends for years."

Wilder also presided with good humor. When a lobbyist delivered a Valentine Day balloon to the desk of Wilder's longtime ally, Senator Peter K. Babalas of Norfolk, Wilder asked a page to remove it, "before the senator takes off."

Wilder even encouraged Republicans to speak. When the usually reticent W. Onico Barker fidgeted with his microphone, undecided whether to join a debate, Wilder exhorted him, saying, "each person is as entitled to the floor as the next. That's why they're here."

And he prescribed senatorial courtesy and decorum. He chastised Republican Wiley Mitchell, normally one of the more decorous members, for uttering the word "hell" during a debate, and he scolded the powerful Willey for trying to cut off Barker during a budget debate "since he's going to vote against the budget anyway." Barker subsequently voted for the budget, and Willey apologized.

Wilder's sense of fair play may have reaped an unexpected dividend: By the summer of 1989, Barker, a mortician from Danville who was disillusioned with squabbling within his own party—he had lost a divisive primary election for an open congressional seat in 1988 that allowed the Democrats to retain the seat—was thinking about supporting Wilder for governor, an action that surely would require him to give up membership in the Republican party. If that occurred, Barker indicated he would probably seek re-election in 1991 as an independent.

The tone set by Wilder was contagious. After Willey referred to Dale Eisman, the Times-Dispatch's political writer, as "that little Jew boy," Senator Elliot S. Schewel of Lynchburg rose on the floor and condemned the statement as "derisive, vulgar, highly insensitive and uncalled for." Willey apologized. He said he was angry with Eisman, who is neither little, Jewish nor young, because he had reported a private conversation. Schewel, one of two Jewish members of the Senate, also was upset when Senator William Fears, waiting in the cloakroom for the daily opening prayer, muttered, "I don't know if I'll go out there; it's probably just a rabbi."

Wilder said Schewel's agitation was merited. "Nobody takes it lightly, nor should they. The repetition showed that people were obviously out of touch." Earlier during the session, in the House, Delegate George Beard (R-Culpeper) had criticized a Jewish delegate, saying he should have "a Star of David put at the top" of his legislation.

Wilder's first year as presiding officer was not without controversy, however. He had to break tie votes on two controversial issues, and in the eyes of some, came down on the wrong side both times.

One of his votes killed a seat belt law. "It's just not enforceable," he said afterwards. "I don't think it would do anything for safety." He also was responsible for rejection of an attempt to strengthen the state's conflict-of-interest law, which was the subject of intense scrutiny as the result of charges lodged against Senator Babalas, one of the Senate's most senior members and one of Wilder's closest allies.

Wilder ducked a stand on whether the state should sponsor a lottery, saying, "How I plan to vote is really not important." He was on record, however, in favor of allowing voters to decide the question, which was to be on the ballot in November.

Wilder was much in demand during his first year as lieutenant governor. Invitations to speak flooded his office from around the country.

The office is largely what its holder makes it—after the annual legislative session ends in March, there is nothing more the lieutenant governor has to do until the next year—so Wilder accepted a number of speaking engagements, inside the state and around the country, at conventions, union meetings, banquets and commencements.

In addition to the working the chicken-dinner circuit, he travelled abroad, to Japan and Taiwan, where he promoted Virginia-made products and urged businesses in those countries to invest in the state, and to the Soviet Union, to observe the Goodwill Games, as the guest of their organizer, network television owner Ted Turner.

The Washington Post reported in April that Wilder was given $1,500 for a Kennedy-King Day speech sponsored by the D. C. Democratic State Committee in Washington, the first indication that Wilder was accepting honorariums. The executive director of the committee, Barbara Garnett, said, "we had to do quite a bit to get him. He was supposed to leave Chicago and go either directly to Houston or Dallas. We begged him to come here first. He's a hot property." Joel Harris, Wilder's chief of staff, declined to discuss what fees Wilder was receiving for his speeches, saying it would be "unfair to those who cannot afford honorariums." The first report that Wilder was charging in-state groups as well came from Jeff E. Schapiro in the November, 1986, issue of the monthly magazine Virginia Business, which reported that Wilder had requested a $1,500 fee to speak at a convention of black ministers in Newport News. Wilder did not fulfill the engagement, in part because of a scheduling conflict.

Suddenly, Wilder was besieged by reporters clamoring for an accounting of his honorariums. The revelation so unnerved the usually quick-witted Wilder that he was speechless when confronted for comment. Pressed almost daily for a answer about how much he had collected, and what he planned to do with the money, Wilder either refused to respond, or resorted to childish retorts, replying to questions with nonsensical remarks such, as "how's your family?" or "how've you been?" When one reporter threatened to print his silly responses, he pleaded for time, saying, "I'll get back to you on that," a response that had employed in other situations for which he had no ready answer.

He suggested that the revelations were part of a plot to embarrass him, most likely planted by Robb or Baliles intimates. "I was threatened this would come out, no question about it," he said. He had received written warnings that "other things were going to happen to me, that a torrent would be unleashed" against him. Whatever happened, he said, would not be a surprise.

The longer he stonewalled, the more information leaked out: Officials at three Virginia colleges confirmed that Wilder had accepted honorariums for speaking at their commencements, including $500 paid by the University of Virginia for a highly acclaimed graduation address.

The full story came out in mid-January, 1987, when Wilder filed, as required by law, his annual financial disclosure statement, which required reporting anything accepted by top state officeholders valued at more than $200. Wilder's report showed that he had accepted $53,000 in honorariums— almost double his $28,000 state salary—plus $34,600 in expenses in the first year of his term. Wilder attached a statement to the report saying that his policy in the future would be not to accept honorariums from in-state groups, other than expenses. He promised to donate the in-state portion of his fees to charity.

To make matters worse, neither Governor Baliles nor Attorney General Terry reported receiving any honorariums, although they had accepted free transportation, via airplanes and helicopters, and Baliles accepted rooms at hotels.

Among the in-state groups from which Wilder took money were the NAACP of Lynchburg, $500; Virginia State University, $1,000; Hampton University, $1,500; the Opportunities Industrialization Council (OIC) of Winchester, $1,000, and Tidewater Area Business and Contractors Association, $1,500. He commanded larger fees outside the state. "I was more shocked than anybody," Wilder said, when he received a check for $5,000 for a speech to the National Association of Letter Carriers meeting in Baltimore.

The Republicans jumped on the disclosure. And in the 1987 session of the General Assembly, Republican Delegate Vincent F. Callahan Jr., of McLean, offered legislation that would prohibit legislators and statewide office-holders from accepting honorariums for in-state appearances, but it was rejected.

On the one hand, observed University of Virginia political scientist Larry Sabato, the payments showed "how significant Wilder's victory was, and what a marketable commodity he is nationally." But because none of his predecessors had accepted money for speaking engagements, "he appears a bit greedy," Sabato added. Robert Holsworth, a political science professor at Virginia Commonwealth University, added that "to the extent they haven't been accepted as part of the political culture in Virginia, it could hurt him."

Common Cause, a watchdog organization on campaign financing, found no fault, however. "As long as he discloses them, which he did, it's fine," said Julie Lapham, executive director of the lobbying group, noting that members of Congress routinely accept honoraria, although the practice has come under increasing scrutiny and criticism. State Senator Joseph V. Gartlan Jr., (D-Mt. Vernon), an outspoken advocate of more restrictive rules on conflicts of interest, also saw no problem, "as long as the fee is somewhat commensurate with the means of the organization."

In an interview in 1988, former governor Robb said that although he had not accepted compensation for appearances he made within the state during his term as lieutenant governor, he was not critical of Wilder for doing so. Robb said he had accepted fees for a small number of out-of-state speeches over the years, although he wasn't certain if he did so as lieutenant governor. The state's financial disclosure law didn't require reporting it in those days, Robb said, so he listed the money only on his income tax returns. "It was not a great moral dilemma," Robb said. "I just thought it didn't look right. There was no prohibition, obviously, and I don't think there is any ethical problem." As governor, Robb didn't accept any remuneration for Virginia appearances, and as a United States Senator, he had pledged to forego all honorariums. "I'm fortunate enough to have the financial independence that it doesn't become a factor," Robb said. "I had the luxury—and that's not fair (to expect that of others who hold the office). A lot of very able people have to be concerned about meeting their bills every month. I'm not posturing on that."

Eva S. Teig, who was chief-of-staff for Dick Davis, Wilder's predecessor as lieutenant governor, said, "I can understand how it happened. It's not fair to say Doug used poor judgment." She said there is "a real difference between what the constitution says about the job, and the reality. You can't do that job just January-March. There are constant invitations, requests to represent the governor. The public expects you to be full- time." As the result of fulltime demands, Teig said there were times during Davis's tenure when there wasn't enough money in the budget to reimburse the staff or the lieutenant governor for legitimate business and travel expenses. "You shouldn't have to be wealthy to seek that office. As it is, it precludes non-wealthy candidates from running in future."

At the time, Wilder defended acceptance of the money, saying, "I am not apologetic for anything that has occurred. The gut instinct serves you well," he said, explaining how he decided whom to charge, and how much. "That has been very much my guide, and it has served me well," adding that he had accepted money from just "a very, very few in-state groups." However, looking back a few years later, Wilder said, "yes, it was a mistake, and I gave it back, to charity. He said he had stopped accepting money from Virginia organizations before the criticism began. He blamed part of problem on the enormous number of requests for appearances, and suggested that some groups that he had to turn down, because of scheduling conflicts, may have decided they were rejected because they didn't offer enough money. "And when I started giving it back to charity, everyone started constituting a charity," he laughed.

Wilder refused to identify the charities to which the money was given, using as an excuse the concern that revealing the recipients would be interpreted as a decision that one organization was more deserving than another. A defensive Wilder said, "The only reason to make it public would be to check on me to see if I was telling the truth," acknowledging that critics could accuse him of pocketing the money. "If you think I'm not telling the truth, all you have to do is show where I wasn't."

43. Taking Credit

As Wilder neared the end of his first year as lieutenant governor, he was engulfed in controversy, nearly all of it of his own making. As a result of challenges, first to former Governor Robb and then to Governor Baliles, he had handed the Republicans sure-fire fodder for the 1989 gubernatorial campaign. He was denounced by fellow Democrats as a coward, a Monday-morning quarterback, a johnny-come-lately and a sandbagger. But Wilder didn't blink, because the attacks were part of a high-risk strategy to establish conservative credentials and to show his independence from Robb and Baliles, who Wilder believed were likely to support Attorney General Mary Sue Terry against him if an intraparty fight developed for the gubernatorial nomination in 1989.

It was less than two weeks after the 1985 election that the Wilder-Robb feud began, set in motion by Paul Goldman, Wilder's campaign manager, when he called reporters to complain that Robb was taking too much credit for Wilder's victory.

Goldman launched his attack on a Sunday afternoon. Continuing a pattern from the campaign, he telephoned reporters at home in the middle of a Washington Redskins football game, and began a whiny recitation of complaints.

From the outset, it was clear that Goldman was calling with the knowledge of, if not at the behest of, Wilder, the latter's revisionist claims not to the contrary. Goldman said Robb "was helpful, as a Democratic governor should be" in the Wilder victory, and in those of Baliles and Terry. But he added that Robb had opposed a couple of ideas—of Goldman's—that turned out to be keys to Wilder's victory, the two-month tour around the state and the repeated citing of Wilder's war record.

Goldman may have been upset because the national media, especially, were pointing to the Democratic sweep in Virginia as a Robb legacy, which would boost Robb's national standing. Goldman suggested the national networks and news magazines were portraying the rainbow victory as part of a grand design by Robb.

George Stoddart, Robb's press secretary, said Robb agreed that many deserve credit. "Sometimes the national press tends to focus on the more identifiable person," Stoddart said, attempting to explain the attention on Robb.

Goldman was correct in pointing out that Robb was getting a lot of credit in the national media. On "The McNeil-Lehrer Report," the nightly news show of the Public Broadcasting Service, Roger Wilkins, a senior fellow at the Institute for Policy Studies, lauded Robb as "an exemplary governor" who helped "usher in the first black lieutenant governor," which Wilkins called "an amazing feat." Thomas Cavanagh, the black studies scholar at the National Academy of Sciences, praised Robb for being "very creative in devising a strategy that includes blacks and women and yet hasn't alienated mainstream whites." United Press International reporter Carolyn Click called Robb "an architect of November's Democratic sweep."

"We're not trying to take away anything" from Robb, Goldman said, but, for example, he said greater credit belonged to Baliles and House Speaker Philpott. "It's a question of trying to show the people of Virginia that they're the ones that made us," Goldman said, adding that "I've gotten more credit than I deserve" also.

Goldman said Robb and his staff did little to assist Wilder with fund raising, and that the governor had not actively campaigned for Wilder until the closing weeks of the campaign, when he made a commercial and accompanied the ticket on the traditional final weekend trip around the state.

As for the national party, Goldman said, "we made three phone calls to Paul Kirk (the party chairman) and none of them were returned."

Robb said Wilder is "a little like (New York Governor) Mario Cuomo" in that "anything that doesn't sound like it's 100 percent supportive gets a reaction." Robb said his relationship with Wilder had gotten to the point that "I pretty well could rely on Doug, but that changed from time to time. That's like all political alliances, there are very few true-blue, lasting relationships." Robb said he has learned not to hold long-term grudges, although he admits he is not immune to reacting to cheap shots. But he usually suppressed his reactions when he read something someone had said about him that was less than flattering, or, even less than true. "Doug seemed to make them (grudges) a little more important," said Robb, in a classic understatement. "Doug'll let you know he had been displeased; he wants to know the motivation."

If anyone might have had a complaint about failing to get credit it was Governor Baliles. Although he was at the top of the ticket, he often was overlooked when the campaign was discussed. Accounts by out-of-town newspapers even confused him with Wilder or Terry, or simply ignored him. One Denver paper's headline said "Virginia Elects First Black Governor," while a Miami paper ran Terry's picture and identified her as Robb's successor as governor.

Instead, Baliles credited Robb with "making it respectable, socially, politically and economically, to be a Democrat. A decade earlier this ticket would not have been successful. I think it's a mistake to try to pinpoint...if Doug had not saved money, he would not have been on television the last thirty days; Mary Sue clearly had qualifications. Her strength was her background..." As for the length of anyone's coattails, Baliles said there was "plenty of credit to go around." Because he was pleased that he had won his race, Baliles said, "I didn't judge anyone else." Luxuries such as worrying about who was getting credit "were denied me because I was working on the transition," said Baliles.

Wilder also admits that "it's highly questionable" that he could have been elected had Robb never been governor. Had Robb lost in 1981, Wilder pointed out, the Democrats would have gone into the 1985 election faced with breaking a sixteen-year Republican hold on the governor's mansion. Instead, Wilder conceded, the Democratic ticket in 1985 was seeking a second consecutive sweep of the top three statewide offices. "And to the extent that Chuck Robb's administration was perceived to have been successful, it was beneficial to Mary Sue Terry, Doug Wilder and Jerry Baliles. We all benefited. To say that I was more benefited than Mary Sue Terry or Jerry Baliles by that might be an overstatement. To the extent that my candidacy might have been a bit more unique, and that Mary Sue's was a bit more unique, to say that we benefited, surely. And I think it helped us greatly to have had a successful administration. And Robb's election and his popularity greatly contributed to it."

It is clear, however, that Wilder believes Robb helped Terry more than him. And there is no question that most of Robb's supporters, his core group, were committed to Terry's candidacy, while cool to Wilder's. The justification for Robb is easy enough: He and Terry had known each other since they were in law school together. It is less easy to understand why Robb's loyalists were so partial to Terry vis-a-vis Wilder; it may have been that she was more closely aligned to their generally conservative philosophy. But for whatever reason, they were, and they knew that if both of them won, the next fight would be between Wilder and Terry.

Wilder said he thanked everyone who was supportive of his effort, and he singled out several members of Governor Robb's staff for special thanks, including special assistant Phil Abraham. What he refused to do, and what he thinks some Robb loyalists expected, was for him to make an "everything-I-am-I-owe-to Chuck" statement.   When he names pivotal individuals and events in the campaign, however, Robb is not mentioned. Wilder cites the tour, the Philpott breakfast, a fundraiser at Lain O'Ferrall's home, which showed he could raise money from the Richmond business community, and some key endorsements, including those from the Fraternal Order of Police, Virginia Education Association and the state AFL-CIO. "But it would be wrong for me to say of any one person or any group, that without any one or the other, my candidacy would have failed."

Wilder said that it doesn't serve any purpose to say who took credit and who didn't, adding, "it's just that I knew what I was doing all through the campaign, and I took a great deal of comfort in knowing that I did. You win it on your own. You get elected independently, run on your own. That's gravy (when you get help from others on the ticket). You do it in a united way, but you do your own thing."

If Wilder is touchy about credit, it's largely because he knows that many of Robb's allies consistently were warning—almost seemed to take pleasure in it—that Wilder was not going about the campaign in the proper manner, was not doing what was necessary to raise sufficient money. Of his critics, he said, "I didn't think to respond to it then, and don't choose to now. I have joked to a couple of people, saying, 'my troubles are over. All I need to do is call on you and you could raise the same mountain of money for me now that you did then.'"

Goldman contends he wasn't offended by criticism from the Robb camp, but it's hard to tell that when he talks about how some people regarded him. "Some people didn't seem to want to give me a chance. I never could understand that. They did a lot of things. At the convention, people didn't want me near Doug. They said it was bad for me to be around him. They wanted me to sit in the bleachers, in a control room with a walkie-talkie." He admits that it hurt him. "It's a helluva thing to say about somebody."

Wilder knew in advance that Goldman was going to take out after Robb, and he made no effort to stop him. "He told me, he told you, he told everyone that he thought the press was giving Robb too much credit," Wilder said.

Two of Baliles' top aides privately said they sympathized with Goldman and Wilder, saying that some of Robb's assistants, particularly chief-of-staff

Taking Credit

David McCloud and press secretary Stoddart, were trying to get more credit for their boss than was warranted.

Jackie Epps may offer the greatest insight into how Wilder views Robb. "I don't think Paul said anything terrible. Paul just said Robb didn't deserve all the credit. He helped, but there were others who deserve more credit. Should we give Robb all the credit, whether he deserved it or not. What really upsets me about Chuck Robb is that when he came in here (to Virginia) and ran for lieutenant governor, he had no statewide experience. The husband of the daughter of a former president—he had star quality because of who he married—he comes in here and Doug helped him. Doug was there for Chuck Robb, then, and when he ran for governor, early on. Frankly, when Robb ran for governor against Coleman, Coleman had black support. Coleman was charming. Blacks had voted for him for attorney general, they liked him. And Chuck said nothing (to woo blacks). Obviously he had to get the conservative vote. Fine. Great strategy. Doug said nothing. He knew what the strategy was. Doug trusted him to be concerned about the needs of black people. Doug had to pull together blacks from all over this state and almost force them to support Chuck Robb. He said, 'there is a difference.' Robb had pulled together conservatives on one end, but you can get all the conservatives in the world, but if the blacks don't go out and vote for you, as a Democrat, you're not going to win. So Doug was instrumental, and I think Robb recognized that, by virtue of the influence that Doug had in the Robb administration. Doug had always been there for Chuck, and Chuck, when he had a chance to be there for Doug, wasn't, initially. Yes, he came on, and I think he did support him. But certainly we could have used a lot more help from him than we got."

As for the DLC meeting, she suggested that Robb wanted Wilder to be able to raise the hands of a black man and a white woman and show them off like trophies. "See what I did. I made these two," Epps said, dripping sarcasm.

"Doug has not gotten where he has gotten by being anybody's patsy. Or anybody's little flunky," said Epps, in an observation that few would dispute. "'He should be so grateful to be there,'" she said mockingly. Does she mean people expect him to shuffle around, droop his head and say "yes suh, yes, suh?" "That's exactly the mentality," Epps said. Although Wilder "pretty much transcended the race issue, it's there in subtlety. It's there. We're not getting rid of it any time soon. Had he been white...."

The fact that both Wilder and Terry had weak opponents, yet Terry got 62 percent of the vote and Wilder 52 percent indicates that "racism was there," Epps said, "But the good thing is, enough people—52 percent—got beyond that. It's always an issue, but hopefully it's not an issue with the majority of people who are voting. It's going to be there this time (1989). It's subtle, ingrained, and you can play on it without actually coming out with it. Doug, having been through all that he had to go through to get where he is, has no illusions about people or politics. He feels it is necessary to constantly make a statement that 'I'm independent. I'm nobody's patsy.'"

Wilder aimed his first broadside at Baliles less than six months into the new administration, on a corrections department policy regarding visits to death row inmates. Under terms of an agreement reached between the state attorney general's office and the American Civil Liberties Union, which had complained about conditions in the death-row section of the Mecklenburg correctional center, the glass that previously had separated prisoners from their visitors was to be removed, allowing the inmates to hold their children and embrace their loved ones, in what was known as "contact visits." The policy was sharply criticized by Republicans as coddling of the worst criminals. Baliles defended the agreement, which had been worked out while he was attorney general, but without his involvement. Shortly before the policy was implemented, Wilder was asked about his view on the controversy. He sided with the opponents, saying the killers had forfeited their rights, and pointed out that families of their victims couldn't kiss and hold their loved ones.

Although the governor's office said Wilder hadn't bothered to warn Baliles to take cover in advance of him dropping the bombshell, Wilder said the governor was aware of his view. He hadn't planned to make an announcement, he said, but when a reporter asked him about it, he responded. "What was I supposed to do, lie, and say I was in favor of contact visits?" He added that he didn't think Baliles was in favor of them either, but was defending the right of the corrections department to strike such a deal.

Baliles didn't react like someone who knew about Wilder's view. Wilder's statement provoked the usually placid governor to complain that common courtesy called for giving him notice of a decision to take issue with an administration of which, when it suited him, Wilder was a part. He said he and Wilder had talked about the policy, but Wilder had failed to mention his opposition to it.

He had never cleared his statements with anyone in his adult life, Wilder responded, and "I don't think the governor is attempting to say that at all."

Nevertheless, prior to his next attack, Wilder gave the governor advance notice—about ninety minutes worth. Chris Bridge, Baliles' press secretary, said the telephone log in the governor's office showed that about ten-thirty on the morning of September 30, someone left the message that "the lieutenant governor is going to give a speech in Northern Virginia on transportation." And some speech it was.

Speaking to the Dulles Area Board of Trade near Washington, Wilder revealed that he did not support the bulk of a tax package that the general assembly had adopted three days before. Baliles had called a two-week special session of the legislature to address the state's mounting transportation crisis. Acting on recommendations from the governor's Committee on Transportation in the Twenty-First Century, the blue-ribbon panel to which Baliles had asked Wilder to serve as his "eyes and ears," the legislators adopted tax increases that would generate $422 million or more annually for the next twenty years, to finance more than $10 billion in highway, mass transit, port and airport projects. Nearly half of the money would come from increasing the sales tax from four percent to four and one-half percent.

Baliles didn't get a copy of the noon speech until four o'clock, by which time news stories about Wilder's remarks were out. The governor couldn't believe what he was seeing and hearing about what his "eyes and ears" thought of the tax package. When he finally caught his breath, Baliles responded that Wilder had missed the point. "The question is whether you're for roads or not.

If you're for roads, you have to look to ways to finance them."

In the speech at Dulles, Wilder denounced the increase in the sales tax and said he also opposed a new $35 minimum titling tax. He pointed out that as chairman of the Senate Transportation Committee, he had favored user charges, such as tolls and the gasoline tax, to fund transportation projects. One of the basic principles to which he had adhered since entering public life in 1969, he said, was that "we must stop piling regressive taxes upon those citizens and businesses least able to afford them."

Wilder said he was "the first person to endorse the plan" when Baliles suggested it might be financed by bonds. But he didn't have a vote on the various subcommittees of the panel that changed the financing method, and didn't even know when they were meeting. Others, however, said Wilder didn't need an invitation, and that he avoided the meetings, stayed away of his own violation.

He noted that three former governors who served on the panel, Albertis Harrison, Linwood Holton and Mills Godwin, had expressed concern about the sales tax increase, although their objections were "so low-keyed you barely heard about it," Wilder noted. Despite their reservations, Wilder said, all three of them voted for the proposal. "I expressed my reservation at the first opportunity I had," Wilder said. "I did not want to kill the package. At that late stage, it would have been misinterpreted." He added that "more than people think, I'm a team player. I wanted to see the measure passed; I wanted to see us get on the way with transportation. I knew what the needs were. I knew if we didn't bite the bullet then, we would be forever putting the pieces together."

Wilder said he had communicated in writing to the governor and the commission's staff director in August that "I would like to see it funded a little differently." But he did not further attempt to influence the outcome because Governor Baliles had said he would "take the bottom line," regardless of how the money was raised.

Wilder pointed out that the tax package passed the Senate by the narrow margin of 22 to 18, with twenty-one votes required for approval. "If I were trying to enlist support to kill it, my legislative record shows that I might have been able to pick up one or two votes. What I'm trying to say, without fear of contradiction, is if I had wanted to kill it, it was dead. But I didn't try to kill it."

He defended his stance, pointing out that as an ex-officio member of the commission, he had no vote. He was in a "Catch 22" situation." He was attacked for withholding his concerns about the taxes increases, yet, "If I had put my views out, I would have been accused of being disloyal. So I stayed quiet, and let the measure pass. There are those who may say that as a Democrat I had an obligation to do whatever the governor asked," he went on, "but that is not how I see the role of the lieutenant governor."

Wilder pointed out that unlike some other states, the Virginia constitution mandates three independently elected statewide officials, and often they are not of the same party. Jefferson wanted it that way, he said. "They wanted officeholders to be free to express their views and to be beholden to no one except the people."

To offset the regressive tax package, Wilder said he would back legislation in the coming year to return a portion of the federal tax reform "windfall" to help offset the burden of the transportation package.

Wilder's late-blooming opposition to the sales tax prompted criticism from friend and foe alike.

The Republicans were gleeful. Wilder was "behaving like a Republican," said Steve Haner, the state GOP publicist. "Of course, that's the strategy. He's intentionally keeping his distance from Baliles, trying to establish the conservative credentials he needs to be governor. But if the thinks he can get the nomination after dumping on Baliles for four years, he's in for a shock," Haner said.

Former state attorney general Marshall Coleman, smiling from the sidelines, noted that the divided administration of which he was a part—two Republicans and a Democrat, got along better than did the Democratic trio of Baliles, Wilder and Terry. Coleman recalled his days in the state Senate when Wilder was "a liberal voice crying in a conservative wilderness. He was combative. He didn't make any apologies and didn't try to hide it. It's been a remarkable transformation on the road to Damascus. You have to wonder about his motives in changing so dramatically and so conveniently. It almost seems an unnatural act."

Edgar Bacon, who had squired Wilder around the southwestern corner of the state at the start of his campaign tour, accused Wilder of "failing to remember all the people who made his great victory possible." Bacon, who had delivered one of the seconding speeches to Wilder's nomination, said in a letter to the Richmond News Leader that Wilder apparently was not "heeding his mother's sound advice" to not let his head get too big. He urged Wilder to treat Robb and Baliles "with kindness...instead of with barbs.

Delegate C. Richard Cranwell of Vinton, a leading Democrat in the House, accused Wilder of "Monday morning quarterbacking," and of paying politically motivated lip service to the poor. Cranwell said a House-passed bill, which would have offered tax relief to low-income families, might have passed the Senate had Wilder gotten behind it. Delegate N. Leslie Saunders Jr., called Wilder "a coward" for waiting to speak out.

Senator Dudley J. "Buzz" Emick Jr. agreed with Wilder that a sales tax is regressive, but said "for those of us who argued so valiantly against it last week, his timing's not too good." But Emick said he makes "great allowances for those running for governor." He had indulged Robb when he was lieutenant governor, and he would indulge Wilder too.

"If he was going to take a vigorous position against it," added Senator Joe Gartlan of Mount Vernon, "he might as well have done it when it was within our power to do something about it." With Wilder's help, Gartlan said, "those of us who were not crazy about leaning so heavily (on the sales tax) might have drummed up a few more allies. It's mystifying," added Gartlan. I don't know who's giving him political advice."

"Doug keeps his own counsel more than anyone I've ever worked with in the legislature," said Senate clerk Jay Shropshire, whom Wilder counts as "as good a friend as I have."

Wilder made no mention of it in his speech at Dulles, but as the 1989 gubernatorial campaign approached, he divulged that he had made a commitment during the 1985 campaign, on a questionnaire from the Crusade for

Voters, to oppose any increase in the state sales tax during the next four years. Whether others knew about his promise was immaterial. "If no one in the world knew about it, I knew about it, and I gave my word," he said later. In answer to another question on the Crusade's questionnaire, Wilder said he would support bond issues for highway improvements if there were agreed upon projects.

An associate of Wilder's confided that there was no political mileage in supporting a tax increase: Proponents would not vote for him simply because they agreed with him on that issue, while opponents would hold it against him.

Amidst all the controversy, Wilder was cool and unremorseful. "I don't know what I was supposed to have done to have to ask for penitence; how I offended tender sensibilities. I don't succumb to flattery, so criticism doesn't crush me," he said, employing one of his favorite aphorisms. He denied that there was a rift between him and Baliles. "He has not been blindsided by me. We consult with each other. There are no hard feelings between us. He knows me, the kind of person I am."

Indeed. Snapped Baliles, "He's indicated that he intends to speak out when he feels it's appropriate and when it suits his schedule."

Wilder said he had no intention of sitting around four years and winding up like his predecessor as lieutenant governor, Dick Davis, who was passed over for the gubernatorial nomination in favor of Baliles. Never mind that Wilder played a role in assuring that Davis was passed over.

"I have not taken anybody by surprise," Wilder said. "I ran to lead discussions on issues. That's a little different from other lieutenant governors, but that doesn't make me a heretic. In the old school, no one cared what the lieutenant governor thought." He said Davis had told him he was never consulted by Robb.

At a benefit roast of Wilder, UVa professor Sabato, borrowing an observation from Steve Johnson in the Charlottesville Daily Progress, noted that "the new lieutenant governor has come down hard on capital murderers, launched a war on drug pushers, voted against the 'big government' mandatory seat belt bill, railed against Baliles' big taxing transportation plan. Just as I predicted, John Chichester won."

Even Chichester agreed. In a note to Sabato, he said, "I believe that our governor is convinced that Wilder has adopted my philosophy and is becoming more of a thorn in his side than I would have been."

Baliles was resigned to the sniping, saying his former running mate would "probably speak out again, especially the closer we get to the 1989 campaign."

237

44. The Robb Letters

About two weeks after Goldman's round of phone calls, a thoroughly piqued Robb wrote a long, personal letter to Wilder.

George Stoddart, Robb's press secretary, said he often found Robb at his desk in the governor's office, pencil in hand, hunched over, squinting (his poor eyesight makes writing laborious) at a yellow legal pad, writing a fiery retort to some perceived injustice to him or members of his administration. Stoddart said he usually was able to convince Robb to wad up the message and toss it in the wastebasket, or absent that, at least slide the legal pad in a desk drawer for a cooling off period. But Stoddart didn't try to stop Robb from sending his letters to Wilder.

The first of Robb's two extraordinary "Dear Doug" letters, written on the governor's official stationery, is a long one—six pages, single-spaced, plus a two-page attachment—dated November 30, 1985, about three weeks after the election.

It said in part:

"This letter is not easy to write, knowing it's one of the first you'll see when you get back from vacation, because I realize it's quite different from most of the congratulatory messages you've been receiving since the election. However, I think it's important that you know how disappointed I am, and that many of your friends and supporters share my concern.

"To say the least, as one who put his reputation on the line for you, worked closely with you for over a year and pulled out all the stops for your election, I was extremely unhappy with the public statements and attitudes attributed to you and Paul Goldman in the various news reports beginning on Monday, November 18, and not corrected. No one I have talked to could offer any rational explanation for why you and Paul did what you did and, as I'm sure you now realize, many others who worked the hardest to help you get elected are equally upset. I can only assume that you were tired and received some very bad advice at some point after all the votes were counted.

"What made this abrupt change of attitude so incomprehensible is the fact that throughout your campaign you were an especially gracious campaigner and on your victory night, when all of us were bursting with pride in your accomplishment, you made even your adversaries feel better about when you invoked your late mother's advice saying, 'Don't get a big head; you didn't do it by yourself.' Regrettably, the most recent sentiments attributed to you stand in sharp contrast to that, as well as to your statements prior to the election.

"Just for the record, let me share a few facts with you: First, and foremost, I never once, publicly or privately, claimed credit for, or claimed to have masterminded, your victory—or Jerry's or Mary Sue's. I said repeatedly, no matter how many ways I was asked, that our ticket won because we had the best-qualified candidates, and I meant it.

"In fact, I repeatedly downplayed my role in your victories, using phrases like 'I'm pleased if I didn't add to their burden' or 'I think I enjoyed the ticket's victory this time as much as I enjoyed the one I was involved in four years ago.' And I think if you'll look at any credit accorded to me nationally, it was for helping create an atmosphere, and a record, on which Democrats could run without being defensive.

"I won't belabor the point. I did everything I could to focus the attention on you and Jerry and Mary Sue for the victories you so clearly earned and deserved. Whether or not you believe I was nonetheless accorded too much credit, you need to know that a great many people worked very hard for you because I asked them to, and they are deeply hurt by what was said last week.

"I really don't need to remind you that you and I spent countless hours over the course of the last year or so discussing your campaign, and I spent even greater amounts of time convincing others, including your fellow legislators, party leaders and the media, that you really could win if you were just given that chance, and that I very much wanted you to win.

"Some believe that early on, when the press was preoccupied with the quixotic nature of campaigns by a woman and a black, the dynamics changed after I devoted most of a news conference to saying, in effect, 'put up or shut up' to those talking about other potential candidates or a draft. I reiterated that I could and would support you and Mary Sue enthusiastically as our nominees. Others believe that the extensive negotiations which I initiated to resolve the gubernatorial nomination right after the mass meetings allowed us to close ranks quickly and be in much better shape for the general election than we'd have been in otherwise.

"Still others believe my repeated references to the entire Democratic ticket as having a clear edge in terms of experience, effectiveness and leadership helped define the election and focused attention away from individual votes or claims that you were the most liberal candidate ever to run for statewide office. Finally, some have said that the three joint ticket swings, which I requested and my staff helped organize, set a nice tone and that my repeated counsel to you and to your running mates, to ignore the pundits counseling the necessity of putting distance between your running mates and you, and to stay together as a team, helped make our sweep possible.

"From the reports I have read, Paul Goldman cited three reasons for your displeasure at what you believe to be the excessive or undeserved credit given to me for your victory. He alleged that: 1) I wasn't with you from the start. 2) I advised against the two-month statewide tour. 3) I advised against emphasizing your Korean War record. As you well know, however:

"1) I declared long before anyone announced their candidacies for any office that I was going to remain publicly neutral until the convention so that I would be in a position to reunite both wings after what we knew would be a hard-fought contest for the gubernatorial nomination. That didn't keep me from meeting regularly and discussing strategy and tactics with all of the candidates for statewide office, however, and I certainly spent more time with you than with any of the other candidates, working on the special challenges you had to meet and conquer.

"2) I told you from the very beginning that the key to your success would be getting out and meeting as many people as possible and speaking before as many groups as possible around the state, to dispel any lingering fears about your candidacy—a strategy with which you credited me publicly on several occasions—and I also advised you repeatedly to avoid taking the bait and overreacting to any criticism of you or your record, no matter how untrue it might be. While I didn't personally conceive of the two-month statewide tour, I certainly supported it enthusiastically from the very first time you mentioned it.

"3) From the very outset, I said your Korean War record was a major plus and I cited it regularly during campaign appearances and in some of the TV commercials I cut for you (without any direction or guidance at all from you or your staff about what I might say). I also included it in a never-used joint TV commercial that I filmed primarily for your benefit, without your knowledge and on my own initiative, several weeks before you first acknowledged you'd be able to afford any paid TV at all.

"Yet in spite of our complete agreement on the above issues which Paul wrongly cited as disagreements, we did have some very real differences about the way your campaign was run, which you and I discussed on any number of occasions and those may well have been the reason for Paul's pique. As you will recall, two matters which you and I talked about privately at almost every meeting concerned the serious difficulties your campaign encountered without a designated campaign manager or a designated finance chairman.

"You told me repeatedly that you recognized the need to have someone at the office on a day-to-day basis implementing a game plan and at least returning phone calls, and you acknowledged that you were missing out on a very significant number of fundraising opportunities by not having a finance chairman to follow up your efforts and the efforts of so many of the rest of us, or organizing individual fundraising events, but you said you couldn't find anyone you were interested in who would take the job. I gave you several suggestions, but in my judgment that was always a glaring and solvable weakness, and we were very lucky reporters never focused on it as a measure of basic, management ability in assessing your potential for governor, if the need ever arose.

"We also differed on the role of the joint campaign—whereas I wanted to channel as much money as possible through that entity for the benefit of the ticket and primarily your race—and underscored my personal preference by contributing $3,000 to that campaign instead of $1,000 to each individual campaign—you and Paul wanted at least a large share of all such joint campaign funds given to you directly rather than sent to or spent on joint activities.

"Notwithstanding these differences, however, I always acknowledged the value of Paul Goldman as a strategist and his frequently innovative and sometimes brilliant ideas, and I placed an extremely high value on his absolute loyalty to you and your confidence in him. Still, as you know, your campaign left many of your hardest-working and strongest supporters quite frustrated.

"In my judgment, you won for many, many reasons, but principally because you were far and away the better-qualified candidate. You made a good personal impression wherever you went, and you used your limited media dollars very effectively (and for that Paul in particular deserves a great deal of credit). You and your ticket mates ran as a team and avoided, prior to the election, even a hint of the attitudes made public last week; and finally, you had a whole army of friends and supporters who voluntarily filled in most of the other gaps in your campaign with virtually no direction from you or Paul, because we all wanted you to win."

Robb went on to say that "there is one part of Paul's recent statement that I wholeheartedly agree with: 'Many people share the credit for Doug's victory.'" Robb said several members of his staff and key advisers "turned at least three fundraisers from what would otherwise have been complete disasters into very respectable events," plus "the countless additional fundraising calls and letters that Lynda (his wife) and I made and wrote on your behalf....

"The letdown from Paul's public statements was universal," added Robb, who said an enclosed attachment, written voluntarily by his staffers, "gives some sense of what a few members of my staff did for you on their own time....

"I could go on," Robb wrote, "but I never expected to have to justify to anyone, and to you of all people, what I and those closest to me did for you in the past campaign, or what so many others did for you at my request..."

Robb told Wilder he was "by no means forgetful or ungrateful for everything you have done for me in the past. But loyalty is a two-way street. If anything was bothering you following your victory, you know you could have told me what it was in person," rather than being evasive during telephone conversations. "Having Paul initiate calls to reporters misrepresenting the facts and completely reversing your attitude during the campaign still makes no sense to me."

Robb suggested that Wilder might have followed the lead of Baliles, who "has done a superb job" in that regard. "For four years" after Baliles' election as attorney general in 1981, Robb said, "he had to listen to pundits and opponents alike say he wouldn't have won without the help of his running mates" on a ticket led by Robb. "He's handled similar comments this time with equal grace, as well as comments about shadows being cast as he puts together his executive team for the next four years....

"You may recall that no little credit and influence were accorded to you for my victory in 1981, which I applauded, and your role in my administration, particularly with regard to black appointments, and your role in the 1982 Senate race, have been repeatedly stated in ways I'm sure you'd agree were advantageous to you and less than flattering to me, but you've never heard a peep from me to try to set the record straight. You may also recall how often my relationship to my late father-in-law was credited with my victory in 1977, even though polls showed he certainly wasn't held in the high esteem then that history may someday accord him."

Robb concluded:

"'Like it or not, we all have to live with the perceptions of others that we couldn't make it alone—and indeed I don't think any of us could. I suspect that was what your mother had in mind in the sentiment you attributed to her in your victory speech.

attributed to her in your victory speech.

"We've been friends for many years, and we've both carried water for each other when it wasn't easy, but friends don't treat friends like you've treated me and those closest to me recently. Unless you can find a way to repair the damage you and Paul Goldman did last week, there are some very large numbers of our mutual friends and supporters who just won't be there again for Doug Wilder, and I'd hate to see that happen.

"I understand that it's not easy being a role model, but increased expectations bring increased responsibilities. Tactics that you may have felt obliged to resort to in the past simply won't work in your new role.

"Your victory sent an extraordinarily positive message throughout Virginia and across the nation, and I urge you not to let your opportunity pass you by, or let the bright potential your victory represents go sour. More people than you may ever know felt an enormous sense of pride in your victory. An awful lot of us put our reputations on the line for you, and we're willing to do it again if you can convince us that our trust is well-placed."

The attachment, compiled by Robb staffer Judy Griswold, listed specific activities that various Robb staffers said they carried out for the Wilder campaign.

The memo said that in the final two months of the campaign, "a day did not pass" when someone in Robb's office did not speak with Wilder or one of his aides about scheduling, speeches, position papers, transportation and fundraising. It expressed frustration that Robb staffers had in arranging meetings with the Wilder strategists. The night of the first such meeting, for example, it said, Wilder kept chief-of-staff McCloud and seven other Robb staffers waiting an hour and a half, during which time they called Wilder at home three or four times to tell him they were waiting his arrival. Once he arrived, "the meeting went very well and everyone agreed to meet weekly," but because of scheduling conflicts with Wilder, no other sessions were held. "This type of episode was not unusual," the memo added, and was "very frustrating to those of us trying to get a little feedback on what we were volunteering to do."

Griswold said that during the last five weeks of the campaign, she was asked to join the Get Out The Vote (GOTV) team operated by the joint campaign. The GOTV effort concentrated on producing a large turnout out in urban areas, especially in black precincts, partly through the distribution of "flusher" money, or "walking around" money," which are campaign funds distributed to party workers to "flush out" the voters by "walking around" their neighborhoods or otherwise seeing that voters get to the polls. Griswold said she met daily at the Baliles campaign headquarters with Bernard Craighead, Ron Moore and Richard Dickerson, three black campaign workers, but rarely with Wilder's contact for the GOTV effort, Michael Brown.

"The most frustrating part of this operation was not having the Wilder campaign's constant participation," Griswold wrote. She said that from the beginning, the Wilder campaign was opposed to a large GOTV effort, believing that with Wilder on the ballot, the black vote would turn out regardless of how much money was spent. Instead, the Wilder campaign wanted the GOTV money turned over for use as it saw fit. "This was a constant strain on most meetings," Griswold said.

As it turned out, Griswold noted, the black turnout "was not that high," but she said "it would have been much lower had the phone banks (financed by the GOTV) not been in existence and the election day flusher operation not been in place."

Griswold concluded that "none of us really expected to get any credit or praise for what we did—we all would have helped no matter where we were or what we were doing—but we certainly didn't expect to get criticized or cause you (Robb) to get criticized."

Robb didn't hear a peep from Wilder about the letter.

Wilder said he didn't give much thought to what has become known, with the familiarity of a long-running soap opera, as "the Robb-Wilder feud." He was focusing all of his energy on his upcoming inauguration.

The second letter to Wilder was written by private citizen Robb from his law office in Vienna, Virginia, in suburban Washington, on August 20, 1986. It noted that Robb and Wilder had exchanged greetings earlier that month in Richmond, at the funeral of former governor John Dalton, but Robb "didn't think that was either the time or the place to talk about matters I want to cover in this letter." Robb said he then delayed writing until after Wilder had returned from his promised rerun of his campaign swing through Southwest Virginia.

Robb went on:

"To get right to the point, I am very much concerned about (1) the way you have treated me and, more recently, [Governor] Jerry Baliles and others who had always regarded you as a friend and ally and (2) the lack of veracity in many of the things you have persisted in saying about my role in your campaign and about the Democratic Leadership Council.

"Whatever short-term mileage you may be getting out of the course you are now following, the long-term effects are bound to be damaging to you. Your credibility with most key participants in the political process is disappearing rapidly and many who have supported you in the past are no longer sure that you can be trusted, or that you can still be an effective team player. In short, the very qualities which helped you win in a statewide election are now being called into question, and I can't believe you want that to continue.

"I am not talking about disagreements on policy matters, or on individual issues where honest differences ought to be raised and discussed. In fact, I commend you for the positions you are reported to be advocating on a number of substantive issues, and I happen to agree with you on many of them. What I am talking about are deliberate distortions and untruths, and the blindsiding of allies without at least trying to resolve differences first.

"Admittedly, a member of your staff did alert David McCloud, presumably to tell me, that you were going to say something about me [and the DLC] in your North Carolina speech, but for me not to take it 'personally,' because it was 'just politics.' When contacted by a reporter, I didn't challenge that charade because I wasn't ready to unload on you— as an increasing number of political leaders and many of our mutual friends have urged me to do. But I do want you to know privately that I have reached the end of my patience.

"You already know how Jerry Baliles reacted to your comments, and you've probably heard, as I have, that Jesse Jackson, while agreeing to ignore your first shot at him, used some very graphic language to describe exactly what he was going to do to you if you ever pulled another stunt like that on him.

"Given the amount and the favorable tone of the media attention you've been receiving since your inauguration, I doubt if you realize the depth of the negative feelings you've aroused in a relatively small but influential group of people, most of whom worked very hard for your election, as well as for the whole ticket. Suffice it to say, many of us are getting tired of repeatedly hearing people say, 'I told you so,' and the temptation to simply acknowledge that we made a serious mistake in going all out for you gets stronger every day.

"So far, I haven't yielded to that temptation, and I've urged others not to do so either, for several reasons. First, I remind them that the facts have not changed—you were unquestionably the best-qualified candidate for the office you now hold, and you certainly deserved to win. Second, your election made an important statement for Virginia, the South, and the Democratic Party that shouldn't be taken lightly, and, with the exception of the way you have treated me and various other allies, that the rest of your message is largely very constructive, and ought to be heard. Third, a lot of us worked too hard for your election to see it all go down the drain without trying to turn things around. In many ways, your success or failure involves not only you, but many of us as well, because of the way we represented you as a candidate.

"Now I'll concede that jettisoning a former friend or two probably won't cause you to lose much public support, but the impact on your credibility is another matter. In my own case, for you to continue to try to mislead people into believing that I ever opposed your candidacy at any stage, or that I opposed your campaign strategy, or that I or the DLC ever claimed or sought credit for either your victory or for those of your running mates, simply doesn't square with the facts, which are well-known to too many people. Nor does it make any sense for you to attack the DLC when your campaign was based on precisely the same appeal to the electorate that the DLC is advocating.

"Your comments several weeks ago regarding Jerry Baliles' policy on corrections, and this week about his transportation package, are equally disturbing. I would concede that you have every right to disagree, privately or publicly, with anyone in government, including the governor with whom you were elected, but when and how you do it can be critically important. As a member of the Baliles-Wilder-Terry team, it seems to me you have an obligation to discuss important differences with Jerry before going public, particularly when it involves an issue as politically sensitive as contact visitation policy in the corrections department. On the matter of his transportation package, I think you have an even greater obligation since you agreed to be his 'eyes and ears' on the commission. I cannot for the life of me figure out why you didn't express your concerns to Jerry before the commission report was adopted, and before he publicly embraced it. Many of us who served on the commission had reservations about individual conclusions and recommendations in the overall package, but all of us were prepared to set aside our individual preferences and vote for the final report because we knew that without that kind of support, its chances of passage in the General Assembly would be greatly reduced. The bottom line is that every member of the commission was prepared to bite the bullet in order to help Jerry and the members of the General Assembly take the heat, and, as the governor's personally designated representative, if you had any doubt about your willingness to do at least as much as the members of the commission, it seems to me you had an obligation to at least let the governor know that ahead of time—not after he'd put his neck on the line.

"Several mutual friends of our have tried to analyze the real reason for your public statements, and most of them remain just as puzzled as I am. Among those possible explanations about which most of the speculation centers are: (1) that Paul Goldman is bitter because I never offered him a job in state government; (2) that you and Paul resented the fact that even though some of my closest friends and supporters worked very hard on your fundraising, that other more conservative friends didn't raise nearly as much money for your lieutenant governor's race in 1985 as they did for my gubernatorial campaign in 1981; (3) that you think I might decide to run for governor again in 1989 and you therefore need to start denouncing me early and often; (4) that you think you can extort my support for your gubernatorial bid in connection with speculation about any national interests I'm alleged to have; (5) that you have decided not to make a serious effort to win the governorship in 1989, but instead to exploit your current role as the highest black elected official in state government for all its worth in publicity and honoraria, and then assume the martyr's role when you don't get the nomination in 1989; (6) that by openly criticizing Democrats, you are setting yourself up to run in 1989 as an Independent, as you threatened to do in prior years; or (7) that you are determined to set yourself up nationally as the black alternative to Jesse Jackson.

"I don't know if any of these suggested motivations are even remotely accurate, but they represent the kind of speculation political insiders engage in when they try to explain why you would try to pick a fight with me, based on allegations that you and I both know simply aren't true, or with Jerry, with whom you have three and one-half years left to serve.

"I am disappointed that you never responded to my lengthy letter last November, and that you have gone on the offense again recently, not on honest differences over issues, but in ways that go to the very heart of your credibility—and mine. However, in an effort to avoid the kind of public exchanges that would surely tantalize the news media, but would only hurt you, me, and our party even more, I thought I'd try one last time to iron out whatever differences we have, before a number of our mutual friends declare open season on you for consistently violating what you recently alluded to as the 11th commandment [though shalt not criticize a member of your own party].

"Whatever the cause of your present feeling, I think it's important that we have a serious talk—like the ones we had so often and so amicably up until a few days after you were elected lieutenant governor. If you'd like to try to resolve our differences, please let me know, but whatever your intentions, please extend me the courtesy of replying to this letter—and to the letter I sent you in November."

Again, Wilder didn't reply.

McCloud, Robb's longtime aide, wrote a letter of his own, to Goldman, saying he hoped that Goldman "might provide some insight into what appears to be a very self-destructive strategy that the lieutenant governor has adopted."

McCloud said "what concerns me most" was that a member of Wilder's staff had come by the governor's office during the summer and suggested that Wilder was going to "say something about Governor Robb" in a speech in North Carolina and that Robb "shouldn't take it personally because it was just politics." McCloud told Goldman, "I may be a little old fashioned, but I don't believe in taking a blindside whack at an ally for the benefit of press coverage. Doug is too smart and knows too well how to manipulate the press for that to have been the reason. I know there has to be a better answer."

McCloud also snidely noted that while he was "equally puzzled about the blindsiding of Governor Baliles" on the issue of contact visits to death row inmates, he chalked that off to "a way to come out on the conservative side of at least one hot topic...given the very significant issues" that the Republicans had raised during the 1985 campaign "about Doug's own voting record on corrections, the death penalty and prison policy."

McCloud told Goldman that before he wrote the letter he had "searched my own mind and the minds of others who have been with Doug since his first state Senate campaign, to try to discover what motive Doug might have had in mind for launching attack after attack on members of his own party; and particularly on the governor and his transportation program. The reasons given range from the perplexing to the ludicrous."

A bizarre theory that McCloud said he had heard was that "since Doug is telling Jesse Jackson to stop fighting with more conservative Democrats, it is a way to camouflage Doug's own record of threatening to run as an independent in the 1982 campaign."

Other reasons proffered by McCloud were that Goldman was smarting from his failure to be appointed to a consumer affairs position in the Robb administration, and as payback for Robb's first letter.

Even after Robb leaked the letters to reporters, Wilder, although furious, refused to comment. Instead, he released a written statement in which he suddenly detoured onto the high road, saying, "If someone wants to write personal letters and later release them to selected members of the press, that is their prerogative. I, however, will having nothing to do with it. The people of Virginia are not interested in negative personal attacks. In 1985, I refused the use of such tactics in my campaign, as I refuse them now as lieutenant governor."

Confronted with the suggestion that the perception is that Goldman's calls were volleys fired as part of Wilder's revolt against his benefactors, Wilder responded, "I think you're right in terms of the perception." But he reiterated that because he had not made the calls, "there is nothing I need to be apologetic for." Told that some of his friends have suggested he could have diffused the issue, Wilder interrupted. "They're not my friends. These are persons that choose not to be quoted. They are people who are brave and courageous to that extent. I call them grim-spinners, who dare not and dream little. If they have said it to you, then you should tell me who they are. I don't fence with shadows. I don't deal with smoke. If I did, I would be engulfed with it. And to the extent that I don't see them, they don't exist, and I don't discuss them."

His real friends, he said, were satisfied once he explained what had happened. He makes a point—another one of those legal technicalities—that when he challenges his detractors to point to instances were he publicly criticized Robb, "no one can. I said to them, 'have you ever seen anything that I have ever said,' and they said no."

As time went on, however, Wilder changed his mind, and in several meetings with reporters, alternately lambasted Robb, and then sounded conciliatory. At one point, he compared Robb's decision to release the letters to nuclear war between the Super Powers of Virginia politics.

"It's like a bomb that's exploded and you're waiting for them mushroom (cloud) to come down from the sky," Wilder said. "The gauntlet has been thrown down...I was accused of being an extortionist, my trustworthiness was questioned."

Going public with the letters might even have had racial overtones, he said. "I don't know whether it's a question of skin or not."

Goldman also had raised the race issues, and infuriated Robb, in a speech to the First District Black Caucus in Williamsburg. Goldman seemed to include Robb among a group of Virginia politicians "whose politics were irreversibly molded by a mind-set that was colored by the pigmentation of Doug Wilder's skin. Politicians whose racially oriented strategies see us in black-and-white terms will never be able to lead America to the full-color portrait we sing about in 'America the Beautiful,'" Goldman said.

Suggestions of racism had an editorialist at the Richmond Times-Dispatch chortling. The newspaper recalled that Wilder had "shrieked racism" during the campaign after former Governor Godwin bemoaned Wilder's attempt to change the state song, and said Robb was now similarly facing ludicrous criticism. It said Robb "has a right to be piqued" about Wilder's behavior toward him, but questioned whether someone "in the big leagues" such as Robb should be observed in Peoria squabbling over sandlot politics. As for Wilder, "his attempt to use his race to deflect criticism should be everyone's concern. It is an intolerable tactic," said a newspaper that not only tolerated, but encouraged, massive resistance and Jim Crowism. A cartoon accompanying the editorial depicted Wilder at a lunch counter yelling at a waitress, "you burned my toast, you racist."

Robb didn't stop with the release of the letters. A few days later, in an interview, on December 2, 1986, he said Wilder's continued criticism of him made it difficult for him to support him for governor. "After you have alienated the former governor and the governor (Baliles) and most of their key supporters and staff, it is fair to assume that they're not going to be allies in the future, if given a credible alternative."

Asked if he meant he would not support Wilder under any circumstances, Robb answered, "I try not to be absolute. Politics takes so many twists and turns. But I clearly thought I would be in a position to support him enthusiastically if he got the nomination, but he has made that very difficult." Robb added that he would "support the nominee of the party," even it were Wilder.

Robb said he had talked to "a number of people, including national leaders, both black and white, and not a single one" could understand Wilder's motivation. Asked why he chose to air his views, Robb said, "you just plain run out of cheeks" to turn.

"I've never encountered anything in politics so difficult to understand or explain. I'm not trying to be vindicative," said Robb, who added that speaking out brought "personal sadness" to him, but it had become a "lost cause" to attempt to retain their relationship.

Robb released the letters to "set the record straight," former press secretary Stoddart said in mid-1988. "For the last year, anytime Doug or Paul Goldman wanted to get in the news, they could call reporters and make some kind of allegations about what Robb did or didn't do" for them during the campaign. By making the letters public, Stoddart said, "people can decide for themselves" whether Wilder had reason to complain.

Intermediaries had attempted several times to get the two of them together, and on one occasion, Robb waited several hours in his law office in Washington for Wilder to come by. Wilder said later that he had not had a firm appointment, and that he had gotten hung up with other appointments.

Wilder avows that the criticism from Robb "runs off my back like water. Notwithstanding all those harsh things that were said, I have no hard feelings toward the former governor. In politics, you've got to learn to be called many things. It does not affect me personally at all."

At times, Wilder and Robb sound more like a couple of self-centered boys arguing over who gets to bat first rather than Super Powers: Robb might not support Wilder for governor? Well, Wilder might not support Robb for president.

Releasing the letters "raised questions in the minds of some people who have talked to me" about what kind of president Robb would make. "One would have to see who was running," Wilder said. "Certain things would have to take place to heal what some have called this rift." On the other hand, "He (Robb) has said he thinks it's a bygone friendship. I don't. I don't let a single act of incontinence ruin a friendship."

Wilder bounces back and forth like a ping pong ball in talking about Robb. One minute he is criticizing him, saying he might not be able to support him for president, then next he is saying, oh well, I understand.

"We are all human," Wilder said, suggesting that Robb's feelings had been hurt. "He's showing no more than the frailties of human emotions."

But with the next breath, Wilder is back jabbing at the DLC and Robb's role in national politics. "When you hear people say that you've got to make an appeal to white Southern males, that's demeaning. And on the other hand, they tell blacks, 'hold on, we're going to do something for you.'"

Governor Baliles attempted the role of peacemaker, saying "sometimes it helps to clear the air publicly," although he made it clear that was not his style. "I have simply indicated that I will do mine (responding to Wilder's broadsides) privately."

The Republicans, of course, weren't going to sit idly by and miss a chance to take a swipe at both men. After first holding their peace—"never interfere in a suicide" quipped GOP spokesman Steve Haner—Donald W. Huffman, the state GOP chairman, said that if Robb's aides indeed had done as much work as they claimed on Wilder's behalf, they were cheating the taxpayers. "It is morally and legally wrong for campaign activities to occur in state offices by state employees on state time," said Huffman, sounding like someone who had never been around politics and politicians. What good is incumbency if you can't use government time for political work?

Huffman's Democratic counterpart, Larry Framme, the state Democratic chairman, doubted there would be long-term consequences of the public airing of the feud. "They're both big boys. And they are friends of long standing. I'm sure at the appropriate time they will be able to work out whatever differences they have."

When, if ever, that appropriate time will arrive, is not clear. It hadn't occurred by mid-1989. At the annual White House Correspondents Dinner in Washington in May, 1989, to which news organizations invite celebrities and politicians, Robb and Wilder were both guests of U. S. News and World Report, and, according to several people associated with the magazine, Robb requested that he not be seated at the same table with Wilder. But he was, and both forced smiles at each other throughout the evening.

45. Rival

Attorney General Mary Sue Terry was next on Wilder's hit list. It was important to either muscle her out of the way, or line up enough support to beat her in a showdown for the gubernatorial nomination. Wilder was prepared to do either. Whatever it took. Nineteen eighty-nine was his shot, now or never; Terry was young enough that she would have other chances.

The rivalry between Wilder and Terry reached its apogee during the 1987 legislative session. It surfaced over a bill, proposed by Terry and supported by the governor, that would require teachers and other school personnel to report to an administrator the names of students suspected of using drugs or alcohol, so the administrator could steer the student to counseling, a measure popularly called a snitch bill. The House version required school officials to notify parents of their discovery in most instances, but allowed them to forego notification if they thought it would be "injurious to the student's health or well-being." The measure, introduced for Terry by Delegate Marian Van Landingham of Alexandria, passed the House of Delegates on a vote of 53 to 46, but when it got to the Senate, conservative opponents, including most of the Republican minority, sought to amend it to remove the notification loophole, and require parental notification in every instance. The amendment was opposed by the bill's backers, who argued that some parents might punish their children instead of seeking help for them. When the amendment was offered on the Senate floor, the vote was 20-20. Wilder broke the tie, joining with all nine Republicans and eleven other Democrats in supporting the amendment.

By that simple act of breaking a tie, Wilder had managed to get himself to the right of Terry on the most important legislation she supported.

The attorney general, who was in bed at home recuperating from a fractured vertebra suffered during a racquetball game, was kept informed of the negotiations on the bill via an open phone line to the Capitol. She told her aides that the amendment was not acceptable. It could "potentially be dangerous or harmful to some children," she said, "and would be counterproductive." Van Landingham agreed and said, "I wouldn't support the bill with that provision." Terry's principal lobbyist, Anita Rimler, said she had talked to Wilder before the vote and "he didn't say he had any trouble with the bill." So the measure went to a Senate-House conference.

Wilder said, "I didn't vote in terms of trying to create a posture....I stand on the vote and its merits." Asked if he worried about going against the administration, he said, "I would like to think I am a member of the team." His vote on parental notification was "the only thing my critics can get a slippery hand on" from the session. Nonetheless, he said, "History shows that I have not had qualms about differing with them. These things happen. They'll happen again."

On the final day of the session, the snitch bill was returned from conference with the original reporting loophole reinstated, and was passed by the Senate on a vote of 20 to 19. Under parliamentary procedure, the bill then was delivered across the hall to the House for its reconsideration. If the House concurred, the bill would go to the governor for his signature.

But the House never got a chance to vote. What happened next became the center of a dispute that was dubbed the "snatching of the snitch bill." As the clock approached the midnight end of the session, Wilder leaned across the two-level podium and whispered to the Senate clerk, who then left the dais, walked across the marble rotunda that connects the two chambers, and retrieved the bill from the desk of the Speaker A. L. Philpott. Ordinarily, when a bill is transmitted from one chamber to the other, it cannot be recalled.

Once it was back in the Senate, it was called up for reconsideration, at which point three senators changed their vote, and it was rejected 22 to 17. That action required the calling of a second conference, and when it returned for the final time—with ninety minutes remaining in the 1987 assembly session—the vote was 18-18, whereupon Wilder broke the tie again and killed the bill permanently.

Although the snatched snitch bill had Wilder's fingerprints all over it, Wilder maintained that did not have the authority or the power to retrieve the bill. When it suited his purposes, Wilder had been able to cite precedents for nearly anything he wanted to do as the presiding officer, but in this instance, he said, "It was not within the power of the chair" to determine how the bill got back to his desk. Once it was miraculously "in our possession," however, he explained that "then this body could act upon it. I never left the podium," he said, suppressing a chortle. "I don't know how it got back. I've been accused of having a long arm, but it isn't quite that long, to reach all the way to the House."

Shropshire said later that Wilder had told him the legislation needed to be retrieved because it contained a technical flaw, but Senator Richard L. Saslaw, the floor manager of the bill in the Senate, blamed Wilder for Shropshire's action. "Doug told him to get it back," Saslaw said.

To Wilder, the whining smacked of sour grapes. Because the outcome was "something that she (Terry) didn't care for, I was blamed for it," Wilder said. "The question is, how did I do it?" When it was suggested that he had ordered Shropshire to get it, he laughed.

"The responsibility for the measure's failure is with the persons who voted against it," he said, conveniently ignoring his own tie-breaking votes. "I wasn't the sponsor. I wasn't the floor manager, I didn't speak against it."

Rimler, the attorney general's lobbyist, put the blame squarely on Wilder, lamenting, "after he called it back, I didn't have a chance to talk to him again." Terry's press secretary, Bert Rohrer, said, "It's very mysterious. There can't have been a philosophical motive" for Wilder's action. Wilder responded that Rohrer was "basically calling me a liar."

"I wasn't trying to see how mad I could make people," Wilder said. "My difference of opinion is an honest one." He insisted that he had voted to kill the bill for philosophical reasons, believing that parents should be informed under all circumstances if school officials believe their children are using drugs or alcohol. During the debate, he said some of the high school students who serve as pages in the legislature said to him, "what principal do you think is going to say, 'I've got a problem with the girls in this school, so I'm going to notify their parents.'" Furthermore, the original proposal "had been turned upside down about fifty different ways," although he said, "I'm not so sure that was all that bad."

The escapade permitted the defeated Terry to take the high ground. "You have to draw the line somewhere on win at all costs," she said.

Legislative observers hadn't witnessed such backstabbing between top state officials since Democrat Lieutenant Governor Robb and Republican Attorney General Coleman squared off in the years before they ran against each other in the 1981 gubernatorial campaign.

Philpott denounced the extraordinary retrieving of the bill from his desk as "highly unethical." Van Landingham said Wilder "didn't play cricket in stealing back the bill. It may not have been motivated by political maneuvering against Terry, but nonetheless it was extra-parliamentary. He didn't follow the rules. It smacks of a character flaw." Wilder insisted he did not know how the bill got back to the Senate. But Senator Richard L. Saslaw of Springfield, the bill's chief patron in the Senate, said Shropshire later told him Wilder had ordered him to bring back the bill.

"Looking at it charitably, Doug was simply uncomfortable with the bill," said one official close to Governor Baliles. "Looking at it cynically, he took Mary Sue down a notch....and won the gratitude of the hard-core conservatives."

"Both sides were right and both sides have a gripe," said Senate clerk Shropshire. "If I were Mary Sue, I'd be crying politics. She had the best two months she had since she was elected. But if Doug had voted for it, he would have been inconsistent."

Despite that setback, Terry had a good session, securing passage of twelve of fifteen bills she proposed. Wilder, on the other hand, backed only one bill—life without parole for first-degree murderers—and it failed. Granted, Terry's job as attorney general is a fulltime one, and her staff numbers more than a hundred, while the lieutenant governor's job is part-time and Wilder's office had only four employees. So who's keeping score? Everybody.

Some Democrats suggested that the rivalry between Wilder and Terry was so fever-pitched that the party might be better off turning to an alternative candidate for governor in 1989, someone less bruised by battle. Two potential compromise candidates mentioned were Richard Bagley, who after withdrawing from the 1985 gubernatorial race had been rewarded by Baliles by being named to his cabinet, as the state's first secretary of economic development, and Congressman Norman Sisisky, who had the advantage of bringing his own money with him—he was a millionaire Pepsi Cola bottler before being elected to Congress.

"I suspect it was part of Doug's effort to establish some credentials on the conservative side of the aisle," said Republican Senator Wiley F. Mitchell of Alexandria. "That's the segment of the electorate where he's the weakest."

If that were the case, it paid off. The News-Virginian of Waynesboro said "one might have guessed that the left-leaning Wilder would have voted the other way. But he didn't, and he was right." It quoted Wilder as saying, "I haven't heard any good reason why parents should be put in limbo."

Several weeks after the session, Wilder cited his vote in speeches around the state. "Parents who do not know what is going on cannot help" their children, he said. The legislation would have, for the first time, put into law a provision saying that parents did not have the right to know something about

Rival

their children. "Our young must be told that drugs are wrong, period...that suicide is the cop-out. It is clear and obvious that what we need is to go back to the drawing board of accountability and to the wellspring of morality and to the fountainhead of responsibility, to set the proper roles for our young people by our actions, by our deeds."

It would be wrong to get the idea that the Wilder-Terry rivalry was a one-way street. The attorney general and her loyal band of aides, who unlike Wilder's, were nearly all on the large payroll of her office, were sniping away at Wilder at every opportunity. Terry was saying privately that if she had it to do over again, she might not have seconded Wilder's nomination in 1985, and her associates were "worrying" that Wilder would not be able to raise the money needed to run a gubernatorial campaign. Terry also said she didn't understand why Wilder wasn't appreciative of the help he got from Robb and Baliles. "What's wrong with coattails?" she said, in a comment designed to keep her good relations with Robb and Baliles.

The most sensitive matter before the Senate in 1987 was the proposed censure of Senator Babalas, who had befriended Wilder when he first came to the Senate. The two men had an affinity that grew out of a sense of being outsiders—Babalas was the brilliant son of Greek immigrant parents who worked his way through Harvard law school.

In a 1985 subcommittee action, Babalas cast a vote for himself and a proxy for Willey to kill a bill that would have harmed one of his legal clients by capping the interest rates charged by second-mortgage companies. At the time, Babalas had been paid $61,000 in legal fees by one of the affected firms, Landbank Equity Corporation of Virginia Beach, which was under federal investigation for fraud in gouging its poor and uneducated customers.

Babalas was acquitted of criminal conflict-of-interest charges the previous August, at which Wilder testified as a character witness for his friend. He said that over the years Babalas had displayed "fierce honesty and integrity, beyond question his word is his bond." But he told the judge, "Had I been Babalas, I would not have voted." The judge who heard the case said he believed that Babalas had a conflict, but that he could not find beyond a reasonable doubt that the violation was willful, a condition necessary for a guilty verdict.

In October, the Senate Privileges and Elections Committee determined that Babalas had violated a Senate rule that bars its members from voting on matters in which they have "an immediate private or personal interest," and in an unprecedented action against one of its own members, voted 12 to 3 to recommend that Babalas be censured, a vague disciplinary action that carried no penalty.

At the start of the 1987 legislative session, Babalas contended he had done nothing more than others, and threatened to embarrass those who sought to punish him, saying the Senate was ruled by an oligarchy. "Is this Russia?" he shouted at one point during the debate over his fate. In return, he was being treated like a pariah by his colleagues, who were upset because his action had prompted calls for a more serious punishment and for tightening of ethical standards.

WILDER: HOLD FAST TO DREAMS

When the report came up on the Senate floor, Privileges and Elections Committee Chairman Joe Gartlan called for its adoption by a voice vote. But Wilder ruled that the form of the report was out of order, and that for a vote to be taken, there had to be a resolution calling for censure, not merely a report recommending it. He said he was relying on rules of the United States Senate in the absence of a Virginia precedent. Wilder's ruling prompted Babalas to celebrate, prematurely, saying, "I am vindicated. They're not going to have a lynching, vigilantism."

Gartlan challenged Wilder's ruling and urged the Senate to overturn it, and on a vote of 20 to 19, with Babalas abstaining, that appeared to have happened. But Senator "Buzz" Emick demanded a second vote, citing a rule that requires all members present to vote. When a second vote was called, Wilder ordered Babalas to participate. Babalas voted to support Wilder's ruling, but his was not the deciding vote because two other senators inexplicably switched position, and Wilder's ruling was sustained by a vote of 22 to 18.

"This is not going to make the Senate as an institution look very good," said Gartlan, who contended that Wilder's ruling exalted "form over substance," and there were private murmurings that Wilder was trying to protect his friend Babalas, hoping that the senators would be reluctant to put their names to a vote that would criticize one of their own.

After much wrangling, however, a resolution of censure was offered by Emick and it was adopted. Afterwards, Wilder said the affair had damaged the Senate's reputation, and admitted that "I was wrong" when in 1983, he had voted against the conflict-of-interest law, saying he was confident the assembly could police itself.

The 65-year-old Babalas, who had been fighting bone cancer for years, did not seek re-election after the censure. He died December 29, 1987.

Wilder's popularity on the national scene helped him become chairman of the forty-member Association of Democratic Lieutenant Governors in April (and before their terms expired, Governor Baliles and Attorney General Terry also headed their respective national organizations).

In August of 1987, Goldman announced that a poll, conducted by an undisclosed source—likely Goldman himself—and paid for by Wilder's friend Louis Salomonsky, showed that he could beat either Coleman or Parris. Dennis Peterson, who was putting together the first stages of Coleman's campaign, scoffed at the anonymous pollster, saying "I've got a poll here that shows us leading by four-to-one. When Goldman was asked why there was no matchup between Wilder and Terry, he said, "Let 'em pay for their own polls."

At the same time, Wilder aides continued to float reports that Wilder was being urged to run for the Senate, by whom was never disclosed, a tactic that the double advantage of keeping his options open and keeping the Robb camp on guard. A short time later, Goldman announced that his poll also showed that three out of four Democrats would like to pick their Senate nominee in a primary, in conjunction with the Super Tuesday voting the following spring. Although Goldman said the lieutenant governor "has nothing to do with it," the finding was interpreted by some as a not-so-subtle message to Robb about the power of black voters in the party, should Wilder decide to seek the nomination.

In yet another chapter of the book-of-politics called it's better to be lucky than smart, Wilder met with Colorado Senator Gary W. Hart in early March of 1987 and appeared to be in line for a role in Hart's presidential campaign. Wilder also was wooed by several other presidential hopefuls, but he made no endorsement.

Hart emerged from a forty-five minute meeting in Wilder's office to say that if Wilder supports him, he would see that the lieutenant governor played a key role in planning overall strategy for his campaign. Hart said he was not looking for paper endorsements "but active involvement from the nation's highest ranking black elected official." Hart said Wilder's election had "sent a signal" of what Democrats had to do to win elections, and Wilder's victory proved that "in key states like Virginia," the party is "not only coming back, but has come back. Lieutenant Governor Wilder can play a very key role in the leadership of his party nationally in the years to come," Hart said. Wilder said he was very impressed with Hart, and said he "left the door open" to a possible future endorsement. Hart had an "excellent chance" of winning the presidential nomination, he said.

That was, of course, was before Hart's involvement with Miami model Donna Rice forced him to withdraw from the race.

Before that occurred, Wilder aide Joel Harris was spreading the word that Hart was ready to name Wilder one of four national co-chairmen, and even suggested that a reporter call the Hart campaign office to see if such an announcement were ready. Wilder's luck held: the announcement was still being worked on when Hart withdrew. And Wilder's good fortune was only just beginning.

46. Mary Sue Withdraws

Wilder's luck came in the form of an announcement in the spring of 1988 by Attorney General Terry that she would seek a second term as attorney general, a reverse way of saying she would not challenge Wilder for the gubernatorial nomination the next year.

Not that, as usual, Wilder hadn't helped make his luck. He had launched a pre-emptive strike in January with a pair of fund-raising events, ostensibly to celebrate his fifty-seventh birthday. The two events, a sedate $1,000-a-couple black tie dinner for lobbyists and assorted heavy-hitters, held in the base of a Richmond monument, and a livelier $100-a-person dance later that evening at the city's convention center, featuring the Four Tops and comedian-activist Dick Gregory, netted about $100,000 for the impending campaign.

Conversely, Terry's luck had been mostly bad. For one, she was the only one of the three statewide officials to have the courage to take a stand on the lottery referendum—she opposed it—only to find out after the election that the overwhelming majority of Virginians wanted it. And unlike Wilder's flirtation with Hart, she went public with hers, in behalf of Tennessee Senator Al Gore Jr., who was soundly rejected by the voters.

Terry made her announcement on March 18, emphasizing that "I really like what I am doing, I am fulfilled. We are making a difference and the task is not finished." A few hours before the public announcement, which came as a surprise to some of her closest associates, Terry called Wilder. She later joked that Wilder "did not express profound disappointment" at the news.

At Wilder's office, there was a sigh of relief. Wilder said he was surprised at the timing, but not at the decision, a typical reaction from a man to whom "you do not give new information," according to one friend, who said Wilder always acts as if he knows everything. His staff, however, openly expressed surprise and elation. Had Terry challenged Wilder, the coming year would have been consumed with lining up support within the party, a time-consuming and potentially divisive endeavor. Now, barring a successful stop-Wilder movement, he and his staff could begin looking beyond the nomination, toward the general election. Laura Dillard, a staff member who became Wilder's press secretary for the gubernatorial campaign, said "Paul (Goldman) was calling every five minutes." While they were excited and pleased, Dillard said it also was "odd, weird" that the battle for which Wilder and his staff had been gearing up for three years would not have to be fought.

Larry Sabato, the University of Virginia seer, said Terry might have won the nomination, "but she realized it would be a nomination not worth having." Sabato said the general election would have been a repeat of 1969, when many blacks stayed home and liberals defected to the GOP, permitting Linwood Holton to become the first Republican governor in Virginia history. Further, Sabato said Terry "probably would have had to make promises in the nominating process that would have sent away conservatives in droves. She made the right decision." Had Wilder lost, Sabato said, he would have gone through the motions of supporting Terry, showing up at an occasional fundraiser or rally, and then, when there was a low turnout of blacks on election day, he could say, "she just didn't excite the electorate."

Almost as soon as the word of Terry's decision was out, some of her supporters began looking around for another candidate, a mini-version of the anyone-but-Wilder drive of 1985. "I think the majority of the so-called Robb-Baliles people will sit back and view the field," said a disappointed Delegate Al Smith. "It's a whole new ball game...and school is still out on how much a team player he is," he added in one of his famed mixed metaphors. "You have to have a big enough team to win."

But as Smith and other doubters quickly learned, Wilder's team was big enough. A few names were mentioned, but there were no takers. Wilder was embedded as the frontrunner.

What little doubt existed about that status was removed a short time later when Governor Baliles, on a trade mission with legislators in Israel, remarked that with Terry out of the running, Wilder's nomination was all but assured, and that he stood a good chance of being elected the nation's first black governor. The remark was interpreted as Baliles' blessing of Wilder's candidacy.

In May, Baliles moved even closer to an official endorsement, telling graduates of predominantly black Norfolk State University of Wilder's upcoming candidacy, "again, he will have a chance to make history in Virginia. Perhaps more to the point," Baliles went on, "Virginia will have the chance to make history, once against demonstrating that enduring values have a home in Virginia—but also establishing that Virginia does not have the time to waste on old fears, the old habits and the old divisions."

Wilder later said that he had never thought the Democratic party "would be rent asunder if Mary Sue and I both sought the nomination. You can fight wars with conventional weapons. You can reach accords when the war is over."

Wilder still wasn't home free. State Senator Daniel W. Bird Jr. had announced his candidacy for governor, on January 29, 1988. Bird, a Democrat from Wytheville in Southwest Virginia, conceded that he was not well know, which he said explained his "early Bird" entry into the race. He was unable to provoke Wilder into responding to calls to debate, however, or taking the bait of a loyalty oath to support the nominee of the party, a reminder to voters of Wilder's threatened independent run for the United States Senate in 1982. Despite a walk across the state that summer, Bird's candidacy didn't fly, and in January of 1989, he withdrew.

Robb was on board early too. Shortly after his election to the United States Senate in November of 1988, he responded to questions about his past differences with Wilder saying, "the problems of the past are just that—past," and assuring inquirers that he would endorse Wilder enthusiastically at the appropriate time. For his part, Wilder shored up his relations with Robb in March of 1989 by attending a meeting of the Democratic Leadership Council, the group that he often had scorned as divisive.

In the 1988 session of the General Assembly, Wilder backed only two pieces of legislation, and fared poorly on both. One of them, to eliminate the sales tax on non-prescriptions drugs, which was opposed by Baliles, was ridiculed as a placebo that would provide only one dollar a month in tax savings to the average family. But even that was too much for Governor Baliles, saying that the state could not afford to remove its overall cost of about $30 million a year without making cuts in its balanced budget. Wilder contended, however, that the state was headed toward a $200 million surplus for the biennium that ended at midyear and could afford removing a tax that "punishes hardest those Virginians in the middle- to lower-income brackets, especially our senior citizens." The other was an anti-crime measure, life without parole for capital murderers who don't get the death penalty, a law-and-order proposal that went too far for even such hard-liners as House Speaker A. L. Philpott, who denounced it as "more inhumane than the death penalty." The speaker, who pointed out he had introduced the legislation that reimposed the death penalty in Virginia, warned that Wilder's approach would create impossible conditions for corrections officials by turning life-term prisoners into "animals who can't be controlled."

At the start of the 1989 legislative session, Wilder backed off his plan to seek repeal of the sales tax on over-the-counter drugs in favor of a broader scheme unveiled by Baliles in his State of the Commonwealth address. There had been some speculation that Baliles would endorse Wilder's plan, which was to be a key ingredient of his campaign, but instead he proposed a maximum $35 tax credit for mostly middle- and upper-income taxpayers as a way of returning about $100 million to taxpayers to offset the extra taxes the state received because of changes in the federal tax code.

Moments after the speech, Wilder said he was so pleased with the governor's approach that he would drop his plan to repeal the sales tax on non-prescription drugs. In answer to a question, he said Baliles had given him "more than half a loaf, more than a loaf." Later that day, however, about the time his office was issuing a statement confirming his decision not to push for his own tax relief, there were reports that Wilder was furious with the governor.

A few days later, in a speech to the Richmond Crusade for Voters, Wilder denied reports that he was angry with Baliles, again implying that the governor's proposal more than compensated for the loss of his tax-relief plan. (Wilder also offhandedly offered his first public explanation for his opposition to the funding of the transportation package adopted by the legislature more than fifteen months earlier, pointing out that in the Crusade's pre-election questionnaire in 1985, he had pledged that he would not support an increase in the sales tax during his term as lieutenant governor.) He called the proposed tax credit "the largest such relief ever advanced in Virginia's history. To paraphrase George C. Marshall's famous words, 'you can accomplish almost anything if you don't care who gets the credit.'"

But as any student of Wilder knows, he cares very much who gets the credit. So it was no great surprise that the next week, a few days before his declaration of candidacy, Wilder announced that he would go ahead with his tax-cutting plan, while also supporting Baliles' measure. Although Wilder said he was renewing his call for the tax repeal because "I think it's clear the money is there," he may also have been prodded into it by Republicans in the assembly, who were threatening to back a similar measure to embarrass him, and by Marshall Coleman, who said Wilder's failure to repeal the tax on patent medicine raised questions about his effectiveness. State GOP spokesman Michael Salster reacted to Wilder's flip-flop saying, "he has been working out on the trampoline again, bouncing all over the place on issues." When Wilder's plan was introduced, by his friend Senator Granger Macfarlane of Roanoke, five Republicans signed on as co-sponsors, including freshmen senators Edwina P. "Eddy " Dalton, the widow of former governor John Dalton, and Joseph B. Benedetti. Dalton and Benedetti subsequently became the GOP nominees for lieutenant governor and attorney general, respectively. But the measure failed again, despite Wilder's personal lobbying and attempts to revive the issue with floor amendments in the closing days of the assembly.

Wilder announced his candidacy on a three-day swing around the state, beginning January 26, 1989, in Richmond. He noted that "forty years ago, working my way through college and law school as a waiter and bus boy, I never dreamed I would have the opportunity to run for governor of Virginia." Even twenty years earlier, when he announced his first try for public office, he stood virtually alone before a few members of the press. Now, two decades later, he was on a blue-and-white bedecked stage surrounded by the governor and attorney general and dozens of other public officials, in front of a crowd of about two hundred cheering supporters.

He pointed out that he had worked with five governors, bestowing special tributes on Governors Baliles and Robb and pledging "to build upon these many accomplishments." He outlined a "three for Virginia" platform that promised permanent tax relief and pledge to "neither propose nor initiate" additional taxes; an attack on drugs and drug-related crimes, and creation of jobs and housing for rural Virginians. And in the way that politicians do, he chose to cite as examples of his legislative career votes that were largely exceptions to his positions in his public career: the drug paraphernalia bill of 1971; a vote for the death penalty in 1977, and support of legislation in 1988 that extended the minimum prison time served by murderers and eliminated parole for escapees. His speech was filled with enough praise of business to satisfy the most rock-ribbed Republican: "Every governor of this state has relied on the keen insight of the Virginia business community. I intend to follow this tradition," including opposition to collective bargaining for public employees and support of the right-to-work law.

The tone of his speech, said Delegate Jerrauld C. Jones of Norfolk, one of ten blacks in the legislature, was designed to assure whites who fear "a whole lot of (blacks) in the governor's mansion eating chicken and chitlins." Delegate Kenneth R. Melvin of Portsmouth, the former roommate of one of Wilder's nephews, said Wilder's visibility as a black politician already was a factor in the contest for governor. "I don't think half the people would be here today if not for the historic nature of his candidacy. People will not vote for him just because he's black, but it does raise interest in his campaign."

Among those in the crowd, which was about equally divided between blacks and whites, was Daniel Perkins Jr., who had known Wilder growing up on Church Hill. Perkins had regarded Wilder as bright, but never in his wildest dream had he imagined that he might someday run for governor. "All judges, all law enforcement people, all public officials were of the white race," he said. "We never gave that kind of encouragement."

Ronald C. Spiggle, the mayor of historic Appomattox, agreed. "He's making history, and that lends credence to his candidacy. He's comfortable in the high-rises of Richmond and he's comfortable in the rural areas where I come from." R. Beasley Jones, a white legislator from rural Dinwiddie County, added, "the feeling is, instead of reading about history, why not make history?"

Wilder was the third black to run for governor in modern times. Los Angeles Mayor Tom Bradley lost twice in California, and Republican William Lucas, the Wayne County executive, lost in Michigan.

Speaking to reporters afterwards, Wilder sought to play down the significance of race. "I want to be judged by my experience and record. I hope (race) plays as little role in election issues as possible."

The closest parallel to Wilder's candidacy was the 1982 gubernatorial race in California, in which Los Angeles mayor Tom Bradley, a black Democrat, lost to Republican attorney general George ("just call me Duke") Deukmejian, by the narrowest margin in the state's history. Bradley's two races for governor—he was drubbed in a rematch in 1986—were the subject of a study for the Joint Center for Political Studies, a black Washington think tank, which published a book, "Tom Bradley's Campaigns for Governor—the Dilemma of Race and Political Strategies," by Thomas F. Pettigrew and Denise A. Alston.

Conventional wisdom, supported by exit polls, suggested that race played little part in the 1982 outcome. Bradley was well qualified—before being elected mayor in 1973, he had served as chief of police—bland and unthreatening; Deukmejian did not make a racial appeal, and Californians already had shown their willingness to elect blacks to high office, including (now Congressman) Mervyn Dymally as lieutenant governor, although Dymally was defeated when he sought re-election. But after a closer examination of voting patterns and post-election interviews, Pettigrew and Alston concluded that race, if not racism, was a key factor in Bradley's defeats.

Deukmejian employed a word that white politicians often use when running against blacks, saying he could represent "all" Californians, the implication being that a black could not. The corollary, the authors pointed out, that a white might not be able to represent all minorities, is of little concern to conservative whites.

The authors said that Bradley "faced the same dilemma as do all black candidates for high office who need strong white support. A nonthreatening demeanor is a necessary, though not sufficient, condition if the black candidate is to appeal to moderate white voters. Yet a person with that demeanor may lack the charismatic appeal required to attract both minority voters and the liberal-left part of the white electorate that is most likely to favor the candidacy of a black."

Bradley's campaign slogan was "he doesn't make a lot of noise, he just gets things done." No one ever accused Wilder of being bland or quiet, and while he's no Jesse Jackson, he's no Tom Bradley either. In both comparisons, that's good for Wilder.

"In hindsight," the authors of the California study concluded, "it is evident that Bradley should have painstakingly courted every possible vote." Instead, he took too many people for granted. He failed to open campaign headquarters in many black communities and didn't bother to address the concerns of black voters in speeches.

Bradley took for granted his "natural constituency"—a term that Wilder lambasted the Republicans for using in 1985 for having racial overtones—for fear that he would be overly identified with liberals, labor, blacks and other minorities. A large turnout from those interest groups could have propelled Bradley to Sacramento in 1982. Fortunately for Wilder, he learned that on his own, in 1985, without having to suffer a defeat for the lesson. (Wilder wasn't the only one who automatically anticipated a large turnout of blacks: Such a hypothesis was responsible for a poll by The Washington Post that overestimated the margin of Wider's victory.)

Wilder said his failure to court the black vote in 1985 arose not so much from a belief that they automatically would vote for him, as from the absence of someone to play the role he had played for others in the past. The Doug Wilder who had gotten out the vote for Chuck Robb in 1981 was busy getting out the white vote for himself, and no one had replaced him in the black community. The situation would be different in 1989, he said with assurance, when, as the head of the ticket, he could command the resources to target any group that could produce large blocks of votes.

One of the raps put on Wilder, usually by Robb and Baliles loyalists, was that he could not raise sufficient money to finance a gubernatorial campaign. He had shown as little interest in wooing such reliable fundraisers as lobbyist Bill Thomas and Delegate Al Smith as they had shown in his campaign.

Thomas said the difference between his enthusiasm for Terry and Wilder over the years was "pretty simple. Mary Sue asked for help, Doug never asked." Thomas did have dinner with Wilder in August of 1988 at a Richmond hotel to discuss strategy, but Wilder could hardly be blamed for not being enthused about what he heard. Thomas told Wilder that unlike Robb and Baliles, who had used their terms as lieutenant governor and attorney general, respectively, to travel the state and line up support of the business community, Wilder had "wasted three years." When Wilder said he was going to start campaigning in earnest after the November election, Thomas said "my mental comment was, 'so you're going to blow two or three more months.'" After that, Thomas said that even if Wilder had asked for his help, he would have been "inclined just to stay out of it, just take a sabbatical."

Wilder took the first steps to put together a campaign team in December, 1988. He discussed strategy with David Doak, who had been Robb's campaign manager in 1981 and Baliles' media consultant in 1985, and hired a Washington polling firm, Donilon & Petts, proteges of Patrick Caddell, who gained his reputation as President Carter's pollster, and who had worked for Baliles four years earlier. In early 1989, he named banker William C. Wiley as his campaign treasurer. Wiley had been state treasurer in the Baliles administration, after serving as co-director of finance in Baliles' gubernatorial campaign. Fundraising continued. Richard S. "Major" Reynolds III, the heir to the Reynolds aluminum fortune who had Wilder's support when he ran against Robb for lieutenant governor in 1977, put together a $1,000-a-person reception at the home of Richmond stockbroker S. Buford Scott Jr., which attracted about fifty paying guests.

261

WILDER: HOLD FAST TO DREAMS

Near the end of 1988, some supporters of the Robb-Baliles-Terry crowd were telling Terry that Wilder's first financial report, due January 15, might be so bleak that party officials might turn to her and ask her if she would reconsider and accept a draft for the gubernatorial nomination. Terry told them absolutely not, that her decision was irreversible.

But like a lot of other concerns about Wilder, that one turned out to be wishful thinking on the part of his detractors.

Wilder's initial report showed he had raised about $850,000, which was more than either Baliles or Davis, the 1985 Democratic contenders for governor, had raised at the comparable time.

Even Al Smith was mildly impressed. "It sounds to me like they've all done pretty well," he said of Wilder and the Republican hopefuls. But Smith couldn't help but add, "The thing to remember is that the first and the last money comes the easiest. It's the in-between that's the hardest."

Wilder may not have been getting his money from the Bill Thomases (although Smith was coming around), but he was tapping new sources and reaching into some deep pockets on his own. One effort was a telephone solicitation of middle-class blacks across the country. Other prominent blacks were hosting fundraisers from coast-to-coast; at one such event, hosted by Alexander Williams Jr., a fellow alumnus of Howard Law School who was the prosecuting attorney in Prince George's County, Maryland, the Washington suburb that may have more middle-class black residents than any jurisdiction in the nation, about a hundred people paid $2,000 a couple to boost Wilder's candidacy. Among his other backers were John Kluge of Charlottesville, the billionaire media mogul listed by Fortune magazine as America's second richest person, and a growing number of nouveau riche developers, led by J. Bahman Batmanghelidj, who calls himself and his corporation Batman. Michael S. Horwatt, one of Batmanghelidj's lawyers, said "it is an identification of sorts with a guy struggling against the odds." The Iranian-born Batmanghelidj and German-born Kluge each produced self-made fortunes.

By summer, after the Republicans had spent more than $10 million in a divisive primary to choose Wilder's opponent, about the only complaint heard about Wilder's money came from the GOP, which said he had too much of it, thanks to being unopposed for the nomination.

On the final day of the 1989 legislative assembly, Wilder's colleagues paid tribute to the end of his twenty-year career in the state Senate.

Senator Stanley C. Walker of Norfolk, who was elected to the House in 1964 and moved to the Senate in 1972, said "there are those here who can recall...the history-making event" of his election in 1970. "You came to this body unafraid of the fray," became known as a great debater and soon found himself among the leaders of the Senate. As a result of his election as lieutenant governor, Walker said, the state received national attention, and "all of us here feel very strongly you have performed with honor to yourself and to all Virginians."

"My total public life has been spent in this chamber," Wilder, in a rare display of emotion, told the forty senators. He recalled arriving "green as a horn" for the 1970 session and receiving "a guiding hand, quiet persuasion and wise counseling" from a hog farmer from the heart of segregated Virginia, the late William Rawlings of Southampton County. "Without Bill Rawlings's steady influence and guiding hand over that time, I would have gone awry," Wilder said. "But he was always there." He also paid a special tribute to "my good friend, (Jay Shropshire) the clerk of this body, who has been fair and always ready to assist all of us."

Only majority leader Hunter B. Andrews and his tennis-playing pal, William E. Fears, had been in the Senate longer than Wilder. Despite occasional clashes with the acerbic Andrews, Wilder said, "those who believe there has been animus and distrust (between them) are removed from the truth." Wilder said that he had relished Andrews' "sometimes bombastic oratory on the floor." Andrews had sent him "my first letter of congratulation" and had taught him how to read between the lines of legislation.

Wilder noted that it was 1983 before a second black, Robert C. Scott of Newport News, joined him, assuring that his race was not represented "just in a token fashion." By 1989, the chamber had three black members: Scott, Benjamin Lambert, Wilder's first campaign manager, and Yvonne B. Miller of Norfolk, the first black woman member. Their presence, he said, "lets the people know that this Virginia Senate is indeed representative in spirit and in capacity of all of us."

Wilder thanked his colleagues for "the opportunities granted to me on this floor, without fear of being punished or without the fear of being somewhat the bad guy."

He said he was "always mindful that while the seats are numbered, the names are typed in," a constant reminder that the members served at the pleasure of the public. Perhaps recalling his long struggle to get approval of the King holiday bill, he said, "it is not important that you are immediately successful, but that you continue to put your best foot forward, and represent the high ideals and aspirations of the people of Virginia."

Waxing poetic, he added, "It is a continuum. As the philosopher says, 'all light comes from pre-existing light; all of the good things that we have ever done comes from some good that was here before us.' I like to think that good was here when I came here, that good is being perpetuated now, and that good will be here when you and I are gone, for posterity."

When the Senate pages presented a resolution telling Wilder, "we are all behind you," his former opponent, Senator John Chichester, jokingly objected. In a similar spirit, Wilder said he once hoped his portrait would hang on the chamber wall, as do all former lieutenant governors who do not go on to become governor. "Now I hope it never appears there."

47. Speeches

While the controversies over Wilder's squabbles with Robb and Baliles offer an insight into Wilder the bare knuckles political infighter, there was another Wilder out there during his term as lieutenant governor, a new kind of black leader, delivering a message of hope and challenge around the state and nation.

Before largely black audiences in Washington, Boston, Baltimore, Hampton and Lynchburg, his message was that blacks should stop making excuses and take control of their destiny. Don't shun menial jobs, he told young people, because any job is better than no job; avoid "black talk," and say "yes, sir" and "yes, ma'am," and accept some of the blame for the plight of their race.

The Lynchburg Daily Advance editorialized that if President Reagan said the same thing, he would have been run out of town. "Former Governor Robb couldn't have pulled it off. President Reagan couldn't have done it with much, if any, credibility. Yet Lt. Gov. Douglas Wilder received a standing ovation for remarks....about the importance of discipline, education, morality and hard work among blacks....it is part of a new candor on race in which some blacks are saying things that immediately would be labeled racist if whites said them...."

Wilder was echoing a theme of Jesse Jackson and other black leaders, preaching against promiscuity, laziness and pornography, but Wilder was delivering his low-key version of the message as an elected official, warning blacks not to expect the government to resolve many of their problems.

"Yes, dear Brutus," he told the NAACP Freedom Fund dinner in Lynchburg, "the fault is not in the stars, but in ourselves."

While he won praise from many, including white conservatives, his remarks upset some blacks. A journalist chided him after a Washington speech, saying he should talk about how difficult it was for him to become the first black elected to statewide office in Virginia.

But Wilder gave no quarter to such criticism. "Some blacks don't particularly care for me to say these things, to speak to values. Somebody's got to. We've been too excusing." He freely conceded that his message was more moral than political, a surprise to those who had watched his adroit dealmaking as a legislator. Wilder does not consider himself religious, (since childhood, he has seldom graced the inside of First African Baptist or any other church as a worshiper), but said what had become his stock speech reflected the precepts of his church-based upbringing and the role models of his youth, including Horatio Alger, Abraham Lincoln, George Washington, Emerson, Cicero and Mary Bethune.

He implored his listeners to "redig the wells our grandfathers dug...not just the rendition of Alex Haley (author of "Roots,") but also of pride in endeavor and accomplishment...discipline of mind and body...and of healthy and competitive challenge, not succumbing to those who talk about taking the shortcuts."

Wilder brushed aside suggestions that blacks need special qualifications to succeed, telling the Blacks Students Law Association at Harvard University, "If you know you have to be doubly prepared, be doubly prepared, and then get on with doing the job."

He pointed to his own election as proof that blacks can succeed, saying, "God knows, if we can do it in Virginia, we can do it anywhere." He said that Virginia voters had done something more than electing the first black, or the first woman, in Attorney General Mary Sue Terry, to statewide office. The voters "picked a poor white boy (Governor Gerald L. Baliles), a poor white girl and poor black boy. None of us was to the manor born."

He expressed concern over illegitimacy and the disintegration of the family, asking, "Where have all the fathers gone? How can future generations sing of their father's pride, when almost an entire generation is going fatherless." He criticized blacks who say it is "necessary to teach in rap talk and rhyme in order for our youngsters to learn," asking, "Can you imagine Lincoln's Gettysburg address being so taught? There is no excuse for those who cannot read and write—none. Nothing worth having comes easy." And he said that censorship is a reasonable response to pornography, declaring: "Our founding fathers never meant to protect the trash our children are subjected to."

Garnell Stamps, chairman of the Lynchburg NAACP, said some in the audience of 400 found Wilder's remarks "strange," and interpreted them as courting conservative support for the 1989 gubernatorial campaign. But most knew, Stamps said, "that Doug Wilder was a liberal before he was elected, and he is still one." Stamps said "someone has to say it," and that Wilder is "one of a kind, a fraternity of one. It's timely, and we applaud him."

In a speech to the black National Medical Association in Washington, he decried an educational system in which 70 of every 100 students drop out in Detroit, and 29 of 100 across the United States while only two of 100 in Japan. He criticized the spending on Star Wars, saying that while education suffers, "We play at Flash Gordon and Superman with SDI and think we can catch a missile after launch. We spend $1 trillion for this play in the sky." At home, he said, young blacks "are assaulted at every level" if they don't want to smoke or drink and if they want to achieve in school. He recalled talking to a young man who sought his aid in getting into college. He had a 3.8 grade point average. "He sat there and said, 'like, I want you to do this for me, man, ok?'" Wilder said after listening to about five minutes of jive talk, he asked, "How did you get out of school talking like that?" The student suddenly began speaking perfect English, explaining that "'people joke us when we speak properly, when we dress properly.' If our black youth are subjected to that kind of destructive peer pressure, it's not their fault, it's our fault," Wilder said to applause.

With federal aid being reduced, he said states will have to rely more on their own programs, and on organizations and individuals, to teach values and responsibility. In his usual convoluted manner, he said, "Until we say that the blight you place on a child by bringing him into the world without a father...and to the extent that some people believe there's nothing wrong with it...Somewhere along the line groups and organizations have to say what has taken place in this country is wrong, and we've got to correct it."

While his audiences were often predominantly black, Wilder rejected the idea that he was addressing black problems. At a conference on the black family at Hampton University, he asked the participants, "are they black problems, or problems that affect us disproportionately because of blackness?

WILDER: HOLD FAST TO DREAMS

The problems of black families, black values, black leadership and black solutions may be overstated. Only when America understands that there are not black problems, but American problems, will be able to solve them."

The Bristol Herald Courier/Virginia-Tennessean agreed. It credited Wilder for sound advice, saying, "countless whites could benefit from his thoughts as well."

His speeches, delivered without Jesse Jackson's fervor, won high marks from his listeners. He was saying "what the black family needs to hear," said Hampton freshman Cedric Harte, "that the family is still the root" for problem solving. "We have to educate our people, education our generation," added Alonso Carter, a Hampton senior, who after hearing Wilder said, "he probably will be our next governor." George McDonald, a political science major from New York City, agreed that "we are at fault, to an extent," but said the message takes a different meaning "when it comes from Lt. Gov. Wilder" rather than from white politicians.

During Black History Month, fourth graders from Berkeley Elementary School in Williamsburg visited the lieutenant governor's office. Asked about his favorite TV shows, they were disappointed that he didn't mention Benson, a sitcom about a black butler who became lieutenant governor, but he won smiles from the children when he said that the Bill Cosby show, in addition to documentaries, was one of his favorites. Their teacher, Pam Lewis, said, "Here is a black man that's making history, who can make Black History month come alive."

Black educators applauded too. Gerald Foster, dean of arts and letters at Hampton, said "incentives and initiatives have been taken away from black people, because they've become so accustomed to the government being there." He said Wilder "did not run a campaign predicated on race. He ran a campaign predicated on experience, knowledge and how he would handle the issues. I think he is correct in calling for black people to take a stronger role in controlling their own destiny. We have to stop blaming racism. We live in a racist society. Saying it's racist is like saying the sun is shining out there today. What else is new?"

Ishmail Conway, a spokesman at Wilder's alma mater, Virginia Union University, agreed with anti-rap sentiments. "We have to take a frontal assault on literacy the same way we took a frontal assault on social ills in the '50s, '60s and part of the '70s. I question whether it (the rhythmic speaking style known as rapping) is abnormal or a real deficiency, but we have to have mainstream and broad-based communication skills. We need to be able to communicate fluently. That's what we are actively moving on here—improving the communication skills of our students."

Conway said the model for today's fatherless families was established during slavery, when slaves in Virginia were barred by law from marrying. "If a man was freed, his family remained slave. If a woman was freed, then her children were freed with her. It may be a contributing factor when you live in a society that's based on that kind of precedent."

The goals Wilder outlined are those of the private black colleges, Conway said. "That was a part of our founders' goals, to found a strong moral and industrial fiber with which people who have been disenfranchised could live. I think we stand in a position to renew that kind of spirit, that kind of concern for morality, family, education and pride."

The Harrisonburg Daily News-Record praised Wilder for speaking about "an unspeakable subject, pregnancy among teenagers and specifically black teenagers. For many years, nearly everyone has been aware of the problem, but black leaders have been reluctant to talk of it....The evil legacy of slavery and racism is certainly a factor, but it does not explain the catastrophic collapse of the black family in the years since World War II. Some blame the welfare system itself, which has disincentives to the formation of families. Whatever the causes, the time has clearly come when the black middle classes have decided to attack the problem. Leadership in the campaign against teenage pregnancy among blacks must come from the black leaders themselves. It is encouraging that Douglas Wilder is speaking out on the subject."

The Richmond News Leader, the state's most articulate and self-important conservative voice, reprinted the entire speech, and in an accompanying editorial, titled "Wilder's Truth," said that "with understated eloquence, the lieutenant governor reminds us of...the existence of right and wrong. The crucial importance of pride. Too many of our politicians spend too much of their time insulating people from hardship. A few, like Doug Wilder, are in the business of leading. What is leadership? It is exerting an influence— and inspiring others to want to do better than they thought they could. Doug Wilder's truths are pure essence."

Wilder was so taken aback at such lavish praise from an unexpected source that he responded in mock embarrassment, "one of us must be doing something wrong."

48. Joel, Jay and Paul

Wilder's closest advisers are three disparate white men who at first blush appear to have little in common with each other, except for their loyalty to Wilder. Thus, Paul Goldman, Joel Harris and Jay Shropshire do not join hands to form an inner-circle, but reach out to Wilder along parallel lines.

Unlike the confidantes of Robb and Baliles, whose devotion to their bosses approaches a spiritual state—the most fanatical Robbites are known derisively as "kool-aid drinkers" after the followers of the Reverend Jim Jones—Wilder's intimates are not above taking a swipe at their guru, if it includes an opportunity to criticize one of the others.

Wilder concedes that it is "a fair characterization" that his trio of confidantes do not get along with each other, and there is plenty of indication that Wilder likes it that way. But he downplays the significance of their infighting, comparing it to reporters for the same news organization competing for a story; it's healthy competitiveness. "They may look at the same thing and see completely different stories, but they also may collaborate. I look at friends like that. They know that I know" that it occurs, he added.

He collects the divergent information he gets from individual meetings and puts it into his mental mixmaster, out of which comes a blend that approaches reality. "Some people tell you every negative thing they ever heard, thinking that makes them closer to you," he said. "There are those who say, 'do this and do that,' and nothing you ever do is right. With others, everything you do is just perfect, sycophants of the first order. As more people know you, the more they'll know you're not interested in hearing flattery. You've got to be smart enough to know what people are saying, why they are saying it; some for their own purposes."

The consensus criticism of Wilder's incongruous confidantes is that Harris can not be trusted because he used to be a Republican; that Goldman is to blame for Wilder's strained relations with Robb and Baliles, and that Shropshire's loyalty occasionally takes a back seat to his insatiable appetite for gossip.

Harris and Shropshire not only are not friends, but go out of their way to snipe at each other, often causing trouble for Wilder along the way. Shropshire admits that he would never spend a social minute with Harris.

Shropshire and Goldman aren't enemies, but they seldom talk to each other, and when they do, it is usually by telephone.

Harris and Goldman could not be more dissimilar in appearance—Harris is a beau brummell who never is seen with a hair out of place, while Goldman is so seldom well dressed that when he is, it invariably evokes teasing. "There is a mythology out there," Harris said, "that I think is derived out of the belief that because Paul and I are very different, that we do not get along. Paul and I talk to each other two or three times a day; we spend a lot of time on the phone 'cutting up,' as my mom used to say." Harris said Goldman is "remarkably different" than the public perception. He is "one of the kindest, most humane men I have ever known. He embodies humanism. I have never heard him say anything unkind about anyone." Does that include Robb? "I've heard him defend himself."

To those who question his loyalty to Wilder, Harris challenges, "I would

Joel, Jay and Paul

be interested in knowing anything anyone pointed to that I ever did that did not have Doug's interest at heart. There is none."

Yet Shropshire says, "Lots of people ask, 'can you trust Doug?' and that's because of Joel," said Shropshire.

"I don't want to get in to a defense of myself," said Harris. "I would only say that Jay is a distinguished clerk of the Senate who is widely respected in state government, and Paul is, despite what he eats, a brilliant and kind man. If I wanted to be unkind, I could pick the principal people of every single political figure in Virginia and within three minutes do to them what that analogy (of oddball associates) does to Doug."

Even if it were true that the three of them were not friends, Harris said, "it wouldn't matter. I don't think that Andy Fogarty goes bowling with Chris Bridge (Governor Baliles' two closest aides)."

One of Mary Sue Terry's most fierce partisans blames Harris for fomenting friction between their two offices, and their bosses. "Joel is a big part of Doug's problem," she said.

"They're all misfits," a member of Baliles' cabinet said of the trio. "I question the company Doug keeps: Paul, Jay and Joel, they're all outcasts," said another member of Baliles' inner-circle.

"I don't understand why Doug runs around with a guy who wears makeup," said a guileless Petey Paige, Wilder's Washington friend, who is dismayed over Wilder's friendship with Harris.

Wilder is aware of the controversy that his three friends generate. As he listened to a recitation of criticisms about them, including their description as misfits, he said, "Now let the record reflect that he (Wilder) laughed," which he did heartily. Without agreeing with the characterizations, Wilder said "I can see how" some of those things are said of Goldman and Harris. But he said, "Jay has been pretty much of an insider. He'd be terribly distressed to hear this."

Even if Goldman, Harris and Shropshire were willing to put aside their differences long enough to work together for the benefit of their mutual choice for governor, Wilder wouldn't want them too. It's part of Wilder's scheme to keep everyone off balance. He doesn't want an inner circle, anymore than he wants a campaign manager or a media consultant. He wants to run the show, to be in full control.

Not only do Wilder's associates not seem to fit together like pieces of a puzzle, they don't easily fit with Wilder.

Bobby Watson, the former state party executive director, said, "If they ever remake 'The Odd Couple,' Joel and Doug will be in the starring roles." (Watson has been in and out of a second tier of Wilder advisers, depending on how close Wilder believes Watson is to Robb at any given moment. When Watson went to work for Senator Robb, as the director of his six in-state offices, Watson was jettisoned as a potential spy.)

So what unites them with Wilder?

"Doug was always attracted to people who don't fit the mold," said UVa professor Larry Sabato, adding that Wilder also was "always grateful when someone sticks his neck out for him," which each of them has done. Criticism of his associates probably only solidifies Wilder's determination to keep them, "just to show his critics who's boss."

With Harris, the appeal to Wilder was the audacity to abandon the GOP to work for the Democrats; with Shropshire, it was defending Wilder in front of the rednecks, and with Goldman it was his eagerness to challenge the establishment. Or, as Sabato put it, "it's the Jewish thing with Goldman; the Republican thing with Harris and the poor white, redneck thing with Jay: Three classes of outsiders joining together with another outsider. They're all beating the system, and having a ball doing it."

Wilder and Goldman "are soulmates," continued Sabato. "What clearly draws them together is that they are both outsiders. They prefer to be outside the tent spitting in rather than inside spitting out." Sabato said that if Wilder loses the governorship, "it will justify all their suspicions. Doug will say, 'I would have expected no less.'"

Wilder and Harris share a sophisticated taste in clothing (they are among the best-dressed men in Richmond) homes (both have stylishly decorated residences) and automobiles (both drive Mercedes), appreciate fine food and wine, and enjoy the company of beautiful companions. By comparison, Goldman is most at home in old clothes, munching from a bag of oats that he carries in his pocket; he is satisfied to borrow a room in a friend's house, and ride in someone else's car.

Further, the twice-divorced Harris and bachelor Goldman are willing and able to devote night and day furthering Wilder's political ambitions. And beyond politics, Harris, Goldman and Wilder share an interest in business and investments, including some mutual ventures.

But most of all, all four of them—Goldman, Harris, Shropshire and Wilder—love nothing better than hatching Machiavellian plots that are at once designed to reward Wilder and punish his enemies, be they Democrats, Republicans or independents.

Joel Walker Harris, who is young enough to be Wilder's son, was born July 7, 1957, in Petersburg, Virginia, the son of a Baptist minister, Richard Evelyn Harris, who later became a general contractor. In 1969, his father, at the request of a local political operative, assigned Joel the job of distributing leaflets for Wilder's campaign for the state Senate. For three days, Joel went door-to-door on Riverside Drive, a fancy South Richmond neighborhood that overlooks the James River, cramming Wilder leaflets in the screen doors. "Doug did not pull a lot of votes in that precinct," Harris laughed. Two years later, Harris worked as a page in the General Assembly, and first met Wilder.

Harris left home three months before his sixteenth birthday and shared a mobile home with three other boys from his high school. He attended school in the morning, worked on construction sites in afternoon and sold shoes in a department store at night. "To this day," he said recently, "I don't like to buy shoes." He attended Virginia Commonwealth University in Richmond, studying political science and business, and graduated in 1977 after three and one-half years. He attended law school at the University of Richmond for a year and a half before dropping out. "I hated it as much as it hated me. I never wanted to be a lawyer; it just seemed like the thing to do."

Harris served as a volunteer driver in Marshall Coleman's 1977 successful campaign for attorney general, and discovered that he had a talent for organization. Of Coleman, who would become Wilder's gubernatorial opponent, Harris said, "he's prodigious, and a very witty guy." The next year, having dropped out of law school, Harris worked briefly as a driver in John Warner's campaign for the United States Senate. A co-worker in that campaign recalled that Harris became so entranced by Warner's wife, actress Elizabeth Taylor, that he attempted to rig the schedule so he could drive her to events, and even sought to be her escort to a fancy campaign event. Taylor that time opted for an ambassador instead.

Politics was fun, but Harris' real interest was, and is, business. The business of making money. His first triumph came as the result of his habit of browsing through the Congressional Record, to which he had gotten a free subscription through the office of Senator Harry F. Byrd Jr. Flipping through its voluminous reports of government actions, he noted that the Environmental Protection Agency was promulgating regulations to ban fluorocarbons. Because "everything was aerosol, virtually nothing was pump," Harris decided that a company that was in a position to capitalize on the new restrictions would make a lot of money in a hurry. He investigated and determined that the Diamond International Corporation, which made matches, "would have a leg up" when the restrictions went into effect. So he "begged, borrowed and pleaded, did everything I could to put together a nice chunk of change," and bought stock options in the company. "The money I put in came back almost seven times," he said. He declined to say how much profit he turned, except that it was "six figures, serious money to me." He said that "nobody tipped me off. It was happenstance. I was a kid."

By 1979, at age 22, Harris was trading bonds and futures full time. He established a partnership with another young man, Taylor Monroe, whom he met through Monroe's mother, Helen Marie Taylor, a rightwing activist (who was so conservative that Senator Barry Goldwater reportedly blocked her appointment by President Reagan as a representative to the United Nations) and heir to the Phelps Dodge fortune.

Harris started a company that he gave the grandiose name of the United States Monetary Corporation, which bought and sold commodities futures, principally gold and silver. He later bought out a one-man company with another grand name, the Virginia Gold and Silver Trading Co., and he branched out into insurance and retailing.

Harris thought of himself as "a very moderate Republican, never held in great esteem by conservatives." He laughed that Mrs. Taylor, for example, was "mildly critical of my 'liberal' views." In 1982, he managed the joint Republican legislative campaign in Chesterfield County and did research on a Democratic incumbent. The next year, in what turned out to be "one of the less enjoyable experiences of my life," Harris ran for the Virginia House of Delegates in Chesterfield County. Although he felt "uncomfortable having to persuade" people to support him, he made the race because his friend, Delegate George Jones, was giving up the seat to run for the state Senate. Harris had grown up in the district, in the Meadowbrook area, and got the nomination without opposition, despite some grumbling "from the Far Right, who knew they couldn't beat me in a primary." Meanwhile, the Democrats met in convention and couldn't find anyone who wanted to run, so Harris appeared to be headed toward election without a contest. Jones was defeated in the GOP primary by former Delegate Robert E. Russell, and in the course of the campaign Russell raised questions about Harris' involvement in the Virginia Gold and Silver Trading Co., whose former owner had gone to prison for fraud.

Shortly after he had purchased the company's client list, Harris said his lawyer, Anthony R. Troy, who had served briefly as the Democratic attorney general when Baliles resigned to run for governor, returned ashen-faced from a meeting with an accountant, saying they had discovered the former owner had been fleecing his customers by writing large checks to himself from their accounts. During the subsequent criminal trial in federal court, Harris, as the holder of the books, testified, for which he said the judge commended him for making his records available to the FBI and cooperating in the investigation.

Meanwhile, Harris said "some extremely conservative, very zealous supporters" of Russell's altered the transcript of the trial to make it appear that Harris had been involved in the fraud, and mailed copies of the doctored document to voters, and Russell called a press conference at the Capitol and read excerpts from the transcript.

"I woke up one morning to read that I was involved in a multi-million dollar gold scam," Harris said. He calculated that it was more important to resolve the questions about his integrity than it was to continue as a candidate, so he withdrew from the race and sued eight of the people who had distributed the altered transcript. Harris won an out-of-court settlement and a public apology, but said the episode ended his interest in elective office. It also was "financially devastating because the business I had been involved with was conducted largely on the basis of affection and trust."

Russell remains unapologetic. He said "the fact is that about a million dollars disappeared and no one ever found it. The gist of my statement was that he could pooh-pooh all he wanted, but five or six people under oath testified that he was actively, daily in charge of keeping customers accounts. It bothered me that a guy like that was offered as a Republican candidate and then tried to silence his critics."

Harris did not sue Russell, but said it is safe to say that he and Russell "are not close."

Harris got back into politics, on the Democratic side, in the 1985 election, when his attorney, Tony Troy, suggested that he could be valuable to Baliles in his run for governor by doing research on the Republican candidates. Harris already had decided he wanted to help Wilder's quest for lieutenant governor, so he accepted. "I tried to advise them (the Democrats) on what the Republicans would do," Harris said. Was he, as was widely rumored, a mole, or spy, within the Republican camp who was welcomed to the Democratic camp when he brought along Wyatt Durrette's briefing book? "I heard there was a belief there was one (a spy)," he said, "but I don't know what a mole is." He added that he had read "a little John Le Carré (the spy novelist)" but dismissed the rumors as campaign paranoia.

Harris agreed to go to work for Wilder after the election "because of my affection for Doug. I enjoy politics, but I do what I do now for a personal purpose. I had never had a real job before, never worked for anybody in my life but myself, or with a partner." Money remains the driving force in his life. "As long as I can make money, I'm happy," he told a co-worker. He perpetually talked about what a financial burden it was to work in state government, how big a pay cut he took when he accepted the $40,000 a year position.

Although his position was called counselor to the lieutenant governor, Harris was the defacto chief of staff. He opted for the title counselor because "I felt it was officious, and an attempt to aggrandize the position, to be a chief of staff of five people." Furthermore, counselor "more properly connoted what I did." Harris left the state payroll in 1989 to work in the campaign.

Laura Dillard, Wilder's gubernatorial campaign press secretary, said the joke around the office is that in a Wilder administration, "Joel's agenda [in a Wilder administration] is getting whatever cabinet post requires the least work," so he could maintain his outside financial interests. The Wilder-Harris relationship is not merely an employer-employee one. They are business associates who have lunch together several times a week, occasionally at the Commonwealth Club, where Harris is a member. Harris is on the board of directors of Interstate Guaranty Insurance Corp., of which Wilder is chairman of the board, and two of Wilder's children have been partners of Harris in business ventures.

"I don't want to know too much about Joel," said Dillard, who interrupted graduate studies in religion at Yale to return to the Wilder campaign. She had worked in the lieutenant governor's office after her graduation from William and Mary in 1986. Dillard admits that she had a gradual falling out with Harris after he hired her. "He told me he could have hired any cookie-cutter off the street" for her job. "We do not care for each other," she said before she left the staff to enter graduate school. "He has strange relationships, a strange background." Nonetheless, Dillard put aside her differences with Harris and came back to work in Wilder's gubernatorial campaign the next year.

In the lieutenant governor's office, Dillard said, "nobody ever stood up to Joel. Candor is not a characteristic of that office. It may have looked on paper like Joel was in charge," she went on, "but the lieutenant governor was in charge. He ran the show." Harris was merely a "royal gopher. Everybody had clerical duties in the office, but he really was the royal gopher," Dillard said. "Joel saw his job as pleasing the lieutenant governor." He performed the tasks that others, of less rank, considered petty. For example, Dillard said, when Wilder wanted a particular desk lamp for his small office off the Senate chamber, Joel saw that he got it. When Wilder speaks out of town, he often gets a key to the city: It was Joel's job to see that the keys were properly framed and placed on the office wall. Wilder, who grew up in the "gentle poverty" of Church Hill, demands first-rate accommodations, whether it is a hotel room, a restaurant or a seat on an airplane. "When the lieutenant governor wants to fly first-class," Dillard learned, "it doesn't matter that there are fifty people in first-class and fifty people on the waiting list, at that moment, it's imperative." For the man who thought he could bluff his way onto an airplane to South America without a passport, what's so difficult about getting bumped into the first-class section. A casual request becomes a very significant matter; it won't be asked twice. "He (Wilder) wants it done. He wants it done now," said Dillard. If the secretary who ordinarily makes Wilder's travel reservations falters in making the booking, it became a job for Royal Gopher. Harris stepped in. "Joel will get him in first class," Dillard said.

Nonetheless, Dillard said, "If the lieutenant governor wants to kick someone, he'll kick Joel. It's an odd relationship." She said she once told Joel, "'I wouldn't take that from anybody.' Joel said, 'it's part of my duty.'"

In early August, with reporters digging into Harris's background and business deals, he resigned, saying he wanted to pursue private interests. His resignation set the Republicans clucking. Mike Salster, the state GOP spokesman, called Harris the "John Sasso" of the Wilder campaign, a reference to the close friend and aide to Democratic presidential candidate Michael Dukakis, who quit under fire during the 1988 campaign. Salster said that the betting at GOP headquarters, however, was that unlike Sasso, Harris would resurface in a Wilder administration. Shropshire and other Wilder confidants had been urging Wilder to distance himself from Harris.

If Joel Harris would seek a soft job in a Wilder administration, Jay Shropshire would seek a powerful one. Shropshire is most often mentioned as a chief-of-staff to a Governor Wilder, a position some say he coveted upon the elections of Governors Robb and Baliles, and because of his failure to be so rewarded, has conducted sniper fire from his office on the second floor of the Capitol.

Shropshire arrived in Richmond in 1966 from his native Martinsville, Virginia, a furniture-factory town on the North Carolina border, and took a job as a self-described "errand boy" for the clerk of the House of Delegates. A short time later, W. Pat Jennings, a fellow Southsider who rose through the ranks to become clerk of the United States House of Representatives, offered him a job in Washington. Shropshire stayed at Jennings' side in Congress just long enough "to learn how to deal with different groups, that to get along, you go along." After eighteen months, at the urging of a Virginia legislator who warned, "come on home before they ruin you up there," he returned to Richmond as an assistant clerk in the Senate.

When Wilder came to the Senate in 1970, Shropshire was among the first to extend a hand in friendship. Shropshire grew up surrounded by unrepentant segregationists, but he remembered Jennings' secret to success—go along. There was nothing insincere about his friendship with Wilder. The two of them hit it off immediately. "I liked Doug when it wasn't popular to like him," Shropshire observed. Although Wilder is fifteen years older than Shropshire, he still was "one of the youngest people around," Shropshire said, and as a result, "there was a natural gravitation. Most of the people who worked here would not go past that barrier (of Wilder's race). There weren't that many people in the building (the capitol) who wanted to be his friend. It was a natural alliance."

Shropshire nodded toward the stern portraits on the chamber's walls as a wall of illustrating the change that Wilder's arrival personified. It was a Senate comprised largely of bankers and lawyers in three-piece suits and wingtipped shoes, and "in walked Doug," sporting an Afro-type haircut, flashy jewelry, a wardrobe that ran the gamut from Nehru jacket to a green suede suit, with a Mercedes sports car outside. "It was culture shock, that's what it was," said Shropshire.

Shropshire got to know Wilder's family, and recalled that when Miss Beulah died, he was the only white person at her wake. "If any of the senators came by, I didn't see them," he said.

Shropshire's boss, Senate clerk Louise Lucas, "didn't even acknowledge Doug existed," Shropshire said. Lucas got her comeuppance, and Shropshire got her job, in the coup that overthrew the old Byrd leadership half a dozen years later. The thirty-year-old Shropshire's initial act as the new clerk was to hire the first black to a staff job in the Senate.

At social functions, Shropshire said, "Doug stood out like a sore thumb in some people's eyes, being black. And of course, Doug was outspoken—he never was a quiet guy. When he did the 'Carry Me Back' bit, the Richter scale went beyond imagination. You would have thought he stood up and said that Robert E. Lee and Stonewall Jackson were communists. It was that kind of reaction: How dare you."

But Shropshire accorded Wilder the same courtesies he did the other thirty-nine senators, and they were considerable. Taking the advice of his mentor Jennings to heart, over the next two decades, Shropshire elevated obsequiousness to an art form. During the annual two-month legislative sessions, he watches the morning news, the evening news and the late news, reads half a dozen daily newspapers, and gives daily reports to members about how their legislation is playing; he provides wake-up telephone calls, a chauffeur service and even an occasional alibi or bail money. Monday through Thursday nights when the assembly is in session, he dines with various senators, trading gossip about the day's activities. And he hosts, without pay, a weekly public television show on which his senators often are the guests. In exchange for his prolonged absence during January and February, Shropshire agrees not to discuss politics at home with his apolitical wife, Anne, who manages a retail store in a Richmond mall.

Although Shropshire doesn't dispute his "Jeeves" role, the shrewdly servile clerk, who in the mid-eighties earned an master of business administration degree in a weekend program for mid-career executives from William and Mary, insists that "I'm no gofer. I'm a professional." When his senators look good, he looks good; when Wilder looks good, he looks good.

Wilder uses Shropshire more as a conduit of information, a clearing house, than as an adviser.

Because he is so often at the center of, if not the central figure in, the latest intrigue swirling around Virginia politics, Shropshire probably gets more credit, and more blame—in equal amounts—for happenings in and around the capitol. For instance, Shropshire's name pops up in any discussion of the infamous Commonwealth Club luncheon date. "If it wasn't set up by Doug," said Governor Robb, "a couple of folks would still think it was a set up by Jay." George Stoddart, who was Robb's press secretary, called Shropshire "one of Doug's least helpful advisers" throughout Wilder's feud with Robb. "Jay feels it's to his advantage, the more turmoil he can create."

Stoddart and other Robb associates contend that Shropshire wanted to be Robb's chief-of-staff, and when the job went to David McCloud, "Jay was bitter, bitter, bitter." Stoddart said Shropshire "so desperately wants to be the executive assistant to the governor." He said he might have been seriously considered for the position when Robb became governor, except that McCloud had worked for Robb for a number of years, during which time "David demonstrated to Robb that sort of blind—'I'll be here to every night to four in the morning if that's what it takes to get the job done'—dedication." Stoddart recalled "what we went through trying to appease Jay when he didn't get David's job." Shropshire wound up with a political plum, chairman of the state compensation board, a part-time job through which he wields tremendous power, as it determines the salaries and staff sizes of thousands of sheriffs, treasurers and other courthouse employees throughout the state. "What he got from Robb probably put him in a more powerful position than any other appointed person in the state, because he has two good state jobs," Stoddart said.

When McCloud left the governor's office for a job in the private sector in the first year of the Baliles' administration, Shropshire again thought he might get the job. Instead, the position was filled by Andrew Fogarty. Shortly after that, Stoddart pointed out that "Doug took out after Baliles (on the transportation tax package)." Stoddart didn't think that was a co-incidence. "It was right when McCloud was leaving," He said. "Again, it was Jay thinking it was his chance to exercise true power."

Stoddart said that during the 1981 campaign, "the silver fox," a name he bestowed on Shropshire because of his prematurely white hair and gray eyes, was "as good a buddy as I had," other than campaign manager David Doak. "I like the guy to death. I just wish he understood which team he was on."

Shropshire isn't after the top job in the governor's office for the money. With his two jobs, he is one of the highest paid employees in state government, and besides that, he doesn't need the money—he is a millionaire as the result of his wife's family's business interests. What Shropshire lusts for is the power of an insider.

Much of Shropshire's power as the clerk of the Senate, a job not inherently influential, is his access to information—gossip, though it need not be negative—that is the currency of the trade of politics. There is no one in the capitol who has a greater appetite for it than Shropshire. With the possible exception of Doug Wilder.

49. The L Word

Try as he did in the middle and late eighties to portray himself as a moderate-conservative, Wilder's record reveals that for the first decade of his service as a legislator, he was a standard-brand liberal. It was a position easily justified, if not out of political conviction, then by the need and desire to represent constituents, largely poor and black, who traditionally have been the beneficiaries of liberal social policies.

"People say I'm a johnny-come-lately to the crime scene," Wilder said, acknowledging a campaign theme of his gubernatorial opponent, Marshall Coleman. "They ask, 'where was Wilder?'" He answers his question by pointing to several bills he introduced during his sixteen years in the state Senate.

The one he most often points to is his an anti-drug paraphernalia bill, enacted in 1972. It made it a misdemeanor to possess, sell or distribute hypodermic syringes or needles and other materials used with drugs. All but three of his thirty-nine Senate colleagues signed up as co-sponsors, and the bill sailed through the assembly. "I felt you weren't going to seriously address yourself to controlling the flow of drug traffic if you didn't have the mechanics controlled," Wilder said. He said the intent of the bill was to require the dispensers of those articles, which in and of themselves were not illegal, to exercise a degree of control and not sell them promiscuously, as they then were doing.

Another lawyer said that after the bill passed some potential clients steered away from Wilder, whose law practice was eighty percent criminal.

Yet Coleman said the bill was so inadequate that it was superceded by more sweeping legislation enacted during the administration of Republican John Dalton.

Wilder initiated legislation that gave police and other law enforcement officials, including sheriffs and agents of the state Alcoholic Beverage Control commission, the right to use vehicles seized in criminal activities for under-cover work.

Although Wilder made his name and fortune as a criminal lawyer, from the beginning of his legislative career he cultivated the support of police officers, an investment that paid off in his endorsement by the state Fraternal Order of Police in the 1985 campaign. Six months after he entered the legislature, lawyer Wilder was retained by a group of police officers in suburban Henrico County to push their claims in negotiations with the county government. Among the officers' grievances was a requirement that they live in the county. In 1972, in federal court, Wilder successfully challenged as unconstitutional the forty-five day suspension of a Richmond police sergeant for disclosing confidential information. Another client was a sheriff's deputy who was charged with giving a key to an inmate in exchange for a watch. After he won the jury trial, Wilder laughed, "I introduced a bill to tighten escapes." He was referring to his 1985 legislation, introduced in the wake of the largest mass escape from death row in American history, from the Mecklenburg Correctional Center, that raised the penalties for prison and jail escapes, and made inmates serving life sentences who escape ineligible for parole. In addition to the sensational escape from death row, Wilder said, inmates were "just walking off on work details, going from courthouse to trial, even in the jails. They were coming out of some of our jails like they were sieves" while some judges meted out sentences for the escapes that were served concurrent with the original sentence. He also backed legislation to provide health insurance for sheriffs and their sergeants, and increased salaries of sheriff's deputy sergeants who pass standard training.

But Wilder also cast scores of votes that provided fodder for his opponent in the governor's race.

For years, Wilder was an outspoken opponent of capital punishment, often a nearly lone voice railing against it on the floor of the Senate. In 1977, for example, he was one of only two opponents to a bill that reinstituted the death penalty in Virginia consistent with U. S. Supreme Court guidelines; in 1980 he was one of five senators who voted against capital punishment for mass murderers; and in 1981 he again voted against a proposal, approved by the Senate by a vote of thirty-two to six, to add mass murder to the list of crimes for which the death penalty was allowed.

In opposing capital punishment, Wilder argued that imposition of the death penalty had been discriminately applied against blacks. He contended that if executions were to be carried out at all, the procedures should be more explicit, including written opinions by the state Supreme Court. He said the standards proposed were too vague for deciding which murders are heinous.

The real problems with the corrections system, he said in 1976, were the overcrowding and understaffing of prisons, which were administered by people with a "callous regard for human beings, who believe in racial superiority, who could not articulate anything past 'tote that bail, lift that barge.'"

By 1985, as a candidate for statewide office, Wilder said he was satisfied that the death penalty was being invoked fairly, and that it was an appropriate punishment in extreme cases. Wilder's own words might be used to question that reasoning however, because, as he said in criticizing former supporters of segregation, including Ed Lane, it was not why they supported it, but simply that they did that was wrong.

Wilder's record on other law-and-order legislation is similarly murky. Until he was elected lieutenant governor, he opposed most efforts to stiffen criminal penalties. In 1976, he opposed a bill that would have imposed a mandatory five-year sentence for using a handgun during the commission of a rape, robbery or murder, saying it had constitutional problems and could be struck down by the courts. Further, he said he opposed a piecemeal approach to gun control. State Senator F. C. Boucher (D-Abingdon), who sponsored the bill, said its purpose was "to control both crime and guns....We have to do something about firearms." But Wilder charged his fellow senators with skirting the issue of gun control. "No one dare bite the bullet of gun control," he said. When the proposal came up for a final vote, on a House version that imposed a one-year mandatory sentence, Wilder cast the lone dissenting vote.

Three years later, he was one of four opponents of a bill that made it a felony to "point or brandish" a fireman in an attempt to escape from a law enforcement officer.

He twice attempted to outlaw the use of dum-dum, or hollow-point, bullets, including by police. He attributed the opposition by law enforcement officials to "a lot of misinformation." The bullets were extremely dangerous, he pointed out, because "they never stop. Swoosh." He said they could pass through the body of an intended target, a criminal, and go on and kill an innocent bystander. There was so much opposition to his legislation, however, that Wilder said that for the only time in his legislative career, he felt he was being stifled in an attempt to get a hearing. At a meeting of the Senate Courts of Justice Committee, Chairman William F. Parkerson Jr., refused to recognize that Wilder was even in the room with a bill to be considered. He said the snub was so obvious that several of his colleagues pointed out to Parkerson that Wilder was waiting. "I was up to here (motioning to his neck) about it," Wilder said. "My theory was, we ought to have a vote here. We don't have to go to anarchy." He finally got a hearing, and the committee rejected it by a vote of eight to seven.

As lieutenant governor, however, Wilder professed a toughest-guy-in-town stance, endorsing legislation that would give juries the option of imposing a sentence of life imprisonment without parole in capital murder cases; the original proposal failed, but an amended version passed that doubled the minimum time, to twenty-five years, a capital murderer must spend in prison.

On other liberal litmus test issues, however, the patch turns blue on Wilder. He favored a limited form of collective bargaining for teachers, sex education, post-card registration of voters, graduated brackets so higher-income wage-earners were taxed at a higher rate, expanding consumer protection laws, establishment of a state minimum wage, including a subminimum wage for sixteen-to-eighteen year-olds employed in school work-training programs; requiring every jurisdiction to adopt a food-stamp or commodity distribution programs; state funding of abortion for the poor; low-income housing; protection from garnishment of wages and ratification of the Equal Rights Amendment. He opposed workfare, which required able-bodied welfare recipients to work up to 20 hours a week in public service jobs.

In consumer matters, he sought to limit the ability of the State Corporation Commission to grant temporary rate increases to public utilities; he succeeded in barring auto insurers from denying coverage on the basis of age, sex, residence, color, creed, marital status or occupation; he tried to limit the cost of pay telephone calls; and expanded warranty protections in consumer sales contracts.

He worked to give greater protection to juvenile offenders. His proposals included requiring that a judge be notified within twenty-four hours of the arrest of anyone under eighteen, so that parents of juveniles knew when their children had been arrested; prohibiting a child from being placed in a detention home before trial unless a judge determined his or her release constituted a threat to the public interest; amending sentencing laws so that children assigned to a detention home at age eleven or twelve, who sometimes remained there until they were eighteen, not serve more time than they would have if they had been convicted as an adult; forbidding placement of juveniles in cells with adults if there were a separate facility for juveniles within fifty miles; and providing in-state services for juveniles who previously had been sent out-of-state for treatment.

In the 1989 gubernatorial race, Wilder found that being on the liberal side of an issue wasn't always a handicap, even in conservative Virginia. Wilder was solidly aligned with abortion rights advocates who wanted to keep intact Virginia's abortion laws, which came under attack after the United States Supreme Court loosened the grip of the landmark 1973 *Roe v. Wade* ruling and returned to the states the authority to enact restrictions on abortions. Coleman's own metamorphosis from moderate-liberal to moderate-conservative had moved him squarely into the anti-abortion camp, which polls showed represented a minority of the population, and which was anathema to the National Organization for Women and other women's groups.

Wilder's most frustrating legislative effort arose from his perennial attempts to remove the sales tax on food and drugs, which would likely be a top priority of a Wilder governorship. Over the years, he proposed making up the loss in revenue, which was the stumbling block, by increasing various other taxes, including those on income, capital gains, inheritance and motor vehicle sales. As lieutenant governor, he got a bite of the apple when the legislature approved an exemption for the elderly that roughly covered the cost of the tax on non-prescription drugs. Even that crumb was ridiculed as little more than allowing retirees to purchase "coughdrops and condoms" tax-free.

"You will find, in examining my legislative record, that I have been involved in almost every subject," he said. "They are like chits, out there waiting to be cashed." Might some of those chits be played against him? "That too."

50. Heroes

The day after the 1988 presidential election, Wilder was in an expansive mood, jumping from an analysis of the election ("never let the other guy be the no-tax guy") to a philosophical discussion of heroes.

Among his personal heroes is his namesake, Frederick Douglass: "That he could be a slave, born in slavery, and be as articulate and educated as he was, means that (slavery) wasn't a barrier." Another was Colonel Charles Young, a black army officer who was denied the opportunity to be a general and told he had to retire because he was unfit. He rode a horse almost across the country to West Point to show there was nothing wrong with him. And Carter G. Woodson, the author of a classic volume on black history, "The Story of the Negro Retold," without whose contributions "nothing would have existed containing the history of black people in this country, or even in the world."

Paul Robeson, who Wilder heard sing as a college student from the black section of the balcony of the Mosque in Richmond, was "a man of great ability. People say, 'oh God, don't mention Robeson or (W. E. B.) DuBois.' Well, DuBois was perhaps the most pre-eminent black scholar we have produced. Robeson never was a communist. No one could prove it. He was a beautiful writer, excellent actor. His vocal accomplishments were unparalleled. Phi Beta Kappa at Rutgers, all-American football player. You name it, he did it. That just impressed me beyond words. Here's a man who in segregation can do all these things. The best he could be in football, in school. He won acclaim everywhere."

Wilder came late to appreciate Booker T. Washington because he disagreed with his famous speech, the Atlanta Compromise, in which he said, "We can be as separate as the fingers on your hand, in all things purely social, but in commerce and equality, we can be together." Wilder said that pronouncement was immediately repudiated by DuBois, setting up years of struggle "that divided the black community more than it helped. Yet Washington's belief that you should work with what you have, rather than worry about what you did not have, caused DuBois to speak about the Talented Tenth, that every tenth black should be educated, because perhaps that was all we could afford, and that one then could lead the others."

The common thread among those men, Wilder noted, was "they all were scholars. Educated. Well read. DuBois's material is exhilarating." By comparison, he found it "frightening to sit in today's classrooms and hear these kids slay the English language."

For all his work in getting a holiday named for him, at the time, Wilder didn't consider Martin Luther King among his heroes because "we were about the same age, coming up. But in reflection, I have considered him a man of far more depth than recorded. Some would like to think he was merely a preacher who enlisted causes, had followers in causes. But nobody has matched him since, his commitment, his lack of reaching for the brass ring for himself, or power. His selflessness is unparalleled. He was a great man."

Wilder also changed his mind about President Harry S. Truman. "I used to think Truman was a man of little account, honor, couldn't be trusted, part of the Pendergast machine. But in reality, he's one of the few political figures who told it like he felt it was; he didn't care. I like that."

Robert E. Lee, the patron saint of the lost Southern cause, is neither hero nor villain to Wilder. "He was tortured over what to do. If you followed the travails of his life, there is more tragedy associated with it, not just the losing cause of war, but a brilliant mind in a dedicated person. I respect his views. Stonewall Jackson. Same way. Men of learning, men of capacity, who, for whatever reasons, a ditch occurred, a ditch where humans were treated as subhumans, and so regarded."

Yet Wilder said the North "shouldn't look with any great degree of sacrosanctity" on its action, which he said was more hypocritical than Virginia's. "Lincoln did what he had to do under the circumstances; Lee did what he had to do, under the circumstances."

Surely Lincoln was a hero. "There are those who question his real commitment to the cause. He knew he had to do certain things. But there is no flip side. I don't deal in overzealous praise, that he struck a real blow, yet what he did was momentous. Without that, it would have been difficult for the nation to have survived. I admire Lincoln because he came from such humble origins. He was able to overcome sickness, a lack of daring, heraldic or otherwise, lack of money, and yet he was a man of great expression. He couldn't have cared, accumulated that, unless it's in you. A remarkable achievement. I always wondered why Lincoln was regarded nationally as such a hero, if he was a villain in the eyes of some. But obviously he wasn't considered a villain, even by the South. But it's not an either-or situation, that you either like Lincoln and hate Lee, or like Lee and hate Lincoln. To the extent that they both represented ideologies, and did so to their best of their abilities, they both would be heroes."

Wilder was asked his feelings about the statues of Confederate generals that line Richmond's Monument Avenue, and the restoration of Johnny Reb, knocked from its pedestal in Alexandria by an automobile. "In defeat, people needed something to feel good about, to rally behind. To the extent some seize upon it for wrong purposes, like the Confederate flag and singing of Dixie, it furthers the misunderstanding that occurs in the North. In addition to glorifying the past, there is a willingness by too many people to live in the past, and to dwell in the past." But the statues and monuments are "a part of our history. They shouldn't be erased or eradicated, but as far as they extol virtues that didn't exist, they are misleading and are not educational." He predicted a gradual disenchantment with the preoccupation with the past that they represent for some. But "it is people, unchanging and unchanged," for which he has the greatest concern, those who "make no apologies for the days of massive resistance, who believed in the separation of the races, that it was not only proper and legal, but intended by God. But they are a vast minority, and I think you'll see a dimunition of it." But Wilder added that "I never had any problem with people who wanted to honor their heroes." He pointed out that when he put the King bill in every year, he never spoke against the Lee-Jackson holidays, or said they were wrong. I have found in life that I don't have to be successful by knocking you; my success doesn't depend on stepping on you. I wouldn't use you as a toehold or a footstool. That would be a more catholic expression of my feelings, tolerating different views, listening to different ideologies."

He offered an assessment of the governors he has served with, beginning with Linwood Holton, who took office the year Wilder entered public life. "He was a courageous man," Wilder said, citing Holton's appointment of blacks to state offices and his insistence that his children attend the integrated public schools of Richmond. (Holton's youngest child, Dwight, worked as the scheduler and advance planner in Wilder's gubernatorial campaign.) Mills Godwin "has always been courtly. I got along well talking with him. I think he recognized that change had to take place. I don't think he believed it would take place as soon as it did. It was an awkward adjustment for him."

Wilder was "very disappointed" with John Dalton's veto of the King bill. "There really was no reason for it," as Dalton had signed a previous version, for its observation on January 1. But "people do what they do. I learned in law, people are presumed to know the consequences of their acts, and I've abided by that. I don't ask them why they did it, and I don't expect people to ask me why I did it, or did I intend to do it. I thought that was something John would one day regret." If Dalton regretted it, he never said so. "I never held it against him. We weren't close, but we weren't enemies."

Without the hint of a grin or sarcasm, he concluded his scorecard of governors by saying, "obviously Robb and Baliles would be my favorites." By the time the 1989 campaign was in full gear, Wilder was saying, with a straight face, that despite their occasional differences, he and Robb "have loved each other."

What about enemies? "Enemies change with the wind. It depends on what the fight is over. I have never really lined up permanently in politics, in such a position as to not be able to shift myself, when the occasion demanded it."

51. Pluses and Minuses

A lot of the conventional wisdom about Wilder includes some of the stereotypes by which Jesse Jackson says African-Americans often are erroneously portrayed. The damaging whispers about Wilder are usually spread by people who don'.t know him well, and often are posed in the form of a question or conjecture, such as, "He may be glib, but I'm not sure how smart he is," or "he's only pretending to be a moderate; beneath it all, he's a typical black liberal," or "Doug doesn't think things through; he shoots from the hip." Others are more blatant racial slurs: "He's late, like Jesse, they run on 'CPT,' (colored people's time)," and "I'm sure if you dig into his background, you'll find skeletons—drugs, women...."

Some of those characterizations are not worth dignifying, and others can be quickly dismissed: Wilder is very smart; he seldom speaks without having thought through the consequences, and other than an acrimonious divorce, which is hardly unique, his private live appears to be typical of a successful lawyer.

Criticisms that cannot be so easily dismissed are that Wilder is distrustful of even his most devoted supporters, and conversely, that he cannot be trusted. Take it from his friends: "You can be with Doug ninety-nine times in a row," said Jay Shropshire, "but if you are against him the hundredth time, he'll say, 'he was never with me.'" Another close friend says, "you wouldn't trust anyone either if you had screwed as many people as Doug has."

At a breakfast meeting with half a dozen Jewish leaders in Richmond in February of 1989, State Senator Richard L. Saslaw, seeking support for his campaign for the Democratic nomination for lieutenant governor, said, "many people say you can't trust Doug Wilder, but I am not one of them."

By the time Wilder got a report on the breakfast, the phrase "many people say" had been dropped. Wilder went wild. "Outside of the Robb letters, it was the angriest I have ever seen him," said Shropshire.

Retribution, as it always is with Wilder, was swift. Presiding over the Senate later that day, Wilder ordered Shropshire to leave the podium and tip off a reporter, in hopes that the story would find its way into print, which it did not because of the murkiness about the context in which it was said.

But the people who know Wilder best, including his colleagues in the state Senate, give him generally high marks. Without exception, they describe him as intelligent, humorous, charming, a superior extemporaneous debater and speaker (although his formal speeches can be wooden and convoluted), and most of them are willing to forgive him if he has changed his views to accommodate a statewide constituency.

They also agree that he is a loner, not a team player; that he holds grudges and seeks revenge, as with Robb, far beyond what is reasonable and that he is second to none—with the possible exceptions of Goldman, Harris and Shropshire—in seeing or planning Machiavellian plots.

Senator "Buzz" Emick, the chamber's resident cynic, said that Wilder is "smarter and shrewder than Robb, and as smart and as shrewd as Baliles." But he also is like former lieutenant governor Henry Howell, the populist who was never quite popular enough to move up to governor, in that "he has a built-in volatility factor."

284

Pluses and Minuses

The caustic Emick discovered that he and Wilder had mutual interests, including debating, shortly after he was elected to the Senate in 1976. Emick recalled that after a floor speech in which he gently castigated Old Guard senator Howard P. Anderson, Wilder whispered, "damn, you took a wire brush to Anderson's ass."

Among all the members of the Senate, Emick said he would probably seek out Wilder if he were looking for someone to either discuss an issue or merely while away time. "He is a great internal gossip and wit. I enjoy the hell out of him." Emick and his wife periodically socialized with Wilder, who had separated from Eunice by the time Emick got to the Senate. "Doug used to bring some really classy ladies" to the legislative parties, Emick said. He recalled leaving a private party at the Commonwealth Club as Wilder and his date were departing. "Marty (Emick's wife) and I were getting into our VW when Doug, in his gray Afro, swept out of the club. He was wearing a cape, swooping it around like Batman, and he opened the door to his Mercedes with a flourish. Marty thought that was just the peaches."

Emick said that if he were part of the business community he "certainly would have misgivings" about Wilder's candidacy, because "Virginia has in my lifetime had basically an oligarchy—a feeling that business leaders in our state drink with the leaders of the legislature, and that they jointly manage this wonderful corporation called Virginia. It's a business orientation. They all serve on boards of directors and they deem the legislature sort of like their board of directors: 'don't get in the way of management, try to stay the hell out, and we'll pay you on time.' I don't think Doug would ever be that kind of governor, so the effect of that is there is going to be some genuine concern. There has never been a governor like that. Jerry (Baliles) had the possibility of doing that, but for whatever reason, he didn't do it."

Emick said "Virginia so keenly needs to experience something remotely approaching a democracy," to show that "a reasonably intelligent, politically honest guy could run a state just as well as another of those 'groomed to bring the great traditions of Virginia to bear.' So naturally I would like to see him win on that basis alone."

Emick isn't sanguine that the voters will look beyond Wilder's race, but even if they do, he said the greater barrier is that Wilder "would represent change in a place that does not like change at all. They begrudge every little bit of change we have had, and race relations is just one illustration of it."

Senator Joe Gartlan, a liberal Democrat from Fairfax County, and Wilder often were the only members of the Senate arguing against the death penalty when it was a hot topic in the mid-seventies, but they made up in rhetorical eloquence what they lacked in numerical backing. "You don't have any doubt what he's talking about," Gartlan said of Wilder's debating style. "It's plain talk. He's able to convey passion, deep feeling, conviction and outrage, and he's persuasive. But prepared speeches hobble him. It always seemed that written words kind of dampened the man down."

Yet Gartlan felt that Wilder "never totally reached his potential" as a legislator. Gartlan sat next to chairman Wilder on the Rehabilitation and Social Services Committee, which has jurisdiction over welfare, social services, corrections and alcoholic beverage control. "That was a natural constituency for

Doug, but the committee just didn't seem to interest him," Gartlan said. The committee did not have a heavy work load, and met only once a week, on Friday mornings, yet Wilder frequently showed up late, or not at all. "He would call in or leave word to get started," said Gartlan, who as the second-ranking member chaired the committee in Wilder's absence. "Whatever it was, whether he had court cases or whatever, he just didn't seem to have a lot of interest in getting up on the work of that committee. Doug is a quick study; you don't have to tell him anything twice, but that committee wasn't his piece of cake."

While Gartlan and Wilder usually were on the same side of an issue, they disagreed in the annual debates about abortion, which Gartlan opposed. After one emotional exchange, Wilder sent a note to Gartlan that said, "Why can't you just let the Supreme Court decision in this thing rest, let it be." Gartlan wrote back, "it's lucky that attitude wasn't widely shared when it came to" the decision that held that separate but equal accommodations on railroad trains was constitutional. Wilder read the note, grinned and tossed it in the waste basket.

Gartlan said Wilder occasionally displayed a quick temper, but didn't go around looking for fights. "He didn't have a chip on his shoulder, but he was ready to go if you challenged him."

It also was not Wilder's style to build or develop consensus, or be a leader of a faction, according to Gartlan. On some issues, where he felt he was the black spokesman in the Senate, Wilder seemed to deliberately to do things on his own, without consulting anyone. "I don't know that he's on any team, permanently." Gartlan said.

But part of Wilder's success was "not taking on Don Quixote issues," said Senator Saslaw, who arrived in the Senate in 1980. He said Wilder challenged death penalty legislation the first year or two he was there, "but around 1983 or 1984, when he knew the vote was going to be thirty-five to five or so, he didn't get up" and rail against it. "He got up when he thought he could make a difference."

As for Wilder's move away from liberalism, Democratic Senator Tom Michie of Charlottesville said "it is no exception to the general rule" that politicians readjust their positions when they run for statewide office. "It's kind of a standing joke. It's occurred at least a dozen times since I've been in the General Assembly, whether you're talking about Marshall Coleman or Wyatt Durrette, or Dick Bagley or Doug. I often wondered if they would have voted that way if they weren't running for something."

James Latimer, who covered politics for the Richmond Times-Dispatch for more than forty years, said Wilder was always pragmatic. "I don't know that he necessarily ever changed his philosophy. He presented a balanced image of himself. He was very smart. He didn't apologize for being black, but he was distinctly above the typical black politician."

In steering a moderate course, Latimer said Wilder may have been entertaining what former governor Lindsay Almond described as that "faint ray of hope" within every legislator that "the star of hope may shine over the humblest trail" and give him a chance to some day run for governor, which in Virginia is considered a higher calling than any office, with the possible exception of the presidency.

Veteran legislative lobbyist E. H. "Judge" Williams Jr. said Wilder "didn't

Pluses and Minuses

flaunt it (blackness) at all. The closest thing he came to it was with the 'Carry Me Back' protest, which Williams attributed to "a need to protect himself in the black community."

The harshest criticism came from a fellow Democratic Senator, one who more often than not has been on the same side of the issues as Wilder. The colleague, who spoke only on condition that he not be identified, called Wilder untrustworthy and two-faced. He said he had been double-crossed by Wilder on several occasions, and recalled that when Robb was lieutenant governor, and presiding over the Senate, Wilder periodically went into the cloakroom and mocked and ridiculed Robb, and denounced him with vile language. No one else verified such stories, however, and another Senator said the critic had a tendency to be self-righteous.

On the other hand, some of the most lavish praise comes from two former Republican colleagues, Wiley Mitchell and L. Ray Garland.

"Doug is one of the smartest politicians I ever saw," said Mitchell, one of the more cerebral members of the legislature. "He's a consummate pragmatist." He called Wilder's handling of the King holiday bill "the most brilliant political maneuvering I have ever seen."

Another sagacious move, Mitchell noted, was the deal Wilder worked out with his senior colleague, Ed Willey, when the legislature adopted single-member districts. Willey permitted Wilder to draw the lines that divided the city into two senatorial districts, one black and liberal, the other white and conservative. While Willey left the partitioning up to Wilder, at one point a wary Willey inquired, "Now, Doug, you sure you didn't give me too many (blacks)."

At the same time, Mitchell said Wilder worked hard at not limiting himself to representing only the point of view of black Virginians. He also gained a reputation as a spokesman for the legal profession, especially that of defense attorneys, and of a lawmaker interested in sound tax policy and good government. "That was the secret to his success," said Mitchell.

Mitchell also credits Wilder for figuring out early that "he was much better off establishing his own identity than trying to latch onto some other political super star." Mitchell said that "the first thing that a politician's got to make certain of that he doesn't frighten people. One of the beauties of having Henry Howell to run against was that he genuinely scared people. Jesse Jackson scares people. Doug Wilder inspires confidence, not fright. He doesn't advocate radical proposals. His deliberate refusal to associate himself with Jesse Jackson, other than to offer his respect and courtesy—he refused to endorse him or his policies—allowed him to establish himself not just as somebody who is independent, but somebody who does not let the black leadership, whoever they might be, think for him. I don't think anybody thinks that Doug Wilder feels he can be pushed or shoved by the Crusade of Voters, or Jesse Jackson or the Rainbow Coalition. He gives me the impression that he considers himself above all that."

Mitchell, who quit the Senate at the end of 1988 because of a job relocation, acknowledged that although he was a member of the opposition party, "I have a problem talking about Doug Wilder because I'm very fond of him, even though I can't recall he's ever done anything for me, or gone out of his way to help me. We have, nevertheless, had a very cordial, friendly and personal relationship." A bemused Mitchell recalled that for twelve years "I sat there and watched him vote against ever capital punishment bill, every bill that dealt with tightening up on the criminal laws that came down the pike for years and years. Then he decided he was going to run for statewide office and he became an opponent of capital punishment and his platform with respect to crime, drug enforcement was more conservative than the average Republican's." Even so, Mitchell said, "that is not duplicitous, any more than my metamorphosis in politics. You learn what works, and you implement, or you get hung up on shoals of politics. He learned where the channel was and he has steered it very skillfully."

Garland, who now is a newspaper columnist, said Wilder's greatest appeal is "his great conviviality and charm." Garland said that Wilder "immediately made his mark (in the Senate) as a flamboyant, very likable, very charming, fashion plate. He was somebody who called attention to himself; someone who you instinctively looked at. He had a winning personality, radiated a great deal of energy—which I personally believe is a key ingredient to success in politics, as it is acting or the ministry. What is it that makes you want to look at Madonna, or Marilyn Monroe? An emanation. Doug Wilder had that in spades. Linwood Holton had it. Gerald Baliles never had it. Robb never had it, except that he had an ironclad guarantee of celebrityhood because of the White House wedding and all the rest of it. But Wilder had it. He had those intonations that caused you to want you to see him, to hear him. You were just glad to see him coming. He always had that radiant smile, a glad hand and a kind word."

Even though Garland was a junior member of the minority party in the House of Delegates when Wilder was first elected, he was extremely cordial to Garland, "and I don't think I was any kind of any exception. After twelve years in the House, when Garland was elected to the Senate in 1980, Wilder "came to see me pretty much as an equal, someone he wanted to groove with." Garland and Wilder shared a love for debate, more often than not against each other. "I believe him to be one of the finest debaters I have ever encountered, and I think he gave me the same courtesy, though I counted him a finer debater than I myself was, on a purely extemporaneous basis. His forte, like many orators, is extemporizing. They are always the best speeches."

Garland said Wilder "is a very intellectual man, up to a point. I don't think he is a deeply learned man, although I once heard him give a speech in Roanoke—if with notes he had only notes—that was one of the most cerebral orations I had ever heard." Garland had forgotten the topic, except for a recurring phrase, though not original with Wilder, in which he spoke of "an educated duncery."

With such high praise, Garland was asked if he might endorse Wilder in his column. "The day I endorse a Democrat, the Methodists will invade hell," he said, "though I have written very warmly of him, and I have come as close to endorsing him as you can come."

Wilder's nomination "says something about him as a very serious, respected person, who has known how to position himself throughout his career," said Garland. Reflecting sentiments similar to Mitchell's, he added,

Pluses and Minuses

that Wilder "had an unassailable political base from he could do anything he wanted. And he positioned himself not to go too far to anti-business. He was never a Henry Howell-type of liberal. He positioned himself as the champion of the underdog, but not as anti-business, big-spending liberal. If you look at his record, he gave labor and the teachers virtually everything they asked for, without exception, but he was never on the cutting edge of their politics or ideas. He limited himself to a lot of technical stuff having to do with criminal law, and symbolic issues such as the Martin Luther King holiday. And going into the lieutenant governor's race, he positioned himself as a fiscal conservative, tough on crime, the latter part which was completely contradictory to his record in the Senate, which was always for the defense lawyers and defendants. He was a trial lawyer."

As lieutenant governor, Garland said, "the only major quarrels he picked were with Robb and Baliles. Part of that was a contempt, particularly for Robb. He wanted to show that he was a conservative on the tax issues, and he wanted them to know he was never anyone who could be taken for granted. A lot was just old combative habits. He reinforced the watchword of his career, as expressed in a speech by Mark Twain on William Dean Howell's birthday in Boston, in which he said, 'I am the doubter of the doubt, he reckons ill who leaves me out.'"

Garland said that "though I hold liberalism in no regard, whatsoever, and on one level, you'd have to say that Wilder is the most liberal" of recent Democratic gubernatorial nominees, "even though for the last four years he has kept that to himself, he also is the most intellectually honest of the group. That's not to say he could always be reached on the basis of intellectual honesty, that he would not just always vote purely a position that was helpful to him, but most of the time he would."

Wilder took a number of advantages into the November election, Garland said. "He has a most attractive skin tone for television, and a friendly manner for television. Those things are important. And the state has changed because of infusion of new people, not tied to the old Virginia traditions. The country as a whole is manfully struggling to cast off some of the shibboleths of the past. You have a man with long experience, very skillful, highly intelligent, with a demonstrated record in public office meeting a moment. So the man meets the moment, and the moment could be his."

52. A Mighty Mountain to Climb

It was a balmy spring day in late March, 1989, and Wilder was attending the formal kickoff of Mary Sue Terry's campaign for re-election as attorney general. The setting for the ceremony was an impressive one, on the marbled south portico of the 200-year-old Virginia state capitol, designed by Thomas Jefferson. Yet as she spoke, Wilder became lost in memories. From his vantage point, he could look eastward, through the magnificent magnolia trees on the lawn, across the industrial valley that connects Richmond's version of Capitol Hill and Church Hill, and see, peaking above the trees, the Confederate soldier atop the monument in Libby Hill Park, where he had played as a boy.

His mind drifted back to those days in the '30s and '40s, when he battled the boys from Fulton for turf, learned to debate in the barber shop, rode the back of the trolley to school and dreamed of making something of himself, as his mother put it.

"Mary Sue was talking," Wilder said, "but my mind was drifting, thinking that from Capitol Hill to Church Hill, it's a short distance to walk, but a mighty, mighty mountain to climb."

As Wilder approached the summit, he reflected on his early days in politics, saying he could envision "someone like Doug Wilder" running for governor. "But I never thought it would be me. It was a faceless person, someone who had paid the dues, who had demonstrated leadership quality, and all other things being possible, perhaps be in a position to receive the nomination." He paused, as if having to convince himself that he was the person he had envisioned. "This is it," he said on the eve of his nomination. "This is absolutely it."

Wilder recalled that a dozen years before, he had called the position of lieutenant governor "vacuous," but said he later realized that it wasn't possible to run for governor without first serving in an entry level position—not even the sainted Chuck Robb had tried that—and although unlike Robb, Wilder had considerable experience in the legislature, to break the barrier of running for governor he and Mary Sue Terry would be required to take what might be considered an extra step. For her, if it were going to happen, it would require her to be elected attorney general, twice, as it turned out. For him, it was lieutenant governor. He also acknowledged that he could not have run for lieutenant governor, much less be elected, unless "the atmosphere prevailed for it," a situation that came about gradually, with the help of governors such as Holton, Robb and Baliles.

"So many people have changed," Wilder said. He recalled "the many nice things" that crusty old Ed Willey said about him before his death, and Watkins M. Abbitt Sr., the long-time segregationist congressman from Southside. Abbitt had, like A. L. Philpott four years before, gotten up early one morning a few weeks before, in May of 1989, and along with his son, Delegate Watt Abbitt Jr., a moderate Democrat by anyone's standards, driven from their home in Appomattox to a breakfast fundrasier for Wilder in Lynchburg. Big Watt, as he was known, was carrying through on a promise he had made a year earlier, while standing in the back of a pickup truck at one of those formerly whites-only, bourbon-sipping, chitling-munching political gatherings at which the remnant of the old Byrd machine anointed it's candidates. "Next year is your turn,"

A Mighty Mountain to Climb

Big Watt had said to Wilder, throwing his arm around his shoulder in welcome-to-the-club gesture.

"I'm more proud than anything," Wilder said, "that in 1985 I could go all over state without fear of rebuke or ugly incidents. That told me a lot. When that was taking place, it was clear that further elective office was not only possible, but probable."

He said it was important to him to win the gubernatorial nomination in an open setting, where others who wanted to contest the nomination could, (although he didn't think that was such a hot idea in 1985). Wilder encountered only nominal opposition, from state Senator Daniel W. Bird Jr. of Wytheville. Bird walked across the state in the summer of 1988 seeking votes, offering himself as an alternative to Wilder, but found few takers. In January, 1989, he ended his candidacy, unable to stir the voters or receive financial backing. But it was Mary Sue Terry's decision to seek re-election, rather than challenge him for the nomination, that was critical to his success. A Wilder-Terry showdown would have been a costly, divisive battle, such as the Republicans went through in their three-way race for the nomination. "I respect her judgment," Wilder said, a trace of a smile creeping across his face. He reasoned, and Terry arrived at a similar conclusion, that waiting another four years didn't hurt her gubernatorial chances. Terry is seventeen years younger than Wilder, who didn't have the luxury of waiting. His opportunity was 1989, and nothing was going to stand in his way. At age fifty-eight, he might not get another shot at the top.

One of the major challenges for Wilder in 1989 was to retain the support of Baliles and Robb loyalists, in the face of his well-publicized criticisms of the two men he hoped to succeed. But to Wilder, it was "not a matter of reconciliation," but rather convincing voters that he could be different from Robb and Baliles without being an adversary.

"Far from being apologetic," Wilder said, he believed voters would see that "in addition to being able to work within those administrations and get things done, they also see a degree of independence" in him that they would consider an asset.

As for Democrats who declined to support him, who might go fishing on election day, Wilder laughed, "I hope they like fish, because they'll be fishing for a long, long time." He added, seriously, "I don't think you'll find that. Fishing is something you do in leisurely pursuit. Most people I know who are involved in wanting something for Virginia don't find that leisurely. It's work, it takes effort. I think you'll find more homogenizing than you may have imagined."

There is a streak of populism in Wilder that extends his appeal beyond blacks and other minorities to people who often feel left out of the process—farmers, shipyard workers, coal miners and clerks, who traditionally have gravitated to the Democratic party, but also to entrepreneurs, small business owners, young professionals and newcomers to the state (many of whom settled in Virginia in spite of, rather than because of, its heritage) who sensed in his candidacy the chance to link arms and gain access to the inside of the tent. He proudly pointed out that some of his supporters are participating in the electoral process for first time, some because they had never before been asked, and others who thought their views would not be wanted. "My door is open," Wilder said. "There is no limit to numbers of people and where they play."

Wilder's appeal extended beyond campaign contributions. Supporting his candidacy gave people an opportunity to feel good about themselves, a chance to cleanse themselves of collective guilt, for themselves or their neighbors or their forefathers. In Williamsburg in the spring of 1989, a woman told Wilder that she and her husband were "Georgia Republicans, and you know what that means," she said. "Yes, I think I do," laughed Wilder. "But we are supporting you," she said. "And she wasn't whispering," smiled Wilder.

At a campaign stop at the country club in Danville, the first person to greet Wilder was House Speaker Philpott, who was "supporting me as openly and strongly as he could."

Nonetheless, Philpott seemed slightly out of place on June 10, 1989, when, as the presiding officer of the convention, he found himself surrounded on the podium by what must have seemed to a former segregationist as a sea of black faces—Wilder and his three children. Although Philpott presided with dignity, he offered no great rhetorical flourishes in behalf of his party's nominee.

Governor Baliles and Senator Robb played major roles at the convention, which attracted about five thousand delegates and guests, including two of Wilder's sisters, Agnes Nicholson and Berthel Penrose, and several nieces and nephews. Baliles gave the keynote address and nominated Wilder, and Robb made one of the seconding speeches. Both men confronted their differences with Wilder, but they chose different ways to express it.

Baliles opted for humor. He posed a series of questions: "Do I like Doug Wilder? Do I admire Doug Wilder? Do I think Doug Wilder is independent?" and answered all three in the affirmative. Baliles said that "when I think of Doug, I think of a poem...

> Voyager upon life's sea,
> To yourself be true,
> And whate'er your lot may be,
> Paddle your own canoe.

"I've looked out the window of the governor's office on more than one occasion," Baliles said, "and, sure enough, there was Doug paddling by. But, he was always nice about it, he always waved."

Robb cited Wilder's leadership and experience as qualifications, and called him a member of the Robb-Baliles team. Then he said, "but some will ask, and some have asked, 'how about your past differences? How about those letters?' Doug and I have had our differences, and I did eventually release a couple of tough letters. But...those letters represent only one year in a relationship that has spanned fourteen years. For almost a decade, Doug Wilder and I were friends and allies. Without Doug Wilder's help and support, I might not have been elected lieutenant governor in 1977 or governor in 1981. That's a fact, and we've campaigned actively for each other in every race either of us has run in since 1975, and don't anybody make a mistake about this race. I'm back in Doug's corner in 1989..."

Despite that bit of revisionist history, Robb clearly understood, as he

A Mighty Mountain to Climb

went on to say, that Wilder's election would send a message "crucial to the continued success of democracy and to our great American experiment. It will demonstrate to Virginia and to America, and to a world that's taking a fresh new look at our system of government, that the Jeffersonian ideal of the 'aristocracy of merit' is alive and well here."

With Wilder's clashes with Robb and Baliles patched over, at least for public consumption, it fell to the Republican nominee, Marshall Coleman, to convince voters that it was a mirage, concocted for the duration of the campaign. Coleman accepted that challenge with jocund suspicion, mockingly praising Robb as "a man of letters" who had recorded his judgment of Wilder for posterity after "calm deliberation."

In his acceptance speech, Wilder praised Baliles and Robb for "unleashing and nurturing the drive and ingenuity of Virginians everywhere. All of us want to preserve our prosperity and to bequeath this good life to our children. We want what we have accomplished to endure the test of time, to become our legacy, to provide for our posterity, just as our ancestors so ably provided for us....I love our state and its people. The past and future of my family are here. This is where my parents raised me; this is where I raised my own children. In my lifetime, I've seen Virginia learn and grow. And like Virginia, I've learned and I've grown....We are all proud of Virginia. Indeed, we hold a most honored place in the annals of American history. Two hundred years ago, we drew the blueprint and set the course for the nation. And now, two hundred years later, America is still following our lead."

Wilder downplayed the significance, and uniqueness, of his candidacy, except to remind the delegates that four years earlier they had "had the courage to stand up with me. You took a chance on an underdog, took a chance that I could take the negative attacks, climb over the hurdles and help this party to its second straight statewide sweep." Now, he said, it was time "for the next step together on our journey." The people of Virginia "do not want to turn back. They know Virginia is moving in the right direction. Four years ago, when I borrowed a station wagon [if people believed it then, they'd believe it still] and drove the back roads through every county, every independent city...I learned a great deal about our people. Looking back, however, one lesson stands out above the others. I learned that Virginia's strength and greatness are found in our very special people."

Wilder wanted his campaign, and should he win, his governing, to be judged as his predecessors had been judged, on his love of state, appreciation of its history and tradition, and his dedication to continuing and expanding its opportunities and prosperity, not just because it's good politics, but because he truly believes in those values. However cunning, suspicious and scheming Wilder may be, he also is truly a Virginian, at least third-generation, and as deserving to claim its heritage as others. There seems little basis to fears, occasionally voiced, that if he were elected he would suddenly pull off a mask of moderation and attempt to make radical changes in state government, whether through the governor's vast power of appointment or legislative agenda.

The national publicity that Wilder's candidacy attracted—he was the subject of stories in the national newsweeklies, major papers around the

293

country, network television reports and at least three books—could redound to his benefit. Self-conscious about their shameful history in race relations, many Virginians were anxious to prove that the state's reputation as a bastion of the Old South, preoccupied with the past, was no longer accurate. With Wilder's election, they could exorcise a collective guilt and claim the mantle of a New Dominion in the New South.

Wilder's election could "transform the state's image forever," said Larry J. Sabato, the University of Virginia political pundit. "Virginia's voters will be on their best behavior. They don't want to be reminded of massive resistance." He said Wilder's slogan from the '85 campaign, "Let's Make History," contained a subliminal appeal. "People like the idea of making history, to be part of the first state" to break a barrier.

Gerald E. Connolly, a Democratic party activist who lives in Fairfax County and works on Capitol Hill, said many of his friends and neighbors in Northern Virginia vote for national Republicans—some moved to the area from the Midwest and Northeast to work in the Nixon, Ford, Reagan and Bush administrations—but don't like to think about, or be reminded, that they live in the South. They settled in Fairfax or Arlington or Alexandria not because those communities are south of the Mason-Dixon line, but because they offered stable neighborhoods, good schools and a proximity to the cultural and educational attractions of the nation's capital.

"At the first hint of race being injected into the race," predicted Connolly, "they'll abandon the Republican candidate and vote for Doug."

Wilder said that his parents would "never believe it, they would be almost anesthetized" at the prospect of their son becoming governor. Yet he was sure his mother would snap out of her dream-state long enough to remind him again to "don't let your head get too big," to which his father would concur with a "hrrump, hrump."

As election day approached, Wilder said "the realization comes in every passing day, and now every passing moment," not just that he was on the brink of a personal breakthrough, but that so too was his state. Such an awesome prospect "requires a constant, strictly measured sobriety," he said.

If he won, from that point on, when the history books talked about the Capitol of the Confederacy and Massive Resistance, they also would talk about the 1989 election, when Doug Wilder became the nation's first black elected governor and the Old Dominion gave way to the New. Yet even then, Wilder's dream would not be fulfilled. As he said on the day the Martin Luther King holiday bill was signed into law, "We are still in the ascendancy, because the journey doesn't stop here...We shall overcome."

ACKNOWLEDGEMENTS

Of the scores of people who made this book possible, Doug Wilder was the most important. He permitted the author to interrupt him during the busiest year of his life, and for every question he declined to answer, he responded to another with candor that a more cautious politician would have ducked. Through hours of interviews, in his office, his home and on the road, we developed a rapport that is likely to survive whatever differences he may have with what has been written about him in these pages.

On one level, Doug Wilder's achievements, win or lose in the governor's race, are remarkable. He has scaled heights achieved by few Virginians, regardless of race, and has left his mark on his native state. On another level, his accomplishments were to have been expected. He is part of a remarkable family. As his mother was wont to point out when people congratulated her on her son's successes, he is from a family of achievers. My wife, Nancy, and I had the pleasure of meeting his sisters in Virginia, North Carolina and Michigan, and nephews in Connecticut and Ohio.

The next generation of Wilders is as accomplished as that of Doug and his siblings. "Our family could run a corporation," observed Doug's sister, Olga Graves. The family includes a federal bankruptcy judge, a dentist, attorneys, accountants, government officials, teachers, photographers, secretaries, two former college deans, an engineer, a designer, an artist and a politician.

Other acknowledgements are owed to:

• Early supporters of Wilder's, who shared those steps with me, especially lawyers Bob Butcher and brothers Jimmy and Phil Morris and investment broker Lain O'Ferrall.

• Public officials, including former Governor Linwood Holton, former Governor Charles Robb, who found time in the midst of his own campaign for the United States Senate; the late George Stoddart, a good friend; J. Marshall Coleman, who is smart enough and confident enough to cooperate on a book about his opponent, not knowing if it would help or hurt his own career; and the many sources who talked freely, both on and off the record, most of whom are named in the index.

• Colleagues at The Washington Post performed a variety of good deeds, ranging from simple encouragement to expert editing. Among those who made special contributions were Ken Bredemeier, who edited the manuscript; R. H. Melton, my colleague in the Richmond bureau, who provided incisive constructive criticism; Mary Lou Tousignant and Wendy Ross, who helped with the final preparation; editors Ben Bradlee, Leonard Downie, Milton Coleman and Doug Feaver, who granted me leave and leeway; Bob Woodward and Bill Raspberry, who offered advice and read portions of the manuscript; Bill Dickinson, who led me to my publisher; former Richmond-based reporters Helen Dewar, Paul Edwards, Glenn Frankel, Mike Isikoff and Tom Sherwood; and Karlyn Barker, Molly Moore, Lee Hockstader and Mary Jordan; and Bill McAllister, who encouraged me to take the assignment in Richmond in 1985.

• My contemporaries in the Virginia press corps, who suspended their competitive nature to help, and even when they didn't, I borrowed heavily from their writings. Among those who rate special thanks are Margie Fisher, Dale Eisman, Bill Byrd, Margaret Edds, Warren Fiske, Nancy Cook, Tyler Whitley, Carolyn

WILDER: HOLD FAST TO DREAMS

Click, Steve Johnson, Dwayne Yancey, Guy Friddell, Bill Wood, Jim Latimer, Shelley Rolfe, Joe Gatins, Mike Hardy, Jeff Schapiro and the late George Bowles.

•Larry Sabato, who allowed me to peruse his voluminous, if disorganized, files at the University of Virginia, and to Curtis Kopf, who made valuable suggestions and contributed mightily to the editing of the manuscript.

•Researchers at the Virginia State Library and Archives, the Richmond public library, the Valentine Museum of Richmond, and the libraries of The Washington Post, The Richmond Times-Dispatch and News Leader, and The Richmond Afro-American.

•Tom Wolfe and Jesse Jackson, who gave freely of their time and talent.

•Lon Savage, who conceived of the project and convinced the author to undertake it.

James M. Morris of Seven Locks Press, who published the book, and Bob Young, Stephen Parrott and Mounir Murad of The Publishers Service Bureau.

•Two special teachers, Virginia Lynch of Warwood High School, who first suggested to me that it was possible to make a living doing something as satisfying as writing, and the late W. L. T. Crocker of West Virginia Tech, who coaxed and cursed me to strive for excellence.

•My family, especially my wife, Nancy, and older daughter, Lisa, who performed numerous tasks, but none as important as providing love and encouragement when it was most needed.

Index

Index

Index

Index

303

Index

Storey, Ken 179
Sutton, Charles 75, 103, 197

Taylor, Elizabeth 94, 271
Taylor, Henry "Buddy" 28,29
Taylor, John "Booty" 29, 223
Taylor, Noel 160
Taylor, Robert L. 8, 13, 21, 22
Teig, Eva S. 120, 173,174, 228
Temple, David L. 13, 22, 163
Temple, Helen 13, 14, 22
Terry, Mary Sue 151-156, 173, 175, 177, 179, 183,184, 211-212, 215, 118,219, 221, 227, 230-232, 236, 238-239, 244, 250-257, 261,262, 265, 269, 290,291
Terry, Nannie Ruth 151
Terry, Nate 151
Terry, Ruth 151
Terry, Sally Ann 151
Thomas, John Charles 124
Thomas, Suzanne 215
Thomas, William G. 117, 118, 120, 123,124, 126,127, 163, 172, 174, 215, 261, 262
Thompson, W. Hale 63,-64
Thornton, William "Doc" 71, 81, 111, 136, 215
Townes, Clarence, Jr. 77
Townsend, W.W. 28
Trible, Paul S., Jr. 126, 136, 149,150, 189, 203
Troy, Anthony R. 272
Tso, James 204
Tucker, Cora 120, 133, 159
Tucker, Samuel W. 69, 195

Underdog Fund 216-218
United Press International 230
United States Information Service 222
United States Supreme Court 59, 130, 287
University of Virginia 53, 99,100, 188

Van Landingham, Marian 174, 250, 252
Viguerie, Richard A. 181,182
Virginia Bar Association 72
Virginia Business magazine
Virginia Education Association 232
Virginia General Assembly 56, 76, 81, 84,85
Virginia State College (University) 234, 36, 52,53, 227
Virginia Supreme Court 76, 124, 194, 196,197
Virginia Polytechnic Institute and State University (Tech) 47, 189, 190
Virginia Union University 1, 28, 34-39, 52, 56, 113, 143, 145, 266
Voting Rights Act 91, 94, 119, 121, 127,128, 130

Index

Illustrations:
Photographs courtesy of Richmond Newspapers Inc., except for the following: Wilder's nomination for governor at the 1989 state convention, by Craig Herndon of The Washington Post; the new administration of Gov. Baliles, with Mrs. Baliles, Lt. Gov. Wilder and Attorney General Terry at inauguration in 1986, by John McDonnell of The Washington Post; personal photographs of Wilder with his sister, with piglets, high school graduation, singing with the band, in Korea, at Stidham's grocery, Jay Shropshire and campaigning with Jackie Epps, Cartoons, on the throne, and firing at billboard, by Brookins of the Richmond Times-Dispatch; and on the road, by Bill Mitchell of the Potomac News; rivals Wilder and Coleman by Dale Ferrell for The Associated Press; cover photo by Mark Charette.

About the Author

Donald P. Baker has been a daily newspaper journalist for thirty-five years, the last twenty at The Washington Post, where he has been a reporter and editor on the metropolitan staff. Since 1985, he has been The Post's Richmond bureau chief, from where he covered state government and politics, including Doug Wilder's tenure as lieutenant governor and his campaign for governor. A native of Wheeling, West Virginia, and a graduate of West Virginia Institute of Technology, Baker worked in Ohio and Indiana before joining The Post in 1970. He and his wife, Nancy, who have two daughters, live in Richmond.